To John A. Ramseyer / *scholar, teacher, and friend*

Educational Administration: selected readings

selected readings

second edition, revised

edited by Walter G. Hack, *Ohio State University* · John A. Ramseyer, *Ohio State University* · William J. Gephart, *Phi Delta Kappa* · James B. Heck, *University of Delaware*

boston · allyn and bacon, inc.

Library of Congress Catalog Card Number: 72–146357

Contents

Preface   vii

I. Building a Concept of Educational Administration   1

II. Educational Administration: A Philosophical Base   9

   1. Inner Direction and the Decision Maker, *Van Miller*   11

   2. Purpose-Defining: The Central Function of the School Administrator, *James G. Harlow*   17

   3. Conflicts in Values, *Harry S. Broudy*   20

   4. Art, Science, and New Values, *Harry S. Broudy*   36

III. Educational Administration: Theory   47

   5. The Nature of the Theory-Practice Relationship, *Arthur P. Coladarci and Jacob W. Getzels*   49

   6. Ways of Knowing, *Andrew W. Halpin*   55

   7. Modern Approaches to Theory in Administration, *James D. Thompson*   69

   8. The Nature and Meaning of Theory, *Daniel E. Griffiths*   85

IV. Educational Administration: The Setting   107

   9. Politics, Economics, and Educational Outcomes in the States, *Thomas R. Dye*   109

   10. Federal-State Educational Relations, *Roald F. Campbell*   129

   11. Organizational Climate, Social Class, and Educational Output, *Alexander M. Feldvebel*   137

   12. Selected Social Power Relationships in Education, *Conrad Briner and Laurence Iannaccone*   144

V. Educational Administration: The Man   157

   13. The Individual and Organization: Some Problems of Mutual Adjustment, *Chris Argyris*   159

   14. Is an Open Mind Necessary? Research Evidence, *C. Gratton Kemp*   178

15. The Manager as a Leader, *L. L. Cummings* 184
16. Who's a Good Principal? *Barry D. Anderson and Alan F. Brown* 193

VI. Educational Administration: The Job 201

17. Doctrines of Administration: A Brief History, *H. Warren Button* 204
18. Political Dimensions of Educational Administration, *Russell T. Gregg* 212
19. New Concepts in Educational Administration, *John Walton* 226
20. Four Definitions of Your Job, *Van Miller* 233

VII. Educational Administration: Organization 239

21. Organizing for Reform in Big-City Schools, *Daniel U. Levine* 241
22. The Authority Structure of the School: System of Social Exchange, *James G. Anderson* 249
23. The Context of Organizational Behavior: A Conceptual Synthesis for the Educational Administrator, *E. G. Bogue* 266

VIII. Educational Administration: The Process 283

24. Use of Models in Research, *Daniel E. Griffiths* 285
25. The Expanding Concept of Research, *Egon G. Guba* 295
26. Toward a Science of Educational Evaluation, *Daniel L. Stufflebeam* 310
27. Toward a Taxonomy of Evaluation Designs, *Blaine R. Worthen* 320

IX. Integrating a Concept of Educational Administration 331

Index 341

Preface

When the first edition of this book of readings was being written, John A. Ramseyer made a significant contribution in both substance and spirit. The initial discussions concerning the revision of the book were underway when John Ramseyer died in August, 1968. It was subsequently decided that the work should continue, and the second edition is a product of that effort. However, it is apparent that this second edition still bears the influence and contribution of John Ramseyer, and is a better book because of it.

A second edition of any book implies that though it will differ from the first in approach the basic purpose will remain the same. The basic purpose or rationale for a book of readings in educational administration has not changed: supplementation of basic texts continues to be widely accepted practice; availability of these materials from libraries continues to pose problems; the needed amplification of essential concepts continues to be necessary for the young administrator's professional development.

The selections best suited to this purpose change as the professional environment of educational administration changes. The editors recognized that the approach taken in the first edition should be updated, retaining, however, certain features of the first edition on the basis of favorable reader reaction.

Over the past six years the editors have monitored the literature in educational administration. It was found that not all relevant supplementary literature was of very recent copyright. Some of the most valuable material which appeared in the first edition has attained the status of "classic" in this field. Thus, ten of the twenty-eight selections in the first edition have been retained in the second.

Another major feature of the first edition which has been retained is the concept of educational administration incorporating seven components or dimensions. Reader reaction suggested this approach was viable and so the seven "substance" chapters remain titled as they were in the first edition.

A third feature we retained is that of the multi-disciplinary approach.

During the life of the first edition, the professional study of education enthusiastically embraced this approach. Scholars from many disciplines have made important contributions and it would be negligent on our part to ignore them.

However, another trend has modified the practice of "borrowing" from other fields of professional study. This second edition reflects a new maturation; more sophisticated and rigorous research is being conducted by scholars of educational administration itself. This is best evidenced by the publication of many of these new studies (as well as those by scholars in other fields) in the *Educational Administration Quarterly*, a journal which made its initial appearance in the winter of 1965, and from which the authors have drawn extensively for this edition.

A significant change is the inclusion of a majority of new selections—a difference greater than merely new readings. The issues and problems of the 1960's and 1970's are dissimilar and this edition is in tune with the times: educational administration is viewed in terms of today's value conflicts; the theoretical orientation of systems; emerging social power relationships; today's leadership requirements; the politics of contemporary education; and problems of organizing for reform in urban schools. What appears to the editors to be the dynamic interests of scholars in the field over the last six years—research in organizational theory and operation, political relationships, and decision-making and, more recently, values, conflicts, and related areas—are given their due, reflecting the changing thrusts of thought, concern, and research in the field of educational administration.

Despite changes in approach, the original and continuing mission of this work is to assist in the development of concepts of educational administration and to provide a source of stimulation to help formulate and test hypotheses as a means of developing concepts.

Special acknowledgment must be given to the publishers of the books and professional journals and to the authors of the selections who have graciously extended to us permission to use their materials. We are appreciative of the help and encouragement of our many professional friends and the candid and valuable reactions of those who used the first edition and encouraged us to update it.

WALTER G. HACK

JOHN A. RAMSEYER

WILLIAM J. GEPHART

JAMES B. HECK

Chapter One

Building A Concept of
Educational Administration

A book, to be a contribution to any field of endeavor, must have a mission. Books of readings are invariably composed of someone's selections. The criteria for the selection of the readings thus becomes the basis for the mission.

Collections of readings drawn together state, either implicitly or explicitly, their rationale. Some books of readings perform a valuable sampling function, e.g., what are writers in a given field saying about the subject. Others try to lay out a taxonomy or classification of the relevant points of view, and thus present a continuum of opinion on the subject. Still other editors develop books of readings which identify current problems and trends in the given field. These types of presentations are valuable in assessing the dynamics of change of thinking in the selected area.

The basis for the selection of readings in this collection is dissimilar to any of those mentioned above. The readings in the following chapters have been carefully selected to enable the reader to better formulate and articulate his own concept of educational administration. The readings are to serve as guidelines so that students may be sensitized to administrative situations, develop effective ways to look at them, analyze them within the frame of reference of other interrelated conditions, make decisions in light of these, and develop an integrated way of behaving while implementing the decisions. Such a process implies the development and use of a total concept of educational administration.

It is indeed a formidable challenge to develop a comprehensive set of concepts of educational administration; much less an integrated pattern of behavior based on these concepts. The scholar-practitioner very soon recognizes divisive influences in his search for comprehensiveness in thought and integrity in behavior. His role is ambiguous; the environment is schizophrenic in its expectations; and his compatriots are idiosyncratic in their relationships to the institution. The challenge to order his world is beset with shifting variables over which strict control is impossible. However, the very nature of this challenge underlines the necessity for the educational

1

administrator to rationally develop for himself a set of concepts for educational administration.

The Nature of a Concept

But what is a concept of educational administration and why is it so difficult to develop? In its most generic sense a concept is an idea. For the purposes of this book of readings, such a simple definition is not very useful as it does not reflect the interplay of variables which must be ordered so that a concept can provide guidelines for the integrative behavior required in the exercise of administrative leadership.

Alternate definitions of a concept appear to have greater relevance for our concern. *Webster's New World Dictionary* defines a concept as "a generalized idea of a class of objects."* This statement connotes the generality of related things. Stephen Knezevich defines the term in the context of educational administration as "an intellectual interpretation or image of a process, event, or thing."** From these, one can synthesize a definition of a concept of educational administration as a generalized interpretation of a class of phenomena *related to and relevant for* educational administration.

The Utility of Concept Building

The above paragraphs suggested in general terms that the concepts of educational administration which the practitioner carries around in his mind influence his behavior as an administrator. Integrative behavior in the administrator role is a result of the development of a comprehensive set of concepts of educational administration.

A characteristic of educational administration reflected in practice as well as in the professional literature is that of change. Definitions have changed; problems, responsibilities, expectations, and behaviors of administrators have changed. As a consequence, the conceptual tools used by the administrator must be able to accommodate these changing conditions and relationships. A set of concepts which provides an ordering of these phenomena is required if the administrator is to tune in the picture of reality.

In the past decade or two the behavioral sciences have effected momentous breakthroughs in the discovery and ordering of new knowledge.

---

* *Webster's New World Dictionary of the American Language* (Cleveland and New York: The World Publishing Company, 1962.)
** Stephen J. Knezevich, *Administration of Public Education*, 2nd ed. (New York: Harper and Row, Publishers, 1969), p. 511.

These have precipitated not only a major restructuring of the disciplines themselves but also have effected revolutionary changes in their applications to the area of our immediate concern, the practice of educational administration. With psychology, sociology, political science, anthropology, and other related fields conducting studies related to perception, role analysis, individual and community decision-making, group dynamics, leadership, and the like, additional variables were injected into the classical debate regarding the dichotomous role of the school administrator.

The original question was: Does the school administrator impose his administration of the school on the community and literally lead the community in the area of school affairs or does the community, through its mores and expectations, impose its pattern of behavior on the school administrator? The new approaches developed in the behavioral sciences suggest that the administrator's function is far more complex than that recognized in the early dichotomy. Recent findings now suggest that the role of the administrator might be that of an initiator of propositions to be tested by the school-community. When the community takes a position on the proposition, these decisions then provide the direction for the school system. Thus the school administrator is not exclusively leader or follower. He functions in either capacity at differing times and circumstances. Many factors determine which is the appropriate role at the given time.

A Process for Developing a Set of Concepts of Educational Administration

The example above of new knowledge forcing the rethinking of one concept of educational administration can be used to illustrate a process which the editors have found to be of value in developing a concept of educational administration. In the new role suggested above, educational administration takes on aspects of a far more complex and dynamic phenomenon than was true in either of the earlier concepts. The new role suggests a new concept, or a generalized interpretation of a class of phenomena relevant for educational administration.

In order to appreciate the relevance of the "new look" in administration, one needs only to consider the dynamic nature of our society and the educational organization which is a part of it. Conditions of every sort are rapidly changing. Technological and sociological change form a constantly spiraling and accelerating set of interactions wherein breakthroughs in one form of change may both demand and produce subsequent developments in the other. In this kind of environment the "pat" answer as assured by tradition, habit, or "the way *good* school districts have done it" becomes increasingly unsatisfactory. Problems emerging in old-line communities with solid, practical administrations provide moot evidence as to the rate of obsolescence of these kinds of answers to contemporary administrative problems.

Change and demands resulting from change are meaningful, however, only as they are perceived by individuals and communities. Thus, the concept of the school administrator as one who directs the community in school affairs is inadequate. This role is not only undesirable from the point of view of our democratic values, but it is politically impossible in the long run. Communities do not often develop the reputation of buying educational services simply because someone says these are good for them. The notion is distasteful philosophically as well as impossible operationally. This type of administrator acting as the source of authority for action provides no means of evaluating the relative merit of proposals other than those criteria which he supplies.

It seems, however, that the answer to the question of appropriate direction is not the converse of the above situation. The desirability of having the community dictate the direction in which schools are to move has some limitations. The community often fails to enunciate rationally and clearly a direction for education, especially in the midst of a welter of rapid and seemingly unrelated or contradictory changes and demands. Under such conditions the problem is still further complicated by the fact that the lines separating lay and professional decisions tend to disintegrate or at least waver and become blurred. Thus it appears that the school administrator must be more than a manager to carry out the tasks defined for him by the community.

Both of the concepts of administration described above have severe limitations. On one hand we cannot be assured that the administrator moves in a direction meaningful to the community. The second concept is limited by difficulties related to having the community determine the direction. In light of these problems some other concept of school administration is needed.

A means of building a concept of educational administration which has proved to be satisfactory to the editors is one which grows out of the observed limitations of the two concepts discussed above. In essence, the school administrator does not function exclusively either as the director of the movement of the educational enterprise or as the implementor of the movement of the system as directed by the community. Instead, the administrator has his primary role in formulating propositions to be tested by the community as a whole, other administrators, the board of education, the staff, and often the students. He further provides the structure within which these are tested, and the results are brought to bear on administrative decisions. These in turn affect or determine the movement of the organization. In such a position the administrator himself is also proposing and testing propositions. It is through this process that the professional competencies of the administration and staff are joined with the community's educational objectives so as to assure the provision for an adequate and meaningful program of education. In this role, administrators are neither string-pullers nor puppets. They are more than catalysts: they are positive influencers of public policy basing their influence on professional competence.

The Theme of Concept-Building as Reflected in the Organization of the Book

In ordering its contents, the editors were concerned with the mission of the book and the way this might best be accomplished by the students who use it. The materials chosen and the methods of presentation were both predicated on the method of developing a concept of administration as stated above. This book is dedicated to the purpose of assisting each reader in the formulation of his own concept of educational administration.

The book is not a collection of answers to given problems but instead is a series of points of view pertaining to a given aspect of school administration. The several points of view on a topic suggest the nature of the propositions the administrator must formulate and test for himself and those which the school-community must do likewise. In this way the idea of educational administration as being that of testing hypotheses may be recognized in the content and organization of the book. In application, one might see a dynamic eclecticism as an integral part of the concept of administration and hence the behavior of administrators.

Each chapter with its own substantive focus presents those problems, questions, and issues which are heuristic. The readings often imply dissimilar ways of viewing these questions and thus encourage the reader to formulate and test propositions in order to develop his own position regarding that particular subject. As the reader moves through the several chapters, the interrelationships among them become apparent. The influence of previously developed positions becomes a factor in the proposition immediately being considered and perhaps makes obsolete the reader's previously developed position. Thus the dynamic eclecticism is demonstrated.

The Sum and Substance of Educational Administration

Administration gives order to the specialized and interdependent activities which characterize an organization. It provides the structure and coordination of these so as to facilitate goal determination and achievement. Teachers and others interested in education develop a general perception of school administration by participating in it, being directly influenced by it, and observing it. In sum, school administration has been, and will be for the express purposes of this volume of readings, conceived of as that phenomenon which coordinates the interdependent activities of individuals in achieving a common goal—the education of children.

The common goal in most schools and school districts is an elusive thing. Not only does the administrator have difficulties in identifying it but he encounters problems in gaining consensus as to how goal definition should be accomplished. Should the institutional goal be derived from the community, from the staff, from the administrator, or from some combination of these?

Secondly, administration is concerned with the activities that go on in order that the goals of the organization, somehow defined, can be met. Again there is a question of who determines the appropriate activities or means for meeting the goal. On what bases are these judgments made?

Administration as defined above presents a very general statement as to what this social phenomenon is all about, but says little of its composition. There are various dimensions of school administration, all recognized as relevant by the editors.

In the experience of the editors the dimension most obvious to the preservice administrator is that of the tasks, e.g., what the administrator does during his "working day." To place these duties in a more meaningful setting a second dimension is explored, that of viewing administration as a complex of roles to be played and perhaps expectations to be filled. A somewhat more abstract look is that relating to the various processes employed and behaviors exhibited. The relationships occurring among the administrator and other role incumbents in that segment of the whole social system involving the educational process delineates yet another dimension of educational administration.

As one looks at this amorphous mass of the substance of educational administration, an urgent need for some ordering is readily felt. Writers in the field responding to this frustration have replied with three basic dimensions.

Educational administration is concerned with:

1. expectations—the "what"
2. tasks   —the "which"
3. method   —the "how"

The above classification is rather generic in character but nonetheless provides an order or a logical classification useful in viewing the several dimensions. To provide a more definitive method for such an observation, the editors developed a prismatic construct (see Figure 1) that might be helpful in viewing the several dimensions or facets of educational administration. Each facet provides a "window" through which the phenomena of administration might be viewed. These facets, as the following chapters suggest, are: 1. philosophical base; 2. theory; 3. setting; 4. man; 5. job; 6. organization; 7. process.

As an educational administrator, *man* has his own unique pattern of values, perceptions, and skills and abilities. In an administrative position he is subject to *antecedent* forces—a philosophy, a theory of administration, and a setting. As these antecedents to administrative action are refracted through the unique construct of *man's* values, perceptions, and skills and abilities, they emerge as *manifestations* of administrative action. At this

INPUTS

ANTECEDENTS

factors that determine what administration is to be.

PHILOSOPHICAL BASE — provides values which give order to the environment.

THEORY — provides guidelines for administrative action.

SETTING — provides expectations and demands.

MAN

SKILLS AND ABILITIES   VALUES   PERCEPTIONS

OUTPUTS

MANIFESTATIONS.

ways in which administration is demonstrated.

JOB — expresses authority and responsibility, and defines limits for action.

ORGANIZATION — expresses the relationship of organizational purpose to needs — satisfactions of members.

PROCESS — expresses the way the organization makes decisions and thus effects organizational movement.

Figure 1

point the job of the administrator is defined, the organization is specified, and the administrative process is determined. Thus, the *antecedents* might be grossly equated with inputs, the *man* with mediating variables and the *manifestations* of administration action with outputs.

From the construct certain fundamental beliefs of the editors can be implied. As we attempt to delineate the administrator's role, we see the *man* as occupying a central and highly visible position. However, he is not the sole determiner of this role. He must define his position in light of the *antecedent* forces. The administrator as a *man* then determines and examines his actions in terms of workability and theoretical consistency.

As the reader moves through the chapters devoted to the seven dimensions of elucational administration, it is the editors' hope that the prismatic construct not only will provide a rationale for the ordering of the chapters but also will lend a thread of continuity to the readings and thought generated by them.

Chapter Two

Educational Administration:
A Philosophical Base

To characterize American education in contrast to that of other nations, we point to the full development of the total person, free to think, to express himself, and to determine how he will use his competence in the service of mankind. Other nations, we argue, place a greater emphasis on societal needs and subject the individual to these needs. Hence, he is less free to realize his potential. We believe that our faith in the individual is a major contributing factor to the strength of our society.

How did we arrive at this principle? Does it stand the test of time? How can we be assured that we are actually applying this principle? What does it mean to say that it is a part of our cultural heritage? Are the present demands upon our society a part of culture? Will these changing demands shake our faith in the worth of the individual and in the free application of his intelligence to the solution of current problems?

The school administrator is a student of the cultural values which we cherish; he knows when and how these values are being challenged. He assesses the forces that impinge upon education in our society. He realizes that culture is dynamic and that the schools and other institutions created by people must also be dynamic. In the present decade change has accelerated more rapidly than in any other time in history. How can education meet the challenge of change? If it does, what happens to our time-honored values?

The school is society's major educational institution. What should be the impact of social, technological, economic, political, and other changes on what the school teaches, and how? Who should decide such matters? What is the function of administration in all of this? Can it be possible that at times such as the present the school administrator may need to devote a major portion of his time to thought about such problems and how these problems are being solved in his school community, the state, and the nation? The editors of this book think so.

No single book can give adequate attention to these concerns. It is expected that prior to this stage in his professional preparation to become an educational administrator, the student would have given considerable thought to value questions and how one resolves problems when a conflict of values is involved. It is also anticipated that, for the educational administrator, this will continue to be an area for serious study and thought.

In the readings quoted in this chapter, the student's attention is drawn to several problems that fall in the philosophical realm—that is, their solutions depend upon how a person, a group, or groups wish to order their values. The first of these problems concerns the individual himself. It is a question of personal integrity. To what extent is a person responsible for the decisions he must make? To what extent may he take refuge for his decisions in the mores, customs, and circumstances of the community in which he finds himself?

Critics of education, both professional and lay, constantly raise the question of what the schools are for. This question must be answered forthrightly. Do schools in America serve a unique purpose? If so, what is it? Is this the most crucial of all value questions to be answered by educational leaders? What other highly crucial value decisions must be made?

Value-oriented problems also surface when communities as well as individuals are subjected to conflicts in values. Of all types of social institutions, schools appear to be among the most vulnerable to value conflict. Administrators of educational institutions must recognize that conflicts in values are indigenous to these organizations. Then they may seek effective means to meet and use conflict to give direction and purpose to the schools.

1 | Inner Direction and the Decision Maker

Van Miller

Miller deals here with the problem of responsibility for administrative decisions. He implies that some administrators shift the burden of responsibility for their decisions to law (interpretations of the intentions of our founding fathers or of the current "American Way"), to codes of ethics or standards established by the profession, to popular support or demand, or to trends. He argues that, while circumstances and customs affect decisions, each administrator should have a "central core of values" that provides him with a philosophical stance from which to assume his responsibilities.

The administrative leader in public education needs both assurance and inner direction at his many points of decision. He can raise the continual questions: "By what right do I take this action? Am I the right person to be doing this? How do I know this is so? Is this the right action to take?" Certainty, in the sense that one can verify a known fact, is never present. The decision has to be based upon probability.

The administrator must call the signal for action and make decisions before the evidence is in from which an historian can determine whether or not it was a good decision. Administration calls for making and staying with decisions. And if it is to be lived with, a decision cannot be the mere spontaneous draw of a straw. The administrator who delegates with confidence is making a decision which the historian may subsequently judge. But he makes it now on the basis of his information about people and purposes, his understanding of group process and social control, his faith in individuals to whom authority is delegated.

Within the limits of policy, public expectation and public tolerance, the administrator is confronted with many decisions—frequently as simple as whether to act or not to act.

One of the most frustrating decisions confronting many superintendents every winter is whether or not to close the schools because of a snow storm. If schools are closed too many days lost time may have to be made up by holding school on Saturdays or by running beyond the end of the

Van Miller, "Inner Direction and the Decision Maker," *School Executive*, Vol. 79 (December, 1959), 27–29. Buttenheim Publishing Corp. Reprinted by permission.

regular term. Since the no-school signal is given over radio stations, there is always the fear that either one's school would be the only one closed or the only one left open and that all of his patrons would be informed of this as they listened to the announcement. Under such circumstances the administrator spends a restless night during a storm, checking late weather reports, looking outside, and possibly calling neighboring superintendents early in the morning to see what they have planned to do. He may also call the school janitor who has been out shoveling the school walks or call patrons living along various points on school bus routes for additional information. But finally, wrong or right, he must decide one way or the other about calling the radio station to give the no-school signal. This crisis is not a policy decision nor even a matter of who is authorized to act—it is simply the implementation of policy by the authorized person.

Since the decisions of an administrator are subject to appraisal and acceptance or rejection by the people affected, and since he has no direct way of securing immediately the properly weighted reactions from each of them, he is left with using his own best judgment. On what basis does he support this judgment which must be at least as good as chance and which should be much better than chance?

The matter of knowing how to decide is at the very heart of administrative leadership. If there were no occasion for decision there would be no opportunity for leadership—there would be little point in the kind of school system we have. Administrators may seek to shift the burden of decision to law or custom or circumstances or pressures of other individuals. Some theorists have viewed the administrative decision as a resolution of a field of forces. This leaves the administrator as a piece of material transmitting action determined elsewhere. On the other hand, administrative leaders may accept the full possibilities of their position with personal responsibility for decision but with support for that decision through one of a variety of means.

One area of refuge is recourse to the orthodox or approved. An explicit source is the law. Through school law and through the precedents of court decisions administrators seek to know what they must do and what is the right decision. Some will do only what the law requires them to do and will not examine the extent to which the law grants permission specifically, or through implication permits them to do. The laws do represent guides to conduct based upon the examined experience of the race but these are man-made and can be changed by men. They provide useful but neither complete nor final guides to conduct. The administrative leader will use school law as a guide to taking action but he will always be alert to the possibility that the law itself needs re-examination in terms of new developments or new problems.

This suggests two other areas of support which have been used formally by the courts in trying decisions, by writers of professional literature, and by the practicing administrator.

One is the consideration of the intentions of the founding fathers or lawmakers. This is again an appeal to the feelings and reasoning of some prior appraisers of human experience. More flexible than the strictly literal interpretation of the law, it also requires personal judgment in determining which founding fathers to look to and which specific evidences about them to consider in assessing their intention. But it is an exercise that provides support for the decision or action and is a method of pondering the matter to be decided.

The other area is recourse to a social interpretation of the "American Way"—which has been variously described as a socially conscious capitalism, a free-enterprise system and the way of equal opportunity. Again, selection of the most pertinent interpreters of the social scene is a decision of the individual who seeks support. The search is a means of reflecting in reaching a decision. Personal support is derived from the feeling that one is acting in accordance with the "American Way."

Another source of approval for supporting a decision is the codes of ethics and the standards established by the profession. If 25 to 30 pupils per classroom teacher is set as a standard ratio by the profession it becomes a guide to the administrator and a source of certainty that he is right in spite of the absence of research definitely clarifying the differences between results in classes of varying sizes. Conformance to the code bears with it the assurance that he can count on support of his professional colleagues or can at least defend his actions to them if he comes under criticism.

Reliance on popular support is another means of seeking guidance and approval. Closely related to reliance on legal authority is the attempt to interpret election results. People vote "for" or "against," or "yes" or "no" in elections. When the votes are counted they have said who is elected and what is approved or disapproved. Those who seek to interpret election results will point out that they may have meant to say much more than could be said in the limited response pattern open to them on the ballot. Instead of voicing approval of the administration they may be saying that there was no acceptable competing candidate available. Instead of saying that they don't want to pay more taxes for a new school building they may be saying that the building proposed was not adequate to meet the situation. By considering not only what the vote was, but what alternatives were posed, what the margin was, how heavy or light the voting was, and who voted (as interpreted through the socio-economic, racial and religious standing of the polling-place neighborhoods) the administrator can find some direction and support for action and decision.

The newspapers provide another sounding board for popular support. The newspaper is dependent upon public interest and good will for its very existence. The press reaction to school problems and administrative decisions will be reflected in the way it handles school news and comments editorially. Its treatment of school news may evoke letters to the editor which provide a further indication of how some of the people feel. The administrator can read the newspapers including the "public pulse" column as a source of guidance and support.

In recent years the use of advisory committees has come upon the scene. These may be lay or student or staff advisory committees. In discussing the contemplated use of such committees, some administrators admit that they have sought to set them up not to get advice but to explain and justify their administrative programs in the hope that the committee would proceed to popularize them. Using such committees as public relations agents will provide only the inner security for the administrator's confidence in his own control over committee members. Representative evaluative discussions can provide guidance and assurance to the administrator. He has, in a sense, sampled through the advisory committee a reaction indicative of the approval or disapproval, enthusiasm or apathy of the larger population.

One other device used to seek guidance and assurance has been the systematic survey. The survey will no doubt include a considerable array of factual information about space and funds and population and test results but it may also include the expression of opinions and sentiments. The findings of such a survey can provide guides for administrative action and inner assurance that the administrator is doing right in the sense that he has popular support.

With the proverbial praise of "the golden mean" or middle ground, both guidance and assurance are also sought in knowing and following average practice or current trends—this by surveying current professional literature. Because educators believe in improvability each seeks to be above average though he may feel insecure if *too* far above it.

On specific issues such as salary schedules, curricular offerings or unit costs of instruction, the local administrator may seek out average practice through a questionnaire addressed to the administrators in school systems with which he would like his system to be compared. Apparently one of the soundest bases of security yet found for teachers' salary decisions is what the surrounding or comparable communities are doing. Sometimes interview or observation is used to seek out average practice.

The corridor and hotel room conversations at professional conventions serve much the same function. The administrator finds out how others are handling some problems with which he is confronted or how they would handle them. He shapes his own judgment by trying it out informally among his colleagues. He has a basis for decision that gives him assurance. If it worked elsewhere it should work for him.

More formally he may seek for himself and his school system the application of established evaluative criteria, of standardized tests, or an inspection visit from an accrediting agency. Perhaps no one will ever know how many decisions in school administration were made and supported because of North Central Association requirements or because of recommendations from the state department of public instruction.

In all of the foregoing bases for deciding and doing the administrator sought to have the actual decision made for him by someone else, to have his own judgment verified through orthodoxy or popularity or being tolerantly close to the average. But there is also an inner strength that arises from feeling that what one is doing is right. This inner strength and personal control comes from some central core of values to which life is oriented and dedicated. It can be either a personal faith—a series of assumptions accepted by the individual and around which his life was organized—or an intellectual formula to be followed in planning and carrying out action.

Some of the formulas are fragmentary and called into play only when difficulty arises. Others represent general rules for administrative behavior. There is the "keeping ahead of the hounds" formula which implies a responsibility for moving off in a new direction before the critics catch up with one and which involves an adeptness in shifting the fields in which public pressures form. Then there is the "leading on" principle which is based on the concept that man was created for activity and that any decision leading to more and better activity is right while any that leads to less or poorer activity is wrong. In the literature of public and business administration particularly there have been a number of descriptions of formulas by which good administrative decision-making is reached with confidence. One writer describes the aspects of "leadership thinking" as "goal thinking," "derivational thinking," "trend thinking," "scientific thinking," "projective or developmental thinking," and "configurational thinking." This represents something of a synthesis of the bases of support discussed as orthodox, popular and standard practice.

The matter of faith is more difficult to describe. The administrative leader who has faith that all things ultimately work out well for those who love goodness, and who believes that it is basically a friendly and orderly world whose people are going to display good will in response to evidence of good will possesses an inner self-confidence and a tolerance for unsettled questions and temporary trials. The inner strength of such a person is based upon his conviction—upon the strength of his personal articles of faith whether these be religious or secular.

Personal experience and observation of the effectiveness of religious faith in the lives of many gives evidence of the personal control and inner strength which stems from such conviction. But neither statistics nor logic are presented to urge anyone without such faith to go to the religious market place and buy what touches his fancy.

Whether through religious views or a secular philosophy, the person who views himself as representative of a larger unity has widened the configuration against which his act is to be construed. This is a view of faith which provides support for right action beyond the span of the immediate situation and the presently participating associates. Social scientists have pointed out how faith in leaders and a system of beliefs, even though these cannot be empirically justified, do keep a society well knit and purposively organized. A system of beliefs also keeps an individual well knit and purposively organized—it provides the personal controls and inner direction.

2 | Purpose-Defining: The Central Function of the School Administrator

James G. Harlow

In this article Harlow raises the question of what is most crucial in administration. He takes the position that the purposes of organizations are really their most crucial distinguishing features. A decision about purpose is a value decision, he says. Therefore, one's approach to decisions about the purposes of an organization must stem from answers to value questions. Harlow, thus, makes a plea for including the humanities in the preparation of school administrators because he believes that the humanities' disciplines provide the best basis for answering questions about purposes.

The principal emphases of the recent past in the study of administration and in the training of administrators—that is the emphases of the last forty-five years—have been placed on the concept of basic process in administration, on organization or structure in administration, and upon human relations in administration. Most recently both in training and in research, there has been a very strong emphasis upon the concept of administration as the name for the interactions of a group of closely interlocking social roles. In research, a substantial intellectual effort has been directed toward the design of models of social interaction through which to describe social roles and their interactions in educational enterprises. The recent past in the training of educational administrators might be described as the period of rise of empirical description of administration, lately coupled with research effort to develop theories which can provide filing systems for the data already collected and direction for the search for new information.

This activity is familiar to students of the history and philosophy of moved as it achieved today's powerful grasp of our physical and biological experience. As this developmental line, borrowed from the natural sciences, has been adopted and consciously exploited by the social sciences, we have

James G. Harlow, "Purpose-Defining: The Central Function of the School Administrator," (in *Preparing Administrators: New Perspectives*, Jack Culbertson and Stephen Hencley, eds.), Columbus, Ohio: U. C. E. A., 1962, pp. 61–71. Reprinted by permission.

gained new insights into problems of social structure and individual behavior—insights which have yielded and are continuing to yield new tech-
science: it is the line of development along which the human mind has
niques and new opportunities for improvement in the quality of the
organizational life of schools.

However, virtually all of the recent efforts at scientific description of
structure, process, and interpersonal relationships in educational administration have neglected the pervasive effects of purpose in organizations.
Perhaps this is as it should be. As workers in the natural sciences freed
themselves from teleological pursuits and began the painstaking aggregation
of fact which is both public and replicable, humanity emerged from individual and social dependence upon ritual and dogma and began the advance which today maintains our amazing lifespan and high levels of
material living. For the last five hundred years, workers in the natural
sciences have sought diligently to avoid asking questions about the purpose
of the structure and processes which they seek to understand, and this effort has certainly been fruitful.

In matters affecting education, however, there is real question concerning the validity of an effort to avoid discussion of purpose—and this
question appears with great brilliance in any discussion of training programs
for school administrators. For public, wide-scale education is not a given
in any social order; it is a creation. It comes into being as the servant of
social purpose. Its content and processes are altered to accommodate
changes in those purposes. And education itself bears most intimately upon
the formation and revision of the purposes which it in turn is required to
serve.

It can readily be argued that it is differences among purposes of enterprises which produce the enormous differences observable among them. The
concepts of division of labor, for example, and administrative process, for
another example, are as applicable to the organization and operation of
fire-fighting groups as they are to schools. The actual modes of operation
of the two enterprises at first glance are so dissimilar as to suggest that
there is no common denominator connecting them. But, on certain occasions, a school looks very much like a fire-fighting group, as, for example,
when it is conducting an emergency drill to train its members in processes
to be used in case of fire, tornado, or nuclear attack. In its training periods,
a fire company is much like the school.

What changes a warm-hearted, permissive elementary school into a
tightly disciplined, rigidly defined set of behaviors upon the sounding of a
specific signal? This is a moot question; it depends of course upon the
definition of "school." The question precisely exemplifies the point to be
made here—that the shift from learning process to processes for the protection of human life in emergencies is a shift in *purpose*. The people remain the same, the school building remains the same. But the purpose of

the enterprise changes suddenly; and in this change of purpose there are born whole new modes of organization and process.

The purpose of preservation of human life, which must be a part of the purpose of every school, is a relatively easy purpose to develop among prospective administrators and is relatively easy to express in organization and in process. But the original purposes for which the school was created are not those of preservation of physical life. They are a different set of purposes altogether, purposes which are literally intangible, often difficult to express effectively, and difficult therefore to communicate to prospective administrators.

Administration is the servant of organizational purpose. Purpose pervades an organization, determining its subordinate and superordinate roles, its governing role expectations and the like. Division of labor and administrative process are determined by organizational purpose. It therefore follows necessarily that one of the principal emphases in the training of educational administrators—possibly the critical emphasis—must be placed on training in educational purpose and in the processes through which such purposes are defined. No amount of empirical description of schools or management, regardless of frame of reference, can supply the insights necessary for this task.

The need for formal, explicit, and extensive training in purpose and purpose-definition for educational administrators can be developed from another set of considerations arising from current organizational structures of schools. Consider the organization chart for the typical high school. A school group may range in size from a half-dozen to perhaps more than a hundred adults, engaged in what is presumably a single task, the education of the young. The group is featured by a very short chain of command. There is a chief executive, typically one or two assistants to him, frequently a small core of special staff usually called counselors, a few middle-management people called department heads or chairmen, and a very large group of relatively independent workers. In a school, the chief executive's span of control frequently is as high as thirty-five, and in spite of the strong departmental organizations found in some large high schools may exceed even that number. The main academic business of the school usually is carried on through a chain of command of two or three levels: teacher and principal, or teacher, department chairman, and principal. Counselors and assistant principals usually stand in staff relation to the principal.

The teachers are characterized by high levels of training—as compared with workers in other kinds of organizations—and by a tradition of great independence of action within their various individual spheres. In the upper levels of the public school activity, this tradition is reinforced by the typical teacher's high degree of specialization in training, a specialization which renders him relatively independent of detailed supervision by his superordinates. As with any worker, each teacher develops a considerable control of his own situation through detailed knowledge of the situations and the materials with which he works; in schools, this natural control is enhanced by the nature of the principal material with which he works, other human beings. It is indeed a brash principal or supervisor who moves swiftly into a classroom with detailed suggestions for an experienced teacher.

In enterprises featured by short chains of command and very highly trained personnel, the principal dependence for effective coordination must be placed upon shared purpose. Production (e.g., the learning of individual students) is maximized in the elementary school when the second grade teacher and the sixth grade teacher are following the same goal, when their institutional and personal value systems are congruent. In the secondary school, production is at peak when the teacher of physics and the teacher of English agree substantially about the contributions to be made by the high school.

Again, the need for training in educational purpose and in the processes of purpose-development emerges as a critical element in the development of the effective administrator.

Yet another line of observation and reasoning leads to the same conclusion. A superintendent or principal is not a free agent, though the mythology of education often urges the contrary view. He is not free to move his school in any direction which appeals to him, regardless of his sophistication and his skill in interpersonal relations. He does not "set policy." As a matter of fact, both the areas of action and the amount of movement possible to any educational administrator are sharply limited. He cannot replace his board. He cannot make wholesale changes in staff. He cannot alter the training programs through which teachers come to him. He cannot swiftly alter the outlooks of the teaching staff itself. He cannot sharply alter the pattern for commitment of funds within his budget. In short, the successful and highly contributive school administrator becomes so through the cumulative impacts of numerous small decisions, for he is permitted to make relatively few large ones. It follows that his success and contribution might well be predicted through measures of his own purposes, his awareness of those purposes, and his ability to relate his daily burden of small decisions to achievement of those purposes. The prospective school administrator must exhibit sophisticated purposes, must be intellectually aware of those purposes, and must be sufficiently committed to them that they actually control his day-to-day work with his board, with the other members of his administrative group, with his teachers, his students and their parents. Again, it becomes clear that training in purpose and in purpose-definition must be a significant part of the formal programs for prospective school administrators.

Even the nature of our times argues strongly for explicit and continued attention to the training of administrators in purposes and purpose-setting. The observation that ours is a time of extremely rapid change has become a cliché—but it should not be forgotten that clichés emerge to describe situations which are so conspicuous as to be widely noted and commented upon. It recently has frequently been observed that the new task of the school is to train young people for living in a world which no one can yet describe—an observation which again brings to the very forefront of discussion that ancient question, what knowledge is most worth? For, in a situation characterized by rapid changes in international relations, in material conditions of living, in the intellectual horizons of much of humankind, and in the understanding of the nature of our physical universe, the imperative for education is to be found in the determination of those purposes, those value systems, those behaviors which can be urged upon our youth, hopefully, in the deep desire to help tomorrow's adults survive the tests of their times. The fact of rapid change in our society, however, has not yet been reflected in the training of prospective educational administrators.

In the symposium, *Administrative Theory in Education*, Professor Talcott Parsons[1] argues powerfully that educational organizations are so different from others that it is virtually impossible to reason from other types of organization to effective educational activity. In his famous *Democratic Administration*, Ordway Tead[2] some years ago argued much the same thing. John Dewey's writings have consistently held the same position; it cannot really be argued that those responsible for training school administrators have not had purpose-definition urged upon them. But formal training in educational purpose and in purpose-definition in programs for administrators remains limited to brief contact with the history and philosophy of education, and receives a typical commitment of about one-tenth of the course time of the graduate program.

One of the more curious features of the landscape of educational discussion of recent years has been the emergence of the term "value judgment" as a frequently recurring element. This term has, relatively speaking, been absent from discussions of administrative training for many years. It appears now most frequently as an epithet indicating intellectual contempt. A vigorous argument can often be won by the timely assertion, "That's just a value judgment." Apparently, this ploy has become standard in educational gamesmanship.

This use of the term "value judgment" is traceable partially to today's scientific emphasis, which hopes to limit the areas of human action in which value judgments must be developed; and it is due in part to a lack of knowledge of the history of value judgments and of the processes through which such judgments are rendered sophisticated and dependable. The fact is that the human race has spent far more intellectual time and effort on value judgments than it has on scientific research. Our delight with our recently acquired scientific methods has caused us to forget the remarkable contributions of our older intellectual tools. We have behaved much like the home workshop addict who buys a wood-turning lathe and for years thereafter turns out nothing but projects which involve spindles.

Neither the democratic way of life nor the Communist way of life is the product of a scientific study. The decision to establish and maintain a system of public schools is not the result of scientific investigation, and the purposes to be served by those schools are not determined through scientific investigations. An individual's decision to marry and to rear a family is not a science-based decision. Our regard for each other and our ways of demonstrating that regard are not products of empirical study and analysis through symbolic logic.

Values and value judgments are the central elements in the selection, extension, and day-to-day realization of educational purpose. Purposes for schools can, perhaps, be inferred from the society at any given time, as for example, the use of colleges and universities as marriage marts for the off-spring of our upper middle-class and upper-class population, or the use of the local high school to provide entertainment for the community through athletic contests. It is the choice among socially-urged purposes which is difficult, complex—and non-empirical. Who will say, certainly, on any basis other than probable employment survival of the administrator, whether it is better in the long run to operate schools and colleges as public entertainment agencies or as intellectually oriented activities and, if the school is to serve both, what makes an appropriate "mix"? This is the kind of choice in which the administrator must be both skilled and sophisticated; the kind of choice-climate in which his daily work is done.

In times like these, the determination of educational purposes is not a matter simply for an exercise in group dynamics. Neither is it a platform for the exhibition of a persuasive and charismatic personality. It is a matter for the most carefully reasoned, most carefully disciplined intellectual effort. It is in this fact that there is to be found an opportunity for the improvement of training programs for prospective educational administrators. For values and the making of value judgments are the domain of one of the major modes of human thought; namely, the humanities. These are the human studies, those which deal with the peculiarly human features of our experience. Actually, the sophisticated formation of value judgments requires a search for first principles, principles from which conclusions can be precisely derived. It requires study of the current and historical experience of all sorts and kinds of human beings exhibiting many sorts and kinds of value judgments. It involves the careful, rational development, explication, and evaluation of social structure and social process designed to realize value systems and to provide a fertile ground from which even more prescient, more sophisticated values can develop.

The academic names of the fields in which value skills and knowledge are developed are old-fashioned names so far as school administrators are concerned. If to improve education, we must speak in terms of discontinuities with previous experience and established knowledge, then there is little that this part of this paper has to offer. If, on the other hand, we can use older knowledge, perhaps there is a useful suggestion here. For, to provide effective training for prospective administrators in value-setting and purpose-definition, it probably is not necessary to create a host of new courses and programs, though some will undoubtedly be necessary. Most universities strong enough to train administrators offer courses at good levels of sophistication in ethics, in esthetics, in history and in general philosophy; and they typically offer courses in the history and the philosophy of education. Nearly any university provides a base for a good "mix" of materials and techniques in these basic humanistic fields. Good courses in literature are available in every major university.

Foreign travel, highly desirable for the correction of parochialism and ethnocentrism, is not a part of the graduate activity of most institutions. However, courses in the history and current practices of cultures other than our own occur widely among universities, though they are not uniform from institution to institution.

Even without the obvious contribution of contact with other cultures to the prospective administrator, there is opportunity in effort directed toward definition of basic content in the humanities for administrators and in the development of new collations of materials for training prospective administrators. And there are contributions which must be made to the selection of administrators, if genuine skill in both the modes of thought characteristic of empirical studies and modes of thought characteristic of the humanities are defined as desirable for a practicing school administrator. Historically, skill in these two kinds of thinking has not very frequently been developed to high levels in the same person. The established differences among the natural sciences, the social sciences, and the humanities are as much differences in tastes for intellectual activity as they are differences in content. It is interesting to note, however, that the recently developed esthetic criteria for theoretical analysis in the physical sciences have begun to attract to those fields larger numbers of individuals who exhibit strong interest in and taste for such activities as music and drama. Today's physicist is much less likely to be a man with wrench, hammer, and coils of wire than a man with oscilloscope, jeweler's screwdrivers, highly developed mathematical skills, and hobbies in classical music.

Perhaps, if we set about seeking them, we could find for school administration equivalents of today's top-flight physicist, men and women with a grasp of empirical techniques in the social sciences, sensitivity to and skill in theoretical constructs, promise in human relations skills, and real awareness of and participation in the rich human endeavor to discover not only what is, but what is of most worth.

Perhaps we should begin to plan for conferences among humanists deeply concerned with education, presently active and prospective school administrators, professors of education, and university administrators in an effort to define humanistic content appropriate to the administrator's purpose-definition function.

Perhaps we could design and initiate working conferences to plan instruments and processes for selection of people who might develop the strong purpose-orientation, aesthetic tendencies, and practical skills suggested earlier.

Perhaps some universities could undertake tryout of behavioral sciences-oriented programs, plus follow-up contact and study as individuals move through the early parts of their administrative careers.

Perhaps support could be developed for really sophisticated and demanding in-service seminars, short courses and workshops in the humanities, designed for working school administrators.

In summary, the proposal here is essentially for division of the graduate work of the prospective administrator into three components of approximately equal size: (1) empirical social sciences, (2) humanities, and (3) technical management skills, culminating in the doctor's degree. Parenthetically, one could well argue against the continuation of the doctoral thesis in the Ed.D. program for administrators, substituting for it an internship of one year, following the medical school pattern, though this sort of arrangement certainly is not central to the argument of this paper. Discussion of reorganization of social sciences content and management skills content has been purposely omitted from this statement because the current literature is so rich in these fields.

Efforts to describe and define the role of the administrator, whether he be department chairman, principal, superintendent, college dean or college president, industrial executive or military officer have proliferated during the past fifteen years. Insofar as the educational administrator has been described, his role clearly encompasses many things. But among these things none stands out with greater clarity than the function of purpose-definition, the function of seeing that the purposes of the enterprise are accurately and explicitly defined, and effectively held up for view by the group.

It is not that the administrator must "set" the purposes. He must know what kinds of intellectual processes are involved in the generation of purposes, he must know what kinds of questions are significant in the development of purposes, and he must be informed as no other member of the group is informed, in the history of human purpose. The United States can no longer afford the simple group addition of assertions such as "I feel that . . . ," and "I believe that . . . ," and "I am convinced that . . . ," as a way to define purpose in so significant a group of institutions as its schools. It is unrealistic to hope that all members of a school staff can be equally proficient, equally sophisticated and equally interested in the problems of setting and maintaining institutional purpose. Purpose defining is the unique intellectual province of the school administrator; train him for it, we must.

Notes

1. Talcott Parsons, "Some Ingredients of a General Theory of Formal Organization" in *Administrative Theory in Education*, Andrew W. Halpin (ed.) (Chicago: Midwest Administration Center, University of Chicago, 1958), pp. 40–72.
2. Ordway Tead, *Democratc Administraton* (New York: The Association Press, 1948), 78 pp.

3 | Conflicts in Values

Harry S. Broudy

In the following article Broudy explores the nature of value conflict in education. He makes a case for administrators having the integrity to recognize a moral issue and deal with it morally when no moral alternative can honestly be entertained. In so doing, administrators must be able to face the omnipresent value conflict between their own value commitment and their obligations in managing the school organization. Broudy calls for administrators to develop their own value scheme to enable them to make the hard choices and by these choices display their own personal commitment.

Just about the most fundamental questions a man can ask are: Can our value judgments be true? Are they about reality? Are they supported by reality? And the most fundamental answer we can give to life is to say "yes" or "no" to these fundamental questions. However, to say that these questions and answers are fundamental is not to say that they are the issues we raise most frequently; indeed, we often go to some pains not to raise them at all.

There have been and are a number of ways of saying "yes." The Aristotelian notion that reality is itself a motion from potentiality to actuality guided by inbuilt norms is a very broad and general "yes" to the question of the objectivity of value. Every living thing and presumably the cosmos as a whole, according to Aristotle, has a telos, a goal that signifies its perfected form. To this end it naturally tends as the plant tends to its fruiting. Man by his very nature not only has a rational telos for his being, but can be aware of it and how well or ill he is achieving it. Moreover, insofar as the human being is succeeding in the human enterprise he feels pleasure, because the good, the beautiful, and the delightful are but different ways of experiencing perfection. Pleasure is not the goal of the virtuous and happy life but rather the accompaniment of it.

The Christian "yes" is even more familiar. A supernatural Being

Harry S. Broudy, "Conflicts in Values," in Harry S. Broudy, R. E. Ohm and W. G. Monahan (eds.), *Educational Administration Philosophy in Action* (Norman, Oklahoma: the College of Education, University of Oklahoma, 1965), pp. 42–58. Reprinted by permission.

through his own nature will provide norms for the human quest. These norms are summarized in commandments and exhortations but also personified in the Christ, the objectification par excellence of the perfection of the man-God relation. Immanuel Kant said that we must say "yes" because, without an unqualified moral law whose sovereignty over our will we freely acknowledge, the moral experience of man would be inexplicable. Only a good will, i.e., a will determined solely by the respect for the moral law, can be an unqualified good, i.e., an intrinsic good.

There are many other ways of saying "yes." Nietzsche looked to the fearless strength of spirit in the Superman and the Romantics found the ultimate "yea" in the strength of passion. The Stoics said it calmly, Nietzsche defiantly, Kant sternly, and Plato beautifully, but they all affirmed the reality of the human quest for value; it was not to be regarded as an illusion.

The variations in the "yes saying" are less important than the posture toward life which the "yes" in any of its forms signifies. It is a strong attitude and, when the chips are down, a rigid one. It is, however, a confident firmness rather than the defiant gesture to which Existentialists feel they must resort. It is a view that makes sense out of striving for endless improvement, out of suffering for ideals, but it also vindicates a certain busybody concern for the improvement of others.

There are also a number of ways of saying "no" to the objectivity and reality of value norms. Skepticism is as old as philosophy itself. Protagoras proclaimed that man was the measure of all things—of what is and what is not, and presumably of what ought to be. By stressing the word "man" he was denying that non-man—God, or the Cosmos, or Reality—was the measure. However, he did not tell us *which* man was to be the measure. The ideal man? The conventional man? The successful man? The educated man? The common man?

Today among philosophers, moral relativism is the popular view. Value judgments, it is argued, reflect the speaker's attitudes and preference; they are not true or false. They are to be construed as ejaculations of pleasure or dismay or as exhortations. As Charles Stevenson might put it: "Generosity is good" means first that I approve generous behavior and, second, that I want you to approve it also. It neither describes nor prescribes anything universally.

Among social scientists and part-time philosophers cultural relativism is the most usual form of saying "no" to the objectivity of value standards. This is merely the belief that value judgments and standards are the product of our culture and valid only to the extent that one wishes to live at peace with that culture. Current cultural relativism has not gone far beyond the observations of Montaigne on cannibalism, but it is better researched and documented.

Of course there are many ways of saying both "yes-and-no." Some say "yes" to means but not to ends; some to ends but not to means; some say "yes" to intentions but not to consequences, and some say the opposite, and to each package of conviction or lack thereof corresponds an attitude toward life. The extreme "no-sayer," if he is consistent, will, like the ancient skeptics, refuse to believe anything and refrain from all judgments about action and from action itself, so far as this is possible. He is more likely to be angered by those who affirm the objectivity of value than by any value in particular that they may happen to affirm. He hates dogmatists, doctrinaires, absolutists, fixity, rigidity, and in all things favors their opposites.

Most of us, as might be expected, have attitudes that go with both "yes" and "no" saying. We live as if at least some of our values are absolute and beyond question, e.g., that the wanton inflicting of pain is unqualifiedly bad, but it is difficult for us to conceive that the judgment, "Beethoven is better than Be-bop," might be universally true. It so happens, I suppose, that none of the persons we respect believe that wanton inflicting of pain is good, whereas many persons whom we respect are not for Beethoven.

At this point it is pertinent to remark that in debating the issue as to whether there are ultimate value norms and objective value judgments we do not use the same criteria as we do in determining whether scientific statements are true. For example, if the natives of Kentucky mountain hollows did not believe in the theory of biological evolution, the community of academic scholars would no doubt conclude that the hollow folk were just plain wrong. But if the same folk failed to believe that what we call lying and cheating were morally wrong, the academic community might take this as a proof that lying and cheating were not really wrong, but only so in certain cultures. In other words, scientific truth is the belief adopted by a consensus of the learned, but a value-truth, so to speak, must be validated by the consensus of everybody. Why the untutored, uncultivated, unreflective man should be a measure of value-truth but not of scientific truth is difficult to understand. Unless, of course, there is an innate moral faculty which validates each man's judgment, whatever it may be.

Our ambivalent attitude toward the truth-status of value judgments reveals itself in our postures toward certain educational issues. For example, we are told in most of our social science textbooks that there is no way of judging whether a society is really good or bad, but at the same time the authors deplore certain tendencies in the culture and praise others. This, although both the norms and failure to live up to them, are "facts" of the culture. They are for reform, although on their own argument there is really no way to justify one form over another. They scoff at any appeal to natural law, but any questioning, let us say, as to the validity of the criterion of democracy or of pleasure they regard as quibbling.

We pronounce solemnly that in our schools there shall be no indoctrination, except that we shall come out boldly and unequivocally for the democratic way of life. Or that there is no fixed truth in science, that all statements in it are held tentatively, and that it is the process of inquiry that is important rather than the product. Nevertheless, there is such a thing as excellence, this same educator insists, and it consists of learning "good" chemistry and "good" biology and insists further that information be accurate, etc. But our hypotheses work because they correspond to a reality independent of them or because of sheer chance. If the former, there is little point in denying truth as a possibility; if the latter, then there is no point in thinking at all.

However, as we shall have occasion to note, even when men do subscribe to a belief in objectivity of value judgment, conflict is not thereby obviated. For we often have to choose among alternatives that offer positive goods and not merely to decide between good and evil. In the ordinary controversies over policy the opponents both seek legitimate goods in a situation where the resources are insufficient to satisfy both. Nor is it very different in the individual's economy of value where many goods vie for attention and effort.

What does this conflict among values mean for the individual who expects to get or give some kind of value education in the schools? What does it mean to the schoolman who is caught in the conflicts of groups that strive to achieve good but incompatible goals?

We as individuals or as participants in the social process can in theory and to some extent in practice subscribe to an egalitarian pluralism in values. By compromise and careful balancing of prudential considerations, one satisfies as many claims as is decently possible, and what more can one be expected to do? Unfortunately, this kind of practical solution on either the individual or social level satisfies nobody. Not simply because everyone is left with somewhat less than he would wish for, but primarily because a mere aggregate of discrete experiences is rarely satisfactory.

A life to be satisfactory over any span of time has to have a dominant theme and interesting variations. This is what is ordinarily meant by an artistic integration of materials and this, in turn, means selection and hierarchial order rather than an egalitarian pluralism. We cannot assign equal volume to every note or equal value to every tone and come up with an interesting piece of music or painting. By indiscriminate variety life can be rendered tolerably diverting and by monotony it can be rendered intolerable, but by neither is it rendered satisfying on any criterion that reflective men have seriously entertained.

It would seem necessary, therefore, that those of us who make motions in the directions of value education seriously consider the notion of gradations or levels within each type of value experience as well as the differences among types of value experience. It makes sense to think of experience as giving a distinctive kind of satisfaction or pain as it varies from the aesthetic to the religious, to the intellectual, to the moral, to the technical, social, physiological and recreational. It takes no tuition to distinguish the inner quality of seeing a gray day from that of bounding good health, or from the sanctity of a holy place, or an act of patriotism, or duty, or solving a problem. He who confuses the joy of victory with duty to one's country or who cannot distinguish the beauty of a garden from the value of real estate is a confused and dull fellow to boot. He who justifies playing games by the duty to preserve one's health and the taking of alcohol by the duty to be amiable to one's host is well on the road to hypocrisy, which is an acute form of messing up the distinctive qualities of experience.

We can distinguish within any one realm of value at least three important levels. At the bottom is the untutored, primitive, rude, but genuine taste. The man likes what he likes and he does not know why and he does not much care. The appeal to his senses or to his sentiments must be direct, gross, and obvious. In a variation of Russell Lyne's descriptions, he drinks when he is thirsty and he prefers beer. Girls are good girls or bad girls; his leaders are good guys or bad guys; his fellow citizens are traitors or patriots.

At a perhaps higher level is the tutored conventional taste and judgment that reflects what the social order will sanction and reward. It is the level represented and approved by a popular play, the best selling novel, the high circulation newspaper and magazine. For a man at this level the guide is fashion, respectability. He is the solid citizen politically, and in most situations can be trusted to do the right thing because he wants to do the right thing. His taste and opinions are not unreflective, but it is not he who has done the reflecting.

The third level (or that of the connoisseur) is the result of self-cultivation. His judgments are his own, so are his tastes, but they are neither the untutored tastes of the peasant nor the conventional tastes of the dominant social stratum. So the connoisseur in any field—baseball to philately, martinis to morals—is a rare person indeed, and yet he is made, not born, and that is most significant for education.

Just as there are connoisseurs in each of the different value domains, so are there connoisseurs of life as a whole who can concoct a life style that witnesses the same sort of sensitivity and taste. The life eminently good is as much a display of interesting variety held in units as is a fine painting, and this analogy is more than a figure of speech.

Such talk about value confronts the schoolman with the question that introduced this discussion, viz., whether types of value and hierarchies of value can be maintained without some kind of commitment to saying "yes" or "no" in value theory. A connoisseur, to establish his authority, must either be right or charming. He can be right only if he can defend his judgments intellectually, and this he cannot do if such judgments are, in principle, neither true nor false. But if they are in any important sense true, or could be true, then his judgments correspond to something objectively present either in human nature or physical nature or in the relation between them.

A commitment to relativism of value judgments, on the other hand, validates the connoisseur's authority if granted at all by his charm or persuasiveness, which may be a fact but is never a validation. A thousand claims upon us, whether they come from individuals, reference groups, or our culture, do not constitute a moral demand until we acknowledge their rightness, and the fact that we can demand the moral credentials of any claim upon us means that sooner or later there have to be self-validating credentials (intrinsic values) and this, of course, means the abandonment of complete relativism.

In a culture where diversity prevents the routine and almost unconscious acceptance of standards that marks a stable simple society, the schoolman cannot count on standards that everyone takes for granted. Nor can he resort to egalitarian pluralism where all values have their day without fear or favor in the school. First, because his patrons will tolerate diversity only within the bounds of a certain life, e.g., middle class value schema. Second, because the school would abdicate the role of educator if it refused to select from the culture and tried to be an indiscriminate reflector of it.

To compound the dilemma of the schoolman and of the individual as well, our culture presents another troublesome choice, still another conflict of values. I refer here to what has paradoxically but not inaccurately been called the choice between the good and the good enough. Excellence is a state that the human psyche inveterately craves and just as regularly does without. Often we settle for less because the culture can afford no more. However, in a culture in which material goods are plentiful even for those not unusually endowed with strength, talent, or energy, the good enough can be quite good indeed. Even with respect to non-material blessings, the situation is hard to cavil at. When has there been so great an abundance of low priced books, magazines, records, radio and television programs? When has the access of the common man to the fine arts been freer?

With relative ease, with only a modicum of self-cultivation and effort, the common man of today can reach the good enough. In such a state of affairs should the school introduce discontent and new conflicts by pointing to "higher" possibilities? Is it not the genius of our age that so many can live so well on the brains of so few? And when so many of our people, despite the plenitude of blessings, still have not achieved the good enough, is there any point in talking about education for excellence? Or is there point in doing so only for the prospective elites whose destiny, like that of the mythological God-King, is to immolate itself for the salvation of the Scientifico-Technological system that it alone can sustain? The good enough is, as my professor of philosophy used to say, the greatest enemy of the good.

In one way or another value conflicts at all levels, metaphysical, societal, personal, within value domains and among them, sooner or later come to roost on the shoulders of the school. And because the highest responsibility rests with the administrator, he must inevitably divide his activity between coping with value conflicts on an institutional basis and acting out his own role as a value witness. His training must inevitably provide for both dimensions, or make the tragic mistake of neglecting to do so. Yet they require skills, knowledge, and attitudes of quite different orders. We are prone to take care of the coping, managing, manipulating, dimension by instruction but to pay our respects to the dimension of self-cultivation and commitment by intermittent exhortation—in ritualistic paragraphs at the opening and closing of the lecture, book, or course. This in a way is understandable, for we know much more about making men efficient than about making them men.

It is easy to become cynical and witty about the way an administrator copes with conflict, especially if one is not an administrator. However, it is a mistake to believe that administrators can or even should always operate at the level of fundamental principle in coping with conflict. The primary function of the administrator is to keep his institution at its job, whereas at the level of controversy about ultimate principle all action stops.

If there is a guiding principle in dealing with conflicts in principle, it is: Don't let them occur. This gives us the rule: Deal with a conflict at the lowest level of principle that the situation and your conscience permits. We might call this the principle of least principle. I would like to generalize this to show why this is not necessarily the result of cynicism but rather a necessity of institutional life in an imperfect society.

We have to go back to the mechanisms by which we make a distasteful but necessary function tolerable. Care of the sick, disposal of the dead, punishment of evil doers, for example, are distasteful but necessary functions in a society. One way of getting people to perform them willingly is to conventionalize the procedures, i.e., depersonalize them into standard procedures performed according to rules. If the rules can be derived from science, so much the better, because in doing so we have arrived at the professional stage of the function. To the professional sickness, death, filth, and corruption are problems to be understood, not ordeals to live through. They are not his troubles and wisely *he* turns to other professionals when the troubles are his own. There is probably no task so revolting that routine, method, theory, a degree, or at least a special uniform and title cannot render tolerable.

The devising of regular and sanctioned procedures for dealing with value conflicts is a standard function of an institution and especially of those administering it. I have heard a noted university president say that his goal was to have a policy, a rule, and a procedure to cover every possible contingency in the conduct of a university. Whether this is an administrative dream or nightmare, I do not know, but the import is clear. Given such a state, no issue of principle would ever have to be raised, and if ever mistakenly raised, could be resolved, i.e., be kept out of the newspapers, by procedural means.

The way in which this device is applied at times has its comic and tragic aspects. Example: Negroes march in protest against housing discrimination. Administrative response: Arrest the leaders for obstructing traffic. Example: A student cheats on an examination, is caught and reported to the administration. Response: Expel him from school because he has not paid his laboratory fees for the semester.

These are examples of what might be dubbed *procedural* irrelevance. Rather than face an issue on its obvious merits, one disposes of it by removing one or more of the parties to the dispute on charges that have nothing to do with the issue in question. Such procedural irrelevance is roughly the counterpart of the logical fallacy of irrelevant thesis.

Another solution might be called procedural interposition. Example: A faculty member protests that he has been dismissed unjustly. Response: File the protest with this and this committee and take X steps in such and such a sequence, if you wish to have your protest adjudicated. This postpones the need to face the value issue for a long time, and, if the petitioner is not a man of courage and persistence, forever.

Or one adopts a diversionary solution. Example: Two valuable members of the faculty cannot agree on departmental policy. Response: Give each his own department or promote one of them to an administrative post.

These gambits, not to speak of the numerous ploys in terms of force, compromise, oblivescence, obfuscation, persuasion, and fatigue, are all devices to avoid raising fundamental issues and especially the moral issue. In such radical problems as automation and federal aid to education, the controversy is kept as long as possible on the procedural griddle in the hope that some sort of acceptable action can be found that will obviate facing the conflict in principle. And this must not be dismissed as cynicism or cowardice, for societies, if not individuals, are well aware that when the issue is reduced to stark "yes" and "no" saying to a fundamental principle, the only action possible is war and the destruction of at least one of the contending parties.

It would be strange indeed if the massive enterprise of formal education did not behave as do other institutions, and if its administrators did not, as all administrators must, seek the knowledge and techniques whereby conflicts in value are managed. It would constitute a remarkable exception to the rule if these techniques for coping with conflict did not employ the principle of least principle in doing so.

And yet the administrator of the educational institution is not in quite the same position as the administrators of other social institutions. The business administrator can fall back on the principle: Business is business, and the politician can fall back on the principle that good politics is what keeps the party in power. The educator, however, deals with nothing but values—human beings who are clusters and constellations of value potentials. Nothing human is really alien to the educational enterprise and there is, therefore, something incongruous about educational administrators evading fundamental value conflicts. A lapse in moral integrity that in a businessman or a politician or a lawyer is merely deplored in an educator becomes intolerable. The public will never quite permit the educational administrator the moral latitude that it affords some of its other servants. For to statesmen and soldiers men entrust their lives and fortunes, but to the schools they entrust their precarious hold on humanity itself.

Whether or not the public is right in this way of looking at the educator is not the point to be settled here, and some people in school "business" undoubtedly chafe under the honor so thrust upon them. The training of school administrators has to take account of a situation in which value conflicts have to be minimized but not swept under the rug. One needs administrative adroitness to prevent raising the moral issue at every turn, but there must also be the moral integrity to recognize a moral issue when there is one and to deal with it morally when no moral alternative can honestly be entertained.

At this point one gets the feeling that this is where Western civilization came in and that this has all been said before. For example, we seem to hear again that precursor of all that is really important both in philosophy and in the philosophy of education, Plato. Plato laid the groundwork for the training of administrators, especially educational administrators, because the instrument of political administration was to be education in both the formal and informal senses of that word. Now the guardians were trained, if you recall, both to know and to be, and to be what they knew. In other words, they not only knew about value and had glimpsed the absolute norms, but they themselves were the embodiments of these norms so far as human beings could embody them. The philosopher-king was expected to be wise as well as well-bred and scholastically apt.

It is easy to dismiss the Platonic training of the guardians as a Utopian counsel of perfection, but the Platonic teaching is more valuable for what it tells us about our problems than for the solutions it proposes. Lacking a rational social order, an administrator will always face a profound existential tension between his own value commitment and the management of the enterprise placed in his charge; a tension between sensitivity to principle and a flight from it. Without efficiency in coping with conflict, the enterprise will collapse dramatically; without a strong commitment to a value hierarchy, the enterprise dies more quietly and gradually but no less surely.

One can end this essay by uttering the truism that there is no easy solution and the equally obvious injunction to train our school administrators in both knowledge and virtue. Whether one could do this and still let them give the ordinary hostages to fortune in the form of fame and family is as doubtful now as it was in Plato's thought. Plato did not think that it was either safe or wise to force leaders to choose between private and public good. In this we are more Utopian than Plato.

Given our times and conditions, about the closest we can come to schooling for a viable union of wisdom and efficiency is a combination of foundational knowledge for the former and science and technology for the latter.

Foundational knowledge, both as to fact and value, is a large scale map with both cognitive and evaluational dimensions. It is formed by really good and thorough general education plus the foundational study of educational problems. It supplies the concepts for building a hierarchy of value. While this does not make our administrator a connoisseur, it does acquaint him with the paths of connoisseurship in the several value domains; and while it does not of itself dictate his own life style, his own pattern of theme and variation, of dominance and subordination, it does expose him to the most distinctive patterns our history has so far turned up.

Whoever interprets his problems and those of the school on such a map does not thereby have a rule for solving them, but he does know in what domain the problems belong. He knows where reality ends and hypocrisy begins. Whoever has a well-developed interpretative map is not automatically happy or serene in his work, but he is not a yokel who perspires too freely and readily in every predicament. He knows when to raise the moral issue and when to divert people from raising it. He can sleep nights and look his colleagues in the eye. This, one might say, is the good enough stage in the development of an administrator.

However, the schoolman, like every other man, cannot forever escape the choice between saying "yes" or "no" to fundamental questions. Like all men, to be somebody he has to be a living witness of this commitment, whether he says "yes" or "no." Whether he persuades by argument or by charm, if he is to lead, he must act out a value schema that makes connection with aspirations and impulses that stir all men—some clearly, distinctly, and compellingly; some only vaguely and dimly, no more than a restless moment in a dream.

4 | Art, Science, and New Values

Harry S. Broudy

Protest movements, especially those directly related to schools, usually provide overt challenges to "established" values. Many educational administrators today are almost completely caught up in such value conflicts. The second Broudy article speaks to this condition and proposes an intellectual posture that may be useful in giving direction to the administrator as he develops his value schema.

A science-based technology has spawned the challenges to established values. However, the author-suggests that science is a source for new values—new values which are essentially new behavioral forms of the old virtues.

There is a familiar saying to the effect that our troubles multiply as our statistics improve. Crime, insanity, and sin in general are blown up—to use a photographic term made notorious by a recent film—by our instant communication systems. We are forced to become conscious of evil and ugliness that our grandfathers were able to keep *sub rosa* and probably subconscious. In those days, it seems, sin and crime and evil could be confined to ghettos of one kind or another, and gentlewomen could be sequestered from them, at least until discreet accounts appeared in genteel novels appropriate to their age, station, and sensibility.

If we are consciously preoccupied with evil and violence, it is not because we choose to be; there simply is no escape from it, not under the mask of decorum, nor under the lid that suppresses the id. It is as if a huge chain of department stores operated by Lucifer flooded us with a stream of unwanted merchandise; as if *Walpurgisnacht* were being staged nightly on our front lawn without so much as a by-your-leave.

I find it impossible to reassure myself that our troubles are caused by nothing more than our increased awareness of them. For one thing, the world is fuller of people than ever before; so absolutely, not merely relatively, there is more likelihood of suicide, divorce, and crimes of violence, including the apparently senseless ones. Furthermore, the closer people are packed together, the more delicately constructed and tuned the social ma-

Harry S. Broudy, "Art, Science, and New Values," *Phi Delta Kappan* 49, No. 3 (November, 1967), pp. 115–119. Reprinted by permission.

chine must be if they are to live without abrading each other. There is little evidence that our social institutions or our individual dispositions have achieved the quality needed to cope with the increased density of men and events.

But all this and numerous other symbols and symptoms of social trouble are familiar to you. Also there is general agreement as to the cause of the trouble: a value breakdown variously described by sociologists, psychologists, the undertaker school of theologians, and artists. There is no need to add to these outpourings, but I shall venture a hypothesis—which there is no time to argue—as to why so much of the protest is so repetitive, so sincere, and so ineffectual. We seem to be in the grip of something like a muscular spasm in which antagonistic muscles keep a limb rigid and its owner in impotent agony. Most of our protest literature is seized by a spasm caused by trying to hold to two antagonistic doctrines at the same time. One is that our ills result from our inability or unwillingness to face reality. The other is that there is no way of distinguishing reality from illusion. How, then, is one to know what attitude to take toward black power, red-necks, purple hawks, and off-white doves? Are they reality or masks for reality?

The scapegoat of this spasm is the middle-class value syndrome, whatever that is construed to be. But is it the values that make the middle class objectionable or is it the holding of them by the middle class that makes the values bad? How embarrassing this situation can be is illustrated by the predicament of the public schools. We are to redeem the disadvantaged, but not presumably by imposing middle-class values and demands upon them. But if one asks in what way the disadvantaged are disadvantaged, we are told they lack the means to achieve what seems suspiciously like middle-class values. Now I think that one can with some consistency hold that class is the criterion of value, as I believe the Marxists do. Or one can maintain that there is a criterion that transcends class and cultural peculiarities. Finally, one can hold to a denial of all value criteria. This is a kind of nihilism, and I take it that some of the protestors profess it. If so, they are chargeable not so much with logical inconsistency as with social ingratitude. For to live in society at all is to live off the common store of Nature's gifts and human labor, and to draw on this store while rejecting the means of maintaining it is a selfishness which issues from a kind of social stupidity. Nihilism, to succeed, must become a club from which most of mankind must be excluded.

So I take the view that the talk about the death of God—the real issue is not whether He is dead, but rather whether He was ever alive—and the more sensational rejection of all value norms is a kind of romantic shock treatment aimed at foolish complacency, mindless cruelty, and muted humanity. This has been solemnized by Existentialists of varying degrees of seriousness and intellectual competence, and it has been exploited by publishers, film makers, and other suppliers of the adolescent market.

My own experience with students has included a number of informal inquiries in trying to ascertain what they really love and hate, and what they would do if the freedom they demand were really given to them. I can only report that only on the most rare occasions have they been willing to accept real liberty to shape their own studies or their lives—especially when the price of liberty was accountability for the wrong choices. I have found that young people—even the wildest protestors—do not reject honesty, decency, kindness, justice, dignity of the person, yes, even chastity. On the contrary, the protests are justified in the name of these virtues. The young do not say, "Down with courage"; rather, they are puzzled and angered by what passes for courage in their time. Neither the young nor the old can reject the generic virtues, for this is not a matter of choice at all. We refuse to let anyone reject them, even if he says he does, because these are the rules of eligibility for membership in the human family. If creatures—on whatever planet we should happen to find them—are really insensitive to these virtues or values, we would simply classify them as nonhuman and treat them accordingly.

The young have the right to expect that the behavioral meanings of the generic invariant virtues be made clear by the elders of their epoch; they have a right to expect an education that will allow them to learn, explore, and appraise these behavioral forms; they have a right to expect from the learned men of their times enlightenment and guidance in the exploration of the new values.

Science a Source for New Values

I shall suggest that if we shift the usual focus of our demands from science and the arts a bit we may get answers that will not make it necessary to seek salvation in contrived happenings, exotic drugs, and dazed surrender to incoherent messages and subtle "massages." I shall argue that science and science-based technology are not merely the source of nonmoral, amoral, or immoral means. On the contrary, I shall invite your consideration of the notion that science is a source for new values, i.e., for the new behavioral forms of the old virtues. Conversely, I shall argue that the arts are not merely the celebrations of values to which we are already committed, and that even though art may need no other excuse for being, it nevertheless is a great instrument for the achievement of whatever values we do espouse. Indeed, without art we do not really perceive the value of anything, for art gives value a perceptible shape and makes it a candidate for imaginative appropriation. In short, I invite you to consider seriously the possibility that science is not our only source of means and the arts our only source of ends.

If the field of our moral obligation is constituted by the value possibilities that we cannot refuse to realize or try to realize, scientifically based
technology is the most dynamic single factor in determining the scope of
our possible duty. Every time new power is put into our hands, a shift in
the moral economy occurs because it changes the domain of what we *can*
do, out of which emerges the domain of what we *ought* to do.

It now looks as if the natural scientists with complicated assists from
technologists have removed "impossibility" as a valid ground of exculpation
in such matters as race discrimination, peace, and social justice. Delaying
actions, counsels of moderation, linguistic evasions are, therefore, seen ever
more clearly for what they are. The brighter the youth, the more clearly do
they see, and the quicker their indignation. Indeed, we must resign ourselves to forfeiting moral credit even when we do move in the right
direction, for it is difficult to distinguish, for example, which factors in
our current war on poverty and inequality are altruistic and which are
motivated by the shrewd realization that if our economy is to leap forever
from strength to strength, it cannot afford pockets of poverty and ignorance.
When humanitarian deeds are economically necessary and politically ex-
pedient, virtue runs rampant. As between a good society and no society the
choice requires little moral heroism.

Since one is never obligated to do the impossible, and since all that is
possible is not necessarily obligatory, the value quest is more than a search
for means to given ends. Both ends and means are transformed by ex-
pansions and contractions in the spheres of possibility. For example, the
fight against cancer and vaccination for smallpox were not objects of moral
obligation for Socrates, but they are for us. The abolition of poverty, over-
population, pollution of air and water, and the abatement of ignorance are
all matters of our obligation, because the power is clearly available for their
accomplishment. Once technology makes social justice possible, we cannot
get by with good intentions.

So, oddly enough, in an age that complains of constraint by vast bureaucratic concentrations of power snarled in red tape, there is really a
surfeit of freedom, more by far than we know how or are willing to use.
The paradox, however, is dissolved rather simply. The power and freedom
we have lost is not always identical with the power and freedom we have
gained. For the power we have gained is likely to take the form of collective,
corporate power, entailing on our part not only a will to use it, but also a
will to unite with others in using it. Much of the power we have lost is the
individual power to shape our own destiny, whether it be in our economic,
political, or social life.

The shift is traumatic in at least two ways. First, it renounces the image
of the moral quest as the slaying of dragons by heroes. It means the de-
valuation of the moral agent in the traditional sense. The scenario of the

good life as a series of donations to worthy causes, memberships in diverse uplifting organizations, and endless attendance at committee meetings is neither dramatic nor exciting. Second, it shakes rudely, rapidly, and repeatedly our convictions as to what we ought to do and want. Conventional morality ceases to be the reliable flywheel of daily life. To be and to remain moral requires moral intelligence, an almost daily reassessment of resources; in short, a nondramatic strenuousness. As we shall see later, the commitments men make are ruled as much, if not more, by aesthetic fitness than logical cogency or even practical efficiency. The Greeks' imagination outran possibility, so they conjured up a set of specialized gods to make up the difference. Our possibilities have outrun our imagination, and we look to the artists to conjure up images of life that would make these possibilities aesthetically interesting and some irresistible.

The responses to this situation are about what one might expect. Middle-aged citizens go through the motions of donating, belonging, and attending, but half-heartedly, for they long for the days when the moral life was an individual encounter between heroes and villains. They have learned that it is vain and naïve to try to fix the responsibility for misdeeds, whether committed on one's automobile or on the state treasury, but that there is no culprit they will not believe to their dying day. They try to understand it all, they endure much, but they forgive nothing.

The half-hearted virtue of the middle-aged is almost correctly diagnosed by the young as complacency, indifference, hypocrisy, and perhaps even cowardice. This, I believe, lies at the root of the more spectacular protests of Sartre, Genet, and the off-Broadway theatre. It lies at the root of the explosive resentment of some of our students—and some of our best students, at that. To them the undramatic mechanics of democratic action is equated with the conventional morality of the middle class, obfuscated by statistics and made corny by sentimentality. They cannot find their identity or reality in it. They feel that a more dramatic, a more dangerous gesture alone will prove their reality and presumably their honesty—to be thrown in jail for civil rights, to shock one's parents, to disgust the community. Even the avant-garde have not apparently gotten beyond the belief that without a hair shirt the claim to moral integrity is a fraud. To those who have found such a shirt, it often becomes a Linus blanket. Integrity without a hair shirt, or more correctly, one with the hair on the inside of our own skin, is a deeper and more serious moral assignment than either the old or the new guard realizes. The proper face of internal suffering may be quite different from what some of our contemporary critics think it is, but art has not yet come up with the new face.

The Moral Meanings of Sex

I shall discuss sexual behavior as one example of the transvaluation of values made necessary by science-technology, because of all the acts in our physiological repertoire, none is so intense in its demands and rewards, and yet, for the individual if not the race, so postponable. It thus comes under the dominion of choice and morality. Further, because it is involved with life-giving and life-sustaining, church, state, and family are inordinately concerned with the most private of intimacies. And in modern times, at least, it has become inextricably woven with romance, glamour, status, and sanity.

But once science made it realiably possible to sever the bond between sex and life-giving, the moral meanings of sexual behavior had to be redefined, for it released the sexual act from a great part of its burden of social consequences. The moral dimension of sex now has to be sought more in personal relations and individual character rather than in social consequences. Sex morality is now personal rather than tribal.

The easy evasion of pregnancy has made it possible to reduce the domain also. The James Bond or Playboy philosophy of sex is not so implausible, if the human context of sex is reduced to the hedonic and aesthetic properties of *love-making*. (Note that one *makes* it.) Can the human context be reduced so radically? The evidence of civilized society seems to be against it. We cannot refrain from humanizing even the most obviously physiological functions: eating becomes dining just as lust, before we know it, turns into love and romance. Birth and death have been ritualized no end; other physiological functions such as digestion and elimination have defied human sublimation, so we devote our efforts to keeping them out of sight and conversation. When these and other vegetative functions get out of kilter to the point where life or death depends solely on them, we are at the nadir of humanness. Surgeons and nurses, in doing what they must under these circumstances, make short shrift of personal dignity. Because civilization consists pretty largely of transforming physiological necessities into human possibilities, science, in makng it possible to demoralize sex, does not make it more plausible that we shall use the new freedom to do so. On the contrary, the new sexual freedom can be used not to demoralize sex but to moralize it far more profoundly than was heretofore possible, once the human relationships that sex engenders become objects of choice rather than forced upon us by biological accidents or the fear of them. Sex relationships become a challenge to integration with all other values, and, above all, a challenge to be consonant with the type of personality one has chosen to become.

But how does one bring about this reflected choice unless the experience is there to be reflected upon? And how does one control the consequences of such experiences so that they remain developmental rather than destructive? What social institutions have we developed for this form of character development? Lacking appropriate institutions—for the ones we have are predicated on equating sex with reproduction—our adolescents have coped with the situation in a clumsy way. Sometimes they establish Bohemian regions within cities or on the unofficial spaces of the campus. Sometimes they leave home for the anonymity and freedom of the city. But by and large it is technology in the form of the automobile and contraceptive devices that furnish the means of escape from parental surveillance, albeit not from guilt feelings.

These solutions are satisfactory to nobody, and I suggest that art has yet to come up with a life style that satisfactorily embodies the new value possibilities in sexual relations. The James Bond and Playboy images are bids in that direction, but they exemplify the demoralization of sex rather than its new moralization. No new life style for the contemporaneous woman has yet emerged. The roles of wife, prostitute, and casual companion we are familiar with, but a variety of free-spirited heroines served up by current fiction and film must still be classified as the probings of art to find such a new form.

Reinterpreting Patriotism, Courage, Heroism

We are in a similar state with respect to war and aggression. Technology has made war logically obsolete and cooperation a moral and practical imperative. Technology has depersonalized and thereby demoralized war, and this has created a need for the reinterpretation of such notions as patriotism, courage, and heroism. These virtues historically have been defined by the exigencies of wars fought by heroes against villains. If war is no longer justifiable, what becomes of these virtues?

Three wars in which the United States has participated in the last 50 years have failed to turn up a convincing heroic life style for the soldier. The glory of battle has been displaced by a dreary resignation to endure what could not be cured. The Vietnam affair is the last stage of disillusionment with military service even among those who do not seek to avoid it. That art has been unable to glorify the modern soldier is a better sign of the bankruptcy of war than any logical argument.

For we do not really lack moral equivalents of war—we have dozens of them, ranging from the conquest of disease to the conquest of injustice, but these all entail peaceful cooperation, which aesthetically is poor stuff, difficult to dramatize. Drama demands personified conflict and danger and publicity. The hero must be sung and glorified. He must overcome real villains. But as I have already mentioned, it is difficult to do poems or paintings about peace and democracy if one is to remain true to their pedestrian complexity. Yet until the new forms of heroism—heroism of an inner, humbler, and deeper sort—are made perceptible to the imagination by art, the moral equivalents of war will not displace war itself.

Science cannot of itself determine the shape of the concrete life styles that can embody the value potentials it creates. For one thing, any number of life patterns could serve as embodiments of the new values or value ideals. Furthermore, science cannot shape ideals out of the possibilities it describes. For an ideal is more than a possibility; it is also a command to take some possibility seriously enough to manifest it. This imperative germinates within the person when a sensuous model of the good seduces him into an irresistible desire to imitate it. But which image will so charm him we cannot even guess. Why the images of Greece and Rome inflamed the youth of the Renaissance to almost ridiculous forms of emulation is hard to say even after it happened; it was impossible to predict it before it happened.

Responsibilities of the Artist

Where do these models come from? First, from the people around us, but when the rate of social change is high, we get a generational gap, and the young cease to look for life models in the population over 30. Yet at best real people are hard to idealize; they forever betray their reality. The inspirational values of biography (especially if truthful) are, I believe, overestimated. The really influential personalities—Socrates, Jesus, Ghandi—are outsize figures, and until their behavior transcends the limits of common sense they do not serve as effective models. But it is precisely their carrying out of an ideal literally and to extremes, that gives their lives a dramatic quality, i.e., makes them suitable for the artistic imagination. Once the myth-making power of the artist fixes on the hero's life as a nucleus, it selects those features of his life that enhance the deviations, and so the hero becomes a legend, a remote but powerful object of imitation. Folk art or popular art, not to speak of Madison Avenue, is forever engaged in the same sort of model building; one wonders how many American men's lives were affected by the 150 or so variants of the Horatio Alger hero. The break in the perceptual habits of the common man demanded by contemporary serious art has, for a time at least, lowered the direct influence of the serious artist, and it is the James Bond, the hippie, the Playboy that tend to shape the aspirations of the adolescent—of whatever chronological age.

The advances in communication technology which have mushroomed the effect of commercial art create a moral responsibility for the educator to narrow the gap between the mass public and the serious contemporary artist. It is encouraging to note that the recent surge of courses variously called the humanities, aesthetic education, and the allied arts in the high school is not abating, and, with luck, aesthetic literacy for the vast majority of our people may be more than a hopeless wish. The fact that serious art is now in fashion, that paintings are being stolen from museums, and that the great mass media magazines feel safe in devoting space to the arts are other good signs. Finally, although government support of the arts creates problems, it recognizes officially the role of serious art in the culture.

Just as the history of science furnishes the great exemplars of our intellectual achievement, so the history of the arts furnish great exemplars of the value commitments of the great epochs of the past. Because adventitious, capricious, and local variations are sifted by history into oblivion, the surviving masterpieces represent the invariants of the human quest—the generic powers of man's intellect and imagination. But it is to contemporary art that we must look for early signs of what is wrong with reality, for the signs that old behavioral forms are no longer suitable, and it is to the artist that we look for the new bottles fit to hold the new wine that science is continually producing. How does art do this?

We touch here upon the great mystique of art. Somehow the early artistic instincts of the people have never lost their potency. The first clue that something is wrong with the world is a sense of aesthetic incongruity. For example, the account of the death of John F. Kennedy given by the Warren Report may have been factually correct, but aesthetically it was an outrage. So great an effect aesthetically demands an appropriate cause with plots and world-shaking personalities for dramatic plausibility. This inveterate susceptibility of man to the aesthetic categories gives art great power, and therefore great responsibility, a responsibility from which serious art understandably but vainly has tried to rid itself.

Yet neither the artist nor the scientist as artist and scientist can be true to himself if he tries to make his science or his art serve the moral quest. To saddle scientists and artists with the task of the educator and reformer is a mistake, and efforts to promote dialogue between them for this purpose or to turn them into political scientists are misguided. If they are any good in thinking about Vietnam or the racial problem, it is not by virtue of their scientific or artistic accomplishments, but by virtue of their general education and the happy circumstances that enabled them to cultivate their human capacities for thought and feeling.

No, the scientist as scientist must exploit science, and the artist as artist must exploit his imaginative impulses to create shapes of life and feeling. The exploration of these possibilities for life is the task of all of us insofar as we are cultivated human beings. Furnishing the contents and forms of thought that bring men to this state of cultivation is the first task of general education.

In closing, I can only reiterate that in these times of trouble not all shouts of alienation, lostness, and meaninglessness are equally significant. For the virtues that define humanity can give us direction and purpose and significance and identity, if we stop making believe that we no longer believe in them. Our moral sphere is enlarged not destroyed, for our power is far greater than our will to use it. This is neither a cheap nor easy optimism, for we have yet to find and define a life form that will make the new heroism, the new courage, the new temperance, the new justice both morally edifying and aesthetically seductive. Thousands of our fellow human beings see no hope of realizing these value potentials and the proper human stance for them is despair—quiet despair, shrieking despair, violent despair, tragic despair. But shouts of despair for mankind on the part of those who have not strained even half of their nerves to do what can be done, who claim to have lost identities they never toiled to establish, who are defiant without risk—this is a comic despair, for it is as if a drowning man roars for help and is rescued by a brigade of life guards—in two feet of water.

Chapter Three

Educational Administration:
Theory

Administrators are men of action. Central to all that they do is the act of decision-making. Under their leadership are formed the policies which guide the organization of which they are a part. Operational decisions, which are actions to achieve the goals determined by policy, are directed and coordinated by administrators. School administrators, like those of other organizations, pride themselves on being "practical" men. By this they mean that the actions performed under their leadership "must work." Just as soon as the controlling bodies of an organization discover that the actions of the people performing the tasks of an organization do not work, attention is given to how well it is being administered.

In the previous chapter we suggested that a decision to act requires a choice among values. The choice was among the several possible alternatives. But what makes one alternative better than another? Knowledge about the consequences of the alternative actions surely plays a major role in all intelligent choices. In educational administration such knowledge is exceedingly important. Yet the scholars in our field tell us that much of the knowledge thus far accumulated is random, applies to limited situations only, and hence is not generalizable. To overcome this weakness it has been suggested that the field of educational administration become more theoretically oriented. In this chapter the readings are directed toward a better understanding of the meaning of theory and of its usefulness in both deriving new knowledge and applying it.

You have heard the expression, "That is good in theory, but it will not work in practice." That *the theoretical* and *the practical* are antithetical has almost become one of the accepted beliefs of administrators. Why is this? How could such a belief have become so prevalent? If good theory is so substantiated in fact that it is generalizable to many situations or that it becomes a dependable predictor of events, how could it be so impractical? Or, rather, how could such theory be reputed to be impractical?

Obviously, if theory works in the sense that it explains events in a wide number of situations and is a good predictor of events to follow, theory is practical. It is the most practical tool that the administrator can possess. The mistaken impressions that we have about theory in administration have undoubtedly arisen from mistaken concepts of theory and of its application to administrative situations. When a fellow administrator (or a person in any other capacity) says, "I have a theory that . . . ," one needs to know whether or not it is sufficiently grounded in fact that it will probably work. One needs to know also that when he applies his theory he has some means for determining whether or not it is working. If such theories turn out to be undependable after systematic study, they surely will be sources of mistrust of theory in general.

Sometimes our references to *the theoretical* carry with them the connotation that a theory will work under ideal conditions. Here again, since most administrators do not work in situations in which the conditions are ideal, such use of the term could cause distrust. Theories that are developed under ideal circumstances need to be tested in the real world to determine what variations must be made in them to increase the probability that they will work in a variety of situations.

The purpose which the editors wish to achieve in this chapter is to present points of view about theory in such a way that the student of educational administration will gain confidence in its use. It should be noted that the authors of the articles quoted here place a heavy emphasis upon a systematic ordering of facts and ideas. This is opposed to a random or *ad hoc* collection of facts and ideas. While random facts, each in its appropriate setting, may be useful in certain instances, it is the relationship among facts that increases their potency as guides to action.

No attempt will be made here to present a theory of educational administration. The field is so broad in scope and it encompasses such a variety of situations that a single theory has little chance of explaining administrative phenomena in general. Rather it seems more useful to present the manner in which students of administration have thought about theory and its usefulness in educational administration. If limited to the areas in which they apply specifically, certain partial theories are useful in explaining behavior in those areas. For example, modest theories about leadership have been useful in explaining the relationship between the administrator and other members of the organization. Role theory has been useful in generating new research and thus extending our knowledge about role incumbents and their behavior in organization. Theories in both these areas of human behavior have been useful in changing practice. Perhaps, all of these uses—explanation of phenomena, generation of new knowledge, and guides for changed behavior—will be noted in the several articles presented here.

5 | The Nature of the Theory-Practice Relationship

Arthur P. Coladarci
Jacob W. Getzels

Coladarci and Getzels declare that theory and practice are not different things; they merely "represent differences in the point at which interest and attention are momentarily directed." Their monograph on the use of theory in educational administration, part of which is quoted here, points up very clearly the nature of the theory-practice relationship. To understand this relationship is an important first step in systematic reordering of administrative behavior.

The Integrity of the Relationship

The inherent interrelationship of theory and practice can be seen in the definition of the former and in careful observation of the latter.

By definition. The term "theory" is often used to mean general principles which seem to predict or account for events with an accuracy so much better than chance that we may say that the principles are "true." But a theory so powerful that it enables an administrator to make better-than-chance predictions regarding the wide range of phenomena with which he daily is concerned does not emerge easily. On one hand it is induced from the world of everyday events. One searches for before-after relationships among the facts, observations, and events of every-day existence on the assumption that they are not independent, non-controllable events and that their future occurrence can be predicted and their past occurrence understood. Such a search, intelligently directed, yields hypotheses (plausible guesses as to what the explaining or predictive principles may be). Note that in this inductive aspect of theory construction no identifiable line can be drawn between the observed events and the hypothesized explaining or predicting principle. The latter was derived from the first and seeks to control it. Furthermore, a theoretical principle arrived at inductively must be

Reprinted from *The Use of Theory in Educational Administration,* by Arthur P. Coladarci and Jacob W. Getzels, with the permission of the publishers, Stanford University Press. © 1955, by the Board of Trustees of the Leland Stanford Junior University.

49

tested by making deductions from it. These deductions are hypotheses regarding the world of events. One thinks, "If the principle is true, this event will occur," ". . . this method of organization will yield a higher level of staff morale," ". . . this grouping of pupils will provide for increased individual progress." If the predicted event occurs, we invest increased confidence in the principle; if the predicted event does not occur, we must re-examine the principle from which it was deduced. Again, we see that there is no theory-practice dichotomy.

A theory attempts to maximize practical predictions and practical understanding. Its validity is judged by the degree to which it can do so. The connecting link between the two is the hypothesis, which is a way of unambiguously relating the high order abstractions in the theoretical principle to the concrete phenomena that we are concerned about.[1] Although the foregoing description of the logical nature of the theory-practice relationship invites the risk of oversimplification, it serves to suggest that the very nature of theory militates against a clear distinction between theoretical and practical concerns.

By observation of practice. Support for the theory-practice integrity is found also in the behavior of the very educators who verbalize a rejection of it. Theorizing is not the exclusive property of the laboratory or of the ivory tower. Everyone who makes choices and judgments implies a theory in the sense that there are reasons for his actions. When an administrator's experiences have led him to believe that a certain kind of act will result in certain other events or acts, he is using theory. If the experiences of others have been roughly similar, his theory will not be unique, even though he has never formulated it in so many words or has never heard it stated by others. Those who learn from their experience in ways which mean revising their judgments and decisions (hypotheses) are modifying their theories in a never-ending process of self-correction. Such people are theorizing—it may be poor theorizing, but it is theorizing nonetheless.

Our point is that such behavior is inescapable. We make decisions on the basis of generalizations and assumptions (hidden or explicit) and, in so doing, we act in terms of a theory. If this is done without full awareness, we run the risk of making poor decisions and are not able to see that the difficulty is not so much with the decision as with the basis for it (the theory). Consider, for instance, the superintendent who may observe that certain desirable curriculum improvements came about in a neighboring district soon after publication of a new course of study; he may then spend a summer writing a course of study for his district, publish it, and expect curriculum improvements to follow. Or consider the principal who, as a classroom teacher, "always did what he was told" and also felt he was successful in that role; he may now believe that teachers who are not in agreement with him cannot be doing anything of much value.

It is not difficult to tease out the implicit assumptions and generalizations upon which such a superintendent or principal is acting. The fact that such a person may not be focally aware of the bases for his actions does not contradict the fact that he is theorizing. In such a case, his theory is implicit and, therefore, unexaminable by him. The fact that the bases for his actions may be invalid, means that his theory is poor theory.

The inevitable presence of theorizing in human affairs must be clear to anyone who has inquired into his own behavior or observed carefully the behavior of others. Reichenbach speaks to this point, basing his argument on the observation that man is a valuing creature:

> In some sense, every human activity serves the pursuit of a goal. . . . In all such activities, however, there are moments where a choice is to be made; it is here that behavior exhibits valuation. The valuation need not be explicitly stated, nor achieved through reflection and comparison; it may be performed in the spontaneous impulse which drives us to read a book or to see a friend or to attend a concert. But in the decisions made we express our preferences and thus indicate through our behavior the valuational order which constitutes the background of our actions.[2]

And Conant, speaking to the more general proposition, notes that:

> Literally, every step we take in life is determined by a series of interlocking concepts and conceptual schemes. Every goal we formulate for our actions, every decision we make, be it trivial or momentous, involves assumptions about the universe and about human beings. To my mind, any attempt to draw a sharp line between common-sense ideas and scientific concepts is not only impossible but unwise.[3]

The administrator, like all human beings, is constantly making choices, decisions, and judgments. Moreover, in his case, some of these choices *are profoundly consequential.* Just as it is inescapable that when he makes decisions he *is* acting from a frame-of-reference, so is it inescapable that he has a moral obligation to make the bases for his acts explicit and examinable.

On the grounds of both the definition and the universality of theorizing, then, the theory and practice functions can be seen as necessarily interrelated aspects of professional behavior. We can dislike this state of affairs but we cannot avoid it. Theorizing and practicing can and do co-exist. Each is an aspect of the process of inquiry and, intelligently pursued, *each constantly re-defines the other.*[4] One who makes his knowledge of this relationship explicit is sharing in the reaffirmation of what Bridgman has termed "intelligent method." [5]

The Practical Values of Theory

Those who can accept the logical bearing of theory on practice, can understand its value in the guidance and evaluation of practice. As Dewey has observed in a well-known statement, "theory is in the end . . . the most practical of all things, because the widening of the range of attention beyond nearby purpose and desire eventually results in the creation of wider and farther-reaching purposes and enables us to make use of a much wider and deeper range of conditions and means than were expressed in the observation of primitive practical purposes."[6] The educator who behaves on a hit-or-miss basis, one whose professional arsenal consists merely of pat techniques for specific situations is operating in intellectual low gear and is denied the self-initiated, self-critical inquiry and innovation that are possible with the wider frame-of-reference available to the theory-conscious or thoughtful practitioner. Intelligent action, in any sense of that adjective, cannot be maximized without some guiding principles tentatively held.

The long history of the physical sciences shows rather clearly that observation and measurements, no matter how precise, cannot lead to stable, practical knowledge except through some guiding principles that serve as guides to *what* to observe, *what* to measure, *how* to interpret. "Begin by collecting facts? Aye, but what facts?"[7] Facts may accumulate without theory but they run the risk of sterility and instability. On the other hand, as Guthrie has pointed out, "theories are the basis of working concepts. They enable men to confront new facts and deal with them successfully. Furthermore, theories are required to direct the search for relevant facts."[8] Larrabee, in our judgment has put this most clearly:

> The advice to "get the facts" is not a blanket injunction to expose oneself to anything in the way of experience that may come along. It leads one to the query: "But what facts?" Certainly, if facts and theories are to be fitted together in such a way as to yield reliable knowledge, "just any old facts" will not do, nor will "any old theory" do either. Relevant facts do not label themselves as relevant. That is an element which must be added by the knower. Unless he is a mere random collector of odds and ends the seeker of knowledge cannot go through life merely looking *at* things; he must be looking *for* something; and that means active inquiry with some directing factor in control.[9]

Perhaps this is the sense in which to interpret T. H. Huxley's admonition that "those who refuse to go beyond fact rarely get as far as fact."

The foregoing is by way of saying that theory is not merely an objective; it is a tool as well; it is a guide to practice. In theory construction there is danger of overlooking this too-like character of theory.[10] A clarified and well thought-out theory, not matter how provisional, is a frame-of-reference that creates some order out of what otherwise might appear to be a disorganized situation that invites something of the order of trial-and-error behavior. Theorizing, as a tool, further provides a check on practice—it offers the administrator a basis for constant, systematic self-criticism and improvement.

> Facts which are . . . interrelated form a system, a science. The practitioner who knows the system . . . is evidently in possession of a powerful instrument

for observing and interpreting what goes on before him. This intellectual tool affects his attitudes and modes of response in what he does. Because the range of understanding is deepened and widened, he can take into account remote consequences which were originally hidden from view and hence were ignored in his actions. Greater continuity is introduced; he does not isolate situations and deal with them in separation as he was compelled to do when ignorant of connecting principles. At the same time, his practical dealings become more flexible. Seeing more relations he sees more possibilities, more opportunities. He is emancipated from the need of following tradition and special precedents. His ability to judge being enriched, he has a wider range of alternatives to select from in dealing with individual situations.[11]

Finally, note should be taken of the fact that, among the most pressing of practical problems is the question of how the practical problems themselves may be identified and adequately defined. (Many have pointed out, Corey[12] most recently, that practitioners are very often impressionistic and casual in the identification of the problems causing them difficulty.) The consequence may be the identification of superficial problems and, frequently, the wrong problems. As Thomas states it, "without the guidance of a theory, the analysis and discrimination which is necessary to convert an indeterminate situation into a formulated problem is severely handicapped, or worse yet, foregone."[13]

Notes

1. Neal E. Miller, "Comments on Theoretical Models: Illustrated by the Development of a Theory of Conflict Behavior," *Journal of Personality*, 1951, 20, 82–100.
2. Hans Reichenbach, *The Rise of Scientific Philosophy*, University of California Press, 1951, pp. 313–14. See also: Albert Ellis, "Valuation in Presenting Scientific Data," *Sociology and Social Research*, Nov.-Dec., 1948; G. Myrdal, *An American Dilemma*, Harper, 1944.
3. James B. Conant, *Modern Science and Modern Man*, Doubleday, 1953, pp. 135–36.
4. V. F. Lenzen, *Science and Social Context*, University of California Publications in Philosophy, 1942, 23, 3–26; B. O. Smith, "Science of Education," in W. S. Monroe (ed.), *Encyclopedia of Educational Research*, Macmillan, 1950, p. 1151.
5. Raymond G. Stone, "Rational-Empirical Criteria of Science and the Problem of Prediction," *Proceedings of the Oklahoma Academy of Science*, 1949, 176–80, p. 176.
6. John Dewey, *Sources of a Science of Education*, Liveright, 1929, p. 17.
7. Morris R. Cohen, *Reason and Nature*, 1931, p. 76.
8. Edwin R. Guthrie, "Psychological Facts and Psychological Theory," *Psychological Bulletin*, 1946, 43, 1–20, pp. 3–4.
9. Harold A. Larrabee, *Reliable Knowledge*, Houghton Mifflin, 1945, p. 82.
10. Melvin H. Marx, "The General Nature of Theory Construction," in M. H. Marx (ed.), *Psychological Theory*, Macmillan, 1951, p. 6.

11. Dewey, *op. cit.*, pp. 20–21.
12. Stephen M. Corey, "Scientific Enquiry and the Practising Teacher," *Canadian Education*, 1954, pp. 9, 31–42.
13. Lawrence G. Thomas, "Mental Tests as Instruments of Science," *Psychological Monographs*, 1942, 54, No. 3 (Whole No. 245), p. 13.

6 | Ways of Knowing

Andrew W. Halpin

*In the following article, Halpin makes a plea for a more balanced appreciation
of various "ways of knowing." He declares that the school administrator has
just as legitimate a way of knowing as does the professor of school administration or the educational researcher. He describes some of the myths that have
grown up during the period in which we have tried to make a science of educational administration. In his own way Halpin takes both the professor and
the administrator to task for the distrust which each exhibits for the other's
methods of gaining knowledge. His plea is that each examine the other's
methods as a means of learning for himself what contributions both can make.*

My thesis is indecently simple: that there is more than one gate to the
kingdom of knowledge. Each gate opens upon a different vista but no one
vista exhausts the realm of "reality"—whatever that may be. It therefore is
important to understand what each vista can and cannot yield. To expect
returns through one way of knowing which can be achieved only through
another is to invite frustration and disillusion. Yet obvious though this
thesis may be, its implications are violated every day. Ironically, they are
ravaged as brutishly in universities as by the man on the street. The pur-
veyors of knowledge in Academe behave like side-show barkers at a carnival,
each shouting that his brand of knowledge is more spectacular and more
dependable than that sold by rival barkers. The midway visitors move from
barker to barker; at the moment a churning awed crowd stands transfixed in
front of the gaudiest tent of all and avidly devours the spiel of the pitchman
of Science. He can easily pack his tent, for science has become a sacred cow
in our culture. Yet the crowd's gullible acceptance of science as a panacea
contains a promise of hidden but inevitable disillusionment. For the pro-
tagonists of science have forgotten the simple thesis which I intend to

Andrew W. Halpin, "Ways of Knowing," *Administrative Theory as a Guide to
Action*, Roald F. Campbell and James M. Lipham, eds. (Chicago: The University
of Chicago, Midwest Administration Center, 1960), pp. 3–20. Reprinted by permission.

develop here: that no one way of knowing is intrinsically superior to all others, that knowing and the specific purpose of the knower must be examined conjointly. All human knowledge is partial, and as human beings none of us is so rich in understanding that he can afford to ignore any of the several gates to the kingdom of knowledge.

But what has this to do with educational administration? To answer this question we must examine briefly the quiet revolution which has been taking place in university programs for training school administrators. Before World War II the training for educational administrators was composed principally of substantive information about the presumed content of the field: courses in educational philosophy, curriculum, finance, buildings, and personnel. What was taught on administration qua administration consisted of maxims, exhortations, and several innocuous variations on the theme of the Golden Rule. The material was speculative rather than theoretical in the true sense of the term, empirical research on administration was slighted, and contributions from the behavioral sciences and personnel research in industry were zealously ignored. With the development of the NCPEA, CPEA, and UCEA programs,[1] professors of educational administration discovered that they could identify a profession of administration qua administration; despite certain content differences, such areas as educational administration, business administration, public administration and hospital administration, did, in fact, share a significant common core. Attention was directed to the social and human skills of the administrator and to the sociology of the organizations in which he operated. The post-war period also saw a surge of interdisciplinary research in the social sciences; at several major universities professors of educational administration participated in this movement. With the recognition that skills and attitudes were as important to an executive as factual knowledge, various forms of internship were incorporated into the training programs for school administrators. The professors sought help from psychologists and sociologists, and discovered that without the support of an explicit theoretical framework their discipline could easily degenerate into a jumble of inert facts.[2]

This emphasis on theory holds great promise. Yet many superintendents get the feeling that an important piece is missing. They ask, "If analytical theory is supposed to be so good for us, why do we feel so uncomfortable in its presence?" The administrator's doubt is justified; there is indeed something missing. The fault is that the scientist's theoretical models of administration are too rational, too tidy, too aseptic. They remind us of the photographs in House Beautiful, the glossy pictures of dramatic and pristine living room interiors. The rooms are beautiful but they look as if they had never been lived in. Nor are the rooms pictured as inhabited by human beings, except perhaps for a vacuous but poised Vogue model who would not even flick her swishy artificial eyelashes were she to catch her husband cavorting on the front lawn with the young blonde widow next door. The superintendent distrusts this tidiness and senses intuitively that the theoretical-analytical approach has left out a big hunk of reality, has omitted much of the palpable stuff which quickens his pulse in his daily job. This is why I think we had better examine afresh our present perspectives in educational administration, had better be sure that our current pitch on administrative theory is taking us, in fact, where we want to go. We will discover, I hope, that we do not have to jettison any recent work, but that we may have to distribute our intellectual cargo more judiciously if we are to keep the ship on even keel.

In the first place, there does not exist today, either in education or in industry, a single well-developed theory of administration that is worth getting excited about. Recent hue and cry on this subject have created a completely false impression; many superintendents and professors of education have been led to believe that our knowledge in this area is more secure than it actually is. Accordingly, I think it is wise for us to check our present bearings. We might just as well start with the theme of the present conference, "Administrative Theory as a Guide to Action." Translated into question form, this becomes "How can administrative theory be applied by the superintendent?" I think that when we pose the question in this form, we invite confusion. This is the wrong question, or at least it is a premature question at this juncture. It would be better to ask, "How can the practitioner use the social scientists' findings to sharpen his analysis of the social situation with which he must deal?" There are some social science research findings which can prove useful to the practitioner. There are also a few ways of thinking about social and organizational phenomena which will help him discern the similarities and differences between day-to-day administrative situations, and thus will enable him to make wiser decisions. And there are ways, too, by which the practitioner and the scientist can each freshen the other's observations. An exchange of ideas in these domains should prove exceedingly fruitful. But an attempt to use the present conference as a springboard for leaping across the chasm which now separates administrative theory from actual practice strikes me as premature and too ambitious. I would be content to have us examine the chasm together, to see how deep it is and how wide, and to determine whether there are some crags from which a leap would be less risky than from others.

We will be in a better position to leap when we have first developed a more balanced attack, by the scientists themselves, upon the problems of educational administration. Much of the present difficulty stems from the fact that the scientists who have chosen to work in this field represent for the most part a parochial view of science. They are social scientists who are intent upon aping the more prestigious physical scientists in building highly abstract, theoretical models. These men have castigated the role of clinical

science and have acted as if anything less than pure analytical science bore
blazoned on its breast the Scarlet Letter. They have disregarded the advice
which Homans gave us a decade ago:

> It is high time we knew the difference between clinical and analytical science.
> Clinical science is what a doctor uses at his patient's bedside. There, the doctor
> cannot afford to leave out of account anything in the patient's condition that
> he can see or test. He cannot leave it out either in itself or in its relation to the
> whole picture of a sick human being. It may be the clue to the complex. Of
> course the doctor has some general theories at the back of his mind, theories of
> the connections between a limited number of physiological factors: what the
> others will do when one is changed. These doctrines may turn out to be useful,
> but he cannot, at the outset, let them master his thinking. They may not take
> into consideration, and so may prevent his noticing, the crucial fact in the case
> before him.
> *In action we must always be clinical.* An analytical science is for understanding
> but not for action, at least not directly. It picks out a few of the factors at work
> in particular situations and describes systematically the relations between these
> factors. Only by cutting down the number of factors considered can it achieve
> this systematic description. It is general, but it is abstract. As soon as he let
> friction out of account, Galileo's science became analytical. To return to our
> medical illustrations, a description of particular cases of anemia is clinical
> science, whereas a theory of blood chemistry is analytical. When progress is
> rapid, clinical and analytical science help one another. The clinicians tell the
> analysts what the latter have left out. The analysts need the most brutal re-
> minders because they are always so charmed with their pictures they mistake
> them for the real thing. On the other hand, the analysts' generalizations often
> suggest where the clinicians should look more closely. Both the clinician and
> the analyst are needed. We ought to be sick and tired of boasts that one is
> better than the other.[3]

At the present stage of our knowledge in educational administration,
the clinically-oriented scientist has as much to give us as the analytically-
oriented man. I do not intend to fall into the same trap that Homans warned
us against: we need both orientations. But right now I think we need to pay
greater heed to the clinical orientation, if only as an antidote against too
heavy and too premature a dose of analytical science.

The key to the issue lies in Homans' observation, "In action we must
always be clinical." Yet even this observation falls short of the mark and it
has remained for Erikson, a distinguished psychoanalyst, to spot the crucial
difference between people and things which most social scientists have
missed completely—a difference which forces the clinician to adopt a personal attitude unlike that of the theoretically-oriented scientist. Erikson
admits that we can learn about the nature of things as we find out what one

can do *with* them. But people are not things; ". . . the true nature of man reveals itself only in the attempt to do something *for* him."[4] But the moment you attempt to do things *for* other human beings, you must assume moral responsibility for what you do. And this is the very responsibility which the analytical scientist has refused to accept, has declared as none of his concern.

The clinician's concern about doing things for humans coincides with the administrator's. It is precisely for this reason that I believe the clinical approach offers hope for greater *rapprochement* between practitioner and scientist. A clinical orientation should prove especially salutary at this time because it will reaffirm an obvious yet often forgotten point which applies to science as well as to all other forms of knowledge-seeking: that the quality and the relevance of our knowledge are determined by the freshness of our observation. (And note that such observation need not be devoid of feeling or emotion.) In graduate courses on research we have made such an ado about the nature of scientific evidence and the use of statistical inference that we have blinded our students to the essential issue: that without fresh, viable observation all the machinations of research methodology become an empty and a self-deceiving ritual. There is no virtue in demonstrating that one can count or that one can compute Pearsonian correlation coefficients on the items he has counted; the trick is to know what things are worth counting in the first place. And no course in research methodology can teach us this. This skill can be acquired only through direct experience with the phenomena we are seeking to understand, and can be matured only by developing within ourselves—as human instruments—the capacity to view with unfettered perception the world around us. This capacity to "see" what is "out there" is imperative for both the scientist and the practitioner. In fact, the superintendent who is highly skilled in sizing up a complex social situation, in observing precisely what is taking place in his school system, exhibits the very essence of scientific method. The heart of the method, I repeat, is the freshness of observation, irrespective of whatever ritual is subsequently performed upon these observations. Yet by emphasizing such rituals and by stressing the parochial aspect of the analytical orientation in science we have foolishly accentuated a false difference between the social scientist and the superintendent. This has not been wise strategy.

But Victorian sighs and even Freudian confessionals are futile. The immediate issue is how we can most constructively alter our course. Since the form of our questions determines our answers, perhaps we should begin asking questions different from those which have guided our recent strategy. Let us therefore examine more carefully how the administrator learns to "know" his job. After we have identified the major "ways of knowing" which the administrator employs, we will be in a better position to try to answer the question which I consider crucial for administrator and scientist alike:

"How can the practitioner and the scientist help each other increase the freshness and the viability of their observations of organizations and of group members within these organizations?"

What are the chief "ways of knowing" which an administrator uses? How does he learn to "know" his job? I believe he relies on three major "ways of knowing," ways which correspond to the three levels of culture defined by the anthropologist Edward T. Hall:[5] the formal, the informal, and the technical. Hall maintains that social learning takes place through a combination of inputs from all three levels.

Formal activities are taught by precept and by admonition. The father corrects his son by saying, "Boys don't do that," and the tone of his voice declares that what his son is doing is unthinkable. The ranch hand yells at the dude, "Hey, not the right side of the horse, the left side! Remember, never approach a horse from the right!" The boss snarls, "Damn it, Jones, if you ever skip channels again, I'll fire you on the spot." Formal patterns are almost always invoked when a mistake is made and someone corrects it. The correction is usually made with personal vehemence and emotion, or through the cold impersonal authority of an institution but with the clear understanding that a violation will be promptly punished. Formal learning teaches us the "rules of the game" as these rules have been defined by a particular culture. The details of formal learning are *binary*, of a yes-no, right-wrong character. You either break a taboo or you don't. You rifle your colleague's desk or you don't. You make a pass at your secretary or you don't.

Informal learning is acquired mainly through imitation. The content of this learning is not explicit, but whereas formal learning is preoccupied with the limits of a role or with the rules of the game, informal learning deals with the details and nuances of the role and with the techniques of one-upmanship within the rules of the game. You find a model and then you try to copy it. "Mother," asks the preadolescent girl, "how does a woman get a man to marry her?" "Well, darling, it's a little hard to describe, but as you get older you'll find out." The daughter correctly translates this reply. "Don't ask questions, look around and see what people do." The earnest graduate student in educational administration says to the superintendent in whose school he has been working, "You know, Dr. Gragg, I admire the way you work with the board of education. I sure hope I'll be able to do as well. How do you do it? How can I learn to handle the board the way you do?" And Dr. Gragg, after choking on his saliva, replies, "Thank you, Jim. But I can't answer your question. I suppose I 'play it by ear.' The only thing I can tell you is to watch. And, Jim, if you do discover how I do it, would you please let me know?"

Technical learning is transmitted in explicit terms from the teacher to the student, either orally or in writing. It usually is preceded by a logical analysis of a body of content which is then organized into a coherent outline form for purposes of presentation. This is how most of our learning in school takes place. When a student asks how he can best understand the administrative process and Dr. Getzels replies by describing his formulation of administration, we have an instance of technical learning about administration.

Now let us look at an example of the interplay among these three modes, the formal, the informal, and the technical, from the standpoint of the learner—or if you will, from the standpoint of the "knower." Let us examine what happens when a beginner learns to shoot pool. His teacher will probably sketch the rules of the game. These are formal stipulations; our boy can be said to "know" how to play pool to such extent as he can recite these rules (e.g., rules about the order of play, scoring, "scratching"). But he quickly discovers a few more formal stipulations: "For Pete's sake, Jack, lift your cue. You're not digging potatoes. If you try to hit the cue ball like that you'll rip the felt into shreds." "Jack, will you please shut up when I'm trying to plan a shot. When the other fellow is shooting don't talk to him, and please don't choose that moment to try out a new cha-cha-cha."

As our boy progresses he watches other players and, using them as models, he consciously or unconsciously imitates their handling of the cue-stick. He notices that Don spreads his fingers to provide a firm bridge, that Harry's body is relaxed, not stiff, when he makes his shot. In the case of his most accurate shots he discovers with delight that at the very moment the cue hits the cue-ball—and even before the ball moves—his stroke "feels right." He can't explicate a lot of his learning at this stage. Yet with his body itself he "knows" when he is in process of making a clean shot and he "knows," too, when he is going to muff. He "knows" not with his frontal lobes but with his gut—with his fingers, his arm, his shoulder. This informal "knowing" is not the same as his formal "knowing," his "knowing," for example, of the rules of the game.

Eventually, dismayed by his opponent's skill in banking the balls and in maneuvering the cue-ball into advantageous position for the next shot, our boy decides to do some reading on the subject, to learn the principles of physics which apply to the control of the cue-ball. He comes to "know" technically why "right-hand English" produces results different from those which ensue when he delivers a sharp "draw-shot." He tries to apply these principles in his play. In this way the theory, in the sense of a theoretical model of how solids respond to forces applied to them, gives him a way of interpreting the results of his direct experience in play. The theory, please note, freshens his observations about his direct experience. But by the same token his direct experience forces him to analyze why the theory doesn't seem to work in every instance, makes him aware of the extraneous variables that the pure form of the theory was not obliged to take into account—variables such as random sources of friction, the worn cushion right below the side pocket, and the cue-stick that is slightly warped. He finds that he often has to "correct" the theory in terms of the particular table on which he is playing. At the technical level what our boy "knows" about the principles governing the motions of the balls constitutes another aspect of his "knowing" how to play pool.

To repeat, then, our boy "knows" the rules of the game. He "knows" when a shot "feels right" and he "knows" the technical principles governing the balls' motion. But though we use the same word to describe each of these "knowings," they are not quite the same; respectively they represent formal, informal, and technical "knowing." Of course these modes of "knowing" are interrelated, and the demarcations between them are not always sharply honed. But it is important that we keep these three categories straight. For example, any attempt to *prove* a formal "knowing" by the same scientific methods which apply to the technical mode of "knowing" is as silly as trying to use the laws of physical motion either to prove or to disprove that the bishop in chess moves on the diagonal.

Just as the three modes of "knowing" operate in what our pool player "knows" so do they apply to how a superintendent "knows" his job. At the formal level the superintendent knows the rules of the game. These are given by the culture. Some rules are historical accidents, some have been devised only after careful planning, while some have literally been drawn from mythology. The scientist can help identify these rules by showing that they exist or do not exist, but he can never *prove* that these rules are either true or false. They simply *are*. In short, these rules represent an order of phenomena different from that with which the theoretically-oriented scientist is equipped to deal.

The superintendent, or any other administrator, knows many things at the informal level in much the same way as a man knows that he loves his wife. He does not love her because of technical or rational reasons or because he is following a set of rules which tell him that he loves her; he simply loves her. Similarly on the job, he "knows" that he feels at ease with some influential members of the community yet also "knows" that there is an invisible screen between himself and certain other figures in the community power structure. After a faculty meeting which seems placid enough on the surface, he still "knows" that something went wrong—the butterflies halfway down his esophagus and his desperate yen for a double martini before dinner give him a genuine piece of "knowledge," but a piece which he can't quite put into words. He does not derive this "knowing" from a rational Q.E.D., but this makes it nonetheless real. However, I believe that he can train himself to become a better "human instrument," can learn to be more acutely aware of subtle cues, and can improve the richness and the quality of what he "knows" on a direct intuitive basis. And in doing this he can freshen his observation of the world around him, and can then share these observations with the scientist. From these raw data the scientist may then devise new hypothetical models which will agree more closely with the "reality" of the superintendent's direct experience. The superintendent's observations in this regard are guided by the clinical orientation in science. At this level of "informal knowing" the administrator and the scientist can help each other in sharpening their observations. The scientist can be especially helpful in devising a language of greater precision for describing the practitioner's observations so that the fruits of the practitioner's experience can be communicated more effectively to new trainees in administration. But at this level of "knowing" the wise scientist will be wary about introducing theoretical models prematurely.

Finally, at the technical level, the superintendent "knows" many things about administration. In addition to substantive information about bond issues, bus routing, curriculum changes, and the care and feeding of board members, he "knows" many things about the nature of administration, is familiar with much technical research on the sociology of organizations and the behavior of executives. He "knows," for example, the work of Chester Barnard,[6] he "knows" certain theoretical formulations of administration such as those devised by Getzels and Guba,[7] and perhaps he knows about the leadership behavior dimensions of "Consideration" and "Initiating Structure."[8] Each of these three "ways of knowing" is derived from a different context and is associated with a different purpose. The "way of knowing" and the human purpose of the "knower" must be treated conjointly. The logic of rationality which is applicable in the case of one human purpose cannot be applied willy-nilly to all other purposes. Nevertheless, what a man "knows" is derived inextricably from all three sources.

There is one foolish notion that we had better scotch right away: this is the belief that different ways of "knowing" can be ranked according to the "realness" of the data with which they deal. When confronted with different "knowings" the naive person is tempted to ask, "Which is more real?" "Which is *really* the truth?" This question is just as rhetorical, just as futile today as it once was in the mouth of Pontius Pilate. Here indeed is the pivot of my thesis: that no one way of "knowing" is any more or any less "real" than what the scientist "knows." The theoretically-oriented scientist can make accurate predictions about uniformities in human behavior, but the very fact that he is dealing with a probability model makes his predictions those of an entirely different order from those made by either the clinically-oriented scientist, the superintendent operating within the complex milieu of his job, or the poet and the playwright. We fall into a trap the moment we assume that one type of "knowing" is better than another. The most we can say is that each "knowing" differs from the other but that the complete human being—to be completely human—must be sensitive to his full heritage of "knowing."

Let me illustrate the point about the "realness" of knowledge with a few lines spoken by the poet, John Ciardi:

> There is no poetry for the practical man. There is poetry only for the mankind of the man who spends a certain amount of his life turning the mechanical wheel. But let him spend too much of his life at the mechanics of practicality and either he must become something less than a man, or his very mechanical efficiency will become impaired by the frustrations stored up in his irrational human personality. An ulcer, gentlemen, is an unkissed imagination taking its revenge for having been jilted. It is an unwritten poem, a neglected music, an unpainted watercolor, an undanced dance. It is a declaration from the mankind of the man that a clear spring of joy has not been tapped, and that it must break through, muddily, on its own.[9]

Is Ciardi's "knowledge" any less "real" than what you might find in a text on psychosomatic medicine? Is his knowledge any less real than a corpus of "knowledge" which I, as a scientist, can pinion to a cross with nails made of means and standard deviations?

Sam Striver, the up-and-coming superintendent of a rapidly-growing community in Westchester County doggedly wades through thick sociological monographs on suburbia, but is oblivious to the short stories of John Cheever![10] Yet I am not convinced that the sociologists' jaded statistics are any more "real" or will be any more useful to Sam than Cheever's compassionate insight into the hearts of suburbanites.

Thus I have returned to the question which I raised before discussing the informal, formal, and technical modes of knowing: "How can the practitioner and the scientist help each other increase the freshness and the viability of their observations of organizations and group members within these organizations?" The first step is for the scientist to rid himself of the prejudice that his skill in constructing theoretical models is somehow more respectable than skill in the direct observation of human events.[11] Never let us underestimate the consummate skill needed for the direct, insightful observation of human behavior. Both skills are needed and neither is less respectable than the other.

But if the scientist has been blinded by the myths of his professional prestige system, so too has the superintendent been blinded by the dry dust of words which has billowed between him and the sentient human beings with whom he must work and *for* whom he must be responsible. Here is a quotation in which the Swedish novelist Frank Heller appraises Benito Mussolini; unfortunately this analysis applies to many administrators:

> If he did not become great it was because he let himself be drugged by a poison which is more dangerous than opium or hashish—by words. He talked so much and so often that at length he took his own words for reality and lost contact with the world.[12]

Consider for example how educators have polluted the word "democracy" in an attempt to apply a political concept to formal organizations which, by necessity, are based upon a rationale different from that which undergirds political institutions. Note, too, how administrators continue to use the fictitious distinction between line and staff as if staff personnel never did, in fact, carry the same force of authority as line personnel. In both these examples the words have been cut loose from their anchors in experience.

If we are to freshen our observations of organizational life we somehow must get hold of some kind of eye-bath—something to cleanse our eyes of an accumulated grit of clichés, slogans, and meaningless words. Ironically, the less aware a superintendent is of the emptiness of his clichés, the more vehemently does he seem to brandish them. This hypnosis by words is one source of "the arrogance of the practical man" who "knows" what he "knows" and is having no part of anyone else's way of "knowing." But he is not alone in arrogance; for totally different reasons the theoretically oriented scientist flees from the "reality" of direct intuitive and observational experience. And he, deprived of the leaven which only such direct experience can furnish, becomes arrogant about his own brain-children, the theoretical models he has constructed. To both groups I can retort with only a well-worn phrase, "A plague on both your houses."

So I conclude with the plea which has threaded its way throughout this paper, a plea for a more tolerant, a more catholic view of various "ways of knowing." I suggest that the crux of all science, of all practice, and of all wisdom lies in a careful, sensitive observation of what is indeed "out there." But it easy to be blinded, whether by the slogans of the practitioners' work-a-day world or by the jargon of the scientists' never never land.[13] How, then, can we break through? How can we learn to see what is "out there?" How can we learn to work more effectively with other human beings? How can we better understand the human heart? How can we sensitize ourselves to a wider range of "knowing"?

Here I shall perform the *coup de grâce* which I suppose will alienate me from the camps of both superintendents and scientists. I suggest that if we are to learn how to observe, how to see what is "out there," we had better avail ourselves of a rich heritage which superintendents and scientists alike have studiously ignored: the heritage of the humanities. For what else is the function of the poet, the playwright, the novelist than to examine and describe the ineffable ambiguity of the human condition? Who other than the creative artist is better equipped to describe man "in the round"? But "the man of letters" has been discredited by the market place, and to such extent that we as educators have adopted the standards of the market place we, too, have discredited him. The voices of the market place have screamed for increased technical specialization and the universities have responded with all the determination of an ambitious salesman anxious to give the customer precisely what he wants. This has resulted in a fragmentation of subject-matter areas in our universities and, in turn, has led to intolerance among the disciplines about the "ways of knowing" peculiar to each area. Our society has given increasing rewards to men in the practical arts and the sciences. But the training in both areas has been partitive. There was a time when a Ph.D. meant precisely that—a Doctor of Philosophy; a man who held the degree was expected to be conversant with philosophy and with the humanities as well as with his specialty. I suggest that, without this broader education, the practical man and the scientist alike are poorly equipped to bring to their observations the freshness and the perspective which their disciplines demand. Fortunately this view of the role of the humanities in freshening our observation of the human condition is now gradually being recognized in business and industry. The most conspicuous example is the training program conducted by the Bell Telephone Company of Pennsylvania. Selected executives are given a ten-month leave of absence with full salary and are assigned to the University of Pennsylvania for a special and extremely rich program in the liberal arts.[14] A recent evaluation of this program, after its first six years, shows that it does, indeed, achieve its objectives.[15] Similarly, Peter Drucker, professor of management at New York University, has noted the inestimable value of courses in creative writing for sharpening the observational skills of executives.[16]

With but few exceptions such as Joseph Wood Krutch and Lewis Mumford, the Renaissance Man has disappeared from our civilization—and we have suffered for it. Perhaps it is time that we, as educators, breed a new twentieth-century Renaissance Man, for without the wisdom of the humanities, I believe that the parochial "ways of knowing" so endemic to practitioner and scientist alike will prove increasingly crippling. We need a reaffirmation of intellectual tolerance, a recognition that "knowledge" about human beings, whether as individuals or as members of formal organizations cannot be secured cheaply and certainly not through the blandishments of a single discipline. Nor does this imply that we must retreat to a position of sloppy relativity in which each of us feels entitled to what he "knows" without responsibility for cross-checking his "knowing" with the "knowing" of others.

My plea is for a more balanced appreciation of various "ways of knowing." In the present context we have touched upon only a few; we have not referred to "knowing" through faith or to the role of myth in our "knowing."[17] Nor have we examined the "no-knowledge" of the East as advocated, for example, in Taoist philosophy.[18]

We must remember that it is impossible to appeal to a neutral principle to determine the rationality of competing systems. This is neatly illustrated in the story of a doctoral examination. The candidate, who had submitted a thesis on Mormon history, was asked whether he, being a

Mormon, regarded himself sufficiently unprejudiced to write a thesis on Mormon history. The student replied quietly, "Yes, if you, not a Mormon, consider yourself unprejudiced enough to examine it."

My remarks have been intended deliberately as a counter-irritant to "sluggish intellecual circulation"—the psychological equivalent of "tired blood." We can start putting this plea for intellectual tolerance into practice right at this conference. No matter what any of us may say, myself included, and no matter how infatuated we may become with our own sense of right-eousness, we will achieve greater wisdom if we are gracious enough to temper our convictions with the admonition once given to Horatio, ". . . there are more things in heaven and earth . . . than are dreamt of in your philosophy."

Notcs

1. National Conference of Professors of Educational Administration, Cooperative Program in Educational Administration, and University Council for Educational Administration. The relationship among these organizations has been described in chap. i of *Administrative Theory in Education,* ed. Andrew W. Halpin (Chicago: Midwest Administration Center, University of Chicago, 1958).
2. Two books in particular serve as markers in the transition from the "old" to the "new" approach in graduate programs for educational administrators. The first is Roald F. Campbell and Russell T. Cregg (eds.), *Administrative Behavior in Education* (New York: Harper and Brothers, 1957); the second, Halpin, *op. cit.* The idea for the present conference arose from the same thrust which produced these two books.
3. George C. Homans, *The Human Group* (New York: Harcourt, Brace and Company, 1950), p. 15. *Italics mine, AWH.*
4. Erik H. Erikson, "The Nature of Clinical Evidence," *Daedalus,* LXXXVII (Fall, 1958), 87.
5. Edward T. Hall, *The Silent Language* (Garden City, New York: Doubleday & Company, 1959). In the following section I have drawn freely from this book.
6. Chester I. Barnard, *The Functions of the Executive* (Cambridge: Harvard University Press, 1938).
7. Jacob W. Getzels and Egon G. Guba, "Social Behavior and the Administrative Process," *The School Review,* LXV (Winter, 1957), 423–442.
8. Andrew W. Halpin, *The Leadership Behavior of School Superintendents* (Chicago: Midwest Administration Center, University of Chicago, Reprinted, 1959).
9. John Ciardi, "An Ulcer, Gentlemen, Is an Unwritten Poem," *Toward the Liberally Educated Executive,* Robert A. Goldwin, ed. (White Plains, N.Y.: The Fund for Adult Education, 1957), pp. 54–55.
10. For example: John Cheever, *The Housebreaker of Shady Hill* (New York: Harper and Brothers, 1958).
11. The argument against this prejudice has been developed most perspicaciously by the French psychiatrist, Pierre Janet. See: Elton Mayo, *Some Notes on the Psychology of Pierre Janet* (Cambridge: Harvard University Press, 1948), especially pp. 99–101. If it is difficult to "see" human behavior, it is sometimes no

less difficult to "see" physical events. For an exquisite example of how even a trained observer can fail to "see" what is "out there" when his vision has been distorted by his own preconceptions, examine the paintings and chromoliths of the Colorado River canyons made by artists who traveled through this region during the 1857–1880 period, and compare these paintings with the meticulous observations of the explorer, John Wesley Powell. These paintings are reproduced in: Wallace Stegner, *Beyond the 100th Meridian* (Boston: Houghton Mifflin Co., 1954), between pp. 92–93. Recall, too, the French public's first shocked reaction to the early impressionists because these artists saw "out there" colors and lines which the public had never before seen.

12. Frank Heller, *Twilight of the Gladiators*, trans. Llewellyn Jones (New York: Putnam, 1944), p. 82.
13. As I read the work of some of my colleagues in the social sciences I am nagged by the memory of Samuel Johnson's comment on Thomas Gray, whom he admired only for *The Elegy:* "He was dull in a new way, and that made many people think him GREAT."
14. Digby Baltzell, "Bell Telephone's Experiment in Education," *Harper's Magazine*, CCX (March, 1955), 73–77. For several other articles on the same general theme, see Goldwin, *op. cit.*
15. Morris S. Viteles, " 'Human Relations' and the 'Humanities' in the Education of Business Leaders: Evaluation of a Program of Humanistic Studies for Executives," *Personnel Psychology*, XII (Spring, 1959), 1–28.
16. Peter F. Drucker, *The Practice of Management* (New York: Harper & Brothers, 1954), p. 375.
17. See, for example, the Spring, 1959, issue of *Daedalus*, LXXXII, No. 2. The whole issue is devoted to the topic of "Myth and Myth-making."
18. See, for example, Chap. IX in R. G. H. Siu's *The Tao of Science* (New York: John Wiley & Sons, Inc., 1959). Note the perceptive insight of the book's subtitle: "An Essay on Western Knowledge and Eastern Wisdom."

7 | Modern Approaches to Theory in Administration

James D. Thompson

The initial question in this article by Thompson is "What do we hope to achieve through theory?" After forthrightly answering this question which has troubled us all, he proceeds to discuss the sources of theory, criteria for administrative theory, and approaches being made to theory. He alludes also to our feelings of inadequacy as we approach theory development, but closes by suggesting how we may become more mature in our professional preparation of administrators by accepting our present stage of growth in the development and use of theory.

Gradually we in our culture are coming to understand that distinctions between theory and practice are artificial distinctions. Men of action as well as scholars entertain notions of cause-and-effect relations—notions which are generalized out of series of specific events and which are employed in new and similar situations. Some of these theories—these notions of cause and effect—may be generated from the personal experiences and insights of the actor, but many are incorporated in what his particular culture and generation consider common sense.

The common-sense basis of our theories does not make them less theoretical, but it may well make them less useful than we would hope. It seems characteristic of common sense that it does not make explicit the conditions under which the relationships it asserts actually hold. When these unknown conditions change, common sense becomes a misleading guide to further action.[1]

In setting about to train students for administration, we assume that there exists generalized or generalizable knowledge about administration which can be imparted. There is the further assumption that common sense does not contain all of that knowledge; otherwise, the student would be wasting his time. Thus theory is a basic aspect of our training programs, even while the courses labeled "theory" occupy minor roles in our curricula.

James D. Thompson, "Modern Approaches to Theory in Administration." Reprinted with permission of The Macmillan Company from *Administrative Theory in Education*, Andrew W. Halpin, ed., pp. 20–39.

Theory per se faces an uphill battle in programs which train future administrators. The situation is different, of course, where future scientists are being trained; here theory is recognized as the core of training. This distinction, I think, reflects the fact that administrators and scientists use theory in opposite ways. The administrator uses theory as a basis for deriving answers or approaches to specific situations; he seeks principles capable of guiding the application of general notions to specific situations.[2] The scientist uses specific situations as a basis for arriving at improved theory. Hence, the same specific situation may have quite a different meaning to the scientist and to the administrator, and it may call forth quite different motivations.

These differing uses for theory do not mean, however, that the theory which the scientist seeks to build and that which the administrator seeks to use must be different theories. Indeed, unless they are basically the same, the accumulated knowledge contained in basic theory must be rediscovered by the administrator—and he lacks both the time and the training to do so. In the more mature fields of applied science, advances have come precisely because teachers and practitioners have learned to employ the systematic theories developed by rigorous science.

We who staff professional training programs have dual needs for theory. We are obligated to equip our students with the best available theory as a guide to their practice. We also need theory to guide our search for better understanding. At this stage in our development these needs are equally pressing.

On the assumption that an adequate theory would serve both purposes, I will attempt to discuss modern approaches to theory in administration from both viewpoints. I will not attempt to judge specific formulations or "models." If these meet the test of internal logic, I know of no other test than that of empirical trial. My remarks will be on a more general level, for it seems reasonable to ask: (1) What do we hope to achieve through the use of theory? (2) What are the sources of traditional theory? (3) What are the criteria for administrative theory? (4) Are we approaching an adequate theory?

What Do We Hope to Achieve through Theory?

Much has been written about the uses of theory in research, less about the potential contributions of theory to the training of future administrators. In my opinion, an adequate theory of administration would go a long way toward preparing students for change. It would condition them to think of the administrative process as a complex of simultaneously variable factors rather than as a set of specific techniques. We cannot expect techniques of administration for 1977 to have much resemblance to those current today. Nor can we predict, with any degree of confidence, the nature of the techniques which will be available and current in 1977. An adequate theory would equip the future administrator to alter the values of those variables subject to his control as other variables beyond his control change in value. Rather than describing currently accepted practices, an adequate theory would explain *why* such practices work and why they might not work, if and when the surrounding context changes.

Perhaps this point can be illustrated by two examples of changing concepts of authority. "Good supervision" of the 1920 variety in America was rooted in a firm paternalism in which fear-inspired discipline had a large role. The same supervisory behavior today is "bad supervision."[3] Why? In part, I think, because the individuals being supervised have more education, are better organized, and place higher value on human dignity.

The military provides another example of changing patterns of authority. Our Air Force grew out of an army where rank and authority were intricately connected. The traditional basis of military authority was appropriate under conditions where work was repetitive and easily divided. Individuals were practically interchangeable, and the supervisor was the one who could do everything other members of his unit did—but could do it all a little better. Each rank was occupied by people who had become experts in the activities they supervised; the various echelons differed primarily in the *scope* of their concern rather than in the *kinds* of work done. The modern Air Force, however, has very complicated equipment and missions, and it employs quite complex processes carried on by a great variety of technical specialists. In such units the supervisor can no longer be an expert in more than one or two specialized processes. Despite assignment rotations, then, it is no longer possible to assume that "any" captain is necessarily competent to exercise authority over "any" corporal. Here, I think, technology is the primary variable undermining what was once an accepted view of authority. Air Force administrators have certainly felt the impact of the changes.

A second advantage which an adequate theory of administration might offer is a system of thinking which would allow the administrator to incorporate knowledge produced by the several disciplines. Even if we could provide the administrator with the most up-to-date knowledge from all related disciplines, this would be woefully out of date long before he left active administration. We do our students a disservice if we lead them to believe that today's psychology, sociology, history, economics, or political science provides him with irrefutable facts. I mentioned above one probable reason for the change in supervisory standards; a second reason, I am confident, is that new knowledge about human motivation challenged older notions about behavior based on fear.

Somehow, in the future, our students must be alerted to the results of new discoveries and interpretations. But it is not enough to bombard them with leaflets or to call them back for "refresher" sessions. We must equip them to trace through the implications and ramifications of forthcoming knowledge about human beings and behavioral processes; we must equip them to alter their own behavior accordingly.

We are learning, for example, new things about the triad and its instability, and game theory predicts that under certain conditions triads resort to coalition behavior. As these lines of inquiry develop, the administrator must see them as more than merely "interesting" new findings. He needs a *systematic* way of thinking which will lead him to re-examine his use of competition and his methods of allocating rewards and resources among groups in his organization.

An adequate theory would also prepare students for further growth through their own later experiences by providing them with economical ways of ordering that experience. By emphasizing the interrelatedness of phenomena, such a theory would help them remain alert to the unanticipated consequences of their actions; it would help them avoid oversimplified explanations of those actions which were successful; and it would caution them to be aware of changing conditions which might call for changed behavior patterns.

If administrators are to profit from their experiences, they must have systems for ordering and generalizing specific events. The more explicit and rigorous the system for ordering experience, the greater the facility in learning.

In short, an adequate theory would direct the student's attention to processes and relationships rather than to techniques. It would provide him with a framework into which he could place both the future findings of the social sciences and his own experiences in administration.

What Are the Sources of Traditional Theory?

There appear to be four primary sources of theory for administration: the comments and reports made by practicing administrators, the survey research of teachers, the deductive reasoning of teachers, and the adaptation of models from other disciplines. These are listed in the order in which they have appeared on the scene. The first two are long established and traditional; the last two reflect newer developments. Because my assignment is to discuss "modern approaches to theory in administration," I would like to comment first on the more traditional sources of theory—to establish some sort of base line for comparing, afterward, the more recent developments.

I have suggested that every administrator uses more or less rigorous theory in meeting specific situations. These theories become of importance to educators only when they are verbalized and, eventually, written—when they can be passed on to others. Perhaps this stating of theory is not central to the role of the administrator, but I think it is evident that much of the reading we now assign to students (and much of our lecturing) is based upon statements of theory made by practicing administrators.

We have a vast machinery for encouraging, facilitating, and disseminating such statements. We hold conferences and training institutes where administrators generalize from their experience. Our trade and professional magazines and journals vie in presenting the views of distinguished administrators; publishers compete for text manuscripts written (or ghosted) by men who "really know" because they do it every day.

These people undoubtedly have much to tell us; we have much to learn from them. Yet they are not necessarily adept at verbalizing their own behavior for purposes of systematic theory. It is not uncommon to find a real discrepancy between what they do and what they tell us to do. On many occasions, I am convinced, our students would do better to "do as they do, not as they say."

We are perhaps handicapped in the behavioral studies, as compared with the biological and physical, by the fact that the things we study— people—are "verbal." The atom and the virus cannot talk, and those who study the behavior of atoms and viruses are forced to learn about that behavior through observation by the investigator. We tend to be content to let the administrator tell us how he behaves, and we are lulled into believing that he has perceived and articulated accurately.[4] In effect, we rely on him to be not only his own philosopher but also his own psychologist, sociologist, anthropologist, historian, political scientist, and economist. The day has long passed when even a full-time scholar can master more than one or two of these disciplines.

This is not to deny that men of action have useful insights. To the contrary, their ingenuity and creativity often would put the academician to shame. I am suggesting, however, that the really creative insights of these people seldom are incorporated into our recorded theory because: (1) They lack the time to record and develop such insights.[5] (2) They tend to force their theoretical thinking into the concepts we have taught them and which we constantly reinforce in our writings and speeches. Our teachings act as blinders. (3) The platforms we afford them are not conducive to reflective critical thought, but rather to the use of journalistic or visual-aid "gimmicks"—three well-illustrated points, seven rules to success, or simple diagrams understandable at the flicker of an eye.

I suspect that in the early development of the various areas of professional training the voice of the practitioner quickly becomes the "voice of authority." Nevertheless, there also develops a pattern of research by faculty members who find it necessary to supplement the pronouncements of practitioners or to systematize their various pronouncements. We now have an extensive literature on the results of such research. With a few notable exceptions, it has been of the descriptive, survey variety. When our teaching materials have lacked details or have appeared out of date, we have interviewed practitioners or have given them questionnaires. From their replies we have developed "modal models"—models which are based on the most common way of handling administrative problems. Our journals and magazines of administration are filled with reports of this type of research.

On occasion we also do "scholarly" research in the libraries. Here we survey, collate, and compare the terminology of the distinguished writers on administration, reducing these materials to their common denominators in order to extract the essentials, or we develop an expanded list of categories which is "all inclusive," or we reorganize the list of categories into memorable slogans such as POSDCORB. Incidently, this can be great fun. I have always found POSDCORB easy to remember but hard to pronounce, and I would like to suggest my own arrangement, which contains all of the letters but is easier said: P–S–C–O–B–O–R–D, pronounced with the P silent.

I repeat, this can be fun; but where does it get us? Whether we have relied on the visiting dignitary or on our own survey efforts, we have seldom produced new knowledge. Rather, we seem to have periodically produced new packages for the same old product. Any honest appraisal of the theoretical literature of administration will reveal that the vast bulk of it is of this "grass roots" variety—a mixture of common sense, descriptive categories one (and only one) step removed from common sense, and slogans and catch phrases which have dramatic appeal but little else.

Within our lifetimes there have been tremendous changes in administrative behavior. Presumably the fundamental process has been constant, but there is no denying that the behavior through which that process operates has changed considerably. Many administrators have responded to new situations, new conditions, and new opportunities by adjusting or adapting their behavior. These responses have not always been consistent or successful, but could we expect otherwise when administrators are forced to rely on hunch and ingenuity, trial and error? These are expensive tools.

The economy of theory has been missing because we have tended to build grass roots theories which "explain" what has been done; we have not examined the outcomes of all possible permutations and combinations of variables and have not generalized the relationships into systematic theories. Our grass roots theories have described the past, but they have not faced the future. In contrast, the abstract theories of physics have had profound effects on human life; they have done more than merely reflect an aspect of reality.

Probably the most damaging criticism that can be made of any theory is that it does not generate new knowledge; I have indicated my belief that this criticism applies to traditional theories of administration. Why? A major reason, I feel, is that we have focused on descriptive categories as pigeon holes for data (for pedagogical neatness), but we have neglected the dynamic relationships among these categories. We have provided, in effect, for electric light sockets and for wall switches, but we have failed to provide the wiring which relates them, and we remain in the dark.

Typically, I think, when we decide to do research, we set aside our verbalized theories of administration and draw on common sense as the source of our research problems. More often than not, it is the common sense of practicing administrators; hence, we do research on the topics which they label as most urgent.

When industrial administrators are vexed by the changing role of foremen, we get a rash of research on this topic; and when these same administrators begin to puzzle over resistance to change, we flood the market with research and theories designed to overcome resistance to change. When the competition for skilled personnel increases employee turnover rates, we shift our research attention to matters of inducements and loyalties. We usually approach these "urgent" topics with the variables stated by the practitioner, hoping that by more careful collection of data and more minute analysis we will find answers for him. In short, I think that we only infrequently undertake research because our theories say a topic is important.

But do our grass roots theories point to strategic topics? Do they in themselves raise new questions to be answered? Do they suggest that since such-and-such relationship holds, we should also be able to find X—or be forced to revise the theory? I think not. Our traditional theories lack this self-correcting feature because they are weak in stating relationships.

My remarks have, of course, been exaggerated. To some extent our theories of administration do pose relationships, at least implicitly. Our theories indicate, for example, that "planning" or "communication" have a positive relationship with performance. Yet, a reading of such theoretical discussions usually leaves the strong impression that the relationship is linear—that twice as much planning (or communication) will double performance—and, of course, we know from experience that this is not necessarily true.

The poverty of our thinking about relationships is indicated by the fact that often we can explain the outcomes of administrative behavior only by value-loaded adjectives—that more or better communication was present, that organization was inadequate, or that planning was democratic. These "principles by adjective" are no better than rules of thumb.

A second serious indictment of our grass roots theories is that they do not facilitate the accumulation and incorporation of new knowledge. As forces from without have changed administrative behavior, have our theories been generalized and expanded to incorporate these new phenomena? Usually, we have added new courses and kept our "theory" or "principles" course intact, with the result that we now offer our students a variety of part-theories but no theory. We have added courses in human relations, operations research, group dynamics, organization and methods, and so on. Our students find a wide assortment in our curriculum cafeteria, but they get no guide to a balanced diet.

. A third weakness of our grass roots theories is that they tend to be special theories of administration rather than general theories. By using the language and concepts of practitioners and by trying to see through their spectacles, we have developed theories of business administration, military administration, educational administration, hospital administration, and public administration. As Litchfield has noted:

> The most serious indictment which must be made of present thought is that it has failed to achieve a level of generalization enabling it to systematize and explain administrative phenomena which occur in related fields. . . . We seem to be saying that there is business administration and hospital administration and public administration; that there is military administration, hotel administration, and school administration. But there is no administration.[6]

Of course there are differences between school systems and industrial organizations, and these differences lead to variations in administrative behavior. But there are similarities of administration which we do not observe when we use grass roots frameworks. Each of these areas has its special concerns, its pressing problems, and its distinctive jargon. When we try to approach administration as the practitioner of a particular area approaches it, we focus on the unique or distinctive, and we join him in taking for granted the underlying bases of administration which are not unique.

What Are the Criteria for Administrative Theory?

I have tried to suggest some of the advantages to be expected of an adequate theory and some of the weaknesses of traditional approaches to theory in administration. Now I will climb further out on the limb and suggest at least a minimum set of criteria for a really usable theory. These are predictions of the characteristics an adequate theory will display when we have it.

The variables and constants for such a theory will be selected for their logical and operational properties rather than for their congruence with common sense. Common-sense terms and concepts gain currency because they are convenient for dealing with frequent events which must be acted upon. To the extent that such terms and concepts are also useful for systematic theory, it would be wasteful to discard them. But where common-sense terms lack precision or clarity, or where common-sense concepts do not order experience in the ways required by systematic theory, then new terms must be invented or adopted. Chemistry did not really begin until it stopped regarding fire, water, earth, and air as the four basic elements. These were "obvious" and "real"; hence, it was common sense to work with them. But what kind of chemistry would we have today if those concepts had not been set aside?

Perhaps I can give an example a little closer to our field. One frequent distinction between "line" and "staff" in complex organizations is that the "line" gives orders while the "staff" gives advice. Now we all know the difference between orders and advice. Or do we? When a staff assistant to my boss indicates that I am doing something inefficiently, have I received advice or an order? In many cases, I am convinced, advice has been given (or intended), but orders have been received (or perceived). The line-staff distinction is common sense to a great many administrators, but, in my opinion, it has seriously interfered with the development of administrative theory.

The selection of variables for logical and operational properties rather than for common-sense properties means that we will face charges of uttering meaningless jargon, but I believe this is an occupational hazard for those seeking new and more useful ways of looking at the world. If we cannot develop thick skins, I doubt if we can develop more useful theory.

An adequate theory will be generalizable, hence abstract. The broader the range of specific events it explains, the more powerful the theory. To regard educational administration as unique is to deny prematurely the relevance of that which is known about business administration, or military, or church administration. The inescapable conclusion in that case would be that the entire task of building a theory of educational administration falls entirely to a pitifully small number of individuals. The only hope, I think, is to approach educational administration as a variety of administration and to incorporate into the theory a variable which will encompass first one, then another, such purpose or task. If relevant knowledge from other types of administration is to be applied to education, then educational administration must be considered as only one special case. Similarly, public school administration, military training education, religious education, adult education, and so on must be considered special cases of education, and a theory adequate for educational administration must be able to encompass them all.

Another reason for abstraction is that an adequate theory of administration cannot be limited by time or place. We cannot afford to be content with a theory of educational administration for America and another for Indonesia, or with a theory of educational administration for America in 1950 and another in 1970. The theory should enable us to deal with different times and places, but again as variables and not as limits to the theory.

The values capable of being attached to education and to administration will not be incorporated into the theoretical system itself; instead, the system will treat such values as variables. The values of "democracy" undoubtedly color both education and administration in twentieth-century America. But if we sincerely want to understand educational (or any other type of) administration, we must not attempt to build a theory of democratic administration into education. Instead, our theory must account for administrative behavior and processes in cases where democracy is highly valued *and* where other political ideals are highly valued. Similarly, we cannot afford a separate theory of profit-oriented administration, although our general theory must be capable of explaining administration where profit is an important concern. Values must be treated as variables, for purposes of theory, rather than as limits to the theory.

An adequate theory of administration will be rooted in the basic social and behavioral sciences. Administration is accomplished through the behavior of administrators in interaction with others. Hence, basic understanding of human behavior must be included in our theory of administration. We cannot hope to start from scratch and develop a psychology of administration, a political science of administration, or an economics or sociology of administration. Yet the subject matters of all of those fields have manifestations in administration. Psychology deals, for example, with motivation, learning, and decision processes, all of which are important in administration. The political scientist's understanding of federalism or of bilateral negotiations, for instance, is pertinent to administration. The administrator in any field has problems of resource allocation and opportunity costs; these are intensively studied by the economist. The sociologist's considerations of bureaucracy and small group processes also are clearly pertinent.

To the extent that such disciplines do not focus on behavioral processes in *administrative* situations, we face the task of extending them. But unless we build on the foundations being laid so painfully by these disciplines we face a hopeless task.

The focus of an adequate theory will be on processes rather than on correlations. Admittedly a theory is valuable only if it simplifies. Still there are limits beyond which simplification is misleading. It seems to me that administration as a self-conscious, definable activity occurs only when the activities to be administered are themselves highly complicated; and, therefore, the behavior which contributes to administration involves chain-like reactions more often than simple cause-and-effect relationships. It helps to know that A leads to B, but if the reality of administration is complex, our theory must eventually not only show that A is associated with H but also show the relations between B, C, and so on to H. In other words, it is not enough to show that a particular pattern is correlated with performance; we must eventually be able to explain how the relationship occurs.

This means, I believe, that we cannot be content with structural concepts—which tell us "what." We must also have "how" concepts.[7] The structural concept "role," for example, gives us guide lines regarding the future behavior of a supervisor, but it does not explain how members of the work group gain understanding of the supervisor's role or how various roles articulate and operate within the work group or how roles change. Structural concepts seem to be indispensable but are not sufficient for a really useful theory.

Are We Approaching an Adequate Theory?

A decade is a short time for which to reckon the development of a body of knowledge; for the immediately preceding decade we do not have sufficient perspective in time to make a firm evaluation of what has been accomplished. Yet I believe that since World War II we have witnessed developments which will turn out to be especially significant. I will have been greatly mistaken if this flurry of activity in theories of administration becomes a passing fad.[8]

The war probably had much to do with this increased interest in administration. Thousands of men and women with administrative experience discovered that at least some of it was applicable in new and quite different kinds of organizations, even as they discovered that their administrative behavior also had to be adapted in some respects. War, as any crisis, placed a new urgency on problems and questions which had only occasionally crossed our minds in more "normal" times. The more mature students who returned to our campuses following the war had experienced this urgency. They were less ready to accept clichés and slogans and were often more eager to disregard traditional boundaries between bodies of knowledge. Their questions challenged complacency, stimulated multi-disciplinary study, and on occasion underscored the need for research.

Whatever the sources, research and theoretical activities increased after World War II in most of the fields of professional administrative training: business, public, educational, social work, hospital, and so on. In each of these fields, more honest-to-goodness field research is going on than ever before, and still more is demanded. New blood in the form of new disciplinary backgrounds has been injected into these fields to the point where we can no longer identify a man's training by his title or his location in the university. Admittedly, interdisciplinary collaboration is difficult, and frequently its results are disappointing. Yet in the overview, I think, the signs are clear that hypotheses are being borrowed back and forth among schools which formerly were isolated. Generalizations and concepts generated by one school turn up a year later in another. Sometimes they are embraced, or they may be bitterly challenged, but they cross boundaries more frequently.

An adequate theory has not yet come out of all this, but there have been several promising starts. The sources of these modern developments, as indicated above, have been two: the deductive reasoning of scholars and the adaptation of models from other disciplines. I doubt that it is possible to identify theories which have been derived exclusively from only one of these sources, but we can identify examples characterized by the predominance of one or the other of these approaches.

There have been a number of deductive approaches to theory—attempts to postulate a few general ideas which for one reason or another appear to be "true," or "plausible" and important, and to arrive by logical steps at more specific propositions. Two approaches of this kind have influenced a great many of us; I refer to the formulations by Chester I. Barnard and Herbert A. Simon. Both men produced books which are as instructive on the second or third reading as on the first, and both have had an influence that extends far beyond the recognized boundaries of administration as a subject.[9] Students usually find these books difficult to read, perhaps because the authors' ideas are more sophisticated and their terms more precise than those we encounter in common-sense language and in textbooks on administration, but readers who exert the necessary effort invariably find these writings extremely challenging.

Also, in the last decade several attempts have been made to formulate administrative theory on the basis of models derived from a number of different sources: learning models, decision-making models, group dynamics models, leadership models, social system models, game models, and so on. Some of these have been more deeply rooted in empirical observation than others; each has started from unique premises. The very proliferation of these models suggests that we are dissatisfied with traditional approaches and are motivated to do something about them. Probably all these models contain some "truth," although my impression is that they are helpful primarily in broadening the scope of our inquiry. Two examples may be briefly noted. Parsons' approach via social system concepts has pointed to the importance of the organization acquiring "legitimization."[10] I think this calls for an expansion of our concept of authority beyond the boundaries of the organization. Game theory, by explicitly calling our attention to the interaction conditions between two or more "organizations" seeking the same or competing goals, forces us to recognize the importance of strategies for dealing with outside forces.

None of these approaches in its present formulation is adequate. Perhaps none can be expanded into an adequate formulation. Yet despite their differences, most of them reveal similar underlying themes, and this convergence is encouraging. One of these common themes is the serious consideration of definitions and of making them operational. There is nothing magic in definitions, and we could bog down in them. On the other hand, when we seek new concepts to be used in logical systems, those concepts must be given labels and precise descriptions. There is much confusion in our current literature over definitions; "role," "status," and "authority," for example, are three terms for which there are conflicting definitions and which therefore confront us with conflicts about how data should be classified. But perhaps confusion is inescapable in moving from an old way of ordering ideas to a new way. At least, I think, the concern over precision and operationalism reflects a search for something more powerful than common-sense concepts.

A second common theme in these modern approaches is that they are *explicitly* relational regarding human behavior. Whether they draw on deductive reasoning or stem from the more empirically based models of the behavioral sciences, these approaches attempt to predict human behavior under stated conditions. Sometimes we complain that the conditions stated are not very lifelike—but it seems to me that we need to observe behavior under all conceivable conditions. The predictions made by the several models may turn out to be incorrect, but if these predictions are explicit enough to be matched against actual human behavior, then the models can be revised accordingly.

Moreover, the predictions contained in the several models are based upon recognition of the fact that human behavior flows out of persons in situations. Some models, as opposed to others, elaborate more on the person and less on the situation. There is a great unevenness here, and each model analyzes its major variables in different ways. One may posit "rational man" and try to determine how the situation interferes with his rationality. Another may posit "robot man" and try to explain how environment prevents his automatic responses. A third may seek group uniformities irrespective of personal idiosyncrasies, thus placing emphasis on the individual's social environment. This is another way of saying that each model tends to be based primarily on one discipline and to include others in subordinate ways. Here again there is confusion and very little uniformity. Nevertheless, I believe that this confusion reflects a searching for ways of incorporating the various disciplines; competing suggestions at this point can protect us from complacency.

A third common theme is that all of these models are or attempt to be generalizable. They differ in degree of abstractness, but they are hypothesized as potentially capable of explaining administrative behavior in a great variety of specific situations and in the several types of administration. Whether the models stress learning, decisions, leadership, group dynamics, games, or something else, they are dealing with phenomena which are not confined to one or two levels in a hierarchical organization; and they are not confined to phenomena unique to the school system, the hospital, or the business firm.

A fourth common theme is the attempt to free these models from culturally defined values, while permitting us to use values as data. The models do not tell us how to be "democratic" administrators or how to be "economically-rational" administrators so much as they predict how administrators will behave if they happen to be committed to one or another of these values. My personal belief is that our models are remiss in not explaining how such values enter the administrative system, but this is correctable by extension, provided that values are used as variables in the models rather than as assumptions upon which the models themselves are predicated.

Thus on four of the five suggested criteria, I think, modern approaches appear to be progressing. On the fifth—the explanation of long chain-like processes—there is less encouraging evidence. We still are fumbling for process concepts, and our models are better at dealing with relations between two variables—with perhaps one intervening variable—than with long sequences. Probably this is largely because these models tend to emphasize a few aspects of administration or behavior in selected types of administrative situations. But it is in the long sequences that complicated "switching" takes place and that outcomes of administrative activities are determined. My personal belief, also, is that we tend to stress internal relations and structures to the point where we fail to see the significance of external relations or the interaction between internal and external activities. There, perhaps, is where we will find the source of the values held by administrators and the impetus for administrative change.

In brief, modern approaches to theory in administration appear to me to be developing more promising concepts of variables which can be defined operationally; they are seeking generalizability and freedom from value-limitations; they are focusing on the sources and the consequences of human behavior. The ultimate criterion of a scientific theory, of course, is its utility in adding to our understanding. Few of these models can yet claim to have made much of a contribution in this respect, but I think there is reason to believe that they are laying the foundation for an adequate theory.

Summary

I believe we are seeing in schools of education, business, public administration, hospital administration, and social work the growing pains and confusion that attend moving from infancy through adolescence. The more mature (but I trust not senile) professional schools—medicine, law, engineering—probably exhibited the same sorts of bewilderment and fumbling at an earlier stage in their development.

Professional schools, however much nurtured and protected by the university, are sired by a clientele of practitioners. They are elaborations of an apprenticeship system and are close to the grass roots.[11] Their first faculties are chosen for demonstrated success and reputation in the professional field regardless of the usual trappings of academic qualifications. Despite their popularity with students and practitioners, however, these people are considered by the rest of the university community as poor relations. They are forced to defend themselves against charges that they are operating trade schools. Under pressure to attain recognized status as a profession and to achieve academic respectability, they therefore raise the academic standards for faculty members. Gradually this encourages them to think that there are other useful approaches to their subject and reduces their subservience to their immediate clientele. Eventually, at least in the cases of medicine and engineering, the professional school incorporates into its own structure representatives of related basic disciplines and seeks to make fundamental contributions to knowledge.

In these terms, we in the fields of administration are not yet mature. But we are fighting back against the trade school charges; we are raising our standards for faculty members; we are considering more abstract materials and de-emphasizing techniques. We have even begun to incorporate into our faculties representatives from the social sciences, although we are not quite certain whether we want the facts they command, the research techniques they have mastered, or the theory in which they are disciplined.

Having presented my own "model" of professional school development, I will climb to the end of the limb and assert that we are on the way toward fashioning a bridge between the basic disciplines of human behavior and the field of administration, similar to those bridges which link medicine to the biological sciences and engineering to the physical sciences. Eventually our theories of administration may lead practice rather than follow it, and in time we may contribute significantly to the behavioral sciences.

Notes

1. For an interesting elaboration of this, see Bernard Barber, *Science and the Social Order* (Glencoe, Ill.: Free Press, 1952).
2. This matter is thoughtfully treated by Harold Guetzkow, "Three Cognitive Barriers in Utilization of the Social Sciences," April, 1957 (privately circulated). See also Philip Selznick, *Leadership in Administration* (Evanston, Ill.: Row Peterson, 1957), and Alvin Gouldner, "Theoretical Requirements of the Applied Social Sciences," *American Sociological Review*, XXII (February, 1957), 92–102.
3. American industry spent vast amounts retraining foremen to the newer concepts and replacing those on whom the training did not "take."
4. Few of us would rely on the centenarian for a prescription on living to a ripe old age.

5. Chester Barnard is a notable exception; he wrote while president of a large corporation.
6. Edward H. Litchfield, "Notes on a General Theory of Administration," *Administrative Science Quarterly*, I (June, 1956), 7.
7. This point is adapted from James D. Thompson, William J. McEwen, and Frederick L. Bates, "Sounding Out as a Relating Process" (paper read at the annual meeting of the Eastern Sociological Society), April, 1957.
8. A recent survey of administrative courses in the field of business illustrates the "boom" in this area since 1945, as well as the newer emphasis on behavioral models. See Charles E. Sumner, Jr., *Factors in Effective Administration* (New York: Columbia University, Graduate School of Business, 1956).
9. See Chester I. Barnard, *The Functions of the Executive* (Cambridge: Harvard University Press, 1938), and Herbert A. Simon, *Administrative Behavior* (New York: Macmillan, 1957). Many social psychologists studying small groups have derived their hypotheses from Barnard and Simon; many sociologists studying formal organizations have done likewise. Both writers are referred to frequently by political scientists.
10. Talcott Parsons, "Suggestions for a Sociological Approach to the Theory of Organizations," *Administrative Science Quarterly*, I (1956), 63–85, 225–39.
11. An interesting set of parallels among various aspects of professional school history and current problems is discussed by Lloyd E. Blauch (ed.) in *Education for the Professions* (Washington: Government Printing Office, 1955). The generalizations made in these closing paragraphs, however, are mine.

8 | The Nature and Meaning of Theory

Daniel E. Griffiths

In the yearbook Behavioral Science and Educational Administration, *Griffiths describes the nature, meaning, and construction of theory as it pertains to educational administration. This statement suggests useful guidelines to both practitioners and scholars for the application and development of theory.*

There is much confusion concerning the concept of "theory" in education since most educationists use the term much more loosely than do those who are working to develop administrative theory. Modern administrative theorists limit the zone of their interests and define in a rigorous fashion the area of their inquiry. Theorists in administration see themselves as social scientists who are greatly influenced by the methodology, the purposes, and the orientation of physical scientists. This chapter aims to set forth the position of administrative theorists as regards the nature, the meaning, and the construction of theory. Since a fundamental belief of these workers is that the adjectival varieties of administration have more in common than not, the substance of this chapter is drawn from business, public, industrial, and educational administration. The methodology is derived from both the social and the physical sciences.

The Nature of Theory

One approach to definition is to state what the concept is *not*. By attempting to exclude certain commonly accepted meanings in an explicit fashion, it may be possible to focus upon the meaning actually accepted.[1]

What Theory Is Not

When the urban superintendents of the country were asked to name the outstanding weaknesses of their preparation programs in graduate

Daniel E. Griffiths, "The Nature and Meaning of Theory," *Behavioral Science and Educational Administration.* The Sixty-Third Yearbook of the National Society for the Study of Education, Part II (Daniel E. Griffiths, ed.). Chicago: The Society, 1964, pp. 95–118. Reprinted by permission.

school, the one which ranked at the top of the list was, "too much theory; courses not practical." [2] Letters were sent to a sampling of superintendents who responded in this way asking what was meant by "too theoretical." The answers to these letters were quite revealing, since they demonstrated many misuses of the word *theory*. Some thought theory was the opposite of practical, thereby equating *theory* with *impractical*. Others had the interesting notion that if a course was *poor*, it was *theoretical*. (The search for the origin of this idea would be a fascinating research project!) The most common use of the concept *theory* was as a synonym for *speculation*, *supposition*, or the *ideal*. These men said that graduate work in school administration was little related to reality, that it was concerned with what "ought to be" rather than what "is." This dichotomy will be discussed in more detail later. To say that theory is not impractical, not poor, nor is it speculation, supposition, nor the ideal, clears away some of the obfuscation which surrounds the concept.

There are other prominent misunderstandings regarding the meaning of theory. It is often contended that theory is a personal affair, a dream, a philosophy, a taxonomy, or common sense, but it is none of these. Since the confusion between theory and philosophy is more prevalent than the others, let us examine the two concepts.

The most commonly held belief regarding theory of administration is that it is a set of "oughts," that is, a set of rules that tells one how to administer. Now, a well-developed set of values, having logical consistency and related to reality, is of crucial importance to the administrator. But this set of values is not a theory. The difference between theory and values is usually discussed in terms of the "is-ought" dichotomy.

Possibly the use of an example from the physical sciences will clarify the difference. If a person jumped out of a window in the thirtieth story of a building, the exact speed at which his body would hit the sidewalk below could be predicted. The force of the impact could be calculated, and it could be predicted that the person would die upon hitting the sidewalk. All this is in the realm of theory. It can be said, "If a person leaps from the thirtieth story of a building, he will die." There is no implication of "oughtness" in this statement. There are no values in the statement. Values can be put in as variables, however. A person might raise the question, "Do I want to die?" If his answer is "yes" (a value judgment), then he might consider the efficiency of leaping from a thirty-story window. Theory tells him this would be very effective (his goal would be achieved in an economical manner).

It can be seen that the "is" deals with two functions of theory. Most obviously it is concerned with *description*. In the above example, an accurate description of the speed of the man's falling body and the force with which he hits the sidewalk can be obtained by reference to the theory of gravitation. In addition, an adequate *explanation* of why the man falls at a certain speed and why the force is what it is can also be obtained from the theory of gravitation. The "is" of the "is-ought" dichotomy refers to both a description and an explanation of the event being considered.

When philosophy is equated to a set of values, the term "philosophy" is being used very loosely. If theory is to be used in a precise fashion, then so too must philosophy. As Butler so concisely states, one would need to deal with the three great problems of philosophy:

> (1) The problem of reality is this: What is the nature of the universe in which we live? Or, in the last analysis, what is real? The branch of philosophy which deals with this great problem is called *metaphysics*. (2) The problem of knowledge is this: How does a man know what is real? That is to say, how do we come by our knowledge and how can we be sure it is true, not error or illusion? The area of philosophy which is devoted to solving this problem is named epistemology. (3) The third great problem, the problem of value is this: What are the important values which are to be desired in living? Are there values rooted in reality? And how can they be realized in our experience? The branch of philosophy dealing with such questions as these is named *axiology*. In addition to these three, but most closely related to *epistemology*, is another branch of philosophy which deals with the exact relating of ideas. This area of philosophy is commonly referred to as the science of *logic*.[3]

Theory is not a set of values, and neither is it a philosophy. Halpin has summed up this argument very cogently:

> . . . some writers have used this term [theory] in the sense of "value theory," to refer not to how administrators *do* behave, but to how they *ought* to behave. This confoundment between the "is's" and the "oughts" of behavior is responsible for a greater failure in communication between educators and social scientists than any other issue. No one will deny that we need normative standards— in the ethical meaning of the term—for how administrators *ought* to behave, but these prescriptions do not constitute a theory.[4]

What Theory Is

A definition.—The confusion as to what constitutes theory has brought forth a motley array of progeny. So that some order might be brought out of chaos, Halpin and Griffiths issued calls asking that there be common acceptance of Fiegl's definition.[5] This definition is rather narrow and is highly restrictive in its scope, but is, however, what is needed, since a word has no value if it can be used to cover all sorts of academic exercises. Fiegl defines theory as follows:

> In order to provide for a terminology which will not constantly involve us in a tangle of confusions, I propose to define a "theory" as a set of assumptions from which can be derived by purely logico-mathematical procedures a larger set of

empirical laws. The theory thereby furnishes an explanation of these empirical laws and unifies the originally relatively heterogeneous areas of subject matter characterized by those empirical laws. Even though it must be admitted that there is no sharp line of demarcation (except a purely arbitrary one) between theoretical assumptions and empirical laws, the distinction, at least in the sense of a gradation, is illuminating from a methodological point of view.

One more terminological suggestion may help: Let us speak of scientific explanation wherever more specific or more descriptive statements are derived from more general or more hypothetical assumptions.[6]

In essence, Fiegl proposes that theory be defined as a set of assumptions from which can be derived by purely logico-mathematical procedures a larger set of empirical laws. A number of questions might be raised concerning the definition: What is the meaning of set? What is the difference between assumptions and laws? Must a theory be tested before any indication of its value is known? What would be a theory which meets this definition?[7]

Terminology.—The language of theory-building is very confusing. Since concepts are used differently by practically all writers and there appear to be no authorities, it would seem that an agreement on basic terminology is essential. With this in mind, the following is offered.

As the term *set* is used here it means a group of assumptions such that (1) no other assumption can be derived from any other combination of assumptions in the group, and (2) the empirical laws cannot be derived without the inclusion of every member of the group.

Presumptions are basic to and precede assumptions in the thinking of the theorist. Some writers call presumptions "principles," but this appears to be too confusing. Let presumptions remain presumptions. What can be said about presumptions? They are not empirical findings and are not directly derived from empirical findings, but they are ways of directing empirical findings. Often they are decisions. The only criterion that can be employed in the selection of presumptions is usefulness. If a presumption gives rise to assumptions upon which theory can be built, then it is retained; if not, it is abandoned. An example of a useful presumption is that administration may be viewed from the perspective of decision-making.

Assumptions grow out of presumptions. One should strive to create a set of assumptions which explains a law in the most elegant and most parsimonious, the neatest, most revealing, and the most relevant fashion possible.

Laws are statements of empirical regularities of phenomena. They have the same form as hypotheses, but have withstood more testing. Examples of well-known laws are the Hawthorne Effect and Boyle's Law.

In an attempt to clarify the terminology of theorists, let us take the terms *assumption* and *laws* and consider them together with some other terms with which they are commonly used. Brodbeck points out that a statement of fact, a concept, a law, and a theory are all different things.[8] A fact is a particular thing, such as Johnny's I.Q. To state a fact is to state that a concept has an instance or a number of instances. When a fact is connected with other facts, a generalization or law is formed. As Brodbeck says, "A law states that whenever there is an instance of one kind of fact, then there is also an instance of another."[9] As an example of a law, note the following: the distance a released body falls varies directly with the square of its time, that is, $d = 16 \, t^2$. A law is always an empirical generalization. To move along with the argument, a theory is a deductively connected set of laws. Certain of the laws are the axioms or postulates of the theory and are usually called assumptions. Their truth is not so much self-evident as it is taken for granted, so that the truth of other empirical assertions called theorems can be determined.

The basic terminology of theory-building is comprised of such words as *fact, concept, presumption, assumption, theory,* and *law*.

Test of theory.—Since a number of physical-science theories have stood for years (sometimes centuries) without empirical proof, the question arises as to the urgency and necessity of proof. Does a formulation have to be tested to be called a theory? The answer is probably "no." What is needed is that the theory must be *logically* capable of proof or disproof whether or not the tools for testing are available at the time of formulation. For example, while the Copernican Theory awaited the invention of a powerful telescope to ascertain parallax, the *logical* test of the theory could have been made at any time. It is not as difficult as it may seem to apply this criterion. Certain theories can be rejected out of hand, for example the following:

1. Theories written so as to make testing impossible as, for example, the caloric theory of heat which postulated "caloric" as an odorless, weightless, invisible substance.
2. Masked tautologies which assume the form of theories; for example, "opium puts people to sleep because it contains dormative power."

The test (at this stage) of a theory is whether or not it is logically capable of proof even if the necessary instruments have not been devised.

An illustration.—Probably the best illustration of a theory in educational administration which approximates the Fiegl definition comes from

Getzels.[10] This theory is hypothetico-deductive in nature and describes administration as a social process in which behavior is conceived as a function of both the nomothetic and the idiographic dimensions of a social system.

Getzels first presented a set of assumptions and then derived a series of hypotheses from the model. Administration is conceived structurally as the hierarchy of subordinate-superordinate relationships within a social system; and functionally this hierarchy of relationships is the locus for allocating and integrating roles and facilities in order to achieve the goals of the social system. The social system is comprised of two dimensions: the nomothetic which consists of institution, role, and expectation; and the idiographic which consists of the individual, his personality, and his need-disposition. Two sets of definitions are presented, namely: *institution* is used to designate agencies established to carry out "institutionalized functions for the social system as a whole,"[11] and *roles* are the "dynamic aspects" of the positions, offices, and statuses within an institution. Roles are defined in terms of role expectations, and roles are complementary.

The set of assumptions is presented diagrammatically in the chart following. In this diagram each term on the two axes is the analytic unit for the term preceding it. In the idiographic dimension, for example, institution is defined as a set of roles, role as a set of expectations.[12]

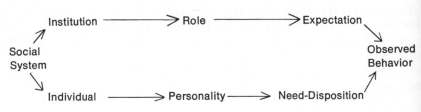

Nomothetic Dimension [12]

Institution ⟶ Role ⟶ Expectation

Social System

Individual ⟶ Personality ⟶ Need-Disposition

Observed Behavior

Idiographic Dimension

It can be seen that a given act is derived simultaneously from both the idiographic and the nomothetic dimensions. The general equation for this relation is $B = f (R \times P)$, where B is observed behavior, R is an institutional role, and P is the personality of the particular role incumbent.[13]

The proportion of role and personality factors determining behavior will vary according to several variables. The accompanying chart should clarify the nature of the interaction between role and personality in various situations.[14] It is obvious that, in the military, behavior is influenced more by role than personality, while, with the artist, behavior is influenced more by

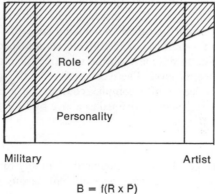

Military   Artist

$$B = f(R \times P)$$

personality than by role. The proportions should be considered as illustrative and not precise.

Getzels hypothesized that there are three types of conflict to be found in organizations: role-personality conflict, role conflict, and personality conflict.

Role-personality conflicts occur as a function of the discrepancies between the pattern of expectations attached to a given role and the pattern of need dispositions characteristic of the incumbent of the role. *Role conflicts* occur whenever a role incumbent is required to conform simultaneously to a number of expectations which are mutually exclusive, contradictory or inconsistent, so that adjustment to one set of requirements makes adjustment to another impossible or at least difficult. *Personality conflicts* occur as a function of opposing needs and dispositions within the personality of the role incumbent himself. It could be demonstrated (or at least contended) that these hypotheses could be called laws, since they appear to be statements of empirical regularities which now have sufficient proof to be accepted. In terms of Getzels' theory, these three types of conflict represent incongruence in the nomothetic dimension, in the idiographic dimension, or in the interaction between the two. Within the framework of the theory, it may be generalized that such incongruence is symptomatic of administrative failure and leads to loss in productivity in both the individual and the organization.

Contemporary Theory

There are many stages in the development of a science. It is rare that any science develops in a sequential set of steps, and administration is no exception to this observation. Contemporary work is proceeding at all of the various stages. There are many ways to discuss scientific work, one of which might be called the "level approach."[15] This means that there are different levels of scientific work, all of which have some value. At the lowest level there are what might be called "sensitizing concepts." They are rather primitive, but serve the purpose of identifying certain specifics which occur in administration. The middle level in the scientific hierarchy may be called the "integrating concept" level. These concepts serve the purpose of relating several lower-level concepts into complex concepts of great power. At the top of the hierarchy is "theory," defined as above by Fiegl.[16]

A Paradigm

The levels of stages of the development of theory can be incorporated into a paradigm (Fig. 1). Theory development begins with certain presumptions in the mind of the investigator. This leads him to make observations of administrative situations, the result being one or more descriptions. The investigator then attempts to explain his observation. He can do this on one of three levels: sensitizing concepts, integrating concepts, or theory. Should he explain his observations at the level of theory, he would create a

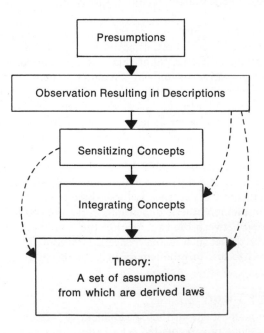

Figure 1.   Paradigm for theory development

set of assumptions, would derive laws from these assumptions, and would be able to predict administrative behavior with a rather high degree of probability.

One should not get the idea that theory-making proceeds in a regular manner through the steps in Figure 1. Generally everyone starts with presumptions. Some skip the descriptive phase, but the resulting work is generally poor when this is done. Some start with sensitizing concepts and jump to theory, while others stay at the level of sensitizing concepts. Some start at presumptions, move to observations, skip to theory, then work back to sensitizing and integrating concepts and then back to description to test their theoretical formulations. The paradigm is used in this chapter merely to aid in visualizing the work of the theoretician.

The remainder of this chapter is devoted to a discussion of concept development and current work at each of the three levels.

Concept Development

Theoretical studies in administration are plagued with the consequences of ill-defined concepts and are thus handicapped in efforts to *describe* administrative situations. Even the most sophisticated students of school administration often resort to homely parables and analogies to talk about administration. As Simon says of administration in general:

> We talk about organization in terms not unlike those used by a Ubangi medicine man to discuss disease. At best we live by homely proverbs: "The important thing about organization is to have the right man in the right place." At worst we live by pompous inanities: "The relationship between delegant and his deputy arises from delegation and is invariable in character."[17]

The first and major task in the construction of a science of administration is the development of concepts which will permit the description of administrative situations. Although considerable progress has been made in recent years, there is still a long way to go before an adequate body of concepts is built.

A definition.—What is meant by a concept? A concept is simply a term to which a particular meaning has been attached. Once the meaning has been attached to the term, the term should always be used with this particular meaning; and, conversely, whenever a particular meaning is intended, the same term should be used. If this single step forward could be made—that is, the use of the same concept by all to describe the same meaning—it would be a giant step. To illustrate what is meant in this situation let us quote a recent book on theory in educational administration. The following two sentences are in consecutive order: "The terms adaptability and quality are used interchangeably in this book. Of course they are not the same." This is an example of what we are talking about. If the two terms are not the same, why should they be used interchangeably? And if the two terms are used interchangeably, why are they not the same?

Operationism.—The lack of appropriate concepts has made it very difficult to adequately describe administrative situations or administrative behavior. In order to solve this problem, theoreticians have turned to *operationism*. This approach is generally credited to Bridgman, a physicist whose book, *The Logic of Modern Physics*, presents the basic tenets of operationism. The idea is very simple and is stated by Bridgman as follows: "In general, we mean by any concept nothing more than a set of operations; *the concept is synonymous with the corresponding set of operations.*"[18] In other words, operationism is the way of thinking which holds that (*a*) concepts are given their meaning by the methods of observations or investigations used to arrive at them, and (*b*) concepts have no meaning apart from their operations. This rigid formulation has been modified slightly, and a concept is now considered to be operational if a link to other operational concepts can be clearly demonstrated. For example, the I.Q. is operational because it is obtained by dividing mental age by chronological age, both of which are operational concepts.

Sensitizing Concepts

Lazarsfeld has contended that the way to approach the relationship between administration and the social sciences is to hold some over-all view of administration and to relate social science to that view.[19] He states that "the social sciences have relevance for administration on a purely empirical level."[20] As a result of his research, Lazarsfeld has developed a number of concepts which can be classified as sensitizing concepts. These concepts are well defined and serve the purpose of drawing attention to specific behaviors associated with administrative activity.

The concept of *visibility* serves as an illustration. This concept is based upon the observation that individuals within an organization are differentially aware of what is going on within the system. Lazarsfeld points out that this is so because organizations are usually set up so as to give the administrator greater access than his subordinates to information about role-performance. He "sees" more, partly because he wants to "see" more and partly because the organization was so designed. Lazarsfeld points out, however, that not all things are equally visible to the administrator: subordinates may act to reduce the visibility of their role-performance, the administrator may not be motivated to try to increase his area of vision, or the organization may lack mechanisms for making certain aspects of role-performance visible.

Lazarsfeld describes a study done by Stouffer to show the significance of the concept of visibility in understanding an aspect of organizational behavior:

> . . . a number of top level people in business organizations were interviewed to find out who it was that helped each of them get to the top. After these "helpers" had been identified, a survey was conducted to find out where they themselves were then located within the organization. Surprisingly, it was discovered that none of these "helpers" had gotten anywhere. It would seem that such people should have been rewarded for their work in developing junior talent. But there was no provision for making this behavior *visible*. If the president of the organization had wanted to do justice to the people who were developing junior talent, in accordance with his wishes, he should have made some provisions for finding out what individuals were doing this part of their jobs. As it was those individuals who spent less time developing their subordinates and more time on their own tasks were the ones rewarded through promotions. An important aspect of role-performance was not visible because there were no mechanisms for making it visible and also, perhaps, because the top administrators were not motivated to make it visible.[21]

From this example, it is clear that the sensitizing concept when well defined is a basic ingredient in the scientific study of administration. There are several examples of sensitizing concepts [included in *Behavioral Science and Educational Administration*]. Carlson . . . creates the concepts of the "domesticated" and "wild" organizations so as to better understand the school dropout and other types of commonly observed behavior. . . . Hemphill discusses numerous scoring categories, which are operational concepts, that help to explain the behavior of school principals. Charters . . . discusses the concepts of task, position, authority-relation, and department—each a concept at the sensitizing level.

Integrating Concepts

The integrating concept is complex in that it orders the relationships among a number of sensitizing concepts. It is powerful in that it enables us to see relationships not suggested by the sensitizing concepts taken singly and, further, in that it offers paths to future inquiry by researchers and theoreticians and guidance to the performance of administrators. The illustration is the concept of anticipated and unanticipated consequences as formulated by Gouldner.

Lazarsfeld's definition of the task of the administrator [in *Behavioral Science and Educational Administration*] forms the basis for the present discussion of Gouldner's concept. To summarize the four phases of the task:

1. The administrator must fulfil *the goals* of the organization.
2. The administrator must make use of *other* people in fulfilling these goals, not as if they were machines, but rather in such a way as to release their initiative and creativity.
3. The administrator must be concerned about *morale* and the idea that under suitable conditions people will do better work.
4. The administrator must build into his organization *provisions for innovation*, for change, for development.[22]

When an administrator attempts to achieve a goal he takes precautions to ensure that the people in an organization act in ways that will gain the

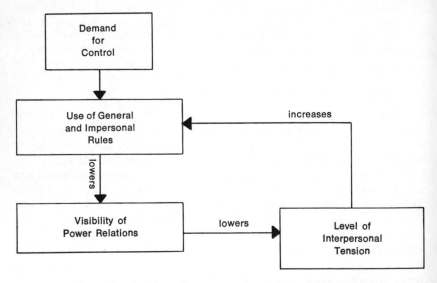

Figure 2.   Anticipated consequences of demand for control

goal. This is often called *control*. The administrator, further, would like to have the people feel "good" while they function in the prescribed manner. This is called maintaining a *low level of interpersonal tension*. He would also like to keep the *visibility of power relations* low and so relies on the *use of general and impersonal rules* rather than on confronting employees personally. The administrator's action and the anticipated consequences of his action can be diagrammed as in Figure 2.

The diagram is read as follows: a *demand for control* results in the *use of general and impersonal rules*, which lowers the *visibility of power relations* between the administrator and other members of the organization while compliance with rules is attained. The lower *visibility of power relations* lowers the *level of interpersonal tension*, which, in turn, increases the *use of general and impersonal rules*.

However, the demand for control may not result in achievement of the desired goal. Something totally *unanticipated* by the administrator may occur. A rule cannot be written to achieve maximum achievement. For instance, a rule concerning the time when teachers should be on the job can state only a reasonable minimum, not a maximum. Therefore, rules give employees *knowledge of minimum acceptable behavior*. Should the employee act on the knowledge of minimum acceptable behavior, this would increase the *difference between organizational goals and achievement*. In order to minimize this difference, the administrator usually, but not always, increases the *closeness of supervision*. This results in an increased

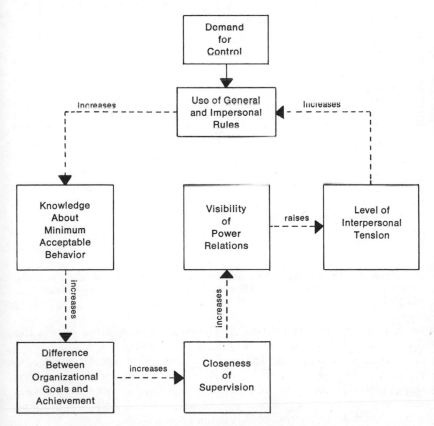

Figure 3.   Unanticipated consequences of administrative act

visibility of power relations, which raises the *level of interpersonal tension* and decreases the value of the *use of general and impersonal rules.* This is pictured in Figure 3. Thus, the very same methods employed by an administrator may bring success in one situation and failure in another. Note, however, that there cannot be "unanticipated" consequences unless there

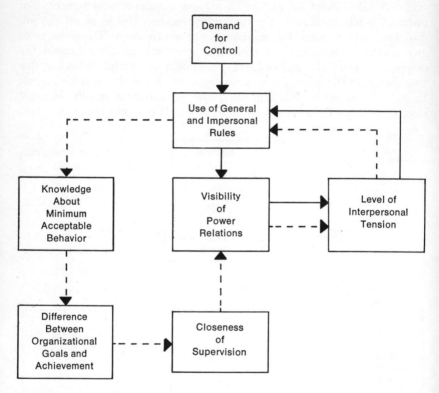

Figure 4.   Unanticipated consequences viewed in the context of an administrator's anticipated consequences. (Gouldner model from March and Simon, *op. cit.,* p. 45.)

are first "anticipated" consequences. The concept has meaning only in the over-all context of the total administrative performance.

Figure 4 indicates the value of the concept of *unanticipated consequences* when viewed in the context of an administrator's anticipated consequences. It gives a way of *ordering* several less complex concepts. One might say that a large segment of administrative behavior takes on meaning when viewed in the context of this major concept.

Several integrating concepts are used [in *Behavioral Science and Edu-*

cational Administration]. Hemphill . . . presents eight basic factors and two secondary factors which are integrating concepts, each of which order a number of sensitizing concepts. Both Iannaccone and Charters . . . present integrating concepts which order several concepts in ways which give these simpler concepts greater meaning. Charters, for instance, uses "organization maintenance" in this way.

Theories

A number of theories of administration have been proposed in the past fifteen years. March and Simon[23] have categorized these theories as follows:

1. Theories of conflict, i.e., role conflict, personality conflict, and role-personality conflict. The Getzels theory, described above, is an illustration of this category of theory.
2. Theories of motivation in which the needs, drives, and motives of individuals are considered. The Barnard-Simon theory of organizational equilibrium . . . illustrates this type of theory.
3. Theories of decision-making in which man is considered as a rational being with certain limitations. The theory of decision-making by Griffiths is an illustration of this approach.[24]

It might be well to look briefly at two theories which go beyond the above categorization to show the direction which theory construction might well take in the future. The first of these is the work of Presthus, in which he uses the Weber bureaucratic model,[25] and the second is the work of Griffiths, in which he employs system-theory as a model.[26]

Organizational society.—Presthus analyzes three distinct levels of modern life: society as a whole, big organizations, and individuals. He views organizations as miniature societies in which traditional social controls over the individual appear in sharp focus. His analysis utilizes the tools of many disciplines—political science, economics, sociology—and turns, ultimately, to Harry Stack Sullivan's interpersonal theory of psychiatry.[27]

Sullivan developed the theory that each person's personality is the result of his pattern of accommodation with people who are significant to him. How the individual accommodates is strongly influenced by the social setting in which the interpersonal relations occur. Sullivan defines personality, then, as a consistent way of reacting or accommodating to interpersonal situations, where social values and institutions play a powerful role.

He argues that most behavior is the result of the individual's search for relief from tension induced by conforming to authority. *Anxiety* is the most compelling of tensions, and much behavior is seen as an effort to escape from it. Sullivan declares: "I believe it fairly safe to say that anybody and everybody devotes much of his lifetime and . . . energy . . . to avoiding more anxiety than he already has, and if possible, to getting rid of some of this anxiety." Sullivan concludes that our personalities are formed as we work out ways of getting along with persons in authority—our parents, our teachers, the police, our bosses—and we bring that method of accomodating with us when we come to work in an organization.

Presthus, in defending the argument that large organizations induce anxiety in their members, first defines a "large organization," using as a model Max Weber's theory of bureaucracy. According to Weber, a bureaucracy is the most efficient form of organization devised by human beings. The personal, irrational, and emotional elements are minimized and the members tend to work with speed, precision, discretion, and technical know-how, without ambiguity or friction. The bureaucracy has the following characteristics:

1. Fixed and official jurisdictional areas, regularly ordered by rules, policies, regulations, by-laws.
2. Principles of hierarchy and levels of graded authority that ensure a firmly ordered system of super- and subordination in which higher offices supervise lower ones.
3. Administration based upon written documents.
4. Administration by full-time, trained officials.
5. Administration by stable and comprehensive general policies.[28]

Clearly Weber's formulation does not completely describe modern organizations. Weber ignores the psychological elements, the goals of individuals, the informal groups, and the influences of the larger society—all of which are taken into account by Presthus. As Presthus says:

> Members are expected to be loyal to the organization, to behave consistently and rationally according to technical and professional criteria and to defer to the authority of the organization's leaders. The social and psychological basis of this accommodation is the major concern of this book.[29]

The big organization, says Presthus, induces anxieties in its members simply because of its fundamental characteristics. Let us examine some of them:

Size becomes a factor when an organization becomes so large that any given member does not have face-to-face contact with most other members.

The larger the organization, the lower morale drops as individuals tend to feel unimportant.

As organizations increase in size and complexity, members must begin to specialize. Such division of labor has both advantages and disadvantages. On the one hand, the technical quality of the work improves. On the other hand, interpersonal relationships deteriorate; so also does the sense of identification with the organization.

"The main function of hierarchy is to assign and validate authority along a descending scale throughout the organization."[30] The hierarchy is of vital importance, since the individual's participation in an organization is always affected by his place in the hierarchy. The weight attached to suggestions, the influence of each member, even the order in which members of a group walk through a doorway is determined by one's hierarchical position.

The importance of status and status symbols is well known. The organization constantly reminds members of their status by the way it distributes salaries, offices, expense accounts, vacations, staff, secretarial help, and titles.

Most bureaucracies are run by a few people; thus they are oligarchies. The "few" are set off from the rest by their "preponderance of power." Their presence in an organization constantly reminds the members that here is a small group with more power than all the others combined. Their presence tends to accentuate the anxieties of the other members.

Presthus states that members accommodate to the demands of the organization in three ways—upward mobility, indifference, and ambivalence.

1) *Upward-mobiles.* These persons are the most successful organization members. The upward-mobile feels friendly toward his superiors and believes that they are friendly and sympathetic toward him. He has little difficulty making decisions in conflict situations because he accepts the organization's values as decisive. He is extraverted and gets along with other people, yet he regards his subordinates with considerable detachment, which leads him to make decisions in terms of the organization rather than the individual. Upward-mobiles enjoy organization life, are successful at it, and reap the rewards of status and salary.

2) *Indifferents.* While the upward-mobile revels in the competition of the organization, the "indifferent" refuses to compete for the organization's favors. The indifferent person comes from one of two backgrounds. Some enter the organization with great expectations but are unsuccessful and react by turning their backs on the organization. Others have a working- or lower-class origin and are taught not to expect much from the organization. The "indifferent" accommodates to organizational demands by doing his

work, arriving on time, and leaving on time—but by developing his major interests *outside* of the organization. His anxieties are reduced to a minimum because he refuses to become involved in the organizational race for rewards. He separates his work from the rest of his living. As Presthus says, "He sells his time for a certain number of hours and jealously guards the rest."

3) *Ambivalents.* The last group is a small minority who can neither resist the appeals of power and success nor play the role required to gain them. The ambivalent finds it hard to get along with authority and cannot play the organization game. As contrasted with the upward-mobile, he places individual friendships above the good of the organization. When confronted with a conflict, he decides in favor of the individual as against the organization. His is, indeed, a miserable lot in the modern large organization.

The Presthus theory deals largely with conflict and motivation yet it also discusses man as a rational being. It is an attempt to explain the behavior of man within an organizational context.

System theory.—The work of Griffiths does not fit the categories either, but for another reason. The model employed, system theory, is designed to be all-inclusive. It is a way of looking at a social organization as a whole. Griffiths uses system theory as a model to investigate the problem of change in organizations.

A system is simply defined as a complex of elements in mutual interaction. Systems may be open or closed. An open system is related to and exchanges matter with its environment, while a closed system is not related to nor does it exchange matter with its environment. Further, a closed system is characterized by an increase in entropy, while open systems tend toward the steady state. (Given a continuous input, a constant ratio among the components of the system is maintained.) All systems except the smallest have subsystems, and all but the largest have suprasystems, which are their environments.

System theory deals only with open systems having the properties of systems in general, together with certain characteristics which distinguish them from closed systems.[31]

1. Open systems exchange energy and information with their environment; that is, they have *inputs* and *outputs*.

2. Open systems tend to maintain themselves in *steady states*. A steady state is characterized by a constant ratio being maintained among the components of the system. A burning candle is often used as an example of a steady state. Upon being lighted the flame is small, but it rapidly grows to its normal size and maintains the size as long as the candle and its environment exist.

3. Open systems are *self-regulating*. In the illustration above, a sudden draft will cause the flame to flicker, but with the cessation of the draft the flame regains its normal characteristics.

4. Open systems display *equifinality*; that is, identical results can be obtained from different initial conditions. Hearn points out that equifinality in human beings (they are open systems) is illustrated by the case of two babies, one born prematurely, the other full-term. While at birth they may look very different and may be in different stages of development, within a few months the differences will have disappeared. Even though the initial states may differ, human beings generally achieve the same stages of development.

5. Open systems maintain their steady states, in part, through the *dynamic interplay of subsystems operating as functional processes*. This means that the various parts of the system function without persistent conflicts that can be neither resolved nor regulated.

6. Open systems maintain their steady states, in part, through *feedback* processes. In general, feedback refers to that portion of the output of a system which is fed back to the input and affects succeeding outputs, and to the property of being able to adjust future conduct by past performance.

7. Open systems display *progressive segregation*. This process occurs when the system divides into a hierarchical order of subordinate systems which gain a certain degree of independence of each other.

A number of propositions concerning conditions aiding or inhibiting change have been derived from the model:

—The major impetus for change in organizations is from the outside.

—The degree and duration of change is directly proportional to the intensity of the stimulus from the suprasystem.

—Change in an organization is more probable if the successor to the chief administrator is from outside the organization than if he is from inside the organization.

—When change in an organization does occur, it will tend to occur from the top down, not from the bottom up.

—"Living systems respond to continuously increasing stress first by a lag in response, then by an over-compensatory response, and finally by a catastrophic collapse of the system."[32]

—The number of innovations expected is inversely proportional to the tenure of the chief administrator.

—The more hierarchical the structure of an organization, the less the possibility of change.

—The more functional the dynamic interplay of subsystems, the less the change in an organization.

System theory is the result of an attempt to develop a general theory which enables the researcher to describe, explain, and predict a wide range of human behavior within organizations. It deals with conflict, motivation, and decision-making so that, like the work of Presthus, it cuts across the three categories of March and Simon. The two theories represent the direction in which theoreticians might move in the coming years.

Conclusions

This chapter is the result of an attempt to depict the place of theory in the scientific study of administration. Stereotyped notions of the nature of theory were discussed, and Fiegl's definition of theory was offered as one which could be accepted. Since the scientific study of administration proceeds on several levels, a set of categories was offered as a way of organizing this work. Sensitizing concepts, integrating concepts, and theories were discussed and illustrated.

Notes

1. For a more detailed discussion of this topic, see Daniel E. Griffiths, *Administrative Theory*. New York: Appleton-Century-Crofts, 1959.
2. *Professional Administrators for America's Schools*, pp. 34–35. Washington: American Association of School Administrators, 1960.
3. Donald Butler, *Four Philosophies*, p. 15. New York: Harper & Bros., 1957.
4. Andrew W. Halpin, "The Development of Theory in Educational Administration," in *Administrative Theory in Education*, p. 6. Edited by Andrew W. Halpin. Chicago: Midwest Administration Center, University of Chicago, 1958.
5. Halpin, *op. cit.*; Griffiths, *op. cit.*, chap. ii.
6. Herbert Fiegl, "Principles and Problems of Theory Construction in Psychology," in *Current Trends in Psychological Theory*, p. 182. Pittsburgh: University of Pittsburgh Press, 1951.
7. I should like to acknowledge the help in clarifying the concept of theory received from participation in the Faculty Seminar on Educational Theory at Teachers College, Columbia University, sponsored by the Horace Mann—Lincoln Institute of School Experimentation, 1960–61. The work of the Seminar was reported in *Proceedings* and other unpublished documents.
8. May Brodbeck, "Models, Meanings, and Theories" in *Symposium on Sociological Theory*, pp. 373–403. Edited by Llewellyn Gross. Evanston, Illinois: Row, Peterson & Co., 1959.
9. *Ibid.*, p. 337.
10. Jacob W. Getzels, "Administration as a Social Process," in *Administrative Theory in Education, op. cit.*, pp. 150–65.
11. *Ibid.*, p. 153.

12. *Ibid.*, p. 156.
13. *Ibid.*, p. 157.
14. *Ibid.*, p. 158.
15. Daniel E. Griffiths, "Response to Paul Lazarsfeld, 'The Social Sciences and Administration: A Rationale,'" in *The Social Sciences and Educational Administration*, pp. 13–19. Edited by Lorne Downey and Frederick Enns. Edmonton: University of Alberta, 1963.
16. Fiegl, *op. cit.*
17. Herbert Simon, *Administrative Behavior*, p. xiv. New York: Macmillan Co., 1957 (second edition).
18. Percy W. Bridgman, *The Logic of Modern Physics*, p. 5. New York: Macmillan Co., 1927.
19. Lazarsfeld, *op. cit.*
20. *Ibid.*, p. 6.
21. *Loc. cit.*
22. This presentation of the Gouldner Model borrows from James G. March and Herbert Simon, *Organization*, p. 45 (New York: John Wiley & Sons, 1958). The method of presentation was suggested by W. W. Charters, Jr., Washington University, St. Louis.
23. March and Simon, *op. cit., passim.*
24. Griffiths, *Administrative Theory*, chap. iv.
25. Robert Presthus, *The Organizational Society*. New York: Alfred A. Knopf, Inc., 1962.
26. Daniel E. Griffiths, "Administrative Theory and Change in Organizations," in *Innovation in Education*. Edited by Matthew B. Miles. New York: Teachers College Bureau of Publications, 1964.
27. Harry Stack Sullivan, "Tensions, Interpersonal and International," in *Tensions That Cause Wars*, p. 95. Edited by H. Cantrill. Urbana: University of Illinois Press, 1950. Quoted in Presthus, *op. cit.*
28. Presthus, *op. cit.*, p. 5.
29. *Ibid.*, p. 7.
30. *Ibid.*, p. 34.
31. For an elaboration of these characteristics, see Gordon Hearn, *Theory Building in Social Work*, pp. 44–50. Toronto: University of Toronto Press, 1958.
32. J. G. Miller, "Toward a Theory for the Behavioral Sciences," *American Psychologist*, X (1955), 525.

Chapter Four

Educational Administration:
The Setting

Practicing school administrators have long been aware of the variability of job settings. Procedures that "work" in one community may not be successful in another. A practice that produces satisfactory results one year might very well fail the next. As a consequence, there has been a continuous search for the factors which are responsible for these variations.

Usually the term "setting" calls to mind the physical characteristics of environment in which the individual finds himself. The administrator thinking about "setting" most often pictures the physical environment, the dimensions and distribution of the population and the nature and rate of change of each of these characteristics. However, sound decision making requires a broader interpretation of the term.

In a deliberate attempt to assess the setting in which he is to work, an educational administrator might also think in terms of the psychological, sociological, political and economic environment. Thus he would consider the environment of individual behavior—the values, needs, and drives that cause individual behavior. The sociological environment is effected by the way groups interact and the relationships among them. The political environment reflects the way governance decisions are made. The economic environment subsumes the phenomenon of the allocation and use of resources to satisfy the needs and desires of the community.

From the classification presented above, it is clear that what we describe as aspects of a setting for educational administration are not discrete components but rather ways of looking at a setting in which an educational program is to be developed. Each perspective has something of all the others. Thus, easily derived or precise descriptions of settings for the administration of schools are rare. The administrator utilizes personal sensitivities and skills to develop his own assessment of the setting in which he is to function. His values schema (philosophical base) and his way of explaining reality and predicting consequences (theoretical base) are fundamental tools in identifying, gathering, analyzing, and generalizing from data pertaining to setting.

The administrator must also recognize that at least two perspectives exist within each of the four settings described above. The first perspective is that seen through the eyes and pictured in the minds of the residents of the community. Through a long and intimate contact there has developed a perception of setting. The newcomer brings with him experiences and perceptions which affect the nature and scope of his conceptualization of the setting in which he is to function as an educational administrator. However, it is possible and important for the administrator to recognize that various persons and groups do see these settings differently. Since we are creatures of our own experiences it is imperative that we recognize the existence and interaction of these two perspectives.

As the educational administrator develops an understanding of the setting in which he operates, he will readily note that he is attempting to understand a dynamic system. None of the above factors which influence the concept of setting remain constant. Thus the administrator is challenged to twofold action: (1) To develop a comprehensive concept of the setting of the school system in which he serves, and (2) to continue the study of the various aspects as they change or may be changed during his tenure as an administrator and study the factors responsible for the changes.

9 | Politics, Economics, and Educational Outcomes in the States

Thomas R. Dye

Decision-making is important to the educational administrator in terms both of his own behavior and of governance decisions. This latter aspect of the setting will influence many actions which the administrator will initiate. Dye investigated the relationship between political variables and educational outcomes. His study characterizes an important application of the assessment of setting as input data for administrative decisions aimed at producing desirable educational outcomes.

Assessing Political Influence in Education

One of the central tasks of political science is the identification of the forces shaping public policy, and this includes educational policy. While the structure and functioning of political systems have always been a concern of political science, the content of public policy is also a variable that political scientists endeavor to explain. The purpose of the research reported below was to explore some of the determinants to the question of whether or not political characteristics of the states independently influence educational outcomes. Does partisanship, party competition, voter participation, or malapportionment have any significant impact on state policies in education? Or are educational policies primarily a function of economic conditions in the states?

Political scientists and educators apparently share a common interest in the identification of the forces shaping policy on public spending for education in the 50 states.[1] Sherman Shapiro correlated educational expenditures with income, industrialization, urbanization, and eight other socioeconomic variables among the states for 1920, 1930, 1940, and 1950.[2] Jerry Miner correlated state per pupil and per capita educational expenditures in 1960 with 22 social and economic characteristics of the states.[3] Edward F. Renshaw examined the effect of increases in the state aid on per pupil expenditures in the states.[4] Research publications of the National Education

Thomas R. Dye, "Politics, Economics, and Educational Outcomes in the States," *Educational Administration Quarterly*, 31 (Winter, 1967), 24–48. Reprinted by permission.

109

Association have also stressed the relationships between socioeconomic variables and educational finance.[5] Thus, educators, and even some economists, have been concerned with the socioeconomic determinants of educational spending in the states.

The most obvious void in the research literature on state educational policies is in systematic efforts to understand the impact of *political* variables on educational outcomes. While both educators and political scientists have been increasingly interested in the political environment of educational decision-making at the community level, research on state politics and education is comparatively rare.[6] Yet it seems fair to say that educational policy is being determined increasingly at the state level and that research into the relationship between state politics and public education is particularly appropriate.[7] Recently, political scientists Nicholas A. Masters, Robert H. Salisbury, and Thomas H. Eliot tried to relate certain characteristics of state political systems to educational policy-making, but their analysis was limited to only three states.[8]

We are still in need of systematic studies of the impact of political variables on educational outcomes in the 50 states. What is the effect of Democratic or Republican dominance on state educational policy outcomes? Does it make any difference in educational policy whether a state has a competitive two-party system or a one-party style of politics? Does the level of voter participation in the states affect educational outcomes? What is the effect of malapportionment on educational policy, and is court-ordered reapportionment likely to bring about significant changes in educational outcomes?

A Systems Model for Analyzing Educational Policy

How can we achieve a better perspective on the relationships between educational policy, political activity, and environmental variables? It is our contention that the conceptual framework developed by political scientist David Easton in A *Systems Analysis of Political Life*, and in other publications, is a useful analytical tool in examining the determinants of policy outcomes in public education in American states.[9] Moreover, it is our contention that the insights devised from a systems analysis approach to educational outcomes will challenge many of the assumptions in political science literature about the effect of political variables on policy outcomes.

Let us use the Easton model to conceptualize the determinants of public educational policy in the 50 states. We shall conceive of educational outcomes as the product of "inputs" brought to bear upon a "system" causing it to produce particular "outputs." The diagram below assumes the socioeconomic character of a state, that is, any condition defined as external to the boundaries of its political system, determine the nature of its political system. The political system is that group of interrelated structures and processes that allocate authoritatively values within a state. Policy outcomes are viewed as the value commitments of the political system and as such they are the chief output of that system.

Within this conceptual framework, the central question presented is whether or not differences in educational outcomes are independently related to characteristics of political systems (see Fig. 1). Do political system characteristics mediate between socioeconomic inputs and educational outcomes (as suggested by linkages A and B), or are policy outcomes determined by

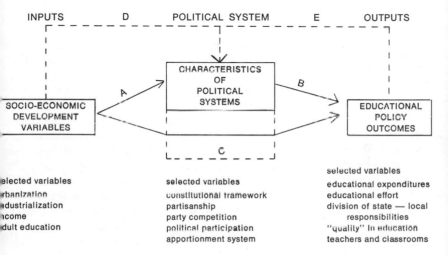

Figure 1. Model for the Analysis of Educational Policy Outcomes

socioeconomic variables without regard to system characteristics (as suggested by linkage C)? To state the problem in another fashion: assuming that socioeconomic variables influence both system characteristics and educational outcomes, can system characteristics be shown to influence educational outcomes once the effects of socioeconomic variables are controlled?

Definition of Terms

Let us turn first to the problem of selecting input variables. Students of politics from Aristotle to the present have recognized that society's economic development helps to shape its political system and determine its public policy. Economic development is defined here to include urbanization, industrialization, income, and the level of adult education.[10]

It is not difficult to justify the selection of economic development as the principal input variable in a model designed to explain educational policy outcomes. The literature on economic development is replete with theoretical postulates and empirical evidence of the linkage between a society's economy and its educational requirements. And the National Educational Association has pressed this point with legislators:

> There is an intimate relationship between schooling and the economic health of a nation and of its citizens. Prosperity demands productivity and productivity demands trained talent. Education develops the intellectual and manual skills which underlie the productive abilities of individuals and nations today. Nations with the highest general level of education are those with the highest development. Schools, more than natural resources, are the basis of prosperity.[11]

What system characteristics should be incorporated into our model? Just as it was necessary to limit the number of environmental variables that could be included, so also it is necessary to limit the number of system characteristics to be incorporated into it. Four sets of system variables were chosen for inclusion in our model of policy outcomes, two reflecting characteristics of the party system and two reflecting characteristics of the electoral system. Party systems are represented in our model by several measures of the level of interparty competition in state politics, and by several measures of the division of Democratic and Republican control of state government.[12] Electoral systems are represented in our model by several measures of the level of voter participation or turnout, and by several measures of the degree of malapportionment in state legislative districts. All four of these system characteristics—the division of the two-party control, the level of interparty competition, the level of voter participation, and the degree of malapportionment—are hypothesized in political science literature as influential in shaping policy outcomes in the American states. In this paper we shall explore the extent to which these system characteristics influence education outcomes.

Educational policy outcomes have been defined to include selected measures of educational expenditures, state efforts in education, organizing, and financing public schools, the status of teachers, and the numbers of dropouts and selective service mental failures.[13] These outcomes measures are described below together with the reasons for their selection.

Measuring Effects of Political and Economic Variables

The method chosen to assess the independent effect of political and socioeconomic variables on state education outcomes was that of simple, partial, and multiple correlation analysis. First, simple correlation coefficients (product moment) were computed for all possible relationships among indexes of economic development, measures of political variables, and measures of educational outcomes. These simple coefficients show the extent to which differences in economic development and political systems are associated with differences in policy outcomes, but they do not establish whether it is economic development or political variables that are primarily responsible for differences in these outcomes. For example, if it is shown that, in general, wealthy states have more party competition than poor states, it may be that differences in the educational policies of competitive and non-competitive states are really a product of the fact that the former are wealthy and the latter are poor. If this were the case, policy differences between the states might be attributable to wealth rather than to party competition. In order to isolate the effect of party competition on educational outcomes from the effect of economic development variables, it is necessary to control for these variables. This required that partial correlation coefficients be computed to show the relationship between party competition and the several measures of state policy while controlling for the effect of urbanization, industrialization, income, and education. If relationships between party competition and policy outcomes that appear in simple correlation coefficients disappear when these socioeconomic variables are controlled, then we may conclude that there is *no independent relationship* between party competition and policy outcomes. On the other hand, if partial correlation coefficients between party competition and policy outcomes remain significant, even after the effects of socioeconomic variables are controlled, then we may conclude that party competition does have an effect on public policy.

The same set of operations was employed to test the independent effect of partisanship, voter participation, and malapportionment.

Economic Development and the Character of State Politics

Before turning directly to the analysis of educational outcomes, it is important to understand the linkages between economic development and political system characteristics. Our model suggests that educational outcomes may be a product of both economic-development levels and political-system characteristics, and that the task of policy research is to sort out the effects of system characteristics on educational outcomes from the effects of economic development.

Neither urbanization nor industrialization correlates significantly with Democratic or Republican party success. However, Democratic and Republican states differ significantly with respect to income and education. States with lower income and educational levels tend to be Democratic states, while wealthier states with better educated adult populations tend to be Republican. These relationships between partisanship and income and education are important to keep in mind when exploring the effect of partisanship on educational policy. Educational differences between Republican and Democratic states may not really be a product of party affiliation so much as a product of their differing income and education levels. To identify the independent effect of party affiliation on educational policy, it will be necessary to control for the effects of income and education.

Party competition is even more closely associated with income and education than partisanship. Parties are more evenly balanced in wealthier states with better educated adult populations; there is less competition in the poorer states. There is also a slight relationship between party competition and urbanization. Participation is also noticeably higher in states with higher income and education levels.

There is also some slight relationship between economic development and the under-representation of urban areas in state legislatures. Industrial high-income states are less likely to discriminate against their urban areas than low-income agricultural states.

Economic Inputs and Educational Outputs

The Cost of Teaching Johnny to Read

Any analysis of public educational policies must begin by explaining educational expenditures. Table 1 shows that economic development is an important determinant of a state's willingness and ability to provide educational services. All four measures of economic development correlate significantly with variations among the states in per pupil expenditures for public education. However, it was the income measure that explained more about per pupil expenditures than any other variables. Almost 70 per cent of the total variation among the fifty states in per pupil expenditures can be explained with reference to median family income. The results are the same even if the southern states are excluded from analysis. Clearly, wealth is the principal determinant of the amount of money a state spends on the education of each child.

State Efforts in Education

Per pupil expenditures measure both the willingness and ability of a state to spend money for education. The next problem is to separate "willingness to spend" from "ability to spend" in order to determine roughly the sacrifice a state is making for education. The desire for education can be expressed in terms of school expenditures relative to some measure of a state's ability to spend money. In this way, states that spend more or less *relative to their ability* can be identified. The most appropriate measure of

TABLE 1   *Relationship between Economic Development and Selected Educational Policy Outcomes in the 50 States*

| | Economic Development | | | |
	Urban-ization	Industrial-ization	Income	Educa-tion
Per Pupil Expenditures	.51*	.36*	.83*	.59*
Expenditure Relative to Income	—.31*	—.44*	—.30	—.05*
Expenditure Relative to Total Expenditure	—.10	—.03	.01	.17
Per Capita Expenditures	.20	—.04	.61*	.75*
Size of School District	.06	.26	—.18	—.37
State Participation	—.10	.18	—.30*	—.35*
Federal Participation	—.36*	—.08	—.32*	—.27
Poverty Impacted School Aid	—.58*	—.43*	—.85*	—.67*
Average Teacher Salary	.69*	.64*	.88*	.57*
Elementary Teachers with B.A.	.42*	.60*	.11	—.04*
Secondary Teachers with M.A.	.54*	.42*	.55*	.42*
Male Teachers	.48*	.26	.63*	.63*
Pupil-Teacher Ratio	—.13	—.19	—.43*	—.50*
Drop-Out Rate	—.40*	.09	—.54*	—.60*
Mental Failures	—.05	.13	—.46*	—.70*

NOTE: Figures are simple correlation coefficients for 50 states; an asterisk indicates
a statistically significant relationship.

ability to pay for education is probably the total personal income of the state.
Therefore, the measure "total public school expenditures as a percentage of
total personal income" really holds constant for ability to spend and more
directly measures a state's willingness to sacrifice personal income for public
education.

Table 1 indicates that increased industrialization, urbanization, and
income actually result in a reduction of education effort. This is in striking
contrast to the effect of these variables on per pupil expenditures: while per
pupil expenditures rise with increasing income levels, school expenditures
as a percentage of personal income declines. This means that the poorer,
less-industrialized, rural states are actually putting forth a greater effort in the
educational field relative to their resources than the wealthy, urban, industrial states. But so great are the inequalities among the states in wealth, that
the poorer states, despite their greater effort, are unable to approach the

wealthier states in per pupil expenditures. Even Mississippi's $229 per pupil expenditure (5.8 per cent of that state's personal income) represented a greater effort than New York's expenditure of $628 per pupil (only 3.7 per cent of that state's personal income spent on education). In short, wealthier states can provide better educations for their children with less of an economic sacrifice than that required of poorer states to provide an inferior education for their children.

Educational expenditures as a percentage of total state and local government expenditures are a measure of public effort in education *relative to other public efforts*. In general, the coefficients in Table 1 indicate that economic development does *not* affect the relative proportion of public funds devoted to education. Wealthy, urban, industrial states do *not* consistently spend more for education than for other public functions. These states simply spend more for *all* public functions without particularly favoring education. The variation among the states in the proportion of public funds devoted to education cannot be traced to any of the indexes of economic development.

One final expenditure variable deserves attention: per capita educational expenditures. Per pupil expenditures are probably a better measure of educational service per unit of "need" than per capita expenditures. However, it might be argued that not only pupils but every member of society benefits from public education, and therefore it is appropriate to measure education service on a per capita basis. Per capita education expenditures are closely related to income and to education levels of adults. It is interesting that education levels of adults appear to be even more influential than income in determining per capita school expenditures.

Centralization in State Education

Major devices for ensuring the implementation of state educational policies are state grants to local school districts. Since these grants are administered through state departments of education, state school officials are given an effective tool for implementing state policies, namely, withholding or threatening to withhold state funds from school districts that do not conform to state standards. Increasing state participation in school finance, then, is an indication of increasing centralization of education in the states. One of the most dramatic reorganization and centralization movements in American government in this century has been the successful drive to reduce the number of local school districts in the United States through consolidation. The extent of state participation in financing public schools and the success of the school-district consolidation movement are both important indexes of educational centralization in the states.

It is in the poorer states and the states where adults have lower education levels that the state governments have played a greater role in the financing of public schools and that the school consolidation movement has made the greatest progress. The negative coefficients indicate that state participation in school finance decreases among the more wealthy states and the states with educated adult populations. Apparently, the lack of economic resources is a stimulus for state participation in school finance and school district consolidation. Affluence, on the other hand, enables smaller local school districts to function more effectively, reduces the need for state aid, and delays the movement toward school consolidation.

The Federal Role

Still another question involving the organization of public education in the nation is the role of the federal government. While large-scale plans for federal aid to education consistently floundered in the Congress prior to 1965, the federal government did contribute to public education through a number of specialized programs.

The total financial contribution of the federal government to public elementary and secondary education through these programs was quite small. Federal funds amounted to only about 4 per cent of the total public school revenues in 1962. However, there is considerable variation among the states in the extent of their reliance on federal funds for public schools. Federal participation in school finance does have a slight equalizing effect among the states. Table 1 shows that the federal government tends to pay a greater proportion of the cost of public education in the less wealthy, rural states. Thus, federal aid tends to equalize educational opportunity throughout the 50 states.

With the passage of the Elementary and Secondary Education Act of 1965, the role of the federal government in financing education will be greatly expanded. This act, among other things, pledges important federal aid to poverty-impacted schools, those schools that enroll children from low income families. It can be expected that the equalizing effect of federal aid will be more pronounced in the years ahead as the federal contributions to educational expenditures increase.

What is the effect of increased state and federal participation on public school systems? Since it is in the poorer states that state government plays the greatest fiscal role, and since these states also have the lowest per pupil expenditures, simple coefficients seem to say that state participation brings about lower per pupil expenditures. The simple coefficient for the relationship between state participation in school finance and per pupil expenditures among all fifty states is —.26. However, once the effects of economic development are controlled, this coefficient disappears; the partial coefficient for the relationship between state participation and per pupil expenditures, while controlling for the effect of economic development, is —.03. Clearly then, it is a lack of economic resources, and not state participation, that brings about lower per pupil expenditures in the less wealthy states.

It is noteworthy, however, that the partial coefficients do *not* permit us to conclude that state and federal participation leads to increases in per pupil expenditures. The partial coefficients are too low to assert any positive relationship between state or federal participation and per pupil expenditures. This tends to confirm the findings of Edward F. Renshaw about the effect of state participation on school expenditures.[14] Renshaw found that increasing ratios of state to other aid does *not* necessarily bring about increased expenditures per pupil. State aid is more a substitute for local support than it is a stimulant to educational expenditures.

States and School Teachers

Let us assume that the proportion of elementary teachers with a bachelor's degree and the proportion of secondary-school teachers with a master's degree are rough measures of the adequacy of teacher preparation in a state school system.

It is interesting to observe that the states that apparently place little emphasis on elementary-teacher preparation are not necessarily the poorer states but the more rural and agricultural states. The coefficients in Table 1 for elementary-teacher preparation show that the state income levels were not related to four-year college preparation, but that urbanization and industrialization were related to this measure. Apparently, years ago, midwestern farm communities did not feel that their elementary teachers needed to be college graduates, and many noncollege teachers remain on their staffs.

The rural states also score low in the preparation of their secondary teachers. However, in the case of secondary teachers, income levels play an important role in the willingness and ability of a state school system to obtain highly trained high school teachers. All four measures of economic development were related to the preparation of secondary teachers.

Economic development is an important determinant in teachers' salaries. Table 1 shows that all four measures of economic development were closely related to teachers' salaries in the 50 states in 1962. It was wealth, however, that was the single most important determinant of teachers' salaries. Median family income explained almost 80 per cent of the variation among the states in average teachers' salaries.

Wealthy, urban states with well-educated adult populations also attract more men into their public educational systems than states lacking in these attributes.

One final measure in instructional quality available for all 50 states is the pupil-teacher ratio, or the number of pupils enrolled per member of instructional staff. Two indexes of economic development, family income and adult educational level, correlated significantly with teacher-pupil ratios in the 50 states.

Drop-Outs and Mental Failures

Given conflicts over the objectives of public education, it is difficult to make any overall evaluation of educational output. Is the goal of public education college preparation, vocational skill, emotional happiness, psychological adjustment, academic excellence, the reduction of automobile accidents, the inculcation of spiritual values, the cultivation of patriotism, the production of engineers and scientists, the training of competent homemakers, or winning the Olympics? How can we tell whether the failure to achieve any one of these objectives is a product of our educational policies or an outgrowth of other national problems?

Two measures seemingly reflective of public education that are available on a state-by-state basis are the percentage of high-school students who drop out of school before graduation and the percentage of selective service registrants who fail the mental examination prior to induction.

Economic development is directly related to drop-out rates and mental failures. Thus, the simple correlations point to a familiar syndrome: wealthy states with well-educated adult populations are the same states that spend more per pupil on their public schools, pay higher teachers' salaries, attract more male teachers, and have better teacher-pupil ratios; and these same states tend to have fewer high school drop-out and selective service mental failures. In contrast, the less wealthy states with poorly educated adult populations spend less per pupil on their public schools, pay lower teachers' salaries, attract fewer male teachers, and have poor teacher-pupil ratios; and these same states have more drop-outs and mental failures.

One final note about the impact of economic development: partial coefficients (not shown) indicated that controlling for political variables did *not* affect the relationships between socioeconomic variables and policy outcomes. This is evidence that these relationships do not depend upon political conditions in the states.

Political Variables and Educational Outcomes

Partisanship

Thus far, attention has been focused upon the relationship between socioeconomic inputs and education policy outcomes. Now we turn to the problem of assessing the influence of political system characteristics on educational policy.

First of all, let us examine the effect of Democratic and Republican party control of state government in education policy. Are the educational policies of states under Democratic and Republican control any different?

Table 2 presents both simple and partial correlation coefficients for the relationships between educational policy outcomes and Democratic dominance in state legislatures and gubernatorial elections. The partial coefficients control for all four measures of economic development—urbanization, industrialization, income, and education.

As the coefficients indicate, there are many significant associations between partisanship and public policy outcomes. The simple coefficients show that states experiencing Democratic party control between 1954 and 1964 were the same states that had lower per pupil expenditures and lower per capita educational expenditures. While these Democratic states had more elementary teachers with B.A. degrees, on several other measures of quality instruction they rank low. They had fewer male teachers, higher pupil-teacher ratios, and higher drop-out rates and mental failures. There was also some slight association between Democratic control and lower teachers' salaries. Finally, Democratic states tended to have larger school districts and to receive greater shares of educational revenues from state rather than local sources. Republican party control of state government, on the other hand, was associated with just the opposite of these educational outcomes.

When economic development is controlled, however, some of the association between partisanship and public policy disappears. This means that part of the association between Democratic party control and educational outcomes was merely a product of the intervening effect of economic development. There seems to be no *independent* relationship between partisanship and per pupil expenditures, educational expenditures relative to income, per capita educational expenditures, average teachers' salaries, the preparation of secondary teachers, or the proportion of male teachers. These important educational outcomes are not affected by the party dominating state government.

On the other hand, even after controlling for economic development, significant associations continued to exist between partisanship and elementary-teacher preparation, pupil-teacher ratios, drop-out rates, mental failures, the size of school districts, and the extent of state and federal participation in school finance. The coefficients for these relationships were noticeably reduced when economic development was controlled, but we cannot reject the idea that there is some linkage between partisanship and these outcomes, a linkage that is not an artifact of economic development.

In spite of these controlled relationships, we are reluctant to infer that a direct causal relationship exists between Democratic politics and higher drop-out rates and mental failures. It seems unlikely that Democratic politics "brings about" drop-outs or mental failures, or even vice versa, especially in

TABLE 2   Relationship between Political Variables and State Educational Outcomes

	Democratic Success		Party Competition		Voter Participation		Legislative Malapportionment	
	Simple	Partial	Simple	Partial	Simple	Partial	Simple	Partial
Per Pupil Expenditures	—.47*	—.06	.51	.08	.49*	.18	.09	.15
Expenditure Relative to Income	.15	.33	.07	—.14	—.19	—.23	—.10	—.06
Expenditure Relative to Total Expenditure	.05	.17	—.15	—.15	.13	.12	.04	—.09
Per Capita Expenditure	—.39*	.30	.43*	.07	.38*	—.08	—.06	—.25*
Size of School District	.64*	.49*	—.51*	—.34	—.45	—.29	—.13	—.15
State Participation	.68*	.61*	—.50*	—.31	—.46	—.31	—.23	—.28
Federal Participation	.27	.60*	—.24	—.30	—.26	—.29	—.07	—.18*
Average Teacher's Salary	—.23	.27	.36*	.11	.35*	—.16	—.01	—.28
Elementary Teachers with M.A.	.62*	.67*	—.38*	—.34	—.37*	—.37	—.12	—.24
Secondary Teachers with M.A.	—.15	.06	.16	.16	.31*	.11	.10	—.04
Male Teachers	—.49*	—.25	.50*	.14	.49*	.22	.01	—.10
Pupil-Teacher Ratio	.72*	.50*	—.55*	—.21	—.63*	—.30	—.15*	—.21
Drop-Out Rate	—.69*	.55*	—.74*	—.53*	—.66*	—.53*	.15	.29
Mental Failures	.71*	.42*	—.64*	—.37*	—.73*	—.63*	—.16	—.14

NOTE: Figures are simple and partial correlation coefficients for 50 states; partial coefficients control for the effect of urbanization, industrialization, income, and education; and asterisk indicates a statistically significant relationship.

view of the fact that Democratic politics does not affect per pupil expenditures or teachers' salaries. The concentration of southern states among the most Democratic states accounts for these relationships; if the southern states are removed, the coefficients disappear. Rural midwestern Republican states, although they share many of the same economic characteristics of southern states, have fewer drop-outs and mental failures. Likewise the midwestern reliance on non-college teachers is probably a product of Republican party affiliation.

The southern states stand high on drop-out rates and mental failures. This standing is not merely a product of their lower economic development levels, since southern states stand higher than nonsouthern states in these outcomes, even after controlling for economic development. This suggests that some attribute of the southern states other than their economic development levels or Democratic politics accounts for these generally undesirable educational outcomes. We can only speculate on what attribute of the southern states is responsible for these educational failures. Certainly a plausible explanation is the system of segregated education in the southern states with its deprivation of educational and cultural opportunities for large numbers of children. Negroes are heavily overrepresented in drop-out rates and mental failures. It is probably not only segregated education that brings this about, but limitations on occupational and employment opportunities and general cultural deprivation.

It seems more plausible that Democratic politics might "bring about" increased federal and state support for education and decreased reliance upon local sources of educational revenue. Controlling for economic development actually increased the correlation between Democratic control and federal financial participation. Moreover, the removal of the southern states did not significantly affect the partial coefficients between Democratic politics and these particular outcomes. Differences between strong Democratic and strong Republican states in the degree of centralization in state educational administration must be related in some way to their differences in party affiliation. The midwestern and upper New England states, which in many ways resemble the South in economic resources, have resisted the consolidation of local school districts and have continued to place the heaviest financial burden of education on local rather than state governments. This suggests that in their policy adjustments to economic deprivation, strong Republican and strong Democratic states takes separate courses. Strong Republican states in the Midwest and upper New England refuse to give up local control over education, while strong Democratic states of the South have consolidated school districts and have looked to the state and federal governments for financial support.

All we can really say on the basis of these operations, however, is that a linkage exists between the partisan character of state politics and several educational outcomes, and that this linkage does *not* depend upon economic development.

Party Competition

In the simple coefficients in Table 2, which do not control for the effects of economic development, party competition appears significantly related to many of the educational variables. States with a high degree of party competition tend to spend more money per pupil on their schools, pay higher teachers' salaries, attract more men teachers, and experience fewer drop-outs and mental failures. These same states have larger school districts and raise more school revenue from local than from state or federal sources. But since we already know that economic development affects both party competition and educational policies, it is necessary to sort out the influence of party competition on educational policy from the influence of economic development. When the effects of economic development are discounted, party competition does not explain differences among the states in per pupil expenditures, educational effort, teachers' salaries, teacher preparation, male teachers, or pupil-teacher ratios. Party competition appeared independently related only to drop-out rates and mental failures, but this relationship is a product of the peculiar influence of southern states.

In short, while competitive and noncompetitive states differ somewhat in education policy, these differences can be traced to the effect of economic development rather than party competition.

Political Participation

The simple coefficients in Table 2 show that there is considerable association between voter turnout and educational outcomes. States with high levels of voter participation are the same states with generally higher per pupil and per capita educational expenditures, higher teachers' salaries, better-prepared secondary teachers, more male teachers, smaller pupil-teacher ratios, and fewer drop-outs and mental failures. They are also the same states with smaller school districts and greater reliance on local school revenue rather than state or federal school aid. However, since we know that these states are also the most wealthy, urban, industrial states with better-educated adult populations, we cannot attribute these educational outcomes to participation levels until we control for the effects of economic development.

When economic development is controlled, most of the association between voter participation and educational outcomes disappears. Voter participation has no *independent* effect upon educational expenditures, average teachers' salaries, male teachers, pupil-teacher ratios, teacher preparation, the size of school districts, or the extent of state or federal participation in school finance.

Interestingly, the coefficients between participation and drop-out rates and mental failures remain significant even after controlling for economic development. This relationship does not depend upon the southern states. It may be that the relationship between participation and drop-out rates and mental failures is a feedback linkage. Participation may not effect educational outcomes; but education outcomes, particularly drop-outs and mental failures, may affect participation.

Malapportionment

Malapportionment of state legislatures has been successfully challenged before the Supreme Court on the grounds that it denies to citizens the equal protection of the laws. This was a normative challenge stemming from firmly entrenched values about political equality. The moral case for reapportionment cannot be tested empirically. However, proponents of reapportionment have occasionally made statements about the effect of malapportionment upon public policy and have predicted consequences of reapportionment.· These statements *can* be tested empirically. In the field of education, it has been argued that malapportionment, with its overrepresentation of rural areas, leads to de-emphasis on education.

However, on the whole, the policy choices of malapportioned legislatures are *not* noticeably different from the policy choices of well-apportioned ones. None of the coefficients under the apportionment score is statistically significant. There is no evidence that malapportionment in its technical sense has any relevance in educational policy decisions.

An Evaluation of a Model

Let us begin an evaluation of our explanatory model by trying to summarize its powers of explanation. To what extent can differences in educational outcomes among the states be explained by reference to our model? Operationally speaking, the question becomes: How much of the total variation in educational outcomes can be attributed to *all* of the economic development variables and political system characteristics considered together?

Multiple correlation coefficients for key policy variables are shown in the left-hand column of Table 3. These coefficients summarize the total effect of four economic development measures and four political system variables on each policy outcome. In other words, these coefficients summarize the explanatory power of urbanization, industrialization, income, education, partisanship, party competition, voter participation, and malapportionment, considered together.

The summary coefficients presented in Table 3 show that our model possesses very substantial explanatory power. Of course, the question of what is or is not a satisfactory level of explanation is always a very subjective one. But it seems safe to conclude that our model has turned out to be a very powerful tool in policy analysis. A multiple coefficient of .71 or above indicates that more than half of the total variation among the states in a policy measure has been explained by our model. Most of our key policy measures are above that level of explanation, and others are quite close to it. This means that our model succeeds in explaining most of the variation among the 50 states in important policy outcomes in education.

Comparing the Effects of Economic and Political Variables

One further set of operations seems appropriate in order to confirm the belief that the character of political systems is less important than economic development in shaping educational policy. We want to know how much variation in educational policy can be explained by *all* of the political system characteristics at once while controlling for *all* of the socio-economic variables at once. Then we want to compare this with the variation in educational policy which can be explained by all of the socio-economic variables at once while controlling for *all* of the political factors at once. The only way to do this is with multiple-partial correlation coefficients. These statistics permit us to compare the influence of all of our economic development variables with the influence of all political system characteristics.

In Table 3 the multiple-partial coefficients in the fourth column from the left show us the explanatory power of all of the economic development variables while controlling for all of the political system variables. The multiple partial coefficients in the fifth column show the explanatory power of all of the political system variables. By comparing the size of the coefficients in these two columns we can compare the effects of all economic development variables, while controlling for all economic development variables.

Again the evidence seems conclusive: economic development variables are more influential than political-system characteristics in shaping educational policy in the states. Multiple and multiple-partial correlation analysis presented in Table 3 confirms the results of simple and partial correlation analysis presented earlier. A majority of the policy variables listed are more closely related to economic variables than to political variables. These are the policy outcomes for which the coefficients in the fourth column are larger than the coefficients in the fifth column. For these outcomes the effects of all economic variables under controlled conditions are greater than the effects of all political variables under controlled conditions.

There is a very interesting parallel between these findings about the 50 states and the results of H. Thomas James' analysis of the determinants of educational spending in 107 cities.[15] James found that socioeconomic

TABLE 3   Comparison of Effect of Economical Development Variables and Political-System Variables on Educational Outcomes in 50 States

	Total Effect Economic Development and Political System Variables	Total Effect Economic Development Variables	Total Effect Political System Variables	Effect of Economic Development Variables Controlling for Political System Variables	Effect of Political System Variables Controlling for Economic Development Variables
Per Pupil Expenditures	.86	.85	.58	.61	.04
Size of School Districts	.69	.52	.67	.05	.28
State Participation	.74	.49	.70	.13	.41
Federal Participation	.74	.50	.37	.48	.40
Average Teacher's Salary	.91	.90	.43	.78	.05
Elementary Teachers with B.A.	.85	.70	.64	.54	.47
Secondary Teachers with M.A.	.64	.60	.33	.34	.08
Male Teachers	.73	.70	.56	.32	.10
Pupil-Teacher Ratio	.80	.70	.74	.24	.30
Drop-Out Rate	.91	.82	.79	.54	.48
Mental Failures	.88	.79	.81	.32	.39

variables in the cities—income, property value, adult education, race—were more important in educational spending than characteristics of school systems—whether the school board was appointed or elected, dependent on or independent of city control. This parallels our findings about the primacy of economic variables over political system variables in shaping educational policy.

There are only four policy outcomes that appear to be more influenced by political variables than by economic variables. These are pupil-teacher ratios, drop-out rates, the size of school districts, and reliance upon state government for school revenue. Two of these variables—the size of school districts and state financial participation—have to do with centralization in education. Political conditions in the states may not "cause" or "bring about" these outcomes. But there is an association between political conditions in the states and these outcomes that is not merely a product of the intervening impact of economic development.

We are not really justified in concluding from this study that political variables do not have any impact on educational policy in the states. We can only say that partisanship, party competition, participation, and malapportionment do not appear to be as influential as economic development in determining most of the policy outcomes we have mentioned.

It may be that the measures employed are too crude to reveal the real impact of political variables on state activities. Perhaps the effect of politics on policy outcomes is too subtle to be revealed in quantitative analysis. Perhaps there are political variables other than partisanship, party competition, participation, and malapportionment that affect policy outcomes. For example, it may be that differences among state populations in political values and attachments can be shown to influence policy outcomes significantly, even after controlling for the effects of economic development. However, it was already pointed out that a great deal of literature in political science *asserts* that partisanship, party competition, voter participation, and malapportionment are influential political variables. Our findings at least warn educators and political scientists against making simple generalizations about the policy consequences of these political variables. Hopefully, our findings will also challenge educators and political scientists to continue research into the linkages between politics, economics, and educational policy.

Notes

1. H. Thomas James, *School Revenue Systems in Five States* (Stanford, Calif.: School of Education, Stanford University, 1961).
2. Sherman Shapiro, "Some Socio-economic Determinants of Expenditures, for Education: Southern and Other States Compared," *Comparative Education Review*, VI (October, 1962), 110–66.

3. Jerry Miner, *Social and Economic Factors in Spending for Public Education* (Syracuse, N.Y.: Syracuse University Press, 1963).
4. Edward F. Renshaw, "A Note on the Expenditure Effect of Aid to Education," *Journal of Political Economy*, LXVII (April, 1960), 170–74.
5. See, e.g., Harold M. Groves, *Education and Economic Growth* (Washington, D.C.: National Education Association, 1961).
6. For the excellent summary of research on politics and educational decision-making at the *local* level, see Ralph B. Kimbrough, *Political Power and Educational Decision-making* (Chicago: Rand McNally & Co., 1964).
7. For a summary of the work of political scientists in state educational politics, see Robert H. Salisbury, "State Politics and Education," in Herbert Jacob and Kenneth Vines (eds.) *Politics in the American States: A Comparative Analysis* (New York: Little Brown & Co., 1965).
8. Nicholas A. Masters, Robert H. Salisbury, and Thomas H. Eliot, *State Politics and the Public Schools* (New York: Alfred A. Knopf, 1964).
9. David Easton, *The Political System* (New York: Alfred A. Knopf, 1953); A *Framework for Political Analysis* (New York: Prentice-Hall, 1965); and A *Systems Analysis of Political Life* (New York: John Wiley & Sons, 1965).
10. The following measures of these variables were employed: percentage of state population living in urban areas; one minus the percentage of the state work to be employed in agriculture, fisheries, and forestry; median family income in the state; and median school year completed by population age 25 and over in the state. All figures are from U.S. Bureau of the Census *1960 Census of Population*, PCI—IC (Washington, D.C.: Government Printing Office, 1962).
11. National Education Association, *National Policy and the Financing of Public Schools* (Washington, D.C.: The Association, 1962), p. 1.
12. The specific measure of partisanship used in Table 2 is the percentage of total seats in the lower house of the state legislature held by Democrats from 1954 to 1964. Similar measures focusing on upper houses and governorships (not shown) produced results almost identical to those in Table 2. (Note that this measure of partisan success is expressed as Democratic percentage; simply reverse the findings to express the effect of Republican success.)

The competition measure used in Table 2 was the proportion of seats in the lower house held by the *majority* party in each state from 1954 to 1964, regardless of whether the majority party was the Democratic or Republican Party. Similar measures focusing on the upper house and governorship produced almost identical results.

The participation measure was the average percentage of eligible voters casting votes in gubernatorial elections between 1954 and 1964. The malapportionment measure was the Schubert and Press "apportionment score"; see Glenon Schubert and Charles Press, "Measuring Malapportionment," *American Political Science Review*, LVIII (June, 1964), 302–27, and corrections published December, 1964, pp. 968–70.
13. From U.S. Office of Education, *Statistics of State School Systems, 1961–62* (Washington, D.C.: Government Printing Office, 1963); and National Education Association, *Rankings of the States, 1963* (Washington, D.C.: The Association, 1963).
14. Edward F. Renshaw, *op. cit.*
15. H. Thomas James, *Determinants of Educational Spending in Large Cities* (Stanford, Calif.: School of Education, Stanford University, 1966).

10 | Federal-State Educational Relations

Roald F. Campbell

Another kind of setting of which school administrators must be aware is the political setting beyond the local community. Many educational influences emanate from the state or federal government. Administrators are also aware that the roles of the state and federal governments are not static but are dynamic. Changes in the relations of federal and state levels to the local level are obvious as well as variance in relationships and exercise of authority between the federal and state levels. This constitutes a fluid setting which must be constantly monitored by the administrator if he is to competently exercise his managerial leadership roles. Campbell analyzes the federal-state relations and makes some suggestions for establishing a creative interdependency.

The announcement of this conference carried the theme, "power-play for control of education." This theme seems to imply that state and federal governments are locked in conflict in an attempt to seize control of our schools and colleges. Despite the differences state and federal governments may have regarding the control of our educational institutions, I cannot ascribe sinister motives to either level of government as they strive to integrate their efforts toward achieving the best possible educational system for our nation and for each of its subdivisions.

With World War II, federal participation in education, always present in a minor way, took a quantum jump. The GI bill of rights represented the largest fellowship program ever attempted. This was followed by the creation of the National Science Foundation, the National Defense Education Act, and the great quantity of more recent legislation. Two of our presidents have made education an important cornerstone in the American dream. Legislation devised to create the Great Society has placed great strain upon American federalism.

All of us find ourselves in a new world of education. Expectations held for schools and colleges have multiplied, our social and economic objectives are increasingly thought to be tied to our educational efforts, costs have risen

Roald F. Campbell, "Federal-State Educational Relations," *Phi Delta Kappan* 49 (September, 1967), pp. 16–20. Reprinted by permission.

even faster than enrollments, more and more our political leaders must take stands on educational issues. In this educational ferment the chief initiative for the improvement of education has passed from local and state agencies to the federal government. The federal government, including its legislative and executive branches, seeks advice as it attempts to formulate and pass legislation and to administer programs designed to bring greater quality to our educational endeavors.

This advice comes from a wide spectrum of spokesmen—the establishment and the non-establishment or, if you wish, the old establishment and the new establishment. In this process schoolmen at local and state levels often feel left out. They note the prominent role played by university scholars, foundation officers, and political leaders. Advice from a variety of sources has led to many federal programs, often with little coordination at the national level but frequently requiring much collaboration at the local level. My purpose today is to analyze some of the relationships between and among federal and state agencies, to note some of the problems and issues that arise out of these interactions, and to suggest that these relations may best be understood when seen as part of a national social system for education.

Let us turn first to some of the problems. I shall mention only two. The first has to do with the programs of the Office of Education itself. Programs appear to be too numerous and too frequently revised. I recognize that the Office must implement each of the titles mandated to it by the Congress. Moreover, I suspect that the USOE has been subjected to considerable pressure from the Executive Office of the President and the Bureau of the Budget. Even so, it seems to me that the Office must insist on some additional integrity for itself.

I have the impression that the National Science Foundation and the National Institutes of Health have more control over their own procedures and programs than does the U.S. Office of Education. If this be the case, the more tenuous position of the Office may be due, in part, to a more diverse mission and possibly to lack of the kind of support other agencies have in the scientific community. But part of the problem seems to reside within the Office itself. The decision to establish a major research training program in 1966 and to cut it back in 1967 seems to have been, at least in part, an allocation decision within the Office. The decision to decentralize post-doctoral fellowship admissions procedures in 1966 and to centralize them in 1967 seems to be another example of uncertainty. Also, some would suggest that the Office has had a vacillating policy with respect to the purpose and financing of regional laboratories.

In any case, it seems that the Office ought to settle down a bit, decide what programs it must offer, develop the necessary guidelines and let them stand a few years, and put its energies into making such programs work. Undoubtedly there was a time for change and effervescence in the Office. The time for stability and accomplishment now seems to be at hand.

The second problem is a related one: the administration of federal programs. Again, much of the problem grows out of the unprecedented growth of federal programs, the rapid expansion of personnel in the Office of Education, and the time limits imposed by congressional action. Even so, lack of lead time, relative instability of programs, and specificity of budgets and reporting procedures have imposed great difficulties on local and state educational agencies. We must all help the Congress understand that a program can hardly begin in July when appropriations are not made until the following December. Moreover, the personnel demands for many of the new programs require careful search, sometimes even the establishment of new programs for training, before people can be put on the job.

The short-run nature of some federal programs creates other staffing problems. Efforts to secure additional, specialized personnel are not encouraged unless there are fair indications that such people can be assured of reasonable employment conditions. Moreover, few states and local agencies are in a position to run all of the budget risks for the continuation of such people on the payroll with uncertain federal assistance.

While the problems of federal aid are essentially those of mission orientation and inadequate administration, the issues in federal-state relations appear to have even greater consequence. The first of these issues is as old as the nation itself: should the federal government play a role in education? Most of us have long since answered this question in the affirmative, but a few politicians find it useful to keep raising the issue. I suggest that education is too closely linked to the national well-being, particularly in terms of trained manpower and economic growth, for any answer other than federal participation.

It should be noted in passing that with the adoption of our Constitution in 1787 we not only created a federal system but also a national government. The welfare clause and the First, Fifth, and Fourteenth Amendments have provided ample constitutional authority for federal entry into educational endeavors, as congressional legislation and a number of our U.S. Supreme Court decisions attest. In a very real sense, then, we have had an incipient national system of education from the beginning. Only within the last two decades, however, have we begun to sense the full implications of the federal role.[1]

A second issue has also been about for a long time: Should federal aid be categorical or general in nature? As can be readily understood, most schoolmen and college administrators prefer general aid. A formula for the distribution of general aid to the several states and universities could be developed. The Congress is currently giving attention to "block grant" amendments to the Elementary and Secondary Education Act (ESEA), presumably as a way of at least reducing the categorical aid proposed by H. R. 7819. One wonders about the motives behind such a proposal. Is it a well-conceived shift away from categorical aid or merely a plan to discredit the administration?[2]

While the arguments for general aid are persuasive, I doubt that the Congress will permit a substantial part of federal assistance to be general in nature. General aid means that any state, even any community, can be as bad as it wants to be. Measures designed to desegregate the schools, to provide compensatory education for the culturally disadvantaged, and to insure that library materials are made available to nonpublic school pupils are illustrations of national needs, as perceived by the Congress, and either through legal mandate or financial inducements no state or locality is permitted to ignore such national needs.

Still another condition suggests that general aid alone is a doubtful solution. By its very nature, general aid provides little political visibility for the congressman. Categorical aid, on the other hand, permits a congressman to stand for something: the education of the poor, vocational and technical training, teaching fellowships, assistance for federally impacted districts, new research and development institutions, and other specific programs. While a combination of general and categorical aid may be feasible, I take the position that the Congress has an obligation to support some specific programs aimed at meeting national needs.

Let us turn to a third issue. Should federal programs make use of established institutions or must alternative arrangements be set up? NDEA assistance in the purchase of science equipment and the provisions of Title I of ESEA are examples of channeling assistance through existing school systems. On the other hand, the Head Start program of the Office of Economic Opportunity (OEO) resulted, in many instances, in the creation of new institutional arrangements. Contracts with business firms to operate Job Corps and other programs is another example of new arrangements. Recently, some have advocated that a new federal school system be established to compete with the existing school systems.[3]

Local and state school systems, like other organizations, public and private, do develop certain inflexibilities over time. Some of these local systems, particularly in the large cities, have become hemmed in with tradition, tradition imposed by bureaucratic administrators and by teachers' organizations. Achieving change in curriculum programs or in teaching practices at times seems well-nigh impossible. When urgent problems such as desegregation of the schools and improved instruction for the culturally handicapped appear to be largely ignored in favor of business as usual, discouragement with the "establishment" is intensified. Little wonder that some members of Congress and representatives of federal agencies seriously consider alternative organizational arrangements.

Without doubt, existing school organizations need, or did need, a shake-up. Titles I, II, and III of ESEA and many provisions of the OEO program have provided some of that shock. Public schools have new partners in nonpublic school officials, art curators, orchestra directors, and university professors. Community action groups are ready to set up Head Start programs if the school is not. If board members and administrators have been loath to identify the educationally handicapped, they are now required to do so in order to qualify for Title I money. If one school district cannot or will not set up vocational and technical programs, a combination of school districts may be formed into a regional vocational district.

Should we persist with these interventions in existing local schools, improving them where need be? Or should we conclude, after our short experience with the new programs, that existing schools and colleges are bankrupt and then set up new structures under federal operation? Clearly, some expectations for school reform have been unrealistic; moreover, schools alone cannot solve all of our social problems. We need to formulate our expectations and our programs in much more realistic terms. But I think the time is here to make what we have already begun work, not to start all over with a new set of institutions. Even new institutions will soon take on their own inflexibilities, and if we give up on local and state participation we may find that the federal bureaucrats soon become even worse than the local variety.

Still another issue has to do with church-state relations. Should federal aid force new arrangements in our historic struggle to keep church and state separate? Nearly all of our state constitutions forbid the use of public money for nonpublic schools, particularly church schools. Moreover, the First Amendment to the U.S. Constitution contains the ringing words, "Congress shall make no law respecting an establishment of religion or prohibiting the free exercise thereof. . . ." Despite these seemingly clear legal demarcations, the doctrine of "child benefit" was evolved by the U.S. Supreme Court in the Cochran case in 1930. The Louisiana practice of providing textbooks at state expense to pupils in church schools as well as in public schools was allowed to stand.

Titles I, II, and III of ESEA have made full use of the child benefit principle. In each of the acts, programs are to be made available to nonpublic as well as to public school pupils. The public library has been used as the model. But the line between benefiting the child and supporting the school is sometimes very hard to determine. When programs for the culturally deprived are provided in church schools as well as in public schools, one wonders if the distinction has not been ignored. Or when books are supplied to nonpublic schools, albeit on a loan basis, one suspects that the loan will never be repaid. Without doubt some of these practices are still to be tested in the courts.

In the meantime one can take any one of three positions. The "separationists" on one end would make no overture at all toward aiding nonpublic schools and probably not even the pupils who attend them. At the other end the "collaborationists" advocate that public money should be allocated to church schools as well as to public schools. I subscribe to neither position; rather, I think we must find some accommodation between these two positions. While nonpublic schools, particularly church schools, do serve some public purposes, I contend that public money cannot be used to support them unless public agencies also supervise their curricula and teaching practices. At the same time, this need not rule out public provisions for books, transportation, health services, shared time, and other arrangements for nonpublic school pupils. Constantly, we need to ask whether or not the practice seems to be helpful to our future citizens and whether or not it does any damage to our public institutions. Such queries may help us formulate necessary adjustments in this difficult area.

Let me suggest one additional issue. Should federal aid require restructuring of educational government? Federal programs appear to accentuate the conflict between special government and general government. At the local level, educational government is essentially special government— special boards, special taxing procedures, and, for the most part, fiscal independence for school districts. At the state level, the education agency represents special government. To some extent, so do the special provisions for the state financing of education. At the same time, the state legislature is the plenary body for education, hence education is inevitably thrown into the arena of general government. At the federal level, with the important roles played by the Congress, the courts, and the Executive Office of the President, all policy questions regarding education seem to be shaped even more within the context of general government.

The USOE and other federal agencies operate within the context of general government or, if you wish, much more as a part of the total political system than do local school districts. The general government context at the federal level suggests that congressmen deal with mayors, not school officials, even on local educational matters. Such approaches, however, ignore the special government context of most school districts. This problem is accentuated when other social measures, such as many OEO programs and possibly the model cities program of the Department of Housing and Urban Development, include educational provisions, some of which affect local school districts directly, but whose administration is tied much more closely to the mayor's office than to the school office.

I have no doubt that some restructuring of educational government is called for. While I am not yet ready to transfer school affairs from boards of education to city councils, at the same time better ways of coordinating efforts in education, planning, housing, welfare, and other social programs, particularly in our large cities, must be found. But the need for coordination and unified effort at the local level is no greater than at the federal level. Some consolidation and reorganization of federal agencies is called for. Moreover, additional stability should be built into the federal agencies which are evolved.

Let me now turn to another consideration. A mind-set or way of looking at the world is a powerful force. If we view federal-state relations within the mind-set of "power-play for the control of education," we shall find some evidence for our position. We all see what we are looking for. We are dealing here with the well-known psychological phenomenon of perception, and there is abundant evidence that much of what a person sees is in his own eyes. Mind-sets or analytical constructs can be useful or harmful. They are useful if they suggest additional insights regarding the real world, harmful if they limit or thwart our understanding of the real world. I believe the power-play concept limits and misrepresents our understanding of federal-state relationships.

I suggest another mind-set or way of viewing these phenomena, namely, an interdependent social system. As a way of provoking our thinking, and not as a precise description of all of these relationships, we may think of the nation as a total system, social in the sense that we are concerned with interactions among persons. Within such a social system we have many subsystems—cultural, religious, economic, political, and others. In federal-state relations we are concerned chiefly with the political subsystem, particularly as it applies to education. In the political subsystem we may envision the states and localities as additional subsystems.

If these subsystems are to function as part of the larger social system, there must be communication between and among the parts and the whole. The subsystems must be strong enough, articulate enough, and wise enough to provide useful feedback to the larger system. The larger system, on the other hand, must be alert to its dependence upon its subsystems, to the need to nurture them, and to the importance of the feedback provided through them.

Within this kind of framework we can understand that during the last two decades the larger social system (representing all of us, I may add) has become more concerned and more aggressive. The equilibrium within the total system seems to have been altered: more influence at the national level, less at state and local levels. Actually, national activity, such as Title V provisions of ESEA for strengthening state departments, may help state and local levels acquire even greater influence. This thrust toward a national system is not well understood, has created apprehensions, and in some instances produces downright resistance. In view of the growing importance of an educated citizenry to the national well-being, I think this shift is inevitable. At the same time, we need to recognize the interdependence of the total system and its subsystems. The nation must depend upon states and localities to operate schools and colleges and to collaborate with other operating agencies in advancing the general good. Vigorous and constructive interaction between state and federal agencies, not recrimination, seems to be the road ahead.

The concept of interdependence provides challenges to both the states and the federal government. States need to become less concerned with structure and legal jurisdiction and more concerned with giving leadership to local agencies and to helping in the formulation of federal policies. Very few of our states are currently staffed to do this; most state boards of education, most chief state school officers, and most state department staffs must be strengthened if they are to meet this challenge. Governors can make a major contribution here particularly in the selection of able, not merely deserving, citizens for membership on state boards of education. No governor should be content until he can say honestly that the state board of education contains as many dedicated and illustrious citizens as does the board for the state university.

The federal government, too, needs to recognize more fully what is involved in interdependence. Federal programs need some consolidation, the missions of federal agencies need further clarification, and additional stability in terms of programs and personnel, particularly in the U.S. Office of Education, needs to be achieved. Communication between federal and state agencies should be extended. Hopefully, over a period of time feedback from state agencies will be improved in quality and in turn influence federal programs more significantly. The federal government has the very difficult task of initiating and implementing programs which support our basic value positions as a nation even though we have some dragging of feet in certain quarters. Such a task requires the utmost in courage, discernment, and tact.

Notes

1. Roald F. Campbell and Gerald Sroufe, "Toward a Rationale for Federal-State-Local Relations in Education," PHI DELTA KAPPAN, September, 1965, pp. 2–7.
2. For another view on the Quie amendment see "Kicking Civil Rights Upstairs." *Saturday Review*, June 17, 1967, pp. 49–50.
3. "Educator Says U.S. Should Start Schools To Challenge Local Systems," *The Washington Post*, April 5, 1967.

11 | Organizational Climate, Social Class, and Educational Output

Alexander M. Feldvebel

The sociological setting for educational administration is a broad and complex concept. However, two components are usually identified early in any consideration of this kind, i.e., internal and external, or the sociology of the school as contrasted with the sociology of the local community outside the school.

The research reported by Feldvebel is illustrative of one way of thinking about the sociological setting of the school and how it relates to one set of purposes of the school.

Much of the literature dealing with morale, satisfaction, and related concepts is based upon the assumption that the social climate of an organization is in some way related to motivation, aspiration, and eventually, job proficiency. The climate of an organization, on the other hand, is often viewed as having its origin, in important part, in the community that the organization serves. Defining organizational climate as in the study by Halpin and Croft,[1] we investigated two possibilities: (1) that organizational climate was a function of the socio-economic status of the school community, and (2) that the output of the school, as measured by standard achievement tests, was a function of the organizational climate as well as the socio-economic status of the school community.[2]

Organizational climates may be defined as patterns of social interaction that characterize an organization. The main units of interaction in this concept of climates are individuals, the group as a group, and the leader. Eight dimensions of organizational behavior are utilized to describe these climates. Each of these dimensions is represented by a subtest in the *Organizational Climate Description Questionnaire* (*OCDQ*),[3] an instrument used to measure climates. The notion of organizational climate has been compared to the concept of *personality* with reference to the individual.

In the analysis of the data of this study an important distinction has been made between the global concept of organizational climates and the

Alexander M. Feldvebel, "Organizational Climate, Social Class, and Educational Output," *Administrator's Notebook*, 12 (April, 1964), pp. 1–4. Reprinted by permission.

137

elements (subtests) of climates considered separately. Climates were designated in the study by the profile patterns described by the eight subtests, of the OCDQ, but it was felt that important relationships might be overlooked if the subtest scores were not analyzed separately, as well. Thus we will refer to the "global concept" of organizational climates (the profiles described by the eight subtests) and to the "elements" of organizational climates (the subtests considered separately).

Perhaps it may be useful to call attention to the design bias which underlies this study, since all research efforts are contingent upon the validity of the assumptions implicit in the theoretical base. Essentially this study focuses upon the organization's efficiency as measured by the ratio between selected inputs and the organization's output. More specifically, the goal which the organization publicly proclaims—academic achievement —is used as the criterion of effectiveness.

Etzioni argues for the need of an entirely different perspective in determining the effectiveness of an organization.[4] He maintains that a major shortcoming of the goals model for determining organizational effectiveness is that the organization has different goals from the ones it claims to have, particularly its publicly stated goals. The public goals are intended to enlist the support of the public to the organization, support which, in all probability, would not be forthcoming for its private goals. Yet, the private goals—organizational maintenance, service and custodial functions—are as essential to the continuing existence and effectiveness of the organization as are the public goals. In short, organizations are multifunctional. Effectiveness in the sense of Etzioni's systems model, is determined by the *optimum* distribution of an organization's resources among its various needs, and over-emphasis on the organization's public goals is considered dysfunctional.

Methodology

Schools within the area described as the Northeastern Illinois Metropolitan Area in the *Suburban Factbook of 1960* and associated with municipalities of between 2,500 and 20,000 residents were divided into three strata based upon a rank derived from four socio-economic characteristics as reported in the *Fact-book*. A random sample was then selected within each socio-economic stratum, proportional to the population of the stratum, so as to produce a total sample size of thirty schools.

In each school, data were collected with respect to the socio-economic status of the school's patrons, pupil achievement levels, and organizational climate. Warner's *Index of Status Characteristics* was used to collect the socio-economic data. Pupil achievement data (based upon a sample of approximately thirty fifth-grade pupils in each school) were secured through use of the 1953 edition of the *Stanford Achievement Test,* and the *Organizational Climate Description Questionnaire* (*OCDQ*) was used to collect the "climate" data.

Findings

Analysis of variance was used to test the relationship between the socio-economic status of the community and the organizational climate of the school. Although neither open nor closed climates showed any tendency to be associated with the social class level of a community, when the global concept of organizational climate was broken down into its elements or subtests (*Disengagement, Hindrance, Esprit, Intimacy, Aloofness, Production Emphasis, Thrust and Consideration*), certain characteristics of the principal's behavior were associated with the socio-economic status of the community. The *Hindrance* and *Consideration* subtests, which describe the principal's behavior, accounted for a majority of the variance in pupil achievement level. In other words, *Hindrance* and *Consideration* seem to be significantly associated with the social class of the community.

Analysis of covariance was used to test the relationship between organizational climate and pupil achievement level, with pupil achievement treated as the criterion measure, organizational climate as the independent variable and socio-economic status as the covariate. Although there was no statistically significant relationship between the degree of openness in a climate and pupil achievement level in this analysis, when organizational climate was broken down into its eight elements or subtests, we found significant relationships between two of the subtests and output. As in the first case, the measures which were associated with variation in output levels were measures of the principal's behavior (*Production Emphasis* and *Consideration*) and not of the group. In other words, when the effects of social class are controlled, *Production Emphasis* and *Consideration* seem to be significantly associated with pupil achievement.

Supplementary data gathered through the use of a questionnaire made it possible to explore several other relationships. A fifteen variable correlation matrix was constructed, relating to the eight *OCDQ* subtests as well as to some school and community characteristics. Eleven relationships were found significant at the five per cent level and four at the one per cent level. Three variables (operating expenditure per pupil, socio-economic status, and a transiency variable), suggestive of a common factor, were involved in eight of the ten highest coefficients of correlation. Two *OCDQ* subtests (*Production Emphasis* and *Consideration*) were included in the ten highest correlations. These two climate subtests, descriptive of the principal's behavior, demonstrate several meaningful associations.

Conclusions

Although there was no relationship between the global concept of organizational climate on the one hand and pupil achievement and social class on the other, three of the elements of organizational climate (*Hindrance, Production Emphasis and Consideration*) were significantly related to these two criterion variables. It is worthy of note that two of these three dimensions describe perceptions of the principal's behavior directly (*Production Emphasis and Consideration*) and one, indirectly (*Hindrance*).

Although it is clear, in this analysis, that social class of the community and certain dimensions of the principal's behavior are related, it is not clear how these relationships should be explained. We may speculate that the principal is more closely identified with the community values than is the organization as a whole. Some support for this viewpoint can be obtained in the literature.[5] Parson's model suggests that the principal is probably more sensitive than teachers to community values because this role demands that he mediate between the organization and the larger community which legitimizes the organization.[6] In addition, the community power structure may play a greater role in the selection of the principal than in the selection of teachers, so that the former choice is more likely to reflect community values. In selecting personnel, superintendents and boards are probably aware that principals are more visible to the community than are individual teachers.

On the other hand, this relationship may be explained in terms of the more direct effect of varying financial support levels associated with the social class level of the community. The more affluent communities evidently do tend to support their schools on a higher level, as evidenced by the correlation of $-.546$ between social class and operating expenditure per pupil (Table 1). Inadequate professional and clerical staffing will probably be reflected in a greater delegation of administrative detail to the teaching staff and a larger burden of custodial duties for the teacher. This would account for the negative association between social class and *Hindrance* (*Hindrance* refers to the teacher's feeling that the principal burdens him with routine duties and interferes with his work).

The association between social class and *Consideration* may be explained in a similar way, since higher support levels in schools will tend to be reflected in higher levels of professionalism on the staff. Principal behavior described by the *Consideration* subtest and the qualities of professionalism are closely related.

Although the global concept of organizational climate shows no significant relationship to pupil achievement level, the dimensions of *Production Emphasis* and *Consideration*, considered independently of the climate structure, do show a significant association. The relationship, although not

TABLE 1   *Selected Variables From the Correlation Matrix*

Socio-Economic Status-Pupil Achievement	.787	
Pupil Achievement-Operating Expend./Pupil	.568	a
Socio-Economic Status-Operating Expend./Pupil	−.546	
Socio-Economic Status-Production Emphasis	.505	
Pupil Achievement-Faculty Experience	.444	
Faculty Experience-Operating Expend./Pupil	.438	
Pupil Achievement-Transiency	−.436	
Socio-Economic Status-Transiency	.427	
Socio-Economic Status-Consideration	−.411	
Pupil Achievement-Production Emphasis	−.399	b
Pupil Achievement-Consideration	.391	
Principal Experience-Disengagement	−.388	
Principal Experience-Aloofness	.378	
Organ. Climate-Operating Expend./Pupil	−.373	
Socio-Economic Status-Intimacy	−.363	
Organ. Climate-Pupil Achievement	−.271	
Organ. Climate-Socio-Economic Status	.197	

a 1% Level   b 5% Level

powerful, tends to reinforce a belief in the significance of the leadership role in organizational goal attainment.

Implications

Since most of the variance in the socio-economic class variable was seen to be associated with dimensions of the principal's behavior rather than with the group behavior characteristics, it appears that there may be a possible source of conflict within schools with respect to the organization's tasks as perceived by teachers and principals. In addition, the biographic and personality characteristics of teachers may turn out to be more important predictors of the group dimension of organizational climate than is the social class of the community; this relationship would suggest the possibility of controlling organizational climate through the selection of teachers.

It also seems that financial support levels, associated with the social class variable, may have a salutary effect upon aspects of the school climate.

The relationship between two of the dimensions of leader behavior and attainment of the organization's goals supports the theory of leadership which conceives of two basic goals for the leader—group maintenance and group achievement.[7] Although these two leadership functions tell us little about the kinds of administrator behavior involved, the *Production Emphasis* and *Consideration* subtests are considerably more explicit. Items in these subtests reflect real situations occurring every day in schools and provide some insights into the kinds of behavior that may be associated with the two leadership functions of group maintenance and group achievement.

The consistently negative results in regard to the relationship between the global concept of organizational climate and pupil achievement level suggest that this relationship may be considerably more complex than assumed here. In this study, the open climate is defined operationally as one in which organizational members derive high levels of satisfaction both from their interpersonal relations with fellow workers and from accomplishment of organizational tasks. Consequently the study hypothesized, in essence, a relationship between satisfaction and output.

Brayfield and Crockett have warned against treating worker satisfaction as a global concept.[8] As a result of their studies in industry they have pointed out that most workers function in a number of social systems within and outside of the job situation, viewing job performance as a means to an end rather than an end in itself. Productivity on the job is seldom a means to satisfying relationships in all of these social systems. For instance, increased productivity is seldom an avenue to status with fellow workers or with the union. Therefore, job satisfaction need not imply a strong motivation to improved job performance. On the other hand improved job performance may be seen by some workers as an avenue to higher pay, promotions, and consequently an enhanced social status. Such differences in orientation toward various social systems between individual workers and between work groups could result in the equal likelihood of positive, negative or no relationship between satisfaction and output.

It is clear, from this analysis, that the recent development of certain conceptual and operational tools has opened an important domain of the school for further investigation. Certain elements of organizational climates are seen as being related to important variables in the school situation. It is also possible that administrators have been provided, in the OCDQ, with an evaluative criterion which goes beyond the more obvious, outward characteristics of schools and provides some guide to organizational improvement. It is believed analysis of the climates of educational systems is essential to the hope of providing a better basis for intelligent choices in education.

Notes

1. Andrew W. Halpin and Don B. Croft, "The Organizational Climate of Schools," *Administrator's Notebook*, Vol. XI (March, 1963), and their *Organizational*

Climate of Schools (Chicago: Midwest Administration Center, University of Chicago, 1963).

2. Alexander M. Feldvebel. "The Relationship Between Socio-Economic Status of the School's Patrons, Organizational Climate of the School, and Pupil Achievement Level" (unpublished Ph.D. dissertation, Department of Education, University of Chicago, 1964).

3. Halpin and Croft, *op. cit.*

4. Amitai Etzioni, "Two Approaches to Organizational Analysis: A Critique and a Suggestion," *Administrative Science Quarterly*, V (September, 1960), 257–78.

5. George Spindler, "Education in a Transforming American Culture," *Harvard Educational Review*, XXV (Summer, 1955), 145–56.

6. Talcott Parsons, "Some Ingredients of a General Theory of Formal Organization," in Andrew W. Halpin (ed.), *Administrative Theory in Education* (Chicago: Midwest Administration Center, University of Chicago, 1958), pp. 43–45.

7. Andrew W. Halpin, "A Paradigm for Research on Administrator Behavior," in Roald F. Campbell and Russell T. Gregg (eds.), *Administrative Behavior in Education* (New York: Harper and Brothers, Publishers, 1957), p. 168.

8. Arthur H. Brayfield and Walter H. Crockett, "Employee Attitudes and Employee Performance," *Psychological Bulletin*, LII (1955), 396–424.

12 | Selected Social Power Relationships in Education

Conrad Briner and Laurence Iannaccone

It is generally accepted that the structure of an organization effects the behavior of its role occupants. Briner and Iannaccone explore the relationships between certain features of the educational organization and the work flow of the organization. From these relationships hypotheses are developed which, when tested, might provide guidelines for the administrator in his attempts to increase the effectiveness and efficiency of the educational organization.

The formal organization in education such as the school or school system, unlike friendship groups which exist to provide psychological satisfaction to members, is the most effective known way of coordinating the behavior of many individuals to achieve the societal goal of educating children. The formal organization in effect influences the behavior of its members putatively, at least according to criteria of efficiency and effectiveness in task accomplishment. The characteristic pattern of operations, such as the hierarchy of offices, system of communications, and compliance system is presumed to be rationally related to accomplishing organizational purposes.

In bureaucratically administered organizations, administrators, supervisors, and teachers continuously influence each other's behavior in quest of compatible and self-satisfying relationships that will also reasonably do the work of the organization. The resulting relationships, though, are sometimes more like uneasy truces than enduring work compacts.

Social organization implies that to some extent the behavior of individuals in the organization will be constrained by the behavior of other organization members. Organizations may then be viewed as limiting and directing the behavior of participants. From this point of view, the individual may lose degrees of freedom.[1]

The discussion presented here depicts the limiting and directing features of an educational organization—the school district—in terms of social power, the influence exerted by some people over others.

Conrad Briner and Laurence Iannaccone, "Selected Social Power Relationships in Education," *Educational Administration Quarterly* 2, No. 3 (Autumn, 1966), pp. 190–203. Reprinted by permission.

The discussion is presented in two parts. In the first part, an empirical study of two administrative roles is reviewed to provide a description of their respective bases of power.[2] In the second part, hypothetical elaboration of the empirical description is used to suggest directions inquiry might take for a better understanding of the work organization in schools and school districts.

Observations

Funk's study of two administrative roles was stimulated by his interest in what appears as a confounding characteristic of educational administration.

The school administrator, in his work, is subjected to at least two distinct influences, (1) the knowledge and ethical disciplines of the profession and (2) the traditional authority structure of the organization. Specifically Funk studied in this context the senior high-school and subject-field supervisor offices in a large city school district.[3] The functional relationships of forty-five principals and eighteen supervisors in the administration and supervision of instruction were described in terms of the bureaucratic environment, operational expressions of legal authority,[4] and patterns of personal contacts in accomplishing work tasks. An overarching question was the extent to which classical, human relations, and revisionist theories of organizations were useful in explaining the personal relationships of the two offices.

Funk used annual reports of the board of education, development studies of the school district, official reports of district offices, and financial and statistical data to document the historical evolution of the administrative hierarchy and the two administrative offices.

A complexity of communication and decision making was revealed by a multi-level hierarchy, centralized expertness, and rigid rules—in essence the bureaucratic prescription of offices by a presumably rational, dispassionate monolithic administrative system. The legal authority of the two offices was compared by determining position level in the administrative hierarchy relative to each other, time measures of responsibility correlated with salaries, promotion practices, and duty statements.

In the chain of command, detailed extensively in personnel bulletins, the principal and supervisor appeared as classical line and staff offices within the secondary-school division of the district. However, supervisors served line functions when interrelating the secondary division with other operating and service divisions such as curriculum and personnel. That is, multiple line-office chains existed in addition to the traditional superintendent-principal-teacher chain. The supervisor thus on occasion acted de facto as a line officer in one authority chain and as a staff officer in another chain.

The legal authority structure of the organization was further delineated using the Stogdill and Shartle method of determining the "level in the organization" for each of the two offices.[5] Identical numerical position scores (7) were derived for the offices, therefore suggesting nearly similar types of legal authority or at least formal opportunity for such. This conclusion was based on the assumption that the normative basis of interpreting such data, established by Stogdill and Shartle in their studies of business and military organizations, was relevant to this school organization. The classical character of the school district's bureaucratic administration encouraged validation of this assumption. Analyses of official statements of office duties, salary schedules, promotion procedures, and license qualifications left little doubt of the extent to which the obvious structural features of the organization could be rationalized by application of the Weberian model of bureaucracy.

The idea of nearly identical legal authority being possible for both the line and staff positions was further affirmed using Jaques' time measure of responsibility.[6] The operational definition of level of responsibility was the time span during which a member of an organization made decisions at his own discretion without accounting to his superior. Jaques' validity criterion was the prediction of salaries. The 1964 maximum salaries for principal and supervisor were $16,459 and $15,899, respectively. Funk therefore concluded that both offices had potentially equal opportunities to influence instruction as superordinates to teachers and as subordinates to common superiors. Officially, teachers related directly to the two superordinate offices of principal and supervisor, which in turn were subordinate to a single office—an associate superintendent.

Review of office duties confirmed both the legal authority duality and differences in functions and sources of personal influence. Official expectations of the principal's office suggested that administrative authority for the direction of instruction and those for the supervisor's office implied the existence of a special expertness capable in itself of influencing instruction. The duties of the principal were characterized by words indicative of command functions such as: organizes, directs, supervises, exercises, administers, plans, allocates, and certifies; the supervisor provides, assists, participates, develops, plans, furnishes, and conducts, suggesting a more indirect influence.[7]

Evidence of status relationships apart from the table of organization and statements of duties indicated the supervisor's office to be subordinate to the principal's. (One aspect of Weber's bureaucratic career emphasis includes "a system of promotions according to seniority or to achievement or both."[8]) Principals and supervisors were in part appointed on the basis of competitive examinations. Despite similar technical prerequisites and salary levels associated with the offices, the promotional status of the principal's examination was perceived as more significant for continuing promotion in administration. Actually, few supervisors had moved into the line-office hierarchy. Only two superintendents had been appointed from other than the principal's position in the past twenty years.[9]

Other status differences were perceived in terms of office space, equipment, and clerical and staff assistants. Principal's offices were larger and better equipped for study and conferences. Clerical and staff assistance was more readily available to principals for planning and conducting professional meetings, opinion surveys, research efforts. These status symbols were visible expression of promotional achievement in the administrative hierarchy—a common feature of corporate life, too.[10]

In summary, the two offices appeared to be traditional line and staff types, but each had both status and exerted authority *and* prestige and exerted influence. That is, each office in working with a common subordinate (teacher) and a common superordinate (associate superintendent) was capable of exercising two bases of social power or sources of influence—(1) status as legal authority legitimated by general acceptance of impersonal rules, and (2) personal prestige derived from the quality of technical knowledge. However, the question of how each office influenced the administration and supervision of instruction remained. Did one basis of social power more accurately represent one office or the other? Using the Weberian bureaucratic model, Funk hypothesized that the unique distinction between the sources of influence would be the differentiation of legal authority and personal persuasion. The principal was expected to represent more completely legal status as a basis of influence; the supervisor was expected to depend primarily upon persuasion stemming from his technical knowledge of the teacher's subject matter.

Funk attempted to validate the functional descriptions derived from examination of official documents and observations of environmental conditions by describing the actual work patterns of both offices in two ways. (1) Incumbents indicated, by choice of descriptive statements, perceptions of their status and practice in carrying out duties involving instructional administration and supervision.[11] (2) Actual work associations were described by responses to the basic question, with whom do you spend the most time in getting work done? A persons-dealt-with instrument was constructed to reveal work-association patterns, both with the professional staff of each high school and with the professional staff within the school district but outside each school.[12]

The RAD scales were scored for principals and supervisors using a frequency distribution for each of six scales, standard errors of mean scores, and critical ratios. Significant differences were established at the .001 level of confidence.

Principals perceived themselves as high in responsibility, authority, and amount of delegation of authority in administering and supervising instruction; supervisors perceived themselves high in responsibility but significantly lower in authority and delegation—the expected responses of line and staff offices, respectively. These sets of responses were consistent with reports of responsibility measures significantly correlated with superordinate-subordinate self-descriptions.[13] The perceptions of high responsibility for both offices were consistent with the results of Browne's study of business executives in which RAD scores and level in organization measures were significantly correlated.[14] Equivalent responsibility scores could have been hypothesized on the basis of previous data, which indicated equivalent level in organization for the two offices.

The perceived differences between the two offices were consistent with the sociometric data. Within schools, the principals spent the most time with assistant principals, secretaries, and head counselors regarding school business and much less time with department chairmen. The supervisors interacted most with teachers and department chairmen and less with assistant principals. Outside the school, the principals spent the most time with the assistant superintendent for secondary education, the administrator of assignments, and those involved with managerial functions. Supervisors interacted most with other subject supervisors, high-school principals, the administrator of assignments, and the assistant superintendent. The work-association patterns of principals and supervisors within schools seemed negatively related. The supervisors spent more time with teachers than with assistants to the principal, whereas the converse was true of principals. Also, the supervisors spent more time conducting their business with principals than did principals with supervisors. Similar amounts of time were spent by both with the assistant superintendent and administrator of assignments.

The nature of work regarding instruction was distinctive for each office. The principal's office dealt mainly with a multiplicity of managerial tasks, which precluded working extensively with department chairmen and teachers on instructional matters. The supervisor's office dealt mainly with instructional matters interacting with teachers, department chairmen, and principals. In amount of time spent, supervisors worked primarily with principals as well as teachers, whereas principals worked secondarily with supervisors and teachers. These relationships existed in spite of the same organizational level of both offices, as indicated by almost equivalent times spent by each with the associate and assistant superintendents.

Discussion

Hypothetical consideration of the nature of work organization in a large school system is presented here. The intention is to draw upon Funk's study and on other observations of organization in education to extend theoretical explanation of dynamic phenomena encountered in administering schools and school systems.

The bases of personal influence associated with the two offices are pervasive and complex. Obviously both are capable of influencing teachers in the manner of line offices. Bureaucratically administered, both can issue directives and commands to teachers, backed up by the authority of a superior office. That is, the legal power of each office can be perceived as legitmate in the sense that it is based on a legitimizing agent.[15] The teacher relates to multiple superordinates, the principal, and supervisor, who relate to a common superordinate, the assistant superintendent. Certain line authority, therefore, is ascribed to both offices to the extent that authority is perceived as delegated by the organization to both offices.

In the context of the authority of office, supervisors, however, have probably achieved formal status regarding specific job duties and responsibilities by personal aggressiveness and demonstrated expertness rather than by administrative mandate.[16] Consequently teachers may be viewed as influenced by a flow of power involving teacher-department head-*supervisor*-superintendent associations as well as by flow of power involving teacher-department head-*principal*-superintendent. In effect, within the sphere of instructional behavior, the staff-office supervisor holds power over the line-office principal by virtue of expert authority without violating the legal character of the administrative authority system.[17] The principals' decision choices regarding instruction may actually be less significant to instruction than the supervisors' choices, thus limiting the power of principals to make decisions basic to instruction.[18]

However, the fundamental relationship of these offices does not involve similar line-office characteristics; rather their incumbents exercise distinctively legitimate and expert power.[19] Principals depend upon the legitimate right of superordinates to influence teachers and the obligation of teachers to accept this influence—essentially a formal role or office relationship. Supervisors must share knowledge with teachers; they must be evaluated as experts making personalized work associations with teachers necessary to the exercise of their power. This distinction is rooted in the nature of specialization as located in the supervisor's office and as this office constitutes a key element in a secondary work-flow in the organization.[20]

An organization's work flow is central to its task accomplishment. Charters has recently used the distinction between division of labor and duplication of labor in work flow to examine schools.[21] Division of labor is characteristic of the primary work flow in industry, where a product is successively and directly worked on by a series of individuals performing specialized tasks. In such a work flow, no one worker is entrusted with the primary responsibility for the product. Instead, it is the flow of work itself which in effect bears that responsibility. As the product flows from operation to operation, the specialized skills of each worker are added sequentially to those earlier in the process. The introduction of new specializations usually proceeds by the insertion of new divisions of labor in this primary work flow.

Duplication of labor is characteristic of the work flow in organizations such as schools where the product is achieved through a series of complex and distinctly different operations performed chiefly by a single individual. Here, a single worker is entrusted with the primary responsibility for the product. The introduction of specialization takes one of two forms. It may change the nature of the primary work flow from duplication of labor to division of labor. Alternately, it may create a secondary work flow which affects the organization's task accomplishment indirectly as it affects the work of the individual having primary responsibility for the product in what continues to be a primary work flow characterized by duplication of labor.

Increasing specialization and division of labor in primary work flows has been a major theme in the history of the industrial revolution. The benefits of this theme are illustrated by the modern mass production of goods and services far beyond what could be imagined simply by means of duplication of labor. The human costs and penalties are only slightly less well known. Among these we note in particular the standardization of products and the alienation of workers from their work. Taking these benefits and penalties into consideration we hypothesize that:

> If an organization's goal achievement as translated into task accomplishment does not permit a high degree of standardization and requires a high degree of psychological engagement of the worker with his work, then that organization's primary work flow will be characterized by duplication of labor.
>
> Conversely, if an organization's goal achievement as translated into task accomplishment permits or favors a high degree of standardization and does not require a high degree of psychological engagement of the worker with his work, then that organization's work flow will be characterized by division of labor.

As indicated above, the introduction of specialized skills must result in new divisions of labor which either bring about or increase the division of labor in the organization's primary work flow or create a secondary work flow. Thus we hypothesize further that:

> If an organization's primary work flow is characterized by duplication of labor, then the introduction of specialists will take the form of a new division of labor which creates a secondary work flow acting on a worker in the primary flow and not directly on the product.
>
> Conversely, if an organization's primary work flow is characterized by division of labor, then the introduction of specialists will take the form of a new division of labor which is inserted in the primary work flow acting directly on the product.

The organization using duplication of labor cannot, however, place the specialist in a line position superordinate to the worker and still gain the benefits of specialization. Specialization, to exist, must be embodied in the specialist as representing a particular aspect of the worker's general task; it must omit some aspect of the general task gaining in depth and uniqueness of skill and insight as it narrows in breadth and generality. To place the specialist in the chain of command over the general worker central to the duplication of labor in the work flow must result either in losing the benefits of specialization or reducing the scope of the worker's behavior to that of the specialist's only. In the first instance, the specialist must become a generalist in order to discharge responsibility for worker behavior as required by his line position. If the specialist avoided this and still continued as the sole line officer to whom the worker was held responsible, we would expect the well known phenomenon Veblen labeled "trained incapacity" to operate so as to remold the worker's behavior into that of a less well trained specialist. Thus to assure the benefits of specialization, the organization has to retain the general line superordinate. Therefore, we hypothesize that:

If an organization characterized by duplication of labor introduces a specialist without changing its primary work flow, then that specialist will occupy a staff office.

A staff office can exist on the same echelon as the worker in the primary work flow, an echelon above, or an echelon below and contribute to the worker's task accomplishment. For particular organizations and tasks, the balance of power between the specialist and worker required by the allocation of responsibility for task accomplishment will determine the echelon on which the staff office is located. Organizations such as schools achieve their goals by means of client-teacher relationships which require a concern for unique aspects of the client's development. The primary work flow of such organizations will be characterized by duplication of labor. To the extent that such an organization seeks to capitalize upon the existence of specialists to enhance its task accomplishment by inserting them into its primary work flow, it must reduce the extent and centrality of the client-teacher relationship.[22] It may instead retain the strength of that relationship without changing the customary structure of its work flow by adding specialists as resources to the teacher who continues to function in the organization's customary duplication of labor. The secondary work flow thus created involves the specialist and the teacher, but only indirectly the client.

The nature of the teacher-specialist work relationship may vary along a continuum involving the amount of discretion assumed by the teacher in allowing the influence of the specialist or the secondary work flow in her work. One end of this continuum gives to the teacher alone the power to initiate the relationship with the specialist and complete discretion concerning whether and to what extent he will be influenced by the specialist in his work. The other end of this continuum gives to the specialist alone the power to initiate the relationship and obligates the teacher to accept the specialist's influence. Ideal types of organizational phenomena seldom exist. However, it would seem logical that the location of the specialist-teacher relationship on this continuum in specific organizations would depend upon the extent to which the organization delegates complete responsibility for the client's welfare to the teacher's discretion. We, therefore, hypothesize that:

> If an organization characterized by a primary work flow involving duplication of labor and a client-teacher relationship delegates to the teacher complete discretion concerning the client's welfare, then the teacher will be given control of the teacher-specialist relationship.

It may be argued that when an organization viewed as a totality itself retains major responsibility for the client's future welfare, introducing a specialist is likely to constitute a decision by the organization to change teacher behavior. But leaving the use of such a specialist to the discretion of the teacher has a high probability of producing only minimally changed teacher behavior. Therefore, organizations seeking to change teacher behavior by the introduction of a specialist will place the specialist in a superordinate position to the teacher. We hypothesize that:

> If an organization withholds a major share of the responsibility for the client's welfare from the teacher, then the introduction of a specialist into a secondary work flow will limit the teacher's choice regarding his use of the specialist's services.

And

> If an organization wishes to insure use of specialized services by teachers, then it will place specialists who embody those services in staff offices on the echelon above the teacher.

Since such officers are expected to influence the behavior of teachers on the echelon below, the term "supervisor" attached to these offices in public schools is an appropriate reflection of the reality. By way of contrast, the line officer (in education the principal) is thus of necessity a generalist or superordinate responsible for general teacher behavior rather than a specialist concerned with limited teacher behaviors. The principal's position representing the legal structure and the probability that this structure is the organization's means of decision-making in the main makes it likely that the principal will use legal authority as the base for his power to influence teachers.[23] It is also likely that this office will not provide leadership but be concerned primarily with administration.

Lipham, following Hemphill, defined leadership as "the initiation of a new structure or procedure for accomplishing an organization's goals and objectives."[24] In contrast, administrative behavior is defined as "concerned primarily with maintaining rather than changing established structures."[25] Thus the line office, by its nature, tends to cause its incumbents to draw upon legal authority in their attempts to influence the behavior of subordinates, particularly in order to maintain existing structures and procedures. The result of this line and staff combination of offices is the placing of the responsibility for changing the behavior of a mutual subordinate on the staff officer's shoulders and for certifying performance and general decision-making on the line officer's.

The potential for conflict between these officers is obvious, but equally obvious are the means of avoiding conflicts and resolving the few which are not avoided. In such an organizational context, the line officers will be responsible for general organizational maintenance. The appeal to legal arrangements and precedent or conventional wisdom by such officers to influence subordinate behavior is quite appropriate and to be expected. In contrast, the specialist supervisors will have the responsibility for leadership, the initiation of instructional change in education. The appeal to expert knowledge, research and science or uncommon wisdom is particularly appropriate to the staff offices instead.

The basis of power is different for each office: the authority of expertise in the one case and of the office and its responsibilities ultimately before the society and its law in the other. Similarly, a "natural" role restriction, preventing the incumbents of each office from encroaching upon the other, follows from the differences in authority and task implicit in each office. The basis for avoiding conflict, which lies in the differences in power of each office, extends beyond the relationship of line and staff officers on their own echelon. Their mutual superordinate can adjudicate conflicts between his line and staff subordinates in terms of the extent to which decisions involve the specialist's expertise or more general organizational issues. For the staff supervisor, cases which he can afford safely to take "upstairs" will be those that clearly involve his expertise. The less this is true the more dangerous his situation. But this is precisely what the organization "wants" in the staff specialist—maximum utilization of his expertise without necessary encroachment upon the general practice.

Similarly, the line officer may not be wise to take upstairs cases that clearly involve the staff specialist's expertise. He must pick his instances of appeal, if at all, involving events as far removed from the specialist's strengths as possible. We hypothesize that:

> If an appeal is taken to a mutual superordinate by a line or a staff officer, then the appeal will be based upon special knowledge or general organizational issues depending upon which office is the initiator.

Instead of conflict, mutual adjustments without appeals to superordinates, patterns of reciprocity and mutual support knitting line and staff together are likely to result from this organizational dynamic. These adjustments involving reciprocal arrangements of unique spheres of interest may also be reflected in the relationship between the staff and line offices on a given echelon and their common subordinates. The teacher faced with conflicting demands between line and staff superordinates will be in a position to avoid letting either control his behavior and may ignore both sets of demands using each of the superordinates to protect himself against the other. The resulting stalemate is hardly desirable for either line or staff officer, and in time may necessitate confrontation requiring the involvement of their superordinate. We hypothesize that:

> If line and staff officers seek to influence a mutual subordinate teacher's behavior, then they will base their attempts to influence on general legal power and special expert power respectively.

The avoidance of conflicts between line and staff officers having a common group of subordinates is more theoretically logical than the classical views of line-staff organization and dual control would suggest. That is, to the extent the staff office does not indeed represent a specialization not available in the line, the delineation of spheres of interest between the line and staff officers will develop. Also in the staff will be superordinate to the line in its influence upon teachers without impairing the legal power of the line officer. The existence and use of different bases of social power by each office will function to reduce and largely avoid conflict between them as the behavior of the incumbents of each office are limited by the other. We thus conclude with the hypothesis:

> The amount of conflict between line and staff officers will be inversely related to the extent each uses a different basis of social power—specifically legal in contrast to expert—to influence common subordinates and superordinates and one another.

Notes

1. While the obverse of this coin will go largely unnoticed in this discussion, it should not be completely ignored. Some of the factors that reduce the probability of certain kinds of behavior also create opportunities not otherwise available for other kinds of behavior.
2. B. Gordon Funk, "Two Roles in the Administration and Supervision of Instruction" (unpublished Ph.D. dissertation, Claremont Graduate School, Claremont, Calif., 1964).
3. Funk delimited the sociological concept "role" by a structural analysis of the organization that emphasized the Weberian meaning of authority as attendant

with the description of "office." The concern was for what authority occupied each of the two offices because of customary behavior or by explicit design prerogatives graded according to hierarchical level.

4. Directives originating from an office perceived as legitimate à la Max Weber, *The Theory of Social and Economic Organization*, ed. T. Parsons, trans. A. M. Henderson and T. Parsons (New York: Oxford University Press, 1947), pp. 324–386.
5. Ralph M. Stogdill and Carroll L. Shartle, *Methods in the Study of Administrative Leadership* ("Research Monograph" No. 80; Columbus: Bureau of Business Research, Ohio State University), pp. 14–17.
6. Elliot Jaques, *Measurement of Responsibility* (Cambridge, Mass.: Harvard University Press, 1956), pp. 32–42.
7. Line offices in education have traditionally conducted operating functions; staff offices have provided advisory and other services. See as examples: American Association of School Administrators, Thirty-third Yearbook, *Staff Relations in School Administration* (Washington, D.C.; February, 1955), p. 22; and Benjamin F. Pittenger, *Local Public School Administration* (New York: McGraw-Hill Book Co., Inc., 1951), pp. 51–52.
8. Weber, *op. cit.*, p. 331.
9. Possibly for one reason Amitai Etzioni reports, ". . . most successful experts are not motivated to become administrators . . . those who are willing to accept administrative roles are often less well committed to professional values than their colleagues." ("Authority Structure and Organizational Effectiveness," *Administrative Science Quarterly*, IV [June, 1959], 55.)
10. For similar examples of executive preoccupation with status symbols see Vance Packard, *The Status Seekers* (New York: David McKay Co., Inc., 1959), pp. 115–127; and *The Pyramid Climbers* (New York: McGraw-Hill Book Co., Inc., 1962), pp. 19, 250–251.
11. The RAD (Responsibility, Authority, Delegation) scales were designed by Stogdill and Shartle (*op. cit.*), to measure different degrees of perceived responsibility, authority, and delegation of authority as exhibited by individuals who occupy administrative and supervisory positions. Funk modified the scales to emphasize instruction. Descriptions of instructional administration included recruiting and assigning teachers, and budgeting and allocating instructional resources; instructional supervision included supervising, evaluating, training, and counseling instructional personnel.
12. This instrument was developed according to the technique used by Stogdill and Shartle (*ibid.*).
13. See Ralph M. Stogdill and Ellis L. Scott, "Responsibility and Authority Relationships," *Leadership and Structures of Personal Interaction* ("Research Monograph" No. 84; Columbus: Bureau of Business Research, Ohio State University, 1957), p. 75.
14. C. G. Browne, "Study of Executive Leadership in Business: The RAD Scales," *Journal of Applied Psychology*, XXXIII (December, 1949), 521–526.
15. An influencer may be seen as legitimate in prescribing behavior because he has been granted such power by a legitimizing agent. See John R. P. French, Jr., and Bertram Raven, "The Bases of Social Power," *Studies in Social Power*, ed. Dorwin Cartwright (Ann Arbor: Institute for Social Research, University of Michigan, 1959), p. 160.
16. Such experience has been described in business management and education. See Chester E. Evans, *Supervisory Responsibility and Authority* ("Research Report" No. 30; New York: American Management Association, Inc., 1957), p. 5; and

Jesse B. Sears, *City School Administrative Controls* (New York: McGraw-Hill Book Co., Inc., 1938), p. 48.

17. Expert authority means conscious professional identification with a specialized subject field. For further indication of personal and organizational ramifications of such identification see Etzioni, *op. cit.*; Blau and Scott, *op. cit.*, p. 63; James G. March and Herbert A. Simon, *Organizations* (New York: John Wiley & Sons, Inc., 1963), pp. 70, 79, 153; and E. W. Bakke, *Bonds of Organization* (New York: Harper & Brothers, 1950), p. 67.

18. This line-staff anomaly has been described in studies of military and hospital units. See James P. Thompson, "Authority and Power in Identical Organizations," *American Journal of Sociology*, LXII (November, 1956), 290–301; and Rose L. Coser, "Authority and Decision-Making in a Hospital," *American Sociological Review*, XXIII (February, 1958), 56–63.

19. Legitimate power is based on an individual's acceptance of a social structure involving a hierarchy of authority—largely a relationship between offices rather than between persons. It is the administration's prerogative to make certain decisions. Expert power is based on perceived credibility of a social agent and the content of a communication; the former involves perception of an individual as an expert; and the latter, informational influence. See French and Raven, *op. cit.*, pp. 150–167.

20. Secondary meaning supportive of teaching—the primary work flow.

21. W. W. Charters, Jr., "An Approach to the Formal Organization of the School," *Behavioral Science and Educational Administration*, ed. Daniel E. Griffiths (Chicago: National Society for the Study of Education, 1964), pp. 243–261.

22. *Ibid.* Charters has pointed out that the balance beween division and duplication of labor may be used as a means for analyzing curriculum changes in schools.

23. For additional discussion of legal structure and decision-making see Laurence Iannaccone, "An Approach to the Informal Organization of the School," *Behavioral Science and Educational Administration*, ed. Daniel E. Griffiths (*op. cit.*), pp. 229–232.

24. James M. Lipham, "Leadership and Administration," *Behavioral Science and Educational Administration*, ed. Daniel E. Griffiths (*op. cit.*), p. 122.

25. *Ibid.*

Chapter Five

Educational Administration:
The Man

In taking an initial look at educational administration, students frequently try to visualize themselves in an administrative position. However, most encounter difficulty because they can find no single uniform mold by which to determine whether or not they "have what it takes." In this chapter the editors propose that the student study the several factors which constitute a multidimensional image of the educational administrator as a man. In so doing, it is our intention to provide a base for the initial as well as the continuing assessment of the student's potential for educational administration

In previous chapters it has been illustrated that there is an interaction among the man, the school, and the social system of which the school is a part. It appears that the degree of success enjoyed by an administrator is determined largely by the quality of this relationship. In this chapter emphasis is given to the man, the key to this interaction.

How can one look at the man to determine the quality of his relationship to this setting? To the most casual observer it is obvious there is no one stereotype of the successful administrator. It is apparent that one must look beyond personal traits to assess the person's effectiveness in an interacting role. A more valid set of criteria for observing a man's relationship to a group is the following:

Values—Man as an individual has his most distinguishing characteristics springing from his pattern of values. Basic values dictate not only what he does but how he goes about doing it.

Skills and abilities—When values determine objectives and the methods usable in reaching these objectives, skills and abilities are brought to bear in the implementation process. The learned skills and abilities constitute the competencies—the "pay-off" in terms of performance.

Perceptions—With values and beliefs providing goals, and with skills, abilities, and competencies providing means for implementation, the man can relate himself to his environment. This relationship is, however, modified by how the man perceives himself, his environment, and his role in the environment.

157

As one looks at the man by means of these dimensions, the role of the man as an administrator in an educational institution becomes discernible. In essence, his role is determined by the nature of his function in the environment, the nature of the man, and the way the man sees himself relating to his function. Administrators of differing characteristics may be classified on a continuum of behavioral manifestations based upon these variables. At one end of the continuum is the director, the administrator as the expert, who sets the goals and assists his subordinates by directing them in their several responsibilities that contribute to reaching the predetermined goal as perceived by the administrator-director.

At the opposite end of the continuum is the group coordinator-implementor. He is occupied with coordinating the work of others, facilitating the work of the composite parts of the organization in order that each can best operate and thus reach the organizational goals generally agreed upon by the group.

In the middle of the continuum is the group-oriented leader. He leads the group by confronting them with propositions regarding both direction and method which are tested in the group situation. He thus enables group members to test their thinking and develop their own basis for action in a way acceptable to the group as a whole.

When viewing administrative behavior along this continuum it is important to remember that none of these examples will describe a specific administrator. Rather, each administrator will operate at varying places along the continuum depending upon the current situation, the individuals with whom he is working, and the point at which he finds himself in his own development.

The careful study of the man in educational administration is necessary in order to assess one's own potential for or competence in such positions. The classroom teacher or the pre-service administrative trainee, as a result of a study of the following materials, may be able to develop criteria useful in determining whether he should consider a career in administration. Likewise, the in-service administrator may also develop criteria for the assessment of himself as an administrator in an existing situation. Such appraisal will bring to light many implications regarding further training, study, and thought.

The following selections lead from consideration of the interaction of the individual and the organization, through the impact of open-closed mindedness on administrative decision-making, to the elements of successful leadership style, and finally focus on leadership behavior as a prime aspect in measure of the effectiveness of the educational administrator. They prove helpful in serving as a screen against which to examine relevant data in assessing both the function of the administrator and the administrator as a man.

13 | The Individual and Organization: Some Problems of Mutual Adjustment

Chris Argyris

In the thinking of the editors, one of the most productive ways to look at the man as an administrator is to consider the interaction of personality and organization. In this article Argyris summarizes (1) research in personality and human development and (2) information on the properties of formal organization. Based on a synthesis of these data, he suggests some propositions useful in explaining difficulties that are created as a result of the differences between the needs of the individual and the demands of the organization. The propositions imply that there is a lack of congruency between these. This incongruent relationship causes personality disturbance characterized by frustration, failure, conflict, and lack of perspective. These difficulties result in the creation of competition, rivalry, hostility, and an inability on the part of the individual to view with broad perspective the problems of the organization. When viewed from the perspective of the behavioral continuum just described, the administrator tends to move toward that place on the continuum where he finds the greatest congruency for meeting both individual and organization needs.

It is a fact that most industrial organizations have some sort of formal structure within which individuals must work to achieve the organization's objectives.[1] Each of these basic components of organization (the formal structure and the individuals) has been and continues to be the subject of much research, discussion, and writing. An extensive search of the literature leads us to conclude, however, that most of these inquiries are conducted by persons typically interested in one or the other of the basic components. Few focus on both the individual and the organization.

Since in real life the formal structure and the individuals are continuously interacting and transacting, it seems useful to consider a study of their simultaneous impact upon each other. It is the purpose of this paper to outline the beginnings of a systematic framework by which to analyze the nature of the relationship between formal organization and individuals and from which to derive specific hypotheses regarding their mutual impact. Although

Chris Argyris, "The Individual and Organization: Some Problems of Mutual Adjustment," *Administrative Science Quarterly*, II (June, 1957), 1–24. Reprinted by permission.

a much more detailed definition of formal organization will be given later, it is important to emphasize that this analysis is limited to those organizations whose original formal structure is defined by such traditional principles of organization as " chain of command," "task specialization," "span of control," and so forth. Another limitation is that since the nature of individuals varies from culture to culture, the conclusions of this paper are also limited to those cultures wherein the proposed model of personality applies (primarily American and some Western European cultures).

The method used is a simple one designed to take advantage of the existing research on each component. The first objective is to ascertain the basic properties of each component. Exactly what is known and agreed upon by the experts about each of the components? Once this information has been collected, the second objective follows logically. When the basic properties of each of these components are known, what predictions can be made regarding their impact upon one another once they are brought together?

Some Properties of Human Personality

The research on the human personality is so great and voluminous that it is indeed difficult to find agreement regarding its basic properties.[2] It is even more difficult to summarize the agreements once they are inferred from the existing literature. Because of space limitations it is only possible to discuss in detail one of several agreements which seems to the writer to be the most relevant to the problem at hand. The others may be summarized briefly as follows. Personality is conceptualized as (1) being an organization of parts where the parts maintain the whole and the whole maintains the parts; (2) seeking internal balance (usually called adjustment) and external balance (usually called adaptation); (3) being propelled by psychological (as well as physical) energy; (4) located in the need systems; and (5) expressed through the abilities. (6) The personality organization may be called "the self" which (7) acts to color all the individual's experiences, thereby causing him to live in "private worlds," and which (8) is capable of defending (maintaining) itself against threats of all types.

The self, in this culture, tends to develop along specific trends which are operationally definable and empirically observable. The basic developmental trends may be described as follows. The human being, in our culture:

(1) tends to develop from a state of being passive as an infant to a state of increasing activity as an adult. (This is what E. H. Erikson has called self-initiative and Urie Bronfenbrenner has called self-determination.[3])

(2) tends to develop from a state of dependence upon others as an infant to a state of relative independence as an adult. Relative independence is the ability to "stand on one's own two feet" and simultaneously to acknowledge healthy dependencies.[4] It is characterized by the individual's freeing himself from his childhood determiners of behavior (e.g., the family)

and developing his own set of behavioral determiners. The individual does not tend to react to others (e.g., the boss) in terms of patterns learned during childhood.[5]

(3) tends to develop from being capable of behaving in only a few ways as an infant to being capable of behaving in many different ways as an adult.[6]

(4) tends to develop from having erratic, casual, shallow, quickly dropped interests as an infant to possessing a deepening of interests as an adult. The mature state is characterized by an endless series of challenges where the reward comes from doing something for its own sake. The tendency is to analyze and study phenomena in their full-blown wholeness, complexity, and depth.[7]

(5) tends to develop from having a short-time perspective (i.e., the present largely determines behavior) as an infant to having much a longer time perspective as an adult (i.e., the individual's behavior is more affected by the past and the future).[8]

(6) tends to develop from being in a subordinate position in the family and society as an infant to aspiring to occupy at least an equal and/or superordinate position relative to his peers.

(7) tends to develop from having a lack of awareness of the self as an infant to having an awareness of and control over the self as an adult. The adult who experiences adequate and successful control over his own behavior develops a sense of integrity (Erikson) and feelings of self-worth (Carl R. Rogers).[9]

These characteristics are postulated as being descriptive of a basic multidimensional developmental process along which the growth of individuals in our culture may be measured. Presumably every individual, at any given moment in time, could have his degree of development plotted along these dimensions. The exact location on each dimension will probably vary with each individual and even with the same individual at different times. Self-actualization may now be defined more precisely as the individual's plotted scores (or profile) along the above dimensions.[10]

A few words of explanation may be given concerning these dimensions of personality development:

(1) They are only one aspect of the total personality. All the properties of personality mentioned above must be used in trying to understand the behavior of a particular individual. For example, much depends upon the individual's self-concept, his degree of adaptation and adjustment, and the way he perceives his private world.

(2) The dimensions are continual, where the growth to be measured is assumed to be continuously changing in degree. An individual is presumed to develop continuously in degree from infancy to adulthood.

(3) The only characteristic assumed to hold for all individuals is that, barring unhealthy personality development, they will move from the infant toward the adult end of each continuum. This description is a model outlin-

ing the basic growth trends. As such, it does not make any predictions about any specific individual. It does, however, presume to supply the researcher with basic developmental continua along which the growth of any individual in our culture may be described and measured.

(4) It is postulated that no individual will ever obtain maximum expression of all these developmental trends. Clearly all individuals cannot be maximally independent, active, and so forth all the time and still maintain an organized society. It is the function of culture (e.g., norms, mores, and so forth) to inhibit maximum expression and to help an individual adjust and adapt by finding his optimum expression.

A second factor that prevents maximum expression and fosters optimum expression are the limits set by the individual's own personality. For example, some people fear the same amount of independence and activity that others desire, and some people do not have the necessary abilities to perform certain tasks. No given individual is known to have developed all known abilities to their full maturity.

(5) The dimensions described above are constructed in terms of latent or genotypical characteristics. If one states that an individual needs to be dependent, this need may be ascertained by clinical inference, because it is one that individuals are not usually aware of. Thus one may observe an employee acting as if he were independent, but it is possible that if one goes below the behavioral surface the individual may be quite dependent. The obvious example is the employee who always seems to behave in a manner contrary to that desired by management. Although this behavior may look as if he is independent, his contrariness may be due to his great need to be dependent upon management which he dislikes to admit to himself and to others.

One might say that an independent person is one whose behavior is not caused by the influence others have over him. Of course, no individual is completely independent. All of us have our healthy dependencies (i.e., those which help us to be creative and to develop). One operational criterion to ascertain whether an individual's desire to be, let us say, independent and active is truly a mature manifestation is to ascertain the extent to which he permits others to express the same needs. Thus an autocratic leader may say that he need to be active and independent; he may also say that he wants subordinates who are the same. There is ample research to suggest, however, that his leadership pattern only makes him and his subordinates more dependence-ridden.

Some Basic Properties of Formal Organization

The next step is to focus the analytic spotlight on the formal organization. What are its properties? What are its basic "givens"? What probable impact will they have upon the human personality? How will the human personality tend to react to this impact? What sorts of chain reactions are probable when these two basic components are brought together?

Formal Organizations as Rational Organizations

Probably the most basic property of formal organization is its logical foundation or, as it has been called by students of administration, its essential rationality. It is the planners' conception of how the intended consequences of the organization may best be achieved. The underlying assumptions made by the creators of formal organization is that within respectable tolerances man will behave rationally, that is, as the formal plan requires him to behave. Organizations are formed with particular objectives in mind, and their structures mirror these objectives. Although man may not follow the prescribed paths, and consequently the objectives may never be achieved, Herbert A. Simon suggests that by and large man does follow these prescribed paths:

> Organizations are formed with the intention and design of accomplishing goals; and the people who work in organizations believe, at least part of the time, that they are striving toward these same goals. We must not lose sight of the fact that however far organizations may depart from the traditional description
> nevertheless most behavior in organizations is intendedly rational behavior. By "intended rationality" I mean the kind of adjustment of behavior to goals of which humans are capable—a very incomplete and imperfect adjustment, to be sure, but one which nevertheless does accomplish purposes and does carry out programs.[11]

In an illuminating book, L. Urwick eloquently describes this underlying characteristic.[12] He insists that the creation of a formal organization requires a logical "drawing-office" approach. Although he admits that "nine times out of ten it is impossible to start with a clean sheet," the organizer should sit down and in a "cold-blooded, detached spirit . . . draw an ideal structure." The section from which I quote begins with Urwick's description of how the formal structure should be planned. He then continues:

> Manifestly that is a drawing-office job. It is a designing process. And it may be objected with a great deal of experience to support the contention that organization is never done that way . . . human organization. Nine times out of ten it is impossible to start with a clean sheet. The organizer has to make the best possible use of the human material that is already available. And in 89 out of those 90 per cent of cases he has to adjust jobs around to fit the man; he can't change the man to fit the job. He can't sit down in a cold-blooded, detached spirit and draw an ideal structure, an optimum distribution of duties and responsibilities and relationships, and then expect the infinite variety of human nature to fit into it.
> To which the reply is that he can and he should. If he has not got a clean

sheet, that is no earthly reason why he should not make the slight effort of imagination required to assume that he has a clean sheet. It is not impossible to
forget provisionally the personal facts—that old Brown is admirably methodical
but wanting in initiative, that young Smith got into a mess with Robinson's
wife and that the two men must be kept at opposite ends of the building, that
Jones is one of those creatures who can think like a Wrangler about other people's duties but is given to periodic amnesia about certain aspects of his own.[13]

The task of the organizer, therefore, is to create a logically ordered world
where, as Fayol suggests, there is a "proper order" and in which there is a
"place for everything (everyone)."[14]

The possibility that the formal organization can be altered by personalities, as found by Conrad M. Arensberg and Douglas McGregor[15] and Ralph
M. Stogdill and Kathleen Koehler,[16] is not denied by formal organizational
experts. Urwick, for example, states in the passage below that the planner
must take into account the human element. But it is interesting to note that
he perceives these adjustments as "temporary deviations from the pattern in
order to deal with idiosyncrasy of personality." If possible, these deviations
should be minimized by careful preplanning.

He [the planner] should never for a moment pretend that these (human) difficulties don't exist. They do exist; they are realities. Nor, when he has drawn
up an ideal plan of organization, is it likely that he will be able to fit in all
the existing human material perfectly. There will be small adjustments of the
job to the man in all kinds of directions. But those adjustments are deliberate
and temporary deviations from the pattern in order to deal with idiosyncrasy.
There is a world of difference between such modification and drifting into an
unworkable organization because Green has a fancy for combining bits of two
incompatible functions, or White is "empire-building" . . . or Black has always looked after the canteen, so when he is promoted to Sales Manager, he
might as well continue to sell buns internally, though the main product of the
business happens to be battleships.

What is suggested is that problems of organization should be handled *in
the right order*. Personal adjustments must be made, insofar as they are necessary. But fewer of them will be necessary and they will present fewer deviations
from what is logical and simple, if the organizer first makes a plan, a design—
to which he would work if he had the ideal human material. He should expect
to be driven from it here and there. But he will be driven from it far less and
his machine will work much more smoothly if he *starts* with a plan. If he starts
with a motley collection of human oddities and tries to organize to fit them all
in, thinking first of their various shapes and sizes and colors, he may have a
patchwork quilt; he will not have an organization.[17]

The majority of experts on formal organization agree with Urwick. Most
of them emphasize that no organizational structure will be ideal. None will
exemplify the maximum expression of the principles of formal organization.
A satisfactory aspiration is for optimum expression, which means modifying

the ideal structure to take into account the individual (and any environmental) conditions. Moreover, they urge that the people must be loyal to the formal structure if it is to work effectively. Thus Taylor emphasizes that scientific management would never succeed without a "mental revolution."[18] Fayol has the same problem in mind when he emphasizes the importance of *esprit de corps*.

It is also true, however, that these experts have provided little insight into *why* they believe that people should undergo a "mental revolution," or why an *esprit de corps* is necessary if the principles are to succeed. The only hints found in the literature are that resistance to scientific management occurs because human beings "are what they are" or "because it's human nature." But *why* does "human nature" resist formal organizational principles? Perhaps there is something inherent in the principles which causes human resistance. Unfortunately too little research specifically assesses the impact of formal organizational principles upon human beings.

Another argument for planning offered by the formal organizational experts is that the organization created by logical, rational design, in the long run, is more human than one created haphazardly. They argue that it is illogical, cruel, wasteful, and inefficient not to have a logical design. It is illogical because design must come first. It does not make sense to pay a large salary to an individual without clearly defining his position and its relationship to the whole. It is cruel because, in the long run, the participants suffer when no clear organizational structure exists. It is wasteful because, unless jobs are clearly predefined, it is impossible to plan logical training, promotion, resigning, and retiring policies. It is inefficient because the organization becomes dependent upon personalities. The personal touch leads to playing politics, which Mary Follett has described as a "deplorable form of coercion."[19]

Unfortunately, the validity of these arguments tends to be obscured in the eyes of the behavioral scientist because they imply that the only choice left, if the formal, rational, predesigned structure is not accepted, is to have no organizational structure at all, with the organizational structure left to the whims, pushes, and pulls of human beings. Some human-relations researchers, on the other hand, have unfortunately given the impression that formal structures are "bad" and that the needs of the individual participants should be paramount in creating and administering an organization. A recent analysis of the existing research, however, points up quite clearly that the importance of the organization is being recognized by those who in the past have focused largely upon the individual.[20]

In the past, and for the most part in the present, the traditional organizational experts based their "human architectural creation" upon certain basic principles or assumptions about the nature of organization. These principles have been described by such people as Urwick,[21] Mooney, Holden *et al.*, Fayol, Dennison, Brown, Gulick, White, Gaus, Stene, Hopf, and Taylor. Although these principles have been attacked by behavioral scientists, the assumption is made in this paper that to date no one has defined a more useful set of formal organization principles. Therefore the principles are accepted as givens. This frees us to inquire about their probable impact upon people, *if they are used as defined.*

Task (Work) Specialization

As James J. Gillespie suggests, the roots of these principles of organization may be traced back to certain principles of industrial economics, the most important of which is the basic economic assumption held by builders of the industrial revolution that "the concentration of effort on a limited field of endeavor increases quality and quantity of output."[22] It follows from the above that the necessity for specialization should increase as the quantity of similar things to be done increases.

If concentrating effort on a limited field of endeavor increases the quality and quantity of output, it follows that organizational and administrative efficiency is increased by the specialization of tasks assigned to the participants of the organization.[23] Inherent in this assumption are three others. The first is that the human personality will behave more efficiently as the task that it is to perform becomes specialized. Second is the assumption that there can be found a one best way to define the job so that it is performed at greater speed.[24] Third is the assumption that any individual differences in the human personality may be ignored by transferring more skill and thought to machines.[25]

A number of difficulties arise concerning these assumptions when the properties of the human personality are recalled. First, the human personality we have seen is always attempting to actualize its unique organization of parts resulting from a continuous, emotionally laden, ego-involving process of growth. It is difficult, if not impossible, to assume that this process can be choked off and the resultant unique differences of individuals ignored. This is tantamount to saying that self-actualization can be ignored. The second difficulty is that task specialization requires the individual to use only a few of his abilities. Moreover, as specialization increases, the less complex motor abilities are used more frequently. These, research suggests, tend to be of lesser psychological importance to the individual. Thus the principle violates two basic givens of the healthy adult human personality. It inhibits self-actualization and provides expression for few, shallow, superficial abilities that do not provide the "endless challenge" desired by the healthy personality.

Harold L. Wilensky and Charles N. Lebeaux correctly point out that task specialization causes what little skill is left in a job to become very important.[26] Now small differences in ability may make enormous differences in output. Thus two machine-shovel operators or two drill-press operators of different degrees of skill can produce dramatically different outputs. Ironically, the increasing importance of this type of skill for the healthy, mature worker means that he should feel he is performing self-satisfying work while using a small number of psychologically unchallenging abilities, when in actuality he may be predisposed to feel otherwise. Task specialization, therefore, requires a healthy adult to behave in a less mature manner, but it also requires that he feel good about it!

Not only is the individual affected, but the social structure as well is modified as a result of the situation described above. Wilensky and Lebeaux, in the same analysis, point out that placing a great emphasis on ability makes "Who you are" become less important than "What you can do." Thus the culture begins to reward relatively superficial, materialistic characteristics.

Chain of Command

The principle of task specialization creates an aggregate of parts, each performing a highly specialized task. An aggregate of parts, each busily performing its particular objective, does not form an organization, however. A pattern of parts must be formed so that the interrelationships among the parts create the organization. Following the logic of specialization, the planners create a new function (leadership) the primary responsibility of which is to control, direct, and coordinate the interrelationships of the parts and to make certain that each part performs its objective adequately. Thus the planner makes the assumption that administrative and organizational efficiency is increased by arranging the parts in a determinate hierarchy of authority in which the part on top can direct and control the part on the bottom.

If the parts being considered are individuals, then they must be motivated to accept direction, control, and coordination of their behavior. The leader, therefore, is assigned formal power to hire, discharge, reward, and penalize the individuals in order to mold their behavior in the pattern of the organization's objectives.

The impact of such a state of affairs is to make the individuals dependent upon, passive, and subordinate to the leader. As a result, the individuals have little control over their working environment. At the same time their time perspective is shortened because they do not control the information necessary to predict their futures. These requirments of formal organization act to inhibit four of the growth trends of the personality, because to be passive, subordinate, and to have little control and a short time perspective exemplify in adults the dimensions of immaturity, not adulthood.

The planners of formal organization suggest three basic ways to minimize this admittedly difficult position. First, ample rewards should be given to those who perform well and who do not permit their dependence, subordination, passivity, and so forth to influence them in a negative manner. The rewards should be material and psychological. Because of the specialized nature of the worker's job, however, few psychological rewards are possible. It becomes important, therefore, that adequate material rewards are made available to the productive employee. This practice can lead to new difficulties, since the solution is, by its nature, not to do anything about the on-the-job situation (which is what is causing the difficulties) but to pay the individual for the dissatisfactions he experiences. The result is that the employee is paid for his dissatisfaction while at work and his wages are given to him to gain satisfactions outside his work environment.

Thus the management helps to create a psychological set which leads the employees to feel that basic causes of dissatisfaction are built into industrial life, that the rewards they receive are wages for dissatisfaction, and that if satisfaction is to be gained the employee must seek it outside the organization.

To make matters more difficult, there are three assumptions inherent in the above solution that also violate the basic givens of human personality. First, the solution assumes that a whole human being can split his personality so that he will feel satisfied in knowing that the wages for his dissatisfaction will buy him satisfaction outside the plant. Second, it assumes that the employee is primarily interested in maximizing his economic gains. Third, it assumes that the employee is best rewarded as an individual producer. The work group in which he belongs is not viewed as a relevant factor. If he produces well, he should be rewarded. If he does not, he should be penalized even though he may be restricting production because of informal group sanctions.

The second solution suggested by the planners of formal organization is to have technically competent, objective, rational, loyal leaders. The assumption is made that if the leaders are technically competent presumably they cannot have "the wool pulled over their eyes" and that therefore the employees will have a high respect for them. The leaders should be objective and rational and personify the rationality inherent in the formal structure. Being rational means that they must avoid becoming emotionally involved. As one executive states, "We try to keep our personality out of the job." The leader must also be impartial; he must not permit his feelings to operate when he is evaluating others. Finally, the leader must be loyal to the organization so that he can inculcate the loyalty in the employees that Taylor, Fayol, and others believe is so important.

Admirable as this solution may be, it also violates several of the basic properties of personality. If the employees are to respect an individual for what he does rather than for who he is, the sense of integrity based upon evaluation of the total self which is developed in people is lost. Moreover, to ask the leader to keep his personality out of his job is to ask him to stop actualizing himself. This is not possible as long as he is alive. Of course, the executive may want to feel that he is not involved, but it is a basic given that the human personality is an organism always actualizing itself. The same problem arises with impartiality. No one can be completely impartial. As has been shown, the self concept always operates when we are making judgments. In fact, as Rollo May has pointed out, the best way to be impartial is to be as partial as one's needs predispose one to be but to be aware of this partiality in order to correct for it at the moment of decision.[27] Finally, if a leader can be loyal to an organization under these conditions, there may be adequate grounds for questioning the health of his personality make-up.

The third solution suggested by many adherents to formal organizational principles is to motivate the subordinates to have more initiative and to be more creative by placing them in competition with one another for the positions of power that lie above them in the organizational ladder. This solution is traditionally called "the rabble hypothesis." Acting under the assumption that employees will be motivated to advance upward, the adherents of formal organizations further assume that competition for the increasingly (as one goes up the ladder) scarcer positions will increase the effectiveness of the participants. D. C. S. Williams, conducting some controlled experiments, shows that the latter assumption is not necessarily valid. People placed in competitive situations are not necessarily better learners than those placed in noncompetitive situations.[28] M. Deutsch, as a result of extensive controlled experimental research, supports Williams' results and goes much further to suggest that competitive situations tend to lead to an increase in tension and conflict and a decrease in human effectiveness.[29]

Unity of Direction

If the tasks of everyone in a unit are specialized, then it follows that the objective or purpose of the unit must be specialized. The principle of unity of direction states that organizational efficiency increases if each unit has a single activity (or homogeneous set of activities) that are planned and directed by the leader.[30]

This means that the goal toward which the employees are working, the path toward the goal, and the strength of the barriers they must overcome to achieve the goal are defined and controlled by the leader. Assuming that the work goals do not involve the egos of the employees, (i.e., they are related to peripheral, superficial needs), then ideal conditions for psychological failure have been created. The reader may recall that a basic given of a healthy personality is the aspiration for psychological success. Psychological success is achieved when each individual is able to define his own goals, in relation to his inner needs and the strength of the barriers to be overcome in order to reach these goals. Repetitive as it may sound, it is nevertheless true that the principle of unity of direction also violates a basic given of personality.

Span of Control

The principal of span of control[31] states that administrative efficiency is increased by limiting the span of control of a leader to no more than five or six subordinates whose work interlocks.[32]

It is interesting to note that Ernest Dale, in an extensive study of organizational principles and practices in one hundred large organizations, concludes that the actual limits of the executive span of control are more often violated than not,[33] while in a recent study James H. Healey arrives at the opposite conclusion.[34] James C. Worthy reports that it is formal policy in his organization to extend the span of control of the top management much further than is theoretically suggested.[35] Finally, W. W. Suojanen, in a review of the current literature on the concept of span of control, concludes that it is no longer valid, particularly as applied to the larger government agencies and business corporations.[36]

In a recent article, however, Urwick criticizes the critics of the span-of-control principle.[37] For example, he notes that in the case described by Worthy, the superior has a large span of control over subordinates whose jobs do not interlock. The buyers in Worthy's organization purchase a clearly defined range of articles; therefore they find no reason to interlock with others.

Simon criticizes the span-of-control principle on the grounds that it increases the "administrative distance" between individuals. An increase in administrative distance violates, in turn, another formal organizational principle that administrative efficiency is enhanced by keeping at a minimum the number of organizational levels through which a matter must pass before it is acted on.[38] Span of control, continues Simon, inevitably increases red tape, since each contact between agents must be carried upward until a common superior is found. Needless waste of time and energy result. Also, since the solution of the problem depends upon the superior, the subordinate is in a position of having less control over his own work situation. This places the subordinate in a work situation in which he is less mature.

Although the distance between individuals in different units increases (because they have to find a common superior), the administrative distance between superior and subordinate within a given unit decreases. As Whyte correctly points out, the principle of span of control, by keeping the number of subordinates at a minimum, places great emphasis on close supervision.[39]

Close supervision leads the subordinates to become dependent upon, passive toward, and subordinate to, the leader. Close supervision also tends to place the control in the superior. Thus we must conclude that span of control, if used correctly, will tend to increase the subordinate's feelings of dependence, submissiveness, passivity, and so on. In short, it will tend to create a work situation which requires immature, rather than mature, participants.

An Incongruency between the Needs of a Mature Personality and of Formal Organization

Bringing together the evidence regarding the impact of formal organizational principles upon the individual, we must conclude that there are some basic incongruencies between the growth trends of a healthy personality in our culture and the requirements of formal organization. If the principles of formal organization are used as ideally defined, then the employees will tend to work in an environment where (1) they are provided minimal control over their work-a-day world, (2) they are expected to be passive, dependent, subordinate, (3) they are expected to have a short-time perspective, (4) they are induced to perfect and value the frequent use of a few superficial abilities, and (5) they are expected to produce under conditions leading to psychological failure.

All of these characteristics are incongruent to the ones healthy human beings are postulated to desire. They are much more congruent with the needs of infants in our culture. In effect, therefore, formal organizations are willing to pay high wages and provide adequate seniority if mature adults will, for eight hours a day, behave in a less mature manner. If this analysis is correct, this inevitable incongruency increases (1) as the employees are of increasing maturity, (2) as the formal structure (based upon the above principles) is made more clear-cut and logically tight for maximum formal organizational effectiveness, (3) as one goes down the line of command, and (4) as the jobs become more and more mechanized (i.e., take on assembly-line characteristics).

As in the case of the personality developmental trends, this picture of formal organization is also a model. Clearly, no company actually uses the formal principles of organization exactly as stated by their creators. There is ample evidence to suggest that they are being modified constantly in actual situations. Those who expound these principles, however, probably would be willing to defend their position that this is the reason that human-relations problems exist; the principles are not followed as they should be.

In the model of the personality and the formal organization, we are assuming the extreme of each in order that the analysis and its results can be highlighted. Speaking in terms of extremes helps us to make the position sharper. In doing this, we make no assumption that all situations in real life are extreme (i.e., that the individuals will always want to be more mature and that the formal organization will always tend to make people more dependent, passive, and so forth, all the time).[40] The model ought to be useful, however, to plot the degree to which each component tends toward extremes and then to predict the problems that will tend to arise.

Returning to the analysis, it is not difficult to see why some students of organization suggest that immature and even mentally retarded individuals probably would make excellent employees in certain jobs. There is very little documented experience to support such a hypothesis. One reason for this lack of information is probably the delicacy of the subject. Examples of what might be obtained if a systematic study were made may be found in a recent work by Mal Brennan.[41] He cites the Utica Knitting Mill, which made arrangements during 1917 with the Rome Institution for Mentally Defective Girls to employ twenty-four girls whose mental age ranged from six to ten years of age. The girls were such excellent workers that they were employed after the war emergency ended. In fact, the company added forty more in another of their plants. It is interesting to note that the managers praised the subnormal girls highly. According to Brennan, in several important reports they said that when business conditions required a reduction of the working staff, the hostel girls were never "laid off" in disproportion to the normal girls; that they were more punctual, more regular in their habits, and did not indulge in as much "gossip and levity." They received the same rate of pay, and they had been employed successfully at almost every process carried out in the workshops.

In other experiment reported by Brennan, the Works Manager of the Radio Corporation, Ltd., reported that of five young morons employed, "the three girls compared very favourably with the normal class of employee in that age group. The boy employed in the store performed his work with satisfaction. . . . Although there was some doubt about the fifth child, it was felt that getting the most out of him was just a matter of right placement." In each of the five cases, the morons were reported to be quiet, respectful, well behaved, and very obedient. The Works Manager was especially impressed by their truthfulness. A year later the same Works Manager was still able to advise that "in every case, the girls proved to be exceptionally well-behaved, particularly obedient, and strictly honest and trustworthy. They carried out work required of them to such a degree of efficiency that *we were surprised they were classed as subnormals for their age.*"[42]

Summary of Findings

If one were to put these basic findings in terms of propositions, one could state:

Proposition I. *There Is a Lack of Congruency between the Needs of Healthy Individuals and the Demands of the Formal Organization.*

If one uses the traditional formal principles of organization (i.e., chain of command, task specialization, and so on) to create a social organization, and if one uses as an input agents who tend toward mature psychological development (i.e., who are predisposed toward relative independence . . . and so on), then one creates a disturbance, because the needs of healthy individuals listed above are not congruent with the requirements of formal organization, which tends to require the agents to work in situations where they are dependent, passive, use few and unimportant abilities, and so forth.

Corollary 1. The disturbance will vary in proportion to the degree of incongruency between the needs of the individuals and the requirements of the formal organization.[43]

An administrator, therefore, is always faced with a tendency toward continual disturbance inherent in the work situation of the individuals over whom he is in charge.

Drawing on the existing knowledge of the human personality, a second proposition can be stated.

Proposition II. *The Results of This Disturbance Are Frustration, Failure, Short-Time Perspective, and Conflict.*[44]

If the agents are predisposed to a healthy, mature self-actualization, the following results will occur:

(1) They will tend to experience frustration because their self-actualization will be blocked.

(2) They will tend to experience failure because they will not be permitted to define their own goals in relation to their central needs, the paths to these goals, and so on.

(3) They will tend to experience short-term perspective, because they have no control over the clarity and stability of their future.

(4) They will tend to experience conflict, because, as healthy agents, they will dislike the frustration, failure, and short-time perspective which is characteristic of their present jobs. If they leave, however, they may not find new jobs easily, and even if new jobs are found, they may not be much different.[45]

Based upon the analysis of the nature of formal organization, one may state a third proposition.

Proposition III. *The Nature of the Formal Principles of Organization Cause the Subordinate, at Any Given Level, to Experience Competition, Rivalry, Intersubordinate Hostility, and to Develop a Focus toward the Parts Rather than the Whole.*

(1) Because of the degree of dependence, subordination,and so on of the subordinates upon the leader, and because the number of positions above any given level always tends to decrease, the subordinates aspiring to perform effectively and to advance will tend to find themselves in competition with, and receiving hostility from, each other.[46]

(2) Because, according to the formal principles, the subordinate is directed toward and rewarded for performing his own task well, the subordinate tends to develop an orientation toward his own particular part rather than toward the whole.

(3) This part-orientation increases the need for the leader to coordinate the activity among the parts in order to maintain the whole. This need for the leader, in turn, increases the subordinates' degree of dependence, subordination, and so forth. This is a circular process whose impact is to maintain and/or increase the degree of dependence, subordination, and so on, as well as to stimulate rivalry and competition for the leader's favor.

A Bird's-eye, Cursory Picture of Some Other Related Findings

It is impossible in the short space available to present all of the results obtained from the analysis of the literature. For example, it can be shown that employees tend to adapt to the frustration, failure, short-time perspective, and conflict involved in their work situations by any one or a combination of the following acts:

(1) Leaving the organization.

(2) Climbing the organizational ladder.

(3) Manifesting defense reactions such as daydreaming, aggression, ambivalence, regression, projection, and so forth.

(4) Becoming apathetic and disinterested toward the organization, its make-up, and its goals. This leads to such phenomena as: (a) employees reducing the number and potency of the needs they expect to fulfill while at work; (b) employees goldbricking, setting rates, restricting quotas, making errors, cheating, slowing down, and so on.

(5) Creating informal groups to sanction the defense reactions and the apathy, disinterest, and lack of self-involvement.

(6) Formalizing the informal group.

(7) Evolving group norms that perpetuate the behavior outlined in (3), (4), (5), and (6) above.

(8) Evolving a psychological set in which human or non-material factors become increasingly unimportant while material factors become increasingly important.

(9) Acculturating youth to accept the norms outlined in (7) and (8).

Furthermore, it can also be shown that many managements tend to respond to the employees' behavior by:

(1) Increasing the degree of their pressure-oriented leadership.

(2) Increasing the degree of their use of management controls.

(3) Increasing the number of "pseudo"-participation and communication programs.

These three reactions by management actually compound the dependence, subordination, and so on that the employees experience, which in turn cause the employees to increase their adaptive behavior, the very behavior management desired to curtail in the first place.

Is there a way out of this circular process? The basic problem is the reduction in the degree of dependency, subordination, submissiveness, and so on experienced by the employee in his work situation. It can be shown that job enlargement and employee-centered (or democratic or participative) leadership are elements which, if used correctly, can go a long way toward ameliorating the situation. These are limited, however, because their success depends upon having employees who are ego-involved and highly interested in the organization. This dilemma between individual needs and organization demands is a basic, continual problem posing an eternal challenge to the leader. How is it possible to create an organization in which the individuals may obtain optimum expression and, simultaneously, in which the organization itself may obtain optimum satisfaction of its demands? Here lies a fertile field for future research in organizational behavior.

Notes

1. Temporarily, "formal structure" is defined as that which may be found on the organization charts and in the standard operating procedures of an organization.
2. The relevant literature in clinical, abnormal, child, and social psychology, and in personality theory, sociology, and anthropology was investigated. The basic agreements inferred regarding the properties of personality are assumed to be valid for most contemporary points of view. Allport's "trait theory," Cattell's factor analytic approach, and Kretschmer's somatotype framework are not included. For lay description see the author's *Personality Fundamentals for Administrators*, rev. ed. (New Haven, 1954).

3. E. H. Erikson, *Childhood and Society* (New York, 1950); Urie Bronfenbrenner, "Toward an Integrated Theory of Personality," in Robert R. Blake and Glenn V. Ramsey, *Perception* (New York, 1951), pp. 206–257. See also R. Kotinsky, *Personality in the Making* (New York, 1952), pp. 8–25.
4. This is similar to Erikson's sense of autonomy and Bronfenbrenner's state of creative interdependence.
5. Robert W. White, *Lives in Progress* (New York, 1952), pp. 339 ff.
6. Lewin and Kounin believe that as the individual develops needs and abilities the boundaries between them become more rigid. This explains why an adult is better able than a child to be frustrated in one activity and behave constructively in another. See Kurt Lewin, *A Dynamic Theory of Personality* (New York, 1935) and Jacob S. Kounin, "Intellectual Development and Rigidity," in R. Barker, J. Kounin, and H. R. Wright, eds., *Child Behavior and Development* (New York, 1943), pp. 179–198.
7. Robert White, *op. cit.*, pp. 347 ff.
8. Lewin reminds those who may believe that a long-time perspective is not characteristic of the majority of individuals of the billions of dollars that are invested in insurance policies. Kurt Lewin, *Resolving Social Conflicts* (New York, 1948), p. 105.
9. Carl R. Rogers, *Client-Centered Therapy* (New York, 1951).
10. Another related but discrete set of developmental dimensions may be constructed to measure the protective (defense) mechanisms individuals tend to create as they develop from infancy to adulthood. Exactly how these would be related to the above model is not clear.
11. Herbert A. Simon, *Research Frontiers in Politics and Government* (Washington, D.C., 1955), ch. ii, p. 30.
12. L. Urwick, *The Elements of Administration* (New York, 1944).
13. *Ibid.*, pp. 36–39; quoted by permission of Harper & Brothers.
14. Cited in Harold Koontz and Cyril O'Donnell, *Principles of Management* (New York, 1955), p. 24.
15. Conrad M. Arensberg and Douglas McGregor, Determination of Morale in an Industrial Company, *Applied Anthropology*, 1 (Jan.-March 1942), 12–34.
16. Ralph M. Stogdill and Kathleen Koehler, *Measures of Leadership Structure and Organization Change* (Columbus, O., 1952).
17. *Ibid.*, pp. 36–39; quoted by permission of Harper & Brothers.
18. For a provocative discussion of Taylor's philosophy, see Reinhard Bendix, *Work and Authority in Industry* (New York, 1956), pp. 274–319.
19. Quoted in *ibid.*, pp. 36–39.
20. Chris Argyris, *The Present State of Research in Human Relations* (New Haven, 1954), ch. i.
21. Urwick, *op. cit.*
22. James J. Gillespie, *Free Expression in Industry* (London, 1948), pp. 34–37.
23. Herbert A. Simon, *Administrative Behavior* (New York, 1947), pp. 80–81.
24. For an interesting discussion see Georges Friedman, *Industrial Society* (Glencoe, Ill., 1955), pp. 54 ff.
25. *Ibid.*, p. 20. Friedman reports that 79 per cent of Ford employees had jobs for which they could be trained in one week.
26. Harold L. Wilensky and Charles N. Lebeaux, *Industrialization and Social Welfare* (New York, 1955), p. 43.
27. Rollo May, "Historical and Philosophical Presuppositions for Understanding Therapy," in O. H. Mowrer, *Psychotherapy Theory and Research* (New York, 1953), pp. 38–39.

28. D. C. S. Williams, Effects of Competition between Groups in a Training Situation, *Occupational Psychology*, 30 (April 1956), 85–93.
29. M. Deutsch, An Experimental Study of the Effects of Cooperation and Competition upon Group Process, *Human Relations*, 2 (1949), 199–231.
30. The sacredness of these principles is questioned by a recent study. Gunnar Heckscher concludes that the principles of unity of command and unity of direction are formally violated in Sweden: "A fundamental principle of public administration in Sweden is the duty of all public agencies to cooperate directly without necessarily passing through a common superior. This principle is even embodied in the constitution itself, and in actual fact it is being employed daily. It is traditionally one of the most important characteristics of Swedish administration that especially central agencies, but also central and local agencies of different levels, cooperate freely and that this is being regarded as a perfectly normal procedure" (*Swedish Public Administration at Work* [Stockholm, 1955], p. 12).
31. First defined by V. A. Graicunas in an article entitled "Relationship in Organization," in L. Gulick and L. Urwick, eds., *Papers on the Science of Administration*, 2d ed. (New York, 1947), pp. 183–187.
32. L. Urwick, *Scientific Principles and Organization* (New York, 1938), p. 8.
33. Ernest Dale, *Planning and Developing the Company Organization Structure* (New York, 1952), ch. xx.
34. James H. Healey, Coordination and Control of Executive Functions, *Personnel*, 33 (Sept. 1956), 106–117.
35. James C. Worthy, Organizational Structure and Employee Morale, *American Sociological Review*, 15 (April 1950), 169–179.
36. W. W. Suojanen, The Span of Control—Fact or Fable?, *Advanced Management*, 20 (1955), 5–13.
37. L. Urwick, The Manager's Span of Control, *Harvard Business Review*, 34 (May-June 1956), 39–47.
38. Simon, *op. cit.*, pp. 26–28.
39. William Whyte, "On the Evolution of Industrial Sociology" (mimeographed paper presented at the 1956 meeting of the American Sociological Society).
40. In fact, much evidence is presented in the book from which this article is drawn to support contrary tendencies.
41. Mal Brennan, *The Making of a Moron* (New York, 1953), pp. 13–18.
42. Mr. Brennan's emphasis.
43. This proposition does not hold under certain conditions.
44. In the full analysis, specific conditions are derived under which the basic incongruency increases or decreases.
45. These points are taken, in order, from: Roger G. Barker, T. Dembo, and K. Lewin, "Frustration and Regression: An Experiment with Young Children," *Studies in Child Welfare*, vol. XVIII, No. 2 (Iowa City, Ia., 1941); John Dollard *et al.*, *Frustration and Aggression* (New Haven, 1939); Kurt Lewin *et al.*, "Level of Aspiration," in J. McV. Hunt, ed., *Personality and the Behavior Disorders* (New York, 1944), pp. 333–378; Ronald Lippitt and Leland Bradford, Employee Success in Work Groups, *Personnel Administration*, 8 (Dec. 1945), 6–10; Kurt Lewin, "Time Perspective and Morale," in Gertrud Weiss Lewin, ed., *Resolving Social Conflicts* (New York, 1948), pp. 103–124; and Theodore M. Newcomb, *Social Psychology* (New York, 1950), pp. 361–373.
46. These problems may not arise for the subordinate who becomes apathetic, disinterested, and so on.

14 | Is an Open Mind Necessary?
   Research Evidence

C. Gratton Kemp

While Argyris looked at the relationship between the individual and the organization, Kemp describes the organization of individual personality. He cites research evidence concerning open and closed minds and such factors as decision-making, intelligence, anxiety, and critical thinking. By exploring such research data, the educational administrator can develop a better understanding of factors that influence both his own behavior and that of others with whom he will be associated. This understanding will promote better decisions about his own personal growth as well as provide a more explicit understanding of the organization of an evolving personality structure.

Among the several necessary abilities for constructive living some are of primary importance among which are capacities to think critically, to synthesize new materials, to make decisions which encompass all the facts and to be open to experience from within and from without.

Such abilities can only be selected for the purpose of description since the quality of thinking is influenced by emotions and emotional reactions, by the products of thought. Feeling and thought are integrally related. As Beck has stated, "Although we cannot know without the intellect, we do not know until we experience with the emotions."[1]

Our recognition of this integral relationship is apparent in many of our expressions. "John has an open mind on the subject," or "When it comes to politics their minds are closed," has become common parlance.

The use of such behavioral descriptions assumes that a discriminable difference exists between those who have relatively open and those who have relatively closed minds, that this difference is overt, recognizable in the performance and the outcome of the interrelationship of cognition and feeling. An individual with an open mind can be expected to differ in his thinking and procedure from one with a closed mind. This difference is apparent in the making of decisions.

In any situation that requires a decision there are relevant and irrelevant factors. The decision depends upon their classification. To use only relevant

C. Gratton Kemp, "Is an Open Mind Necessary? Research Evidence," Walter G. Hack *et al*, (eds.) *Educational Administration: Selected Readings* (Boston: Allyn & Bacon, Inc., 1965), pp. 183–190.

factors requires evaluation and action based on the intrinsic elements in relation to the requirements of the situation. Irrelevant factors in many forms, such as anxiety and the need to be accepted, are heightened by the external pressures of reward and punishment that may be exerted by parents, peers, other authority figures, cultural and institutional norms.[2] The extent to which a person's system is open is "the extent to which that person can receive, evaluate, and act on relevant information on its own intrinsic merits and unencumbered by irrelevant factors in the situation, arising from within the person or from the outside."[3]

Postman and his associates[4] concluded from their research that irrelevant factors function as a perceptual defense against inimical stimuli. Anderson[5] from experience in working with the Stanford Binet Intelligence Test has provided examples of this perceptual defense. Allport[6] observed in his study of rumor that what leads to obliteration of some details and falsification of others is that the force of the intellectual and emotional content existing in the individual's mind leads to the assimilation of ideas in accordance with the values resident within the individual. This, Maslow[7] concludes, wards off the threatening aspects of reality, while at the same time providing the individual with a compensatory feeling that he understands it.

The closed-minded do not approach a new experience openly; they are defensive, insecure, and threatened. They are inclined to ignore, rationalize, project, distort, or narrow in their attempts to deal with it.[8] Rokeach[9] concluded that as the individual tries to handle new experience ideational or otherwise through identification, rationalization, denial or projection, his thinking becomes a tightly woven network of cognitive defenses.

The Open-Closed Mind and Intelligence

The influence of the emotional factors on thinking is present at all intellectual levels. Rokeach[10] compared the scores of 30 persons who were open and 30 persons who were closed-minded or highly dogmatic. He correlated these scores with the scores of the American Counsel on Education Test. The correlation was —.02. Kemp[11] found no significant relationship between dogmatism and the scores on the Otis Test of Intelligence Form A of 104 senior college students. Ehrlich[12] using a sample of 100 college students correlated scores in dogmatism with those on the Ohio State Psychological Examination. He obtained a correlation of —.001. The highly intelligent may be as closed-minded as those of lesser ability.

The Open-Closed Mind and Critical Thinking

Dogmatism influences the quality of the higher levels of thought. Kemp[13] using a sample of 150 with closed minds and 150 with open, chosen from a sample of 500 students from three colleges and one large university administered the Dogmatism Scale Form E and a 50-item test of critical thinking and found that those who had relatively open minds were superior (.01 per cent level) in critical thinking to those with closed minds. It was concluded that the highly dogmatic (closed minds) have difficulty in tolerating ambiguities and are thus impelled toward a "closure" without full consideration of each piece of contributing evidence. This may result in the perceptual distortion of facts and a conclusion that ignores some elements of the problem.

Rokeach and his associates explored the difference in the thinking of those with rigid and closed minds with reference to analysis, and the difference between open and closed-minded thinkers with reference to synthesis.

Using the miniature cosmology of the Doodlebug Problem and 60 subjects he found that those who were low in rigidity differed significantly from those who were high on measures of analysis but not on synthesis. Highly dogmatic or closed-minded subjects experienced to a significant degree greater difficulty in synthesizing or integrating beliefs but did not differ from the open-minded subjects in analysis.[14]

From a group of 249 sophomores Rokeach selected the 30 most open and 30 most closed for the experiment in synthesis. Using the Chessboard Problem he explored the rate of synthesis of those who played chess and therefore were familiar with the principles and those who did not. For those who played chess he found no significant difference in synthesis between the open and closed but for those who did not play chess the open-minded synthesized more rapidly (.01 per cent level). He concluded that when the task is familiar those with open and closed minds synthesize equally well, but when it is unfamiliar those with closed minds apparently resist the formation of new systems.[15]

This body of research suggests that those who are closed-minded may be handicapped in those situations requiring critical thinking especially if the situation requires a synthesis of unfamiliar ideas.

The Open-Closed Mind and the Party-Line Thinker

Although it may be necessary for an individual to be flexible, it is unfortunate if he is tossed about by every wind of doctrine. This is the condition of the party-line thinker. Rokeach describes the party-line thinker as a person "who not only resists change but can also change only too easily. What he does, depends on what his authorities do, and his changes and refusals to change conform with authority."[16]

In his experiments Rokeach used the Doodlebug Problem which required the overcoming of three beliefs (direction, movement and facing) for its successful solution. In one of these, the No Canopy Problem, Joe the Doodlebug could land on the food to eat it, but in the Canopy Problem, due to a canopy over the food, he had to jump backwards in order to eat the food from the edge. That is, the Canopy required the overcoming of a belief which had been used in the No Canopy Problem.

One change was introduced; necessary hints for the working of each problem were provided on 3" x 5" cards in advance. This was for the purpose of making analysis unnecessary and to focus upon the problem of the synthesis of the hints given to find the solution.

Twenty extremely closed and 20 extremely open-minded subjects chosen from a pool of 600 participated in these experiments. Using the hints presented on the cards for the No Canopy Problem it was found that the Open and Closed completed the task in approximately the same length of time.

They were then presented with the hints for the Canopy Problem. Once again each group took about the same length of time. When all the hints were presented at the commencement of the problem the rate of solution was approximately the same for each group. This result was puzzling to those conducting the experiments until they realized that the closed-minded subjects accepted the hints, whereas the open-minded subjects worked them through before they accepted them.

To check on this conclusion, the hints were supplied one at a time instead of all at once. This of course required a synthesis and procedure based on it before a second hint was given. The results now were different. The closed-minded group took longer to do the problem when the hints were presented one at a time, approximately 60 minutes as compared with 45 minutes for the open-minded group.[17]

These experiments illustrate the degree of uncritical acceptance of authority of the closed-minded and their inefficiency in synthesizing because of the dynamic resistance due to the isolation among beliefs.

The Open-Closed Mind and Personality Adjustment

As might be expected the closed-minded individual has more personal problems. A significant difference (.01 level) was found between those with open and those with closed minds in the number of personal problems "of concern" and "of most concern" checked on the Mooney Problem Check List.[18]

In a study of self perception of the degree of anxiety, 25 with relatively open minds were compared with 25 who had relatively closed minds. They were administered the Zuckerman Affect Adjective Check List[19] for the measurement of anxiety immediately prior to a midterm examination.

Before they were given the results, the theory, norms and method of scoring the Check List were explained and discussed. Each subject then estimated his degree of anxiety.

For those with open minds there was no significant difference between the measurement and their perception of their anxiety. For those with closed minds there was a significant difference between the measurement and their perception of their anxiety (.001 per cent level). Almost two-thirds over-estimated and one-third underestimated their degree of anxiety.[20]

From these results it may be inferred that a person with an open mind is more likely to have fewer personal problems and to be more cognizant of the true nature of his internal state of feeling.

Conclusions

Individuals vary from relatively open to relatively closed belief systems. There are many in responsible positions with relatively closed minds whose ability and efficiency may seldom be questioned. However, research indicates that they may distort the situation in satisfying their cognitive and emotional needs. They may avoid a synthesis of ideas from various sources if these endanger any aspect of their belief systems. Their tendency is to make a judgment and then look for evidence to support it. They are also disposed to arrive at a conclusion which is not threatening and which may not always encompass all the facts. They are inclined to feel more or less anxious concerning the material which a status person presents than the situation warrants.

The more open-minded person is more reality-oriented. His ability to use all presented ideas and his own insights improves the quality of each synthesis and therefore of each evaluation. Since new experience is not threatening he is open to all the indications of adjustment in others. He is unlikely to underestimate the gravity of what a disturbed friend, counselee, husband, employee, patient may reveal and is not inclined to reject or distort because of the perception of his own anxiety. He has fewer personal problems and therefore has not only more expendable energy but others less frequently "tune in" on his anxiety-arousing personal concerns.

He is able to tolerate ambiguity and does not dichotomize experience. Since he does not feel impelled by the threat of authority or anxiety to decide he can wrestle with a problem more easily, and longer, entertaining and sorting all relevant information and hunches. Likewise he can permit himself to recognize and to accept "the world of greys," to include in his cognitive structure the realization that experience is a continuum.

He is less threatened by authority and since there is no exaggerated need to discover and conform to the party-line he has more ability and energy to devote to the discovery of his thoughts and feelings about the important issues in his life.

Since he is more reality-oriented he is more genuine. Therefore, associates are likely to feel that they know him and can discuss with him matters of importance and concern.

Notes

1. Beck, Samuel J., "Emotional Experience as a Necessary Constituent in Knowing," in *Feelings and Emotions*, edited by Martin L. Reymert (New York: McGraw-Hill, 1960), p. 106.
2. Kemp, C. Gratton, "Critical Thinking; Open and Closed Minds," *The American Behavioral Scientists*, Vol. 5, No. 5, January 1962, p. 10.
3. Rokeach, Milton, *The Open and Closed Mind* (New York: Basic Books, 1960), p. 57.
4. Postman, L., Bruner, J., and McGinis, E., "Personal Values as Selective Factors in Perception," *Journal of Abnormal and Social Psychology*, 1948, pp. 43, 142–154.
5. Anderson, Gladys L., "Qualitative Aspects of the Stanford Binet," in *An Introduction to Projective Techniques*, Anderson, Gladys L. and Harold H., Eds. (New York: Prentice-Hall, 1951), pp. 581–605.
6. Allport, Gordon W. and Postman, Leo, *The Psychology of Rumor* (New York: Henry Holt, 1947), Chap. 6.
7. Maslow, A. H., *Motivation and Personality* (New York: Harper and Bros., 1954).
8. Kemp, C. Gratton, "Influence of Dogmatism on Counseling," *The Personnel and Guidance Journal*, April 1961, O. 662.
9. Rokeach, *op. cit.*, p. 69.
10. *Ibid.*, p. 190.
11. Kemp, C. Gratton, "Changes in Patterns of Personal Values in Relation to Open-Closed Belief Systems," (Ph.D. diss., Michigan State University, 1957), p. 59.
12. Ehrlich, Howard J., "Dogmatism and Learning: a Five-Year Follow Up," *Journal of Abnormal and Social Psychology*, 1961, Vol. 69, No. 1, pp. 148, 149.
13. Kemp, C. Gratton, "Effect of Dogmatism on Critical Thinking," *School Science and Mathematics*, April 1960, pp. 314–319.
14. Rokeach, *op. cit.*, pp. 191–193.
15. *Ibid.*, p. 222.
16. *Ibid.*, p. 225.
17. *Ibid.*, p. 231.
18. Kemp, C. Gratton, "Influence of Dogmatism on Counseling," *The Personnel and Guidance Journal*, April 1961, p. 663.
19. Zuckerman, Marvin, "An Affect Adjective Check List for the Measurement of Anxiety," *Journal of Consulting Psychology*, Vol. 24, No. 5, October 1960.
20. Kemp, C. Gratton, "Self-Perception in Relation to Open-Closed Belief Systems," *Journal of General Psychology*, 1964, Vol. 70, pp. 341–344.

15 | The Manager as a Leader

L. L. Cummings

Another approach to the understanding of "the man" and his relationship to educational administration is provided in this article by Cummings. It is particularly useful to the student because of its multi-disciplinary support for many of the concepts presented by the editors and explored in various ways in several sections of this book. Cummings' primary focus is on the "leadership" dimension which he defines as the process of influencing thoughts, behavior, and feelings of others in pursuit of common goals. As formulated by Cummings, the "leadership" dimension is a combination of personal behaviors which result in leadership styles which are heavily situationally influenced. The suggested elements of successful leadership style provide a clear-cut point of view which students in educational administration can readily identify and translate into possible behaviors of educational administrators. The article also provides useful data for discussions of the appropriateness of these behaviors in the school situations.

One of the many challenges of the job of the modern executive consists of his continuing need to update himself regarding new ideas, theories and findings of relevance to management. This problem presses particularly heavily on those who strive to attain professional competence in manpower management, largely due to the tremendous growth of literature in the social and behavioral sciences in recent years. Much of this literature contains significant insights of practical utility in the management of manpower. As Professor Dale Yoder recently wrote:

> The effective manager is a gap-spanner. He will build and maintain a bridge across the wide chasm that separates the relevant sciences on one side, from the practice of management on the other . . . . The practice of management is not the scientific study of people and organizations any more than the practice of engineering is the scientific study of physics or the practice of medicine is the scientific study of physiology. . . .
>
> On the contrary, there is a wide gap between the laboratory, on the one hand, and the . . . factory on the other. And the essential function of every

L. L. Cummings, "The Manager as a Leader," *The Personnel Administrator*, X (September-October, 1965), 32–37. Reprinted by permission of *The Personnel Administrator*, official journal of the American Society for Personnel Administration.

practicing manager is to bridge this kind of gap. . . . They must translate the relevant theory and laboratory experiments of the sciences into clues and hunches and suggestions for management policy and practice.

The professor's assignment is to build the other half of the same bridge to span the gap from laboratories and new theories to management policy and practice.

My purpose in this paper is to at least begin to build part of the bridge. On the one side we find the practice of management as a leadership process. On the other, we find a growing literature on leadership theory and its empirical underpinnings. Both parties to the common endeavor (the manager and the concerned educator) will benefit by the building of bridges.

What Is Management?

Historically, management and the job of the manager have been viewed from various perspectives. A brief review of these approaches to the study and practice of management will provide an introduction to our primary theme.

Management has been variously interpreted as a group, a function, or as a position in a hierarchical system. As a group, management has been conceived of as all those employees, either within a given organization or across many different organizations, who perform management tasks. Management is defined as the group any member of which carries out certain functions or behaves in specific ways which, in turn, allow this person to be identified as a member of management.

The important point for our purposes is that management is viewed as the group—not as the functions which are performed or the processes through which these tasks are accomplished. From the functional point of view, management can be thought of as a series of functions performed by those in management positions; e.g. definition of objectives, determination of policies, planning, organizing, directing, motivating, controlling, etc. The functional approach attempts to answer the question "What does the manager do?" by postulating or identifying functions. Management is the performance of these functions and is thought to be a universal, generalizable activity across most goal-seeking organizations.

To others management can be defined in terms of organizational theory and terminology—drawing particularly from those areas of sociology concerned with the study of bureaucracy. Viewed within this perspective, management is a constellation of positions (with associated statuses and roles) within an organizational hierarchy. All those occupying certain positions within the hierarchy are said to be in management—regardless of who they are or, some would say, what functions they perform. A positional definition of management projects an impersonal image and is generally associated with bureaucratic theory.

Obviously, these orientations toward management are interrelated both in theory and practice. Those groups of employees referred to as management occupy managerial positions in which they perform managerial functions. To focus exclusively on a single viewpoint means a loss of perspective and a biased understanding of management as an overall discipline for study and practice.

Question of Leadership Style

Still another focus looks at management as a process—a process of leadership. Leadership is the process of interaction wherein one person influences thoughts, feelings and behavior of another person or persons (e.g., a group of subordinates) in the pursuit of a common goal. The manager as a leader utilizes the resources at his command to motivate and direct the activities of others toward the achievement of the aims of a goal-oriented organization (or of a unit within the organization). Viewing management from this perspective allows us, *and encourages us,* to draw upon the great wealth of theory and findings in the leadership literature in our pursuit of the most effective utilization of manpower. We can study those variables which have been shown to exhibit a significant impact on the leadership process. Furthermore, this approach encourages us to search for and apply the meaning of this research for the selection of a management or leadership style. The continued training of present managers or potential managerial personnel may also be enriched by pursuing this approach.

Range of Styles

1. Production-centered versus employee-centered.

There are numerous descriptions of the types of leadership styles available to and actually implemented by executives in managerial positions. Professor Rensis Likert and his colleages at the Survey Research Center, University of Michigan, have attempted to define leadership behaviors engaged in by more effective managers (versus the less effective) in a variety of work environments.

They have distinguished two approaches to the manager's job as a leader:

1) a production-centered approach and
2) an employee-centered approach. These researchers have characterized the production-centered approach as: concentrating on keeping their subordinates busily engaged in going through a specified work cycle in a prescribed way and at a satisfactory rate as determined by time standards.

In terms of actual behavior, the production-centered manager utilizes close supervision (continually checking on his subordinates and zealously restricting their attention to the task at hand), autocratic decision-making methods (infrequently utilizes the capabilities of his subordinates in arriving at work-related decisions), and a strict man-to-man relationship between himself and each of his subordinates (he tends not to attempt to create and utilize a work team among his subordinates). On the other hand, Likert has characterized the employee-centered approach as focusing attention on the human aspects of their subordinates problems and on endeavoring to build effective work groups with high performance goals.

In contrast to the production-centered manager, the employee-centered leader utilizes general supervision, democratic or participatory decision-making methods and attempts to build a group or team spirit among his subordinates.

When we look at the result of pursuing each of these styles or approaches to leadership we find that the employee-centered orientation appears to be more effective. The Michigan studies report that the employee-centered supervisors achieve higher productivity, higher job satisfaction, lower turnover, lower absenteeism and generally more effective work behavior among their subordinates than do the production-centered managers. Likert explains these findings in terms of the opportunities which the employee-centered supervisors allow for the expression and development of self-fulfillment needs among their subordinates.

Even though it is beyond the scope of this paper, it is interesting to note that these findings have led Likert to question many of the traditional assumptions and practices of management. Likert has proposed as a feasible alternative a "modified theory of management" based on his findings concerning motivation and effective organization of work groups.

Several questions have been asked and reservations expressed concerning the Likert findings. One of the more important of these for the practicing manager concerns the question of whether employee and production-centered leadership are really at opposite ends of an effectiveness continuum. Some have suggested that the most effective style of leadership will vary with the situation; and that perhaps the most successful general style will encompass some combination of the behaviors characteristic of both the employee and production-centered manager. We will return to this momentarily.

2. The authoritarian, democratic, laissez-faire dimension:

Lewin, Lippit and White (1939) experimentally studied the impact of three leadership styles or atmospheres on the performance of young boys in organized play. The researchers trained the three types of leaders to behave as follows:

"Authoritarian": "The authoritarian leader determined all policies, techniques, and activities, maintaining his autonomy by remaining aloof from the groups . . ."

"Democratic": "In the democratically-led groups all policies were determined by group discussion with the leader taking an active role." The democratic leader served as a source of help and guidance. He facilitated the interaction between himself and the group members as well as among the members.

"Laissez-faire": "In the laissez-faire groups the leader did not take an active part, but the group members were free to reach individual or group decisions."

In general, the leader assumed a posture of aloofness and indifference toward the group. The three styles produced the following types of behavior among the group members:

"Authoritarian"—great dependence on the leader, frequently an aggressive reaction to the leader, horseplay when the leader was absent, group members demanded attention of the leader, little freedom to make suggestions as perceived by group members.

"Democratic"—a cooperative-effective relationship between the appointed leader and the group members, freedom to give ideas and make suggestions, high proportion of work-related conversation, levels of productivity maintained in absence of leader, etc.

"Laissez-faire"—initial reaction of asking for and seeking information and structure from the leader, a gradual movement toward apathy, eventual chaos and disorganization among some groups.

Once again, one has the impression that the important question is not *which style* is best, but rather *which combination of behaviors* incorporating dimensions of two or more styles is most appropriate under a given set of conditions. This immediately raises the question of what cues are available to the manager which will help him to select that combination of styles most suited for a given problem. The Lewin, Lippitt and White studies do not help us a great deal in this regard. A third approach to this question of a continuum (or perhaps dichotomy) of leadership styles gives us some intuitive clues to our complex question.

3. Boss-centered versus subordinate-centered.

Robert Tannenbaum and Warren Schmidt (1958) have suggested that the possible range of leadership behaviors available to a manager can be described on a continuum with "boss-centered" leadership at one end and "subordinate-centered" leadership at the opposite end. They have suggested that two variables underlie this differentiation of styles:

1) the amount of authority utilized by the manager and
2) the area of freedom available to the subordinate.. For example, a leadership style located at the "boss-centered" end of the scale would be characterized by the manager merely making a decision and announcing it to his subordinates (high use of authority by the manager and little freedom available to the subordinates).

A leadership style located approximately midway between the ends of the continuum might be characterized by a manager presenting his ideas and asking for questions or presenting the problem to his subordinates, getting their suggestions and then making the decision. Tannenbaum and Schmidt suggest that this represents an intermediate position on both variables—use of authority by the manager and area of freedom for the subordinates.

Finally a "subordinate-centered" leadership style might be characterized by the manager defining the constraints which must be fulfilled and then allowing the group to actually make the decision. It can also be done by actually allowing the subordinates to define the problem, delineate the constraints and make the decision as to the most appropriate solution. This would represent a minimum of authority utilization by the manager and the maximum area of freedom for the subordinates.

Based on intuition and their perceptions of actual leadership situations, Tannenbaum and Schmidt suggest that in selecting a style the manager should be sensitive to and aware of certain forces which operate to determine the effectiveness of any given style. Certain forces "in the manager" are suggested as important, e.g., his value system, his confidence in his subordinates, his own leadership inclinations, and his feelings of security.

Other "forces in the subordinate" which might influence the leadership style selected are the need for independence exhibited by the subordinates, their willingness to assume responsibility, their knowledge and intelligence, their expectations as to how their boss should behave, etc. Finally, it is suggested that certain forces "in the situation" should exert an influence on the selection of a leadership style; e.g. the type of organization (the tradition and mores of the organization concerning appropriate leader behavior, the size and geographical dispersion of the work units of the organization, etc.); the effectiveness of a superior's work group (its commitment to a common goal, its cohesiveness, etc.); the nature of the problem (its complexity, its routine or unique nature, etc.) and the pressure of time (considerable time pressure is not likely to lead to the use of any significant amount of participative freedom by the boss).

Tannenbaum and Schmidt have given us a description of another dichotomy (or continuum, depending on your perspective) of leadership styles. They also provide some intuitive clues as to the variables important in the selection of such a style. However, we are left with two problems:

First is the need to abstract from the boss-centered—subordinate-centered scheme with its emphasis on authority (of the boss) and freedom (of the subordinate) to a level of generality which allows us to deal with explanatory variables which are conceptually independent. One of the problems with the Tannenbaum-Schmidt analysis is that once we have specified the authority of the boss we have simultaneously defined the degree of freedom given the subordinate. In essence, this means the scheme is a univariant description of leadership style. A multivariant analysis would seem to be more powerful analytically as well as more realistic. Secondly, we need to review the research which empirically validates or refutes the suggestions made concerning the variables of importance in selecting a style. We now have enough research available to make this a profitable venture.

4. Initiating Structure-Considerations.

Several researchers originally involved in the Ohio State Leadership Studies have developed two measures highly useful in the study of leadership behavior. One of these measures, the Supervisory Behavior Description, yields scores on initiating structure (IS) and consideration (C) for a supervisor as perceived by others, particularly his subordinates, peers and superiors.

The initiating structure scale has been found to be *positively* related to a supervisor's ratings of proficiency by his boss, the absenteeism of his work group, the formal grievances submitted by his subordinates, and the turnover among his subordinates. On the other hand, the consideration score has been found to be *negatively* related to absenteeism, accidents, and in some cases proficiency ratings by the supervisor's boss.

It should be noted that the IS and C scores are independent of one another; i.e. the score of a supervisor on one scale cannot be predicted from a knowledge of his score on the other scale. The reasons for this independence emerge when one notes how these measures or scales have been defined:

Initiating structure—a leader high on IS is concerned with organizing and defining the relationships between himself and the group, with defining interactions among group members, establishing ways of getting the job done, scheduling, criticizing.

Consideration—a leader high on C scale is concerned with behaving in a manner indicative of friendship, mutual trust and respect, and good "human relations" between himself and his group; he tends to make those under him feel at ease when talking with him; he is friendly and can be easily approached; he attempts to utilize the suggestions of those under him.

A second measure (the Leadership Opinion Questionnaire) has been developed by Fleishman to measure leadership attitudes. This scale gives a measure of the supervisor's or leader's opinion concerning how frequently he thinks he *should* do what each item in the scale describes. It yields not a description of the leader's behavior but an assessment of his attitude. Again one finds two independent scales—initiating structure and consideration, defined in much the same manner as in the Leader Behavior Description Questionnaire.

Supervisors may be high in the amount of consideration they feel should be shown their subordinates, but at the same time may be either high or low in the amount of planning, criticizing, pushing for production and general "structuring" of behavior that they feel they should engage in. The supervisors rated best in terms of proficiency tend to score high on both the IS and C scales. Those scoring high on one scale but low on the other tend to be rated as better leaders in specific kinds of leadership situations; e.g. those high on the (IS) scale tend to emerge as successful leaders in situations requiring the reduction of uncertainty and ambiguity while those high on the (C) scale tend to emerge when maintenance of the group and harmony are important to the work group.

Thus, the Ohio State Leadership Studies have given us at least a two dimensional measure of leadership behavior and attitudes. We are also beginning to accumulate more information concerning the performance correlates of these measures (Cummings and Scott, 1965).

Implications for the Manpower Manager

The basic conclusion emerging from our discussion would seem to be that the most effective leadership style is situationally influenced. This, however, is not a particularly new or startling point. What is new and exciting is our movement toward specifying some of the variables which apparently do have a dramatic and predictable impact upon the effectiveness of any particular leadership style. The challenge, from the research viewpoint, is to study and, if possible, specify the specific conditions (values) of each of the variables influencing the determination of a "best" style. As evidenced by our previous discussion, we are making progress toward the development and verification of an applied science of leadership.

From the perspective of the practicing manager, there appear to be several keys to the successful selection, development and implementation of a leadership style. These might be summarized as follows:

1. The consistently effective leader develops a sensitivity to (awareness of) the important variables or factors in his environment which are known to exert a significant impact upon the effectiveness of any given leadership style.

2. He develops an ability to weigh or balance the relative importance or contribution of these factors in a given situation.

3. Given his estimate of the relative weights of the factors, he has the courage to select that style which seems to be warranted, (this style may not agree in all respects with his usual or habitual leadership behavior).

4. He maintains a desire and willingness to be flexible, even though he may perceive that others interpret him as somewhat inconsistent and superficial.

An intelligent, rationally selected strategy of flexibility will be the most rewarding in the long run in terms of individual effectiveness and the productivity of your work group.

16 | Who's a Good Principal?

Barry D. Anderson and Alan F. Brown

Anderson and Brown describe a study which made use of the "Leader Behavior Description Questionnaire." It was designed to identify specific leader behaviors which are effective in school settings. The article suggests, among other things, that the type of leader behavior is less critical than the frequency of leader behavior that is related to staff satisfaction. In addition the data suggest that neither type nor frequency of leader behavior are related to the background data of leadership personnel. Perhaps the most significant finding of the study is that a good principal is one who leads his staff with considerable frequency. The article is particularly effective in relating educational research to the concerns of developing educational administrators by its identification of various dimensions which influence leadership behavior in school principals.

Leadership is a manifold of concepts. By tradition, the leadership manifold has tended to enshrine whatever a notable and established authority has declared that leaders should be, or that leaders should do. He should for example be alert and aggressive, agreeable and responsible, or should share decision making responsibilities and move his unit toward its goals. Such maxims although inspirational and informative are not very instructive and what scant research exists in their support is frequently conflicting. Now and again, so are the maxims themselves. But whatever the ambiguity surrounding the notion of leadership, the emphasis it has received from practitioner and researcher alike has served to consolidate firmly one simple, yet fundamental point: the primary task of the administrator lies in leadership.

Co-operative Research and Development

Consequently, there has emerged the problem of mapping out in greater detail the entire domain of behaviors called leadership, and of charting a few major thoroughfares through its conceptual domain.

In the process to this time, considerable progress has resulted from turning to teachers themselves for some of the answers and from utilizing

Barry D. Anderson and Alan F. Brown, "Who's A Good Principal?," *The Canadian Administrator*, VI, No. 3 (December 1966), 9–12. Reprinted by permission.

the enthusiastic participation of school administrators in combined research-and-development projects. A recent example of one such project was jointly sponsored in Alberta by the Council on School Administration and The University of Calgary. Called the 1966 CSA Leadership Seminars, this two-stage activity attracted over 170 administrators, largely school principals, who volunteered their staffs in the penetrating analysis of leadership perceived in these schools.

Twelve Tasks of a Leader

The first stage of the project required the completion, scoring and analysis of a research instrument, *The Leader Behavior Description Questionnaire*—Form 12 (LBDQ-12).[1] This instrument measures how frequently an administrator exhibits each of twelve leader behaviors to his staff: representation, demand reconciliation, tolerance of uncertainty, persuasiveness, initiation of structure, tolerance of freedom, role assumption, consideration, production emphasis, predictive accuracy, integration, and superior orientation. Widely used in industry and in education, the LBDQ-12 was herein completed by ten anonymous members of each participant's staff (or by the entire staff in schools of four to ten teachers).

At the same time staffs answered seven additional questions dealing with aspects of the school situation and staff morale. Administrators, using a separate device, answered six questions dealing with aspects of the school situation, staff morale and some biographical characteristics.

Two sets of data were thus available for analysis: (1) the LBDQ-12 results and (2) the background information describing the school, staff morale, and the principal. Specific background information items sought the following data:

i. *Situational Factors.* Size of school, type of school (elementary, junior high, senior high, combined), social class of school community, number of half-days of released time for principals' administrative duties, and staff qualifications in terms of years of university preparation and years of experience.
ii. *Principal Biography.* In terms of age, sex, years of university preparation and years of administrative experience.
iii. *Staff Morale.* Staff expressions of job satisfaction, staff rating of principal's effectiveness, staff estimate of overall school performance, and the principal's rating of staff morale.

System Leaders and Person Leaders

When LBDQ-12 data were compiled and the scores of the twelve leader behavior subscales were intercorrelated, a principal components factor analysis was performed in order to simplify the conceptualization of leadership. This analysis led to the identification of two major factors running through the subscale scores from each school. These two factors, accounting for three-fourths of the test variance, Brown[2] labelled "system-oriented leadership" and "person-oriented leadership",[3] and, with the help of subscale factor loadings, suggested that school staffs tend to distinguish three clusters of effective principals:

(a) those responding chiefly to system needs (high scores on initiating structure, production emphasis, representation, role assumption);
(b) those responding chiefly to the need for effective transaction between the institution and the person (high integration, predictive accuracy, superior orientation, demand reconciliation scores); and
(c) those responding chiefly to idiosyncratic needs of staff (high tolerance of freedom, tolerance of uncertainty, and consideration).

A Circular Model of Leader Behavior

In the historical sequence of events the second stage of the leadership project took place at this point. This stage consisted of seminars which the participating administrators, together with interested members of their staffs, attended. A choice of two sites, Calgary and Edmonton, was offered to the administrators, and the seminars were held on subsequent weekends. The interim results presented to the administrators at that time were largely personal and interpretive in nature in that they applied to individual situations. Some of the overall findings are readily generalized to all school systems, however, and are thus reinterpreted here on the basis of a more intensive analysis of the data.

This analysis is based on a circular model of leader behavior developed by Anderson.[4] In developing the model, the data from 159 of the schools whose principals took part in the leadership project were studied. The leadership in each of these schools was placed into one of nine categories of the model with the aid of the factor scores on each of the factors "system" orientation and "person" orientation (see figure).

Thus, after plotting the two factor scores of a school on the System and Person axes, the leadership of a school could be said to be high on one factor but neutral on the other (sectors 1, 3, 5, 7), high on one factor but low on the other (sectors 4, 8), high on both, low on both (sectors 2, 6, and area 9).

Aided by such a model, a principal may begin to answer questions on the administrative significance of the various kinds of leader behavior ascribed to him by his staff. What, for example, is the likelihood of one or

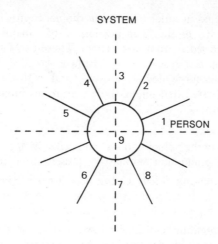

Figure 1. Model of Leader Behavior.

another leadership situation occurring in my particular school? How will it affect my administrative outputs like staff morale?

Type of Leader vs. Frequency of Behavior

To answer these and related questions, two rough methods of grouping the leadership categories of the model were attempted. One, the "Type of Leadership" method, threw together (a) categories 1, 8 and 7 into a person-leader type, (b) categories 3, 4 and 5 into a system-leader type, and (c) categories 2, 9 and 6 into a mixed type. These three types of leader behavior are known respectively as idiographic, nomothetic and transactional after the work of Moser.[5] But none of the background measures were sensitive to this sort of leadership typology. That is, factors of school situation, principal's characteristics, and staff morale failed to be associated any more strongly with one leader type than with another.

A second grouping of the categories may be called the "Frequency of Leader Behaviors" method. The frequency method carves up the model along a different diagonal, again into three groups. When a principal's factor scores plot in categories 1, 2, or 3 they got there because their staffs claimed (via LBDQ-12) he *frequently* exhibited leader behavior listed in the test. Scores plot in categories 4, 9 and 8 because the principal is seen as *occasionally* manifesting these behaviors, and when leadership is *seldom* if ever seen by staff the factor scores by definition must plot in categories 5, 6, or 7.

Using frequency of behavior as the method of analysis, it is again found that the situational matters in a school generally are not determinants, i.e., frequency of leadership is not a function of size or type of school (with one exception) or staff or principal's qualifications. But the opposite is true of morale. Morale differences that are statistically and administratively quite significant were found between pairs in the three frequency groups: the greater the perceived frequency of principal leader behavior, the higher is the staff rating of job satisfaction, overall school performance, and confidence in the effectiveness of their principal.

Discussion

In general these findings indicate that the *type* of leader behavior that a principal exhibits is in itself relatively unimportant. On the other hand the *frequency* of leader behavior is important insofar as it is positively associated with measures of staff satisfaction and their confidence in the principal. Frequency of perceived leader behavior however was not associated with the principal's own estimate of the level of staff morale, a point that is easily understood when it is realized that the correlation between the principal's rating of staff morale and the staff estimate of its own satisfaction was a low .36.

The finding that both type and frequency of leader behavior are unassociated with the background data on the principal has interesting implications for those who select, promote, or train future principals. Age, sex, past experience and training are all traditionally considered important in the selection of principals, yet on the basis of leadership criterion these factors are unimportant.

In view of the emphasis placed upon academic training this finding deserves some explanation. The most plausible seems to lie in the fact that the principals who took part in the project possess a diverse background of educational training, little or none of which was aimed at developing leadership qualities. Had a high proportion of those with additional training devoted considerable of it to leadership development programs, intensive T-group training or related procedure quite a different effect might have been evident.

The lack of association between situational factors and type of frequency of leader behavior also deserves exploration. Principals in their private conversations occasionally express the feeling that, while they realize their leadership is not all it could be, factors in their own school situation such as size, grade inclusion and so forth, render good leadership impossible. Since no association exists between these situational factors and leader behavior it may be assumed that any type or frequency of leader behavior can be utilized in any situation.

An exception to this finding exists. Staffs of combined schools, those composed of grades one to eleven or twelve perceive less frequent leader behavior in their principals than do staffs of other school types. Evidently the principalship of a combined school does present obstacles to good leadership, a finding which is corroborated by Andrews.[6] It would therefore appear that the principals of combined schools or of otherwise fragmented structures must make stronger efforts to exhibit leadership to their staffs if they are to compensate.

Implications for Practice

What are the implications for practice? First, a concern with leadership is important. This concern, this desire to lead, should result in more frequent leader behavior and in turn should result in a more confident and professionally satisfied staff. Second, the study indicates that debate over the relative merits of a "system" or a "person" oriented approach to a leadership problem is unwarranted. A school staff accepts either form of leadership, so long as strength in one form is not cancelled out by a disproportionately poor showing on the other. Third, a principal who wishes to lead his staff effectively need not dwell at length upon the situational or individual factors which he feels will impede leadership. By and large the influence of such factors in individual cases will be felt because they cause inaction on the part of the principal, not because they actually impede his leadership. This inference is of special import to principals of combined schools who must put extra effort into the leadership aspect of their job. Finally, it will be unusual for a principal to be regarded by his staff as a good leader if his own perceptions of staff members as individuals or as a group are inaccurate, distorted, projected or oversimplified, as has recently been found true of principals who generalize their own attitudes and values to staff.[7]

Who is a good principal? The responses of 1551 Alberta teachers offer no answer that is final or absolute but do strongly suggest that the good principal—in their terms of staff satisfaction, confidence in the principal, and feeling of school success—is simply he who frequently leads his staff.

Notes

1. Stogdill, Ralph M., Manual for the Leader Behavior Description Questionnaire—Form XII (Columbus: Bureau of Business Research, Ohio State University, 1963).
2. Brown, Alan F. "Reactions to Leadership," Educational Administration Quarterly, (vol. 3, no. 1, Winter, 1967).
3. Working independently with 48 Ontario elementary principals Punch has corroborated this factorial structure of the LBDQ-12.
4. Anderson, Barry D. "Leader Behavior Styles of Alberta School Principals" (Calgary: Unpublished M.Ed. thesis, The University of Calgary, 1966).

5. Moser, R. F., "The Leadership Patterns of School Superintendents and School Principals," Administrator's Notebook (vol. 6, no. 1, Sept. 1957).
6. Andrews, John H. M., "Some Validity Studies of the O.C.D.Q.," Canadian Education and Research Digest (vol. 5, no. 4, Dec. 1965) pp. 317–334.
7. Brown, Alan F. "A Perceptual Taxonomy of the Effective-Rated Teacher," The Journal of Experimental Education (vol. 35, no. 1, Fall 1966) pp. 1–10.

Chapter Six

Educational Administration:
The Job

The orientation which a man brings to the job he is to perform determines in large measure what he does. Educational administration, like any job involving a complex of activities and relationships, can be viewed from many stances. Some conceive the job of the administrator by focusing their concern upon the purposes of the institution and thus adopting functions and methods in terms of this criterion. There are others who observe that organizational purposes can be achieved only as certain critical tasks are performed. To them, the job of the administrator is centered on these tasks. A third group views educational administration largely as process. Thus, this group visualizes administration as being primarily concerned with making arrangements for the implementation of these processes. While yet a fourth group may view leadership as the essence of the job, others maintain that the primary purpose of administration is management and control—getting the most done at least cost.

In a sense all of these groups are right, but in another sense each of them has oversimplified the task of educational administration by limiting the perspective from which to view it. No administrator can afford to do this. He must come to his task with the realization that, since no absolute definition of his job has been made, he will have to define it. This he must do in the setting of a conflict of definitions made by the various reference groups with whom he comes in contact. This he must do in terms of the realities of the situation in which he works, and finally in terms of what makes sense to him, what he can live with.

We are not talking here of the rights and privileges of administrators. We are simply saying that no matter what influencing factors play upon the definition of an administrator's task, in the last analysis, the significance of his behavior is dependent upon what gets done (the job he performs)— what results from his understanding, his values, his skills, and his acts. It can be no other way. A man can perform only within the realm of his understanding, his values, and his skills. However, this does impose upon him a tremendous responsibility—that of broadening his understandings, appraising his values, and improving his skills. This he does in the setting of the expectations of his reference groups and the realities of the situation in which he works.

Certainly one significant group that will affect the administrator's decision about his task is the lay citizens. We, in America, give great credence to the principle that "the schools belong to the people." The people pay for them; they demand a voice in determining the nature of the education they are buying. As they express their views locally, through state legislative bodies, or in national agencies, they, in a very real sense, set some limits for the administrator's work. More than that, they establish certain expectations for the schools and for those who lead in the continuous development of them.

Another group whose thinking the administrator must consider is his professional colleagues. They, too, have perceptions of the administrator and his role. Some wish to limit his function to that of mere expediter. Others see him wielding great influence in the crucial decisions that are made to move our schools forward. Between these two groups are many others whose perceptions of the administrative job are as varied as the experience which they have had with past administrators.

But there is a broader view than any of these. This particular view encompasses the concerns of others, the limitations and opportunities of the situation, and the capabilities of the personnel of the school including the administrator. Considered singly, these influencing factors suggest expectations which appear to be discordant or even conflicting. Thus it is imperative that these be viewed not as dimensions of the same job, but instead as inputs for the man to relate and reconcile in terms of his perceptions and values, skills and abilities. Through such a process, the man works to rationalize (reconcile) the separate and often discordant notes of the component elements into the harmony of an integrated and complementary pattern—the administrator's job.

In attaining this formidable goal of job definition, the administrator faces several challenges:

1. He must recognize the reality and function of self as well as the three components of lay and professional expectations and situational factors.

2. He must be wary of oversimplification—the determination of his concept of job by the dictates of one element alone.

3. He must recognize that tasks are affected or determined by the interaction of all three and that in the interaction conflict is almost inevitable.

4. He must look to himself—his own values and perceptions, skills

and abilities—to find the common denominator which puts the components into perspective and determines what his job is to be in the given setting.

Because of the variable nature of these factors, it is clear that the job of educational administration is indeed complex. This fact has led to the perplexity which is in evidence on the part of both practicing educational administrators and professors of educational administration. The selected readings for Chapter VI are designed to focus thinking on this problem in terms of the job of the administrator in a historical and political perspective as well as from a perspective of the essential functions and the scope of responsibilities faced by the practicing educational administrator. It is hoped that this range of consideration will provide the developing administrator with general criteria for job selection and the understanding necessary to retain the position which he selects. Finally the development of a personalized conceptualization of educational administration will serve as the basis for continued study of the job and lead to the personal satisfactions which are derived from knowing that one has reconciled the expectations of the institution, significant publics, and self in a rational manner.

17 | Doctrines of Administration: A Brief History

H. Warren Button

In the initial article of this chapter, Button describes educational administration in terms of a series of themes or doctrines which have characterized the field over the past century. These doctrines, strongly influenced by forces outside the field, provide a justification for the administrator and his work. Such a historical review of the progression and definition of educational administration by time period pinpoints the development of a professional field in search of the maturity to be found in a sound theoretical basis.

In most contemporary texts on school administration, and in many articles and addresses about it, there is a common theme, a shared justification for administration. Twenty years ago there was also a common theme, but it was a different one. There have been a series of these themes, or doctrines, during the past hundred years. Each except the current one has lasted for twenty years more or less and has then been suddenly superseded.

The men who speak for administration and the men who train administrators need, and always have needed, a simple statement of what an administrator should be and do, and why. This has served as a justification of administrators and administration to the public and to the school staff, as well as a guide to administrators themselves. To be successful, the statement must be brief and simple, and it must have an appeal. Necessarily, it simplifies. It describes what should be and what is purported to be, and the good and the true, without distinguishing between them. If only an individual subscribed to it, we could call it a private credo, but the theme is shared. It is not simply the belief of an individual, but the generally shared statement of the public belief of spokesmen for school administration. It is an ideology, in a certain sense of the word,[1] or what I shall call here a "doctrine."

A description of doctrines of administration in historical sequence might be only an antiquarian's innocent pleasure. It turns out to be somewhat

H. Warren Button, "Doctrines of Administration: A Brief History," *Educational Administration Quarterly* II, No. 3 (Autumn, 1966), 216–224. Reprinted by permission.

more than that; by understanding why these doctrines have been accepted and then later supplanted, one understands somewhat more about administrators and their worlds and, somewhat more abstractly, about the social functions of doctrines.

As a historian sees it, American public school administration has appeared rather recently. Until the end of the Civil War, there were only scattered school administrators here and there, not enough of them to constitute anything even remotely resembling a profession. With the multiplication of public schools and the growth of large cities and their school systems, the number of administrators increased. The Department of Superintendence, ancestor of the American Association of School Administrators, was organized in 1866.

Teaching of Teachers: 1870–1885

The first semblance of a doctrine of school administration was commonly heard from about 1870 until about 1885. It never won complete acceptance, but it does suggest one of the properties of school administration doctrines generally. Three of the first spokesmen were E. E. White, Francis W. Parker, and Thomas H. Balliet. All of them were administrators at one time or another. White was most prominent at the time, and Parker is historically most important (as a precursor of Dewey). Balliet was superintendent of schools in Springfield, Massachusetts. He expressed the new doctrine most succinctly:

> The superintendent must be, first of all, a *teacher of pedagogy*. His most important work will be to train his teachers to do thorough and clear thinking in all lines of educational work. . . . The superintendent must do work that is almost identical with that of the teacher of pedagogics in a normal school or college.[2]

It was the kernel of an ideal concerning the way a superintendent could improve instruction, by making a contribution that none of his board members could expect to make. Too, it was something which could be done with even extremely limited authority, no more authority than superintendents at the time had. It was appropriate for a time when teachers were poorly prepared. It was credible enough, although it probably did not confer very high status on the administrator, who confessed to being a teacher.

This was the first doctrine of administration, though never unanimously accepted. It abstracted from reality what a teacher of teachers might have hoped to do and passed over the possibility that some teachers might be inept pupils. Administration was very simple, really; administration was supervision (the two words were even used interchangeably), and supervision was the training of teachers. The doctrine of the "teaching of teachers" lasted until about 1885, when a new doctrine appeared.

Administration as Applied Philosophy: 1885–1905

By 1885, matters other than teaching were also receiving much attention by superintendents in the large cities. Courses of study needed development and refinement, school houses had to be built, and policies concerning finance and staffing had to be formulated. As to teachers who did not know how to teach, the gentle thing was to teach them. But the more direct approach, and perhaps the more practical one, if there were many such teachers, was to tell them how to teach as specifically as possible. What was required was a good deal more than the teaching of teachers and a new doctrine to justify it.

The new doctrine described administration as applied philosophy. More than anyone else, W. T. Harris and, in a somewhat more pedestrian way, W. H. Payne, were the most important of many new spokesmen. Harris was superintendent of schools in St. Louis; later, after a pastoral interlude spent philosophizing, he was long-time U.S. Commissioner of Education. Payne was the first professor of education. The doctrine asserted that truth, concerning all things and all matters, was eternal and to be discovered. As in all other fields, this was necessary in education. It therefore followed that the learned administrator, who could discover relevant truths, was the best authority on all matters concerning education, and that the problem of administration was the application of philosophical knowledge to schools. It was roughly the same argument Hutchins has used concerning curriculum, applied far more generally than Hutchins has ever cared to. It still has a certain attractiveness, supposing that one shares the philosophy of the administrator and does not object to the centralization of authority implied. Payne was quite explicit about the latter:

> If there is to be a plan, someone must devise it, while others must execute it. As members of the human body execute the behests of the supreme intelligence, so in human society the many must follow the directions of the few. It is not possible to conceive of a state of society in which there are not inequalities based on gradations in the ability to govern. . . . The assignment of the course of study, the examination of the pupils, their oversight and correction, the oversight of teachers, the compilation of records—these are some of the items on which depend the success of the system, and which require the attention of a single head.[3]

The administrators-as-philosophers had replaced the administrators-as-teachers as spokesmen. A new doctrine, resting on new premises, had replaced the old. Perhaps the administrators-as-philosophers had more drive and need for authority than the teachers of teachers had. Those who formulated this new and later doctrine were not opportunists, but simply of another mind. Innovation in doctrine has always been too hazardous to be a good risk. Those who have accepted the doctrine later, when it has permeated the field and risks have grown small, have demonstrated only that they, like most men, have been human. Perhaps the evolution of schools and school systems has successively brought new types of men into prominence, and men who have accepted the new doctrine have been, because of this, more successful.

The doctrine of administration as philosophy had its advantages. It offered justification for what had to be done, and was a better "fit" than the old one had been. With its emphasis on eternal wisdom and moral judgment, it made the administrator into something like the clergyman and borrowed for him some of the clergyman's status. An administrative doctrine which has placed administrators with a high-status group has always had its advantages.

Business Management: 1905–1930

The doctrine of administration as applied philosophy was successfully defended in the 1890's, when it was proposed that empirical studies offered the best basis for decisions concerning instruction and the schools more generally.[4] However, administration as philosophy was superseded a few years afterward, about 1905. The new doctrine of school administration as management defined school administration as being like the management of a business or factory. This is the era which was described in Callahan's *Education and the Cult of Efficiency.*[5] The appropriate basis for decision-making then was ideally a fiscal one. Like a business enterprise, the schools were to be operated at minimum cost. Like factories, they were to be operated at maximum efficiency. The child was first the raw material and then the product; the teacher was the worker; and the school was the factory.

During the thirty years it was accepted, the doctrine of school administration as business management was widely voiced. Frank Spaulding, a magnificently successful superintendent, and Franklin Bobbitt were among the first; Ellwood Cubberley's work appeared a little later and was probably most widely studied and read. Spaulding, speaking as a business manager, said:

> I know nothing about the absolute value of a recitation in Greek as compared with a recitation in French or in English. I am convinced, however, by other very concrete and quite logical considerations, that when the obligations of the present year expire, we ought to purchase no more Greek instruction at the rate of 5.9 pupil recitations per dollar. The price must go down, or we will invest in something else.[6]

Bobbitt, in *Some General Principles of Management Applied to the Problems of City-School Systems*, 1913 N.S.S.E. yearbook, started with these two principles:

I. *Definite qualitative and quantitative standards must be determined for the product* [the pupil].

II. *Where the material* [the child] *that is acted upon by the labor* [the teacher] *passes through a number of progressive stages* [grades] *from the raw material to the ultimate product* [the graduate] *definite quantitative standards must be determined for the product at each of these stages.*[7]

The change in doctrine from that of the administrator as philosopher to that of administrator as business manager occurred within a few years. The immediate cause of the change was a wave of public criticism of the schools and the increased "vulnerability" of the administrator, which Callahan describes. Less immediate but additional important reasons for the adoption of the new doctrine come to mind. First, perhaps the school really was more like a business enterprise or factory than it was like a church, to push the clergyman analogy. It was a better "fit" once again. Second, the new doctrine justified administrative control over a wider variety of matters. In practice, the extent of administrator control had been increasing, and there were social advantages in a doctrine which would support the increase. Third, the new doctrine allied the administrator with a high status group, the businessmen.

Technical Experts: 1935–1950

The business-management doctrine of administration succumbed in the 1930's. The techniques of administration (budgeting, accounting, purchasing, plant construction and maintenance, etc.) had been enormously developed and refined since 1905, but the justification for administration was almost unchanged.

In the 1930's, during the Depression and the New Deal, the business-management doctrine, along with businessmen, fell into disrepute. The purpose of the school, it was said, was not to operate with the greatest efficiency and economy but to strengthen the democracy. Jesse H. Newlon had raised the point in the 1920's but was much more influential in the 1930's. His *Educational Administration as Social Policy* (1934) was the first important denial of the business management doctrine by an administrator. In 1939 he wrote:

> Education should, of course, be efficiently and economically administered, but it should be kept in mind always that efficiency and economy must be defined in terms of purposes and responsibilities and that economy and parsimony are not synonyms in the parlance of public affairs. The fundamental desideratum is that the schools be kept free if they are to serve their primary purpose of social education.[8]

If the purpose of the schools was to serve democracy, the first essential was that the schools be democratically organized and controlled. Decisions were to be made by everyone involved. The old justification for administration, to assure economy and efficiency in the operation of the school, was gone, and for a time no new one took its place; there was no justification for control by administration. In 1946, in an N.S.S.E. yearbook titled *Changing Concepts in Educational Administration*, Grayson N. Kefauver wrote:

> Actual leadership, as judged by the contribution made or the solution arrived at, may come from a classroom teacher, a parent, or the administrator. The role of the administrator may or may not involve the introduction of the idea finally accepted. In many situations, the administrator's leadership role will be that of encouraging others to participate effectively.[9]

It is not surprising that the business-management doctrine was abandoned. In the 1930's the businessman was no longer in high repute. Democracy in the schools, which followed the business management era, left the administrator in a position of diminished power and esteem, although the technical services which he could provide were still required. (Indeed, many of the technical devices of administration in the 1960's are only refinements of those developed half a century ago.) Under some circumstances, he might serve as an "expediter of planning," but this role was claimed for supervisors and curriculum planners. The antecedent organizations of the Association for Supervision and Curriculum Development had been inconspicuous in the 1920's, but the A.S.C.D. grew into prominence in the 1940's.

Administrative Scientist: 1955–

The doctrine that has won almost complete acceptance in the last decade holds that much of administration can be conceptualized in the terms of the behavioral sciences, and that a science of administration generally is emergent. These were Griffiths' points in the introduction to *Behavioral Science and Educational Administration*, a 1964 N.S.S.E. yearbook.[10] They need not be repeated nor elaborated upon here.

The current doctrine has undoubtedly risen from a variety of circumstances. By 1950, relevant concepts from the behavioral sciences were more plentifully available, and additional ones would appear soon. The scientist, physical and behavioral, was rising in esteem. In part, the new doctrine was an honest attempt to restore the prestige of administrators. Briefly and approximately, the logic went like this: If the status of administration was to be repaired and improved, it was necessary to "professionalize" it. The first step in professionalization was to improve the preparation of those entering the field and to incorporate "basic" knowledge; knowledge of the behavioral sciences was the best choice.

The doctrine of school administration as applied behavioral science is not fully accepted yet—and of course may not be. There are still writers who deal with administration as techniques and technology, and at least until recently there have been writers who have attempted to formulate a rationale of administration within the circa 1940 formulas for democratic schools. There is still some support for democratic supervision and methods of developing curriculum. Nevertheless, there are good reasons why it probably will be fully accepted. For many administrators it is a good "fit," which is to say that in the here and now many administrators find it comfortable. It may be highly acceptable to boards and the public, too, partly because it borrows status from the behavioral scientists, who have a higher status than ever before.

Next?

It would be safer not to predict future changes in the doctrine of administration. Changes have in the past been sudden and unpredicted. If one were to predict change, the least hazardous prediction would probably be no change in the near future. Since previous doctrines have lasted roughly twenty years before being supplanted, and the present one is not much more than a decade old, it seems rather unlikely that it will be replaced very soon.

The form a new doctrine might take cannot be predicted from the present one. New doctrines have been radically different, not evolved from old doctrines. Certainly there are at least latent disadvantages in the present one. Its fortune, or at least its prestige, depends upon that of the behavioral sciences, which may well be overshadowed. Coming from the behavioral sciences, it has a certain deterministic mindless air. Things seem to have a certain inevitability (as they may have in this paper, which is in a generally behavioral framework). The inevitability can be denied, but the feel of it is there. If you believe that improvement of schools can and should be planned, the feeling of mindless inevitability is difficult to live with. It could be much more difficult to live with in an era of change by plan and policy.

It is a hope rather than a prediction that the next doctrine of administration will be indigenous. It would rest upon "pure" knowledge in the way that the present doctrine does. The "pure" knowledge, however, would not be borrowed from philosophy, business management, behavioral science, or another field seen as related to administration. It would be, rather, a knowledge of schools and administration and of educational policy. Such a doctrine might lessen the sometimes painful gap between doctrine and reality. A doctrine that did not borrow status would be a symptom of maturity of the profession. One might hope, too, that a new doctrine would distinguish more exactly between what is good and what is true, and that it would say more and imply less.

There is one prediction that seems safe: There will continue to be a doctrine of administration, as there will continue to be doctrines in other fields, within and outside education. Doctrines of administration have been social and psychological necessities.

Notes

1. F. X. Sutton et al. in *American Business Creed* (Cambridge, 1956) provide a definition of "creed" which could be appropriate.
2. T. M. Balliet, "The Work of the City Superintendent," *NEA Department of Superintendence Proceedings*, 1889, pp. 182–184.
3. William H. Payne, *Chapters on School Supervision* (Cincinnati: Wilson, Hinkle and Co., 1875) pp. 13, 17.
4. H. W. Button, "Committee of Fifteen," *History of Education Quarterly*, V (1965), 253–263.
5. Raymond E. Callahan, *Education and the Cult of Efficiency* (Chicago: University of Chicago Press, 1962).
6. E. E. Spaulding, "The Application of Principles of Scientific Management," *NEA Proceedings*, 1913, p. 265.
7. Franklin Bobbitt, *Some General Principles of Management Applied to the Problems of City School Systems*, Twelfth Yearbook of the National Society for the Study of Education, Part I (Bloomington, Ill · Public School Publishing Co., 1913), p. 11. (Italics are Bobbitt's)
8. Jesse H. Newlon, *Education for Democracy in Our Time* (New York: McGraw Hill Book Co., 1939), p. 129.
9. Grayson N. Kefauver, "Reorientation of Educational Administration" *Changing Concepts in Educational Administration*, Forty-fifth Yearbook of the National Society for the Study of Education, Part II (Chicago: University of Chicago Press, 1946).
10. *Behavioral Science and Educational Administration*, Sixty-third Yearbook of the National Society for the Study of Education, Part II (Chicago: University of Chicago Press, 1964).

18 | Political Dimensions of Educational Administration

Russell T. Gregg

The thesis of this article by Gregg is that the educational system is also in the political system. He argues against the classical conception of politics as equal to government and instead defines politics as the study of power and influence, both formal and informal. Gregg advocates the development of awareness in the educational administrator of the political nature of his role, and suggests the development of skills which make it possible for him to work effectively in such an area. He also attempts to identify with some clarity the "political" facets of educational administration. While it can be suggested that this perception of the job of the educational administrator is somewhat narrow in scope, it nevertheless is an excellent delineation of a critical aspect of the job of the educational administrator.

In spite of the well known facts that public schools are an important part of government, that they are financed by public funds, and that boards of education and school administrators are frequently caught between conflicting pressures and demands, the generally prevailing attitude has been that politics has no relationship to the schools. It is not surprising, therefore, that most lay citizens and many school people give little or no thought to political aspects of public education and of its administration. Until quite recently, even scholars in administration, and particularly those in educational administration, concentrated their attention on formal organization, such as line and staff and span of control, on finance, and on technical efficiency in fulfillment of tasks. During the past decade, however, there has been particular stress on socio-psychological aspects of administration, such as informal organization, decision-making, communication, and conflict.

For many decades there were more school districts in the United States than all other units of government combined; even today, local school districts constitute nearly half of all existing units of government. In the light of this fact it is surprising, indeed, that political scientists did not seem to take cognizance of public school government until as late as 1959, when Eliot published an article that attracted the attention of educationists

Russell T. Gregg, "Political Dimensions of Educational Administration," *Teachers College Record*, LXVII (November, 1965), 118–128.

as well as political scientists (16). Also in 1959, Monypenny (33), a political scientist speaking to a group of professors of educational administration, referred to local school districts as an area of government about which political scientists were uninformed. He stated:

> In moving from state and national government to the local school district, consideration is largely beyond the purview of students of political science. Few political scientists, outside of their own districts, have any knowledge of the structure of education or of the kinds of issues which arise in the politics of the local educational unit.

Monypenny expressed the opinion that little or no initiative would be taken by anyone not in the field of education with respect to educational purposes or programs except with respect to questions of financial support, and then only in fiscally dependent school districts. Since political scientists themselves have given only slight attention to the politics of education, the question arises whether public education is actually devoid of politics or whether it is an arena of political activity that has been unjustifiably neglected. To the author, it is encouraging to note that during quite recent years political scientists, sociologists, and educational administrators have given increasing attention to the politics of education (4, 6, 10, 25, 29).

Traditional Attitudes

Most American citizens hold a narrow, and sometimes a not too wholesome, concept of "politics." For most of them, politics probably connotes only partisan (political party) activity. Some of them may think of politics as synonymous with spoils and patronage, with decisions made in smoke-filled rooms by a few powerful politicians, with unscrupulous behavior and bossism. If "politics" retains such meanings, it is not surprising that so many citizens want the public schools to be kept out of an environment characterized by such "muck and mire."

Throughout most of our educational history the government of public education has been organized separately from, and often fiscally independent of, other local governments. One reason for such separation was the people's desire to disassociate the schools from partisan politics and thus to keep educational issues as non-controversial as possible. This means, of course, that laws relating to the government of public schools are, in general, distinct from those relating to municipal governments. As one political scientist has stated:

> Education is generally held apart, its personnel distinct, its function highly valued and visible, its need judged by different criteria. The tradition of separation is strong and, one may guess, growing. While the geographic space of

school district and municipality may coincide or overlap, the two do not occupy the same "political space" (31).

It may have been the desire of citizens and schoolmen to place schools in a distinct and protected "political space" that resulted in the separation of school government from other types of local government.

Members of elective boards of education are usually elected at non-partisan elections; also they are elected at large rather than by geographical areas of the school district. Citizens' advisory committees, as well as most local groups which concern themselves with the schools, ordinarily are organized on a strictly non-partisan basis. Some of the major reasons for a separate, non-partisan organization for public education appear to be the avoidance of political party conflicts, freeing the schools of the possibility of having their welfare rise or fall with the fortunes or misfortunes of a particular political party, and reduction of competition among community political leaders with respect to public education—in short, to keep party politics apart from the schools. Most citizens will assert that party politics has no legitimate place in education; it is the scholars in the social sciences who are sometimes critical of this idea.

A political scientist recently pointed out that "freedom from politics has become a fundamental tenet in the educational credo" and then proceeded to argue against the appropriateness of the tenet (28). A sociologist has stated that "non-partisan elections appear to favor the well organized minority (usually the middle class) against the relatively unorganized mass" (37).

In our society there are no political parties, or influential organizations with recognized ties to political parties, which are known to be "anti-education" in their purposes and programs. This is probably another reason why citizens seldom look upon educational decisions as "political" decisions. There is the tendency for the citizen to think that public schools and politics constitute two quite different worlds and that in the interest of good education this situation should be maintained.

The Nature of Politics

There is no doubt that politics means different things to different people. As pointed out above, the average layman's concept of politics is restricted largely to the activities of partisan politicians. A dictionary definition of politics states that it is the science or art of political government. Political scientists, however, are in accord that politics in a democracy is importantly related to power and influence, both formal and informal, and that it is not restricted to political party activities. Lasswell stated that "The study of politics is the study of influence and the influential" (26). Bone wrote that ". . . politics is a struggle for power, the attempt to influence the course of public policy and public decision" (7). Politics, then, is the process of influencing, being influenced, and the translation of resulting pressures into public policies. It is equivalent to the broadest conception of public decision-making. Politics, as defined here, is public, not private, in the sense that its aim is the influencing of decisions relating to public issues within a political system.

All political systems exist to maintain control over policies, programs, and events which have an effect on people. In a democracy, the ideal political system is one which makes available the greatest benefits possible to all the people involved in the system. At the heart of the political system, of course, is government, but governmental structure is by no means the whole of it. An important aspect of the political system is the activity of influential individuals, groups of people, and the people as a whole as they strive to influence the nature of public policy and public programs. Politics, then, can be defined as the *relationships* among individuals and groups as they seek to exercise their power, whether formal or informal, in such a way as to influence the thinking and acting of other persons and groups concerning public problems and issues. It is evident, therefore, that politics is, or certainly may be, every citizen's business; it is also obvious that any person responsible for the administration of government which is to serve the people must of necessity be engaged in politics.

In a democratic society there are many avenues by which people may participate in political activity. Political parties represent only one avenue, and probably not the most important one, particularly at the local level of government. Other ways of participating in politics are voting, carrying on individual activities such as making personal contacts and writing letters to the editor, participating in organizations and associations which are organized to promote common interests, and developing informal relationships with friends and acquaintances for the purpose of influencing public decisions.

It is true that many citizens do not seem to have any real interest in the political process. Numbers of them do not even take advantage of the opportunity to vote at elections. On the other hand, if the citizen really wishes to influence public policy, he is not content merely to vote and to make incidental personal contacts; he joins with others who share his interests and points of view. There are, of course, numerous special interest groups which do not attempt to influence public policy, but the many which do are known as "pressure groups" because they pressure governmental bodies and agents to adopt and implement particular policies.

Perhaps because an occasional pressure group works hard for the narrowest kind of class gain, and may resort to questionable methods to achieve its ends, pressure groups generally enjoy a poor reputation. It is paradoxical that they should do so, for they are not only an indispensable but a desirable part of the political process in a democratic state. Like political parties, they form part of the essential machinery of democracy. They give the citizen the opportunity to make his influence felt, to let his voice be heard, to participate in the political process in a meaningful way (9).

Pressure groups are probably not as effective at the local level of government as at higher levels. Moreover, governmental representatives probably look upon some of them as "good" and some "bad," depending on the kind of influence they attempt to effectuate.

Are Schools Political?

Is the common belief that public education is not within the realm of politics fact or myth?

Local school districts are legal government entities created by the state to carry on the education function at the local level. They are governed by the laws of the state and have only such powers as are delegated to them. School districts are governed by boards of education, usually elected, which are responsible to the people of the local districts and of the state. Educational policies and programs must gain public acceptance and school budgets must be financed by public taxes. The schools are public—they belong to the people.

A large number of public policies of widespread interest must be determined in school districts. What shall be the major purposes and goals of the schools? What shall be the nature of the curriculum? Shall intellectual or social development of pupils receive priority? What quality of teacher personnel shall be attracted and retained? What new school buildings shall be built? How much tax money shall be allotted for the operation of the schools? In most school districts there will be divergent interests and points of view with respect to these policy questions. The decisions relating such questions are not merely technical ones to be made by the school professionals. They are major public policy decisions to be made by the citizens; more specifically, they are political decisions. In the making of these decisions there is the probability that many sorts of influences and pressures will be brought to bear upon those who have legal responsibility for legitimizing them. Minar (32) made clear the fact that the school district is a political system when he wrote:

Though seldom considered from this point of view, the suburban school district—in terms of function, structure, and legal standing—actually is, both formally and explicitly, a political system. It has a defined geographical jurisdiction, a specific range of purposes, a recognized public character, a constituency, mechanisms for the popular selection and control of decision-makers, a legislative body, an executive, a bureaucracy, and fiscal powers. Like other local political jurisdictions, it is established and run according to the laws of the state.

Not only are school districts political systems because of their responsibility for making decisions concerning the public policies for which they are responsible, but also because of their relationships to public policy issues which must legally be decided by other units of government. Some examples of such policy issues are those relating to general community planning: zoning, sewage disposal, types of taxes to be utilized, road and street construction, and the level of expenditures for non-educational services. Most citizens recognize these policies to be political matters, but the school district, in terms of its educational interests and goals, cannot isolate itself from them.

Influence and Policy

It is obvious that political influences may profoundly affect educational decisions relating to such policy matters as finance, programs, and services. Some of the sources of influences are internal to the school district, such as local organizations, influential individuals, elections, and the school bureaucracy, while others are external, such as the state and national governments, foundations, and voluntary bodies and individual prophets concerned with education. Some of these influences are formal and some are informal; but all are political, for they are attempting to shape decisions regarding public education. It seems absurd to think that decisions concerning the level of expenditure for public schools are any less political than those relating to the level of expenditures for social security or for public highways.

In summary, a quotation from Bailey appears to be a defensible answer to the question of whether public education is within the realm of politics. Bailey wrote:

> Education is one of the most thoroughly political enterprises in American life. More public money is spent for education than for any other single function of state and local government. No public school in America exists without state legislative sanction. All over the United States school boards are elected or appointed through a highly political process. The size, location, cost, looks, and facilities of school buildings are frequently matters of heated political controversy (3).

Regardless of the frequent disavowal that public education is associated with politics, it is a fact that local school administrators often play a central role as educational policy makers in their school districts. These administrators are not only well-qualified schoolmen but they are also influential policy determiners. Each of them has developed an understanding of the nature of the political environment of his school district. Each has the skills to organize individuals and groups, and to build coalitions of groups who are knowledgeable and concerned about establishing and maintaining appropriate educational policies and programs. Each influences the various persons and groups to exert efforts to these ends. In short, these administrators are engaged in political, and entirely legitimate, activities for the improvement of educational opportunity. Cunningham colorfully described the bureaucratic political behavior of some superintendents of schools when he stated that their skills "in the shifting and blending of pressures among the board of education members, among central staff assistants, among line personnel, when sharply honed, is a thing of beauty" (11).

Power and Decision-making

Since politics has been defined in terms of power, it is necessary to examine the nature of power and its relationship to public decision-making. Hunter wrote that "Power is a word that will be used to describe the acts of men going about the business of moving other men . . ." (22) while Dahl stated that "A has power over B to the extent that he can get B to do something that B would not otherwise do" (14). To the extent that a person influences others to behave in terms of his own interests and goals, he possesses social power. Although a single individual may be able to exert very great power, under usual circumstances power must be structured into clique, associational, or institutional patterns in order for it to be most effective.

Three major approaches or methods have been used to study power relationships in community decision-making. These are the positional, reputational, and decisional methods. The different methods of studying community power are based upon different basic assumptions as to the nature of power and its role in decision-making.

The positional method was the one most often employed before the 1950s (20, 27). It was based upon the assumption that incumbents of executive offices or positions in local government, institutions, and organizations were the key decision-makers of the community. This point of view is a "common sense" one generally accepted by lay citizens; however, the many studies of community power structures conducted during the last decade or so have raised serious questions about its validity.

High and Low Reputation

Hunter was the first among many to use the reputational method to study the structure of community power (22, 18, 30, 36, 39). Knowledgeable persons in various sectors of community affairs are asked to nominate persons who are influential in determining community decisions. The method is based upon the assumptions that men of power may not hold public offices, may not be recognized by typical citizens as decision-makers, but make de-

cisions about a wide range of problems, and may behave in a structural relationship with one another. Many criticisms have been directed at the reputational method (*13, 24, 35, 40*). Among these criticisms are: the method
does not identify men of actual power but only those of potential power;
it assumes an elite, monolithic power structure which may not exist; and
interviewees' perceptions of the meaning of power may vary widely. Of import to educators is the almost universal finding of reputational studies that
educational administrators are almost never ascribed a high-level reputation
for influencing any type of critical community decisions.

The decisional method of studying community power is most commonly
associated with Dahl and other political scientists (*15, 5, 34, 38*). The proponents of this method believe that the proper way to find out who exercises
power in decision-making is to make a study of the behavior of the actors
who are found to be involved in the actual process of making decisions. Particular decisions are selected for study. Data are obtained by direct observations, by interviews, and by the study of records, documents, and newspapers.

Proponents of the decisional method are critical of the assumptions
underlying the reputational method and, in turn, make assumptions that in
a democratic society there is a pluralism in decision-making and that realistic
bargaining among competitors takes place. It is thought that the actors in
decision-making vary from one type of decision area or scope to another. A
number of investigators have found that educational decisions usually are
not made by the same people who make municipal decisions. A more important role is attributed to the professional administrator by this view of
decision-making than by the reputational view. Adherents of the decisional
method also maintain that it is more productive of insights relative to the
processes of leadership and power than either the reputational or positional
methods. Critics of the decisional method maintain that it is too time consuming and expensive to be practical, that no satisfactory criteria have been
developed for the selection of issues nor for the time periods during which
the issues should be studied, and that it tends to ignore those unseen actors
who may not only be influencing the observed actors, but also may be responsible for preventing certain latent issues from rising to a level of controversy (*8, 21*).

Patterns of Leadership

The many studies which have been made of decision making in particular communities have revealed that there are always leaders and followers
but that the patterns of leadership appear to be extremely varied. A study of
Lansing, Michigan, indicated that the most powerful organizations in that
city were the Chamber of Commerce, the labor unions, the local newspaper,
the Board of Realtors, the service clubs, and other business organizations in
the order stated (*19*). In another city the situation might be very different.

No adequate typology for the comparative study of community decision-making and power structures has yet been developed (1); however, several analyses of the problem and suggestions for its solution have been reported (2, 8, 12, 17, 37). Until comparative studies have determined relationships which obtain between dependent community variables and decision-making, little generalized knowledge will be available for the use of administrators. There is promise that more progress will be made in developing understanding of these relationships during the next decade than was the case during the past one.

The many studies of power indicate that there are numerous sources of potential power that individuals may utilize. Among these are wealth, office or position, social. prestige, control over information, expertness and knowledge, persuasive talent, rate of upper mobility in occupation, family relationships, popularity, and length of residence in the local community. A person may have available several sources of power but fail to use his power because he does not care to do so, because he is ineffective in the employment of his power resources, or because he lacks certain resources which make it difficult or impossible for him to use the resources he does possess. Power, of course, implies sanctions, *i.e.*, rewards or punishments, which may be applied to obtain compliance. It is not always necessary to make actual use of sanctions; the threat of their use as perceived by individuals may be sufficient to cause them to behave as expected by the holder of power.

Almost all of the studies reported support the conclusion that the most powerful community leaders tend to be older persons, probably most of them over 50 years of age and a considerable percentage 60 or over. This may mean that in the typical community one can expect the decision-makers to be conservative and somewhat hesitant to approve the adoptions of new policies and methods.

Practically all of the many studies of community decision-making give no special attention to the role of administrators in relation to that of designated influentials. Jennings (23), however, has recently reported a comparative study of "top-level" administrators and "first-level" influentials in the cities of Atlanta, Georgia, and Raleigh, North Carolina. Considering both cities, the superintendent of schools in the city of Atlanta was the only one of 28 selected administrators who was also nominated as one of the 35 influentials. Among Jennings' conclusions were the following:

> First, the comparison of administrators from the two communities is more striking for the likeness shown than for the dissimilarities . . . . A second conclusion is that while there are some similarities within each community between administrators and the influentials, the differences are more pronounced. The influentials rank considerably higher than the administrators in socioeconomic status . . . . the administrators tend to be involved in fewer and sometimes different issues and to be performing different kinds of roles than the influentials

. . . . In Atlanta significant numbers of both administrators and influentials were key actors in the resolution of major issues, but when more than one issue was considered, the administrators had less overlap . . . . Thus the behavior of persons with the status of administrator diverges from that of persons with the status of influential. But this difference does not necessarily mean separate arenas of action, for certain behaviors are common to both status groupings, and close working relationships between the two groupings gives grounds for believing that interdependency develops between the two on many issues.

Implications for Administration

The foregoing discussion of politics, power, and influence in community decision-making has considerable relevance for the administration of public schools. There can be no doubt that the bringing of influence and pressures to bear upon issues in public education represents political activity with respect to both those who influence and those who are influenced. The public nature of education insures that it is a political realm and that those persons involved in its administration are politicians in the sense that they cannot escape being engaged in a political process. This process may be, and often is, largely non-partisan, but from time to time educational issues will take on definite partisan characteristics. It is well known that political party platforms ordinarily have important sections relating to education and it appears that these are being accorded increasing relative importance by the voters. A first implication, therefore, is that educational administrators should recognize the political nature of their jobs and strive continuously to develop the knowledges and skills to be effective in the political process. Furthermore they should be aware that the politics of education will inevitably be related, to some degree and at some times, to the politics of other public agencies in the school district.

The many case studies of community decision-making and power structures which have been reported do not provide validated generalizations of how status leaders and other influentials are related to the process of decision-making. Such generalizations will have to await the findings of comparative studies of various communities over a period of time. The case studies have, however, indicated that there is a comparatively small group of identifiable leaders who hold power over decisions in any community. They may or may not be public officials, known to typical citizens, influence a wide range of decisions or work in harmony with one another. These are the individuals, the men of power, who will have most to say about what decisions will be made and how they will be made. They will serve as referees over the demands of the welter of pressure groups which are to be found in school districts of considerable size. These influentials will most likely interest themselves in educational proposals which involve concepts of economics, finance, and relationships of government to private enterprise.

Administrator and Influential

Another implication, then, is that the educational administrator should be aware that there are influentials in the school district and make every effort to learn just who they are, what values motivate them, what power resources are available to them, and what the patterns of interaction are which may exist among them. He must develop knowledge of the personalities, organizations, and other power agents operating in the school district who have interests in educational policies because of the need to identify those aspects of the power structure which will be most effective in influencing the district to accept a desired decision. As far as possible, he must understand the critical behavioral norms of the individual leaders, or of the leadership group, and be careful to operate within the tolerances of these norms in the decision-making process. Suggestions for developing such understandings are to be found in the literature which has been cited. Not only does the superintendent of schools need to develop these understandings himself; it is also his responsibility to assist other leaders in the school organization to do so.

The educational administrator must not only know about the power structure but he must be able to make effective use of it in developing an environment in which the public schools will enjoy favorable attitudes and a satisfactory level of financial support. He will have to develop effective interaction patterns with all types of influentials in the district. Through these interaction patterns, he will win the confidence and support of certain influentials to the extent that they will actively support educational policy proposals. Also, he will identify likely opponents and attempt to neutralize their behavior as much as possible. The really big test of the leadership of the administrator is the extent to which he can gain consent and support from likely sources of opposition. In order to do this, it is often necessary to develop actual or potential widespread popular support, possibly through such school-oriented organizations as the PTA, to define the issue in non-controversial terms, and to take all precautions to assure that it will not be detrimental to any group of people. Citizens' committees composed of community influentials (including potential opponents) should be organized to study and advise on major educational issues. Fortunately, top influentials will often serve on such committees, one reason being that so doing is frequently considered to be a symbol of prestige by other influentials.

Expertise Carries Influence

It may be that decision-making in school districts is unique in nature because they have characteristics different from other arenas of government. Study of decision-making in school districts has been undertaken only recently and by a relatively small number of investigators. Although some of the studies describe decision-making in much the same terms as do the general studies (25, 39), others have suggested reasons why decision-making may be a different kind of process in school districts (6, 31, 37). One of these reasons may be that power in the school district is less closely tied to the economics of the local community than it is in the general municipality. Another may be that the role of the state is often dominant over the local school district with respect to educational policy; the federal government also appears to be playing an increasing role in local educational decisions. Also, there is probably no other area of local government where the administrator and his staff are credited with as high a degree of professional *expertise*. Minar stated that "the monolithic-pluralistic distinction as it is ordinarily used makes little sense in a substantially unifunctional, single 'scope' polity," such as the school district (31).

"Expertness" is probably the greatest power resource available to the school superintendent; consequently it behooves him continuously to develop specialized knowledge of concepts and practices of education as well as the ability to communicate this knowledge to others, and particularly to the influentials of the community. Because many school administrators do possess such *expertise*, the writer believes the idea that they are not influential in educational policy making is a myth. Both political scientists (28, 31) and sociologists (6, 37) who have given especial attention to decision-making or power structures in public education report that the educational administrator is, or can be, an influential decision-maker. Martin stated that "Nowhere else in American public life is the professional accorded greater deference than in the public school system" (28), and Minar stated that when the board of education and community leaders "trust and value *expertise*, he (the school superintendent) is likely to have much discretion and initiative right up to the highest policy level" (31). A part of the expectations for the role of persons who head community institutions is that they should continuously propose appropriate changes in institutional goals, programs, and services. Moreover, these executives, for example the superintendents of schools, do or should hold the self-image of a constant innovator of defensible policies and changes in the public schools. All this adds up to the inescapable conclusion that educational administrators do, indeed, live and work in a thoroughly political environment.

Notes

1. Adrian, C. R. (Ed.) *Social science and community action*. East Lansing, Mich.: Inst. for Commun. Develpm., Michigan State Univer., 1960.
2. Anton, T. J., Power, pluralism, and local politics. *Adm. Sci. Quar.*, 1963, 7, 425–547.

3. Bailey, S. K., Education is a political enterprise. *NEA J.*, 1964, *53*, 13.
4. Bailey, S. K., Frost, R. T., Marsh, P. E., & Wood, R. C. *Schoolmen and politics: A study of state aid to education in the Northeast.* Syracuse, NY: Syracuse Univer. Press, 1962.
5. Banfield, E. C., & Wilson, J. Q. *City politics.* Cambridge, Mass.: Harvard Univ. Press, 1963.
6. Bloomberg, W. Jr., & Sunshine, M. *Suburban power structures and public education.* Syracuse, NY: Syracuse Univ. Press, 1963.
7. Bone, H. A. *American politics and the party system.* (2nd ed.). New York: McGraw-Hill, 1955.
8. Bonjean, C. M., & Olson, D. M. Community leadership: Directions of research. *Adm. Science Quar.*, 1964, *9*, 278–300.
9. Booth, D. A. *A guide to local politics.* East Lansing, Mich.: Michigan State Univ., 1961.
10. Cahill, R. S., & Hencley, S. P. (Eds.) *The politics of education in the local community.* Danville, Ill.: Interstate Print. Publ., 1964.
11. Cunningham, L. L. Community power: Implications for education. In Cahill, R. S., & Hencley, S. P. (Eds.) *The politics of education in the local community.* Danville, Ill.: Interstate Print. Publ., 1964, 27–50.
12. Dahl, R. A. The analysis of influence in local communities. In Adrian, C. R. (Ed.) *Social science and community action.* East Lansing, Mich.: Inst. for Commun. Develpm., Michigan State Univer., 1960.
13. Dahl, R. A. A critique of the ruling elite model. *Amer. pol. Sci. Rev.*, 1958, *52*, 463–469.
14. Dahl, R. A. The concept of power. *Behav. Sci.*, 1957, *2*, 202–203.
15. Dahl, R. A. *Who governs?* New Haven, Conn.: Yale Univer. Press, 1961.
16. Eliot, T. H. Toward an understanding of public school politics. *Amer. pol. Sci. Rev.*, 1959, *52*, 1032, 1043, 1046–51. (Reprinted in *Teach. Coll. Rec.*, 1960, *62*, 118–132.)
17. Fisher, S. *Community-power studies: A critique. Soc. Res.*, 1962, *29*, 449–466.
18. Form, W. H., & D'Antonio, W. V. Integration and cleavage among community influentials in two border cities. *Amer. soc. Rev.*, 1959, *24*, 804–814.
19. Form, W. H., & Sauer, W. L. *Community influentials in a middle-sized city.* East Lansing, Mich.: Inst. for Commun. Develpm. Serv., Michigan State Univer., 1960.
20. Hollingshead, A. B. *Elmtown's Youth.* New York: Wiley, 1949.
21. Hunter, F. *Adm. Sci. Quar.*, 1962, *6*, 517–519.
22. Hunter, F. *Community power structure.* Chapel Hill: Univer. No. Carolina Press, 1953.
23. Jennings, M. K. Public administrators and community decision-making. *Adm. Sci. Quart.*, 1963, *8*, 18–43.
24. Kaufman, H., & Jones, V. The mystery of power. *Public Adm. Rev.*, 1954, *14*, 205–212.
25. Kimbrough, R. B. *Political power and educational decision-making.* Chicago: Rand McNally, 1964.
26. Lasswell, H. D. *Politics.* New York: Whittlesey House, 1936.
27. Lynd, R. S., & Lynd, Helen Merrell. *Middletown in transition.* New York: Harcourt, Brace, 1937.
28. Martin, R. C. *Government and the suburban school.* Syracuse, NY: Syracuse Univ. Press, 1962.
29. Masters, N. A., Salisbury, R. H., & Eliot, T. H. *State politics and the public schools.* New York: Knopf, 1964.

30. Miller, D. C. Industry and community power structure: A comparative study of an American and English city. *Amer. soc. Rev.*, 1958, 23, 9–15.
31. Minar, D. W. Community characteristics, conflict, and power structures. In Cahill, R. S., & Hencley, S. P. (Eds.) *The politics of education in the local community.* Danville, Ill.: Interstate Print. Publ., 1964, 125–143.
32. Minar, D. W. School, community, and politics in suburban areas. In Chandler, B. J., Stiles, L. J., & Kitsuse, J. I. (Eds.) *Education in urban society.* New York: Dodd, Mead, 1962. 90–104.
33. Monypenny, P. A political analysis of structures for educational policy making. In McLure, W. P., & Miller, V. (Eds.) *Government of public education for adequate policy making.* Urbana, Ill.: Bur. Educ. Res., Univ. of Illinois, 1960. 1–21.
34. Polsby, N. W. *Community power and political theory.* New Haven, Conn.: Yale Univer. Press, 1963.
35. Polsby, N. W. The sociology of community powers: A reassessment. *Social forces,* 1959, 37, 232–236.
36. Presthus, R. *Men at the top: A study in community power.* New York: Oxford Univer. Press, 1964.
37. Rossi, P. H. Theory, research, and practice in community organization. In Adrian, C. R. (Ed.) *Social science and community action.* East Lansing, Mich.: Inst. for Commun. Develpm., Michigan State Univer., 1960, 9–24.
38. Sayre, W., & Kaufman, H. *Governing New York City.* New York: Russell Sage Found., 1960.
39. Thometz, Carol E. *The decision-makers: The power structure of Dallas.* Dallas, Tex.: Sth. Methodist Univer. Press, 1963.
40. Wolfinger, R. E. Reputation and reality in the study of community power. *Amer. soc. Rev.*, 1960, 25, 636–644.

19 | New Concepts in Educational Administration

John Walton

In this article, John Walton describes the job of the educational administrator in terms of functions. He takes the position that these may be delineated in terms of (1) management elements, (2) goal identification, and (3) instructional generalism. The differences in expectations implied by these functions suggest to the student in educational administration not only the necessity of assessing the various expectations but also the crucial need for developing a means to reconcile the varying expectations within and among the several publics with which he must deal.

It is a truism to say that educational administration is influenced by general social and intellectual developments. But it should be said, lest those of us who are forced to witness rather sudden and sharp changes in the conduct of education should stand by puzzled and uncomprehending. The far-reaching changes occurring today in both education and administration are largely the result of changes in our highly corporate and technological society. For example, less than a century ago, no society could support more than a small percentage of highly educated people; today, in most societies highly educated men and women are the central productive resource. This changed condition has brought on an educational revolution. Similarly, but more silently, a revolution has been going on in administration; our highly organized society demands an elaborate administrative machinery and numerous capable personnel to maintain its institutions, including those devoted to education. It is no accident that the Weberian model of bureaucracy continues to fascinate us, that organization theory is a leading topic in the social sciences, and that administrative theory is now given recognition in the curriculum for the preparation of educational administrators. From all this activity, new and clearer ideas and concepts about educational administration are emerging. It is about some of these that I want to talk today.

First, however, I think we should remember that most of us in education came out of a simpler age. Most, if not all, of us have been teachers, and

John Walton, "New Concepts in Educational Administration," *Canadian Education and Research Digest*, II (September, 1962), 205–211. Reprinted by permission.

our professional preparation has been that of teachers. I have no intention of introducing here the problem of what kind of training educational administrators should have; rather, I want only to point out that most educational administrators who devote full time to administration in education were trained primarily as teachers and continue to lament the fact that their present assignments leave little or no time for teaching. We may well ask: Why should they be doing one job when they say they prefer another, especially since teachers are desperately needed? The answer, I think, lies in our continued reluctance to admit that the modern educational organization, with its complexity and its crucial role in society, demands a full-time administrative class. Once we are willing to recognize the importance of administration in education, there will be less ambivalence about the job and less nostalgia, real or pretended, for the classroom.

Let us now look at the kinds of responsibilities that are thrust upon the modern educational administrator. Obviously, there are three major ones. First, he is required to maintain the organization so that formal education can be carried on. To do this, he must be a manager and engage in the traditional and modern managerial activities. It would be absurd to think that the highly complex educational organization of today can be maintained without powerful managers. Second, the educational administrator must be able to discern the present and future educational needs of society. To do this, he must look outside the organization and be able to appraise the significance of social change for overall educational policy. And, third, he must deal intimately with the substantive and specialized activities of educational organizations, with curriculum and instruction.

The mere mention of these responsibilities stirs up a great many questions. Where, for example, does the primary responsibility lie? Is the educational administrator mainly a manager, whose chief task is to keep the organization running smoothly? Is he primarily a setter of goals and purposes? Or is he now, as in a simpler age, a schoolman, a "principal-teacher," whose distinctive abilities lie in the field of instruction? He is, in some sense, all three. What is involved in these three roles, individually and collectively, will be described briefly in the discussion that follows.

The most obvious and, perhaps, the most urgent task of the educational administrator is management. This aspect of school administration has been neglected, and, in fact, denigrated in recent years. However, today, it is the subject of a new concern, particularly as the demands of modern organizations for administrators become more insistent. Bureaucracy seems to have a curious fascination, despite the fashionable opposition to it. There seems to be a growing realization that the formal organization, which provides the means and setting for education, requires full-time administrators. Also, since the educational organizations enter into complex relations with other social institutions, administration becomes more crucial and more strategic.

What, precisely, is management in educational organizations? I think that it is not unlike management in other organizations, although it is forced to adjust to the kind of substantive activities that are carried on. The schools, like all organizations, must be staffed; the fact that they employ professional personnel does not distinguish them from a vast number of other organizations, such as hospitals, research institutions, and art museums. The schools must have buildings, buses, and books; the administrator has an inescapable responsibility for obtaining them. If he does not want to assume this responsibility, he should not become an administrator. The schools must have material and moral support; the educational administrator has a major responsibility for public relations. The varied activities within the school must be directed in such a way that they do not conflict with one another, and this calls for decision-making under severe pressures of time; the administrator who cannot make decisions on the basis of incomplete information and assume responsibility for them is miscast. These are all very general and familiar duties, but they comprise a great part of the administrator's job. Much of this work is routine, much appears to be trivial, but it represents the paradox of the trivial becoming important. Also, since much of the managerial function is strategic, we need more vigorous, tough and effective men in administrative positions.

There are some new developments in the managerial aspects of educational administration. I do not need to review here the classical literature on administration as management; most of us are familiar with *Papers on the Science of Administration*, including essays by Gulick, Urwick, Fayol, Mooney, and others; with Frederick W. Taylor and the scientific management movement; with the Hawthorne experiments; and with principles of budgeting and control. All these efforts have added to our knowledge of administration, but as scholarship moves on, new developments bring new knowledge and new problems. One of the most interesting developments today is the experimentation with the machine as a decision-maker. Herbert A. Simon, in his *The New Science of Management Decision* (Harper and Brothers, 1960), argues that modern computers will eventually supplant human beings in making innumerable routine and repetitive decisions. Even now, computers are preparing airline schedules, turning out payrolls, registering students in our mammoth universities, and diagnosing diseases. They can execute any sequence of operations for which precise directions can be written, and they can execute them more reliably than human beings. We can expect a computer revolution in organizations, including educational organizations.

Since there seems to be no practical limits to the number of variables and their myriad interrelationships that can be handled by the computers, they can lead to the centralization of routine and repetitive decision-making. They make possible larger and more centralized organizations; we shall have to decide what aspects of our work we want to become standardized and transferred to higher and higher echelons of administration. For example, through the use of computers, schedules for all the high school students in Canada can be made out within a few minutes; and, by modern means of communication, transmitted to all the schools in due time. Of course, the schools would have to feed into the computer all relevant information.

This prospect for the use of the machine is the source of much fantasy and fear. We hear predictions of monstrous automata, or robots and mechanical brains that may usurp the dominion man has had over the living things on the earth. It is comforting to know that, for the present, at least, the computers cannot cope with unprecedented problems for which programs have not been written. Nor can they do creative thinking. However, we may be on the very rim of a breakthrough; Simon prophesies that machines will be able to make non-programmed organizational decisions.

Enough of management. Let us now look at the second major responsibility of administrators—the discernment of the goals and purposes of the educational organization. Here, I shall present my own dogma rather than that of others. Briefly, it is as follows: If we define overall policy as goals and purposes, a clear distinction can be made, both theoretically and practically, between policymaking and the execution of policy. Furthermore, in my theory, the administrator is viewed, not as an innovator or reformer, but rather as the executor of accepted policies, and as the patient and deliberate reader of the public will and needs for education. He may be the translator of society's needs into organizational purposes, but he does not impose his will on the educational organization. In one respect, the educational administrator is conservative; he must see to it that the educational organization does not abandon purposes that are not spectacular or urgent—but nonetheless necessary—for those that are more dramatic and popular. On the other hand, he must preside at the councils which go through the solemn business of modifying the purposes of educational organizations in the matrix of social conflict and clashing interests. The educational administrator is not the policy-maker, either deliberately or inadvertently through the acts of administration. However, I believe that the distinction between administration and policy-making can be maintained through a value-fact schema, which would allow value or purpose commitments to remain constant under a series of factual decisions which are made in light of the continuing value commitment. (See my *Administration and Policy-making in Education*, The Johns Hopkins Press, 1959; p. 50.) Also, I think there is evidence from recent events in American education. The administrators of American schools were not in the forefront of the recent change to a more academic emphasis, nor are they the ones with suggestions about the school's responsibility for the unskilled unemployed youth who may become the continuing responsibility of the schools, as Conant suggests in his *Slums and Suburbs*.

It would be less than fair not to remind you again that the vast preponderance of opinion in both public and educational administration stands firmly against my views. There is also impressive philosophical opinion against the means-ends schema that provides the basis of the separation of functions theory. But I can give a concrete illustration that I think will make both clear and plausible my ideas. One of the purposes of the educational organization is to teach the young to read. Now every educational administrator accepts this purpose, this end, of the organization, once and for all, at some time before he assumes his position. This decision does not have to be made again; it continues in force; and, in the light of it, factual or purely administrative decisions are made; e.g., the adoption of a method of teaching reading. A rather curious, partial, and somewhat left-handed support for this view is found in Charles E. Lindbloom's "The Science of 'Muddling Through' " (*Public Administration Review*, Vol. 19; pp. 79–88 [1959]); he says that since goals—and I think he must mean new or modified goals—can be only dimly perceived and that one cannot accurately forecast their preference in long-range situations that are different from the present ones, changes in goals are only incrementally different from those already adopted. Although I am not sure of all the implications and I have many differences in both ideas and vocabulary, I think Lindbloom's thesis has great relevance for the study of administration.

The third and final responsibility of the educational administrator lies in the area of instruction, the intrinsic activity of the educational organization. In addition to his managerial responsibility, and his ambiguous role in the determination of overall educational policy, he must make innumerable decisions involving a great variety of technical and professional matters. He may, for example, be responsible for the adoption of teaching methods, and the new mathematics curriculum, or the employment of a new physics teacher. He cannot absolve himself of the responsibility for the results. Herein lies one of the most troublesome issues of our time—the management of organizations devoted to professional, technical, and creative pursuits. The administrator must be good at management and make decisions about a variety of highly technical matters, about which he can know little. In the words of Sir Eric Ashby ("The Administrator: Bottleneck or Pump," in *Daedalus* for Spring, 1962; pp. 264–278):

> The secret of good administration (that is, of administration which benefits that sector of society which the administrator serves), lies not in the administrator's vast and exact knowledge, but in his skill at navigating areas of ignorance (p. 269).

We no longer expect the educational administrator to be an expert in all the arts and sciences about which he has to make decisions. How then can he make intelligent choices? I think that he should have a general familiarity with the technical system within the organization; that is, with education in all its aspects, and he should be able to use the minds of other men. Both are difficult and rare qualities, and more attention should be given to their cultivation. There are brilliant specialists in all educational organizations who never acquire a sense of the whole enterprise, of its varied activities and their interrelationships, nor do they have good judgment in assessing the opinions of men in other specializations. They have neither the abilities nor the sympathies required of good administrators.

In this age of specialization, we have been reluctant to admit that any kind of "generalist" knowledge has any real intellectual standing, and administrators in educational organizations, facing the scorn of narrow specialists, have often acquired and practiced a specialty to the detriment of both administration and their special field.

This quality of "generalism" may be a relatively new concept. Certainly, it is not the same as the idea of universal knowledge that was once associated with administration; the "principal-teacher" was expected to know more about the different specialties than the specialists themselves. Nor is it just common sense, good judgment, and decisiveness in their everyday employment. Rather, I view it as the ability to draw from all fields of specialized knowledge, either directly or through the use of interpreters, that information which is relevant to the making of intelligent decisions about the role of the various specialties within the organization.

This analysis of the administrator's job has been, I fear, rather abstract and over-simplified. We have viewed administration as management; and, in addition to attempting to restore prestige to this aspect of administration, we have hinted at some new developments in organization through the use of the computers in decision-making. We have attempted to reduce the ambiguity in the policy-making-administration dilemma, by a theoretical distinction. And we have introduced a new concept of "generalism" which seems requisite to making decisions about a variety of specializations. Now, the administrator, as he faces myriad problems, would be unwise to attempt to classify them in one of the three categories of responsibilities; the kinds of problems do not correspond to the kinds of responsibilities. However, in the solution of all problems, I think the administrator asks the following three questions; and, perhaps, in the following order:

1. How will my decision affect the organization, *qua* organization?
2. How does it correspond to the accepted purposes of the organization?
3. Is it based on accurate knowledge?

The hierarchy of these questions is disturbing and represents one of the greatest threats of a highly corporate society: the possibility that the requirements of organization will take precedence over all other considerations. A smoothly-running organization is *prima facie*, but often spurious, evidence of administrative success. To be sure, chaos and collapse are genuine failure, but the administration may be extremely successful if it only barely maintains the organization and accomplishes well its purposes. There is no foreordained exact correspondence between good educational practice, for example, and good organization, *per se*. Since education is institutionalized, organization is necessary and must be maintained. But beyond this, it may be necessary to sacrifice purely organizational excellence for the attainment of excellent education.

20 | Four Definitions of Your Job

Van Miller

Van Miller, in the following article, presents a classification of job definitions for the educational administrator. Instead of relating this classification to functions as was done in the article by Walton, Miller bases his four definitions on the scope of responsibility. In describing jobs as (1) inclusive, (2) exclusive or restrictive, (3) the division of labor or standardized type, and (4) the integrative or relational type, the author provides the student of educational administration with a means of identifying and understanding factors necessary in the development of his own concept of the job.

The task of defining the school administrator's job has changed considerably during the past fifteen years. A common concern has developed among the most knowledgeable, responsible educators for adequately defining the nature of school administration as a basis for communication and collaboration.

School district reorganization is dramatically changing the proportion of isolated districts served by single or part-time administrators; newcomers are more frequently starting their careers as staff members of other administrators. Conurbanization (predicted to attract ninety percent of the population into urban strips) will bring school administrators into closer relationships. They will be unofficial "team-mates," although each may serve a separate district. Even now, the complexities of these close relationships are evident in urban or metropolitan area programs for juvenile delinquency, minority groups, special education for exceptional children, adult education, community or junior colleges, and urgently needed technical-vocational education. At the same time, the Cooperative Project on Educational Administration, the Committee for the Advancement of School Administration, the Project on Staff Utilization, the University Council for Education Administration, and corresponding developments are seeking to define the nature of school administration.

Periodically, some group or individual has attempted to define the school administrator's job. These definitions have taken such forms as *the*

Van Miller, "Four Definitions of Your Job," *Overview*, I (November, 1960), 50–51. Buttenheim Publishing Corp. Reprinted by permission.

inclusive type, the exclusive or restrictive type, the division of labor or standardized type, the integrative or relational type.

The *inclusive* definition has been most common. Any or all of the responsibilities or characteristics of school administration are included. The definition grew virtually as school administration grew. As the small three-R school took on new functions and expanded, so did the administrator's job. Given the wide variety of situations and people in administration, a massive and impressive list of responsibilities was easy to come by. The inclusive definition had its golden age of small districts when the single administrator was everything to everyone, although he must have wondered how much of *anything* he was to anyone! He could not be certain which competence or attribute got—or perhaps lost—him the job.

The inclusive definition probably reached its ultimate in a list of personal characteristics and professional responsibilities drawn up by the National Conference of Professors of Educational Administration at their Madison, Wisconsin, meeting in the late forties. It was a glorious list calling for more than any human being could be or do. But, as Dwight Waldo asked in *The Administrative State*, can the administrator be a specialist of "things-in-general"? On reflection it would seem that an all-inclusive list describes the responsibility and character for which administration is accountable, rather than describing what the administrator must be and do.

The *excluding* or *restrictive* definition attempts to correct a list that has become too general and too all-inclusive. Some of this was a reaction to progressive education (especially to life adjustment education). Some of it came from tax conservatives who felt there was a limit to what they could support. Some came from fundamentalists who wanted to restrict the school to narrower, traditional tasks in the hope that this would maintain quality in the face of booming enrollments and new responsibilities. Restrictive definitions placed the emphasis on school-*keeping*, rather than on school-*using.*

A current version of the restrictive definition separates administration from policy-making. Here the administrator is a managerial chore boy for the public; educational leadership is left undefined, free-floating, or non-existent.

The *division of labor* or *standardized* type represents another approach to correcting errors in the all-inclusive definition. However, it has its own difficulties. It implies that what a school is and what education is must be standardized apart from the community. (Hence, the community must also be standardized as to its size, its people, its purposes, and its cultural-socio-economic activities.)

In order to relate special positions to the field, the definition of each is developed by a survey of those who hold it. Given the variety of situations and people in principalships, directorships, and supervisory positions, the result is likely to be a new all-inclusive list. The composite of administrative definitions in a school system could be even more confused and overlapping than in the inclusive definition of school administration. The desirable competencies and characteristics for today's various positions seem to be much more similar than different. If the standardized definition is used, more attention must be given to identifying differences and to relating these differences to each other. (Anyone assigning jobs must also relate the jobs to each other.) At present, this particular type of definition has been directed mostly to newcomers in school administration; it tells them how to get started and leaves further development to their own experience.

During the past fifteen years work on the *integrative* or *relational* type of definition has begun. Administrators, scholars, and professors of school administration are phrasing it not for novices but for each other. It provides the common basis for theory, experimentation, and research and for selection and preparation of administrative personnel. When properly worked out, it should provide the basis for helping the nation to use—not just keep—educational institutions.

In working out this type of definition it is not the multiplicity of school tasks that is important; it is the attempt to find a unifying pattern. Work on this definition is really a search for the specialist who integrates and stimulates education within the institution and with the supporting community.

A key characteristic of central administration is its integrative nature. Some define it as the point at which pressures are resolved so that active but conflicting interests can move forward together. Others call it the point at which interests and resources are identified and organized to bear upon objectives which must also be identified and arranged in order. Ability to comprehend and communicate an overview of the whole enterprise would certainly be a key feature in the integrative definition. This comprehension must bear on what the times and context can do to education and what education can do to the times and the context.

The basic competence is a shorthand system (a sampling of representative clues) and a staff to provide it. Whether statistical tables, graphic representation, or other form, the administrator needs a kind of chart room to show him what is going on and with what effects. Current facts must be available in descriptive form and in terms of relationships from which inferences can be drawn. The rare administrator in the small school district can walk around his district and quickly see what he needs. But the large urban school system needs its own chart and staff room similar to that of the top command of a military enterprise or of the board of directors of a big corporation.

A sense of basic purpose of education would be a second element in the integrative definition. Basic purpose balances and arranges special purposes, encourages coalition, and motivates to action those who have special purposes. Evaluation is also necessary. Energizing and stimulating are other elements in the integrative definition.

Comprehending the overview, ordering values and purposes, signaling and accomplishing action all depend on understanding and skill in interaction systems. The administrator must know how to design and use organization. He must know the nature of communication systems and how to enhance their effectiveness.

Free interpretation of the work of several current writers leads us to a description of the integrative type of definition as *the development, management, and maintenance of decision-making and action-taking.* Three classes of decisions and actions have been identified:

> Those pertaining to goals and purposes in the policy-making and policy-interpreting realm; called *creative* or *initiative* decisions.
>
> Those pertaining to operation; called *intermediary* decisions, *authoritative* decisions, the passing along of orders and commands.
>
> Those pertaining to adjustments within the system and adjustments of the system to the community context; called *appellate* in that they arise most frequently through the complaints of subordinates. The three classes must be integrated through the overview.

Such a definition recognizes that many tasks are done: financial and business management; management of physical facilities and educational material; ordering of relationships through schedule-making, form construction, laying out of routes; program development and appraisal; internal relations with staff or students; and external relations with public, state authorities, the profession at large. These functions operate everywhere and represent different patterns of staff organization (depending upon the situation and the task). It is entirely possible that they may provide the basis for differentiation in the organization of a team of administrators.

As the definition of the school administrator's job is worked out, the initial experience and orientation to administration will absorb elements of the integrative definition of school administration. There will doubtless be many more specialist roles in functional areas of school administration. The chief administrator or the central administrative staff will ultimately be specialists in the integrative functions; but such personnel will have attained status in administration not by being jacks-of-all-trades but by having competence in at least one or more of the aforementioned areas. Personnel selection and training will involve a much closer interrelationship of training institutes and school systems, and conceivably, provide the basis for studying top personnel in other recognized professions.

Chapter Seven

Educational Administration: Organization

The study of organization in education, as in other fields, is undertaken to determine the manner in which a group of people and materials are brought together to achieve some purpose as well as to assess the effectiveness of the given combination. In such a consideration four factors are primary: (1) the purposes of the organization, (2) its structural characteristics, (3) the behavior of its members, and (4) the efficiency of the organization.

Purposes of the organization devoted to public education are many and varied. As is true with any social institution, and especially one subject to close "local control," the tides of social change have caused attitudes pertaining to purposes of educational institutions to ebb and flow. Formal statements and pronouncements have been many and have emanated from widely divergent sources, from the Educational Policies Commission to small local pressure groups in a given school district or neighborhood. Each statement or attitude has carried with it implications for the way in which schools are to be organized.

The basic structural arrangement of educational organization is that of the governing levels. These are traditionally thought of in terms of local, state, and national levels. Each of these has attached to it a set of purposes, and concerns for the structural, behavioral, and efficiency aspects mentioned above. Thus, regardless of the level being considered, the same organizational concerns are present although viewed from a different perspective.

Other structural variations worthy of consideration are those related to plans of vertical organization, i.e., what kind of grade or school unit divisions should be developed for a given system? Should these be elementary, junior high, and senior high schools; elementary and secondary; or primary, intermediate, and secondary?

The issue of the appropriate degree of centralization of authority and control has marked structural implications for educational organization. Again this concept is manifest in questions of purpose as well as in control or governing levels of educational organization.

The third major factor to be considered in educational organization is the behavioral dimension. Here, the relationships of people within the organization are examined. Concepts relating to formal and informal organization, line and staff relationships, authority and responsibility, rewards and sanctions, communications, job expectations, and morale may be considered. In this aspect of organization the interaction of the job and the man is demonstrated.

Organizational efficiency, the fourth major factor to be considered, is of prime importance to educational administrators. Too often, however, it is considered in an excessively narrow frame of reference and prior to other decisions. Consequently, the editors broach the subject only after an examination of purpose, and a discussion of structural and behavioral aspects. It is the contention of the editors that, fundamentally, organization refers to the arrangements that are made to bring institutional structure and human behavior together to achieve a given purpose. Efficiency or effectiveness of organization results when optimum use is made both of structure and of the people who make up the organization. Thus, in considering the importance of an understanding of organization we give major emphasis to the concepts of structure and human behavior, and the mechanisms that are used to relate them to promote efficiency in achieving the purpose of the enterprise.

The challenge of organization to the individual administrator is two-fold: (1) to provide for the constant maturation of his conceptualization of organization; and (2) to assure the continued examination of the four major factors of organization. To meet the first challenge the educational administrator will find it imperative that his concept of educational organization be developed in a way consistent with his own philosophy and the philosophy of those with whom he works. To meet the second challenge he must further understand that institutional purposes are affected by the other three major factors (structure, behavior, and efficiency) involved in organization, so that there is a resultant need for continued reorganization in order to approach optimum efficiency. Thus organizational modification is constant and tends to be cyclical.

To maintain the effectiveness of the educational organization the administrator must be sensitive to societal changes and shifts and be able to understand them and their implications for the four dimensions of organization; he must also be able to initiate appropriate organizational modification and to effect the leadership necessary to implement and incorporate the changes in the total organization.

21 | Organizing for Reform in Big-City Schools

Daniel U. Levine

Organization is purposive. Administrative organization in education may well demonstrate the utility of a basic tenet of modern architecture: form follows function. In the following article Levine proposes a rationale for this concept as he examines the necessity for reform of urban schools and then describes organizational features required to meet this purpose.

Despairing over an apparent inability to correct the serious dysfunctions which permeate the big-city schools, a number of individuals and groups have expressed serious doubt that the public schools are capable of undertaking the profound reforms which would enable them to provide an adequate education for the disadvantaged youth of the big cities. Several of these observers, as a consequence, have recommended the establishment and support of a competing network of nonpublic schools which might be less resistant to change than are the public schools.[1] Most educators have not taken this recommendation very seriously, if, indeed, they have been aware of it at all.

Now, however, with the recent publication of the report on "The Disadvantaged Poor: Education and Employment" by the task force on economic growth and opportunity of the generally conservative United States Chamber of Commerce, it is no longer so easy to ignore this recommendation and the reasoning behind it. For the task force, as noted in an advance summary in *Education U.S.A.*, concluded that because "the present institutional structure in education may not be the best way to organize it," the government should "consider continuing to finance education for all children—but that it offer them, as an alternative to public education, financial support for private education up to the amount of the average expenditure in local public schools."[2]

We should not take lightly the opinion of respected and knowledgeable observers who are pessimistic about the possibility of significantly reforming present educational patterns in the big cities, but at the same time we are

Daniel U. Levine, "Organizing for Reform in Big-City Schools," *Phi Delta Kappan* 48, No. 7 (March, 1967), 311–315. Reprinted by permission.

justified in being equally skeptical about proposals which are likely to create as many problems as they solve. More specifically, we would do well to withhold judgment on whether the big-city schools can be significantly reformed until a really meaningful attempt has been made to revitalize education in the big-city districts. No such effort has yet been made anywhere in the United States.

Clearly, any potentially effective plan for reforming education as it is practiced in the big cities would have to be many-faceted. One of its central components would have to be a program of teacher retraining far larger than has heretofore been imagined. Nor could such a plan of reform begin to be adequate unless it provided for administrator training and retraining on a scale much more massive than now envisioned in any of our school districts and universities. Similarly, an equally indispensable element would be a set of arrangements to ensure that members of boards of education acquire an adequate understanding of where and why the big-city schools are in such deep trouble. The remainder of this paper is concerned primarily with how this latter goal might be achieved.

A school board determined to come to grips with the functional inadequacies and mismanagement which now characterize the big-city school districts could move almost at once to introduce a system for uncovering and highlighting information without which the system can never operate effectively. More concretely, among the many steps a board might take, one in particular has great promise for bringing about significant and continuing improvement in the big-city schools. A department of inspections should be created outside regular administrative channels to systematically collect information on educational conditions in the big-city district. The fact that blatantly dysfunctional situations in the big cities often go unrecognized by officials responsible for the adequacy of the educational program means that neither the superintendent nor board members can rely on traditional channels for identifying and correcting points of weakness in the schools. The present grievance system, for one thing, is likely to be concerned primarily with issues on which an individual feels personally mistreated, whereas many if not most dysfunctional situations involve more general failings on which individuals are less willing to register complaints. Second, grievance procedures as defined here use present channels through which complaints are considered first at the local level where many can be quickly solved and then are directed in prescribed steps up the administrative hierarchy only if the persons involved are unable to work them out. The educational problems in the big cities are too serious, however, to rely on procedures which require individuals to communicate their feelings to their superiors in the organization, for as William G. Scott points out in his book on *The Management of Conflict:*

The difficulty with many formal programs of redress is that their values and the values of the organization in which they function are not perceived by participants as different. This is why a grin is often provoked when a person is told he can go over his superior's head if he has a problem. He is telling you that he does not believe it will do him any good. . . .[3]

Because most people are aware that major inspections in the armed forces are conducted by inspectors from autonomous units, a good deal of hesitation can be expected concerning the wisdom of adapting a "military" procedure to a public school system. In my opinion objections based solely on such grounds would be gratuitous. For one thing, the rationale behind the pattern of inspections in the armed forces has become increasingly applicable to schools in the great cities: In both cases the survival of society may depend on whether the organization is functioning adequately. In addition, arrangements for systematic and penetrating inspections are characteristic of other kinds of organizations as well as the military. Thus many national firms, particularly those which operate through local franchises, depend on unannounced but regular inspections to acquire feedback on organizational problems. Similarly, the Catholic Church, as Scott points out, has long made use of such arrangements:

> . . . settlement of disputes . . . is accomplished through the function of visitation. The best way to describe the "visitor" is as an ecclesiastical inspector general. Canon law requires the performance of this activity as a check on the temporal and spiritual activities of parishes and religious communities.[4]

Recommending an inspection system does not imply that schools can simply borrow all procedures which may be appropriate in business, religions, or military organizations. What the recommendation does imply is that many school districts are very large organizations susceptible to the same kinds of dysfunctions as are other large organizations, and that the ways problems related to size, complexity, and data collection are handled in other fields are worth the consideration of the educator.

It should also be kept in mind that school districts already are subject to inspections conducted by state departments of education as well as regional accrediting associations, but these arrangements simply do not supply the kinds of information and analysis that need to be acquired within the local system itself. The state departments almost everywhere are too short of staff to delve very deeply into local situations, particularly in the large cities in which they are reluctant to interfere. Regional accrediting procedures, for their part, are concerned almost entirely with education at the secondary level. While the regional associations perform a very useful and important function, they, too, do not throw sufficient light on the basic educational problems in the big cities. In their annual 1963 reports to the North Central Association of Colleges and Secondary Schools, for example, all but one of Chicago's 39 secondary school principals marked "yes" in response to the question, "In your opinion, do you have an adequate number of teachers employed to provide effective instruction, direction of extra-class activities, counseling, and other educational services?," and the lone dissenter remarked only that a vacated assistant principal's position had not yet been filled.

To operate most effectively, the department of inspections should consist of two separate units. Personnel in both units would have the authority to probe as deeply as necessary into whatever situations they were currently investigating. Personnel in one unit would periodically visit the schools as well as the central office units which provide supporting services to the schools in order to determine where and why the organization is functioning less effectively than it should. Most of these visits would follow a regular schedule, but some of them would be unannounced and un-expected. Personnel in the second unit would investigate specific complaints and reports of mismanagement arising either within or outside the organiza-tion. The processing of grievances in this unit would differ from normal grievance procedures in that complaints to the department of inspections would be handled outside regular channels which lead up through the ad-ministrative hierarchy to the superintendent and his staff.

The importance of providing opportunities to express grievances and have them investigated independently of channels now existing in the ad-ministrative hierarchy cannot be overemphasized. Although the concept of an independent official with the authority to investigate and take action when an individual or group believes a government organization to be functioning improperly is still somewhat novel in the United States, such inspectors have become a valued element in social and political life in several Scandanavian countries, and, more recently, in England. Under the name *ombudsman*, such officials have functioned in Sweden since 1809. In general terms, the *ombudsman* investigates complaints to determine whether a citizen has been done an injustice by a government official, and in one way or another takes steps to prosecute offenders or otherwise correct mistreat-ment where it does exist. The possibility of instituting such a system to guard the rights of citizens in our increasingly impersonal society has been receiving a good deal of attention in recent years, and the first American *ombudsman* is now serving a suburban community in the New York area.

The grievance-handling unit here being proposed would differ from the office of the *ombudsman* in that it would process complaints originating within the organization as well as from the public served, and it would be established as much or more to bring needed information to the attention of school board members and (eventually) central office executives as to correct injustices done to individuals. This need to systematically acquire and bring to light information which is presently submerged and repressed within the labyrinth of the large city school district has been documented in Joseph Pois' book on the Chicago Public Schools. Pois, a professor of public administration and formerly a member of the Chicago Board of Education (1956–1961), points out that board members—at least in the large cities—have a very difficult time finding out what is happening in the schools. As a result, he argues, most of them occupy themselves primarily with trivia having little relevance to the real problems in the schools and the community. Pois' experience as a board member convinced him, moreover, that board members in Chicago could hardly be adequately informed as long as they had to depend on currently existing arrangements for bringing important matters to their considered attention:

> Manifestly, a board should avail itself of the factual material and viewpoints emanating from the general superintendent and his subordinates. Yet, if this is the exclusive source of systematic inquiry and analysis concerning the school system, the board's decision-making must inevitably be determined in large measure by the attitudes and concepts of the bureaucracy. . . . The Chicago Board, when it does seek to tap the informational, statistical, and research resources of the school system, is ordinarily expected to use its general superintendent as the point of contact. Although this may be justified on the basis of protocol or recognition of lines of responsibility in the administrative hierarchy, the end result is that the flow of information is subject to screening, selection, or restatement by the general superintendent. As organizations expand in size it becomes less tenable to contend that the chief administrative or executive officer should be the sole conduit for the transmittal of data or analysis to the governing body. . . . [Even a subordinate duly authorized to deal directly] with a board . . . will be prone to proceed with considerable caution lest he incur the displeasure of his superior.[5]

The difficulties in the organizational and administrative relationships in big-city schools, Pois thus argues, justify giving serious consideration, "to the feasibility and desirability of the board having research and analytical facilities entirely apart from the regular administrative staff." He admits that the "elimination of the confidential assistants who formerly served the members of the New York City Board of Education and whose activities apparently made for board conflict with, or usurpation of, the superintendent's authority" provides an argument against having such a unit, but he rightfully insists that "whatever the experience in New York, it would be regrettable if this were regarded as having conclusively demonstrated that it is injudicious to provide school boards in large urban areas with staff services of their own."[6]

Whether the department of inspection—or either of its units—should function as a direct arm of the board of education is an open question. In my opinion it would be wiser to have this department report to a special committee composed of several members of the board, the superintendent and several of his staff, several teachers and representatives of teacher organizations, and a small number of additional lay citizens drawn from various community groups. However, the tenure of the department's personnel, and particularly its director, should be determined by the board of education taking into account only the recommendation of those board members on the special committee and not the advice of others who serve on the committee. In any case, a board of education in a big city, as Pois points out, "cannot justifiably be very critical" of the behavior of the many teachers who bombard it with unsolicited, often anonymous, pleas for help, in view of the fact that as of now it has "failed to provide adequate means for the expression and resolution of grievances."[7]

The information provided by the department of inspections could be significant in galvanizing school board members in the big cities into decisive action. No one can say how well the average board member really understands the ineptness with which education in the big city is generally conducted. Most of them must be aware of instances in which something has gone awry in the schools, but board members have no real basis for appreciating the degree to which the educational programs in many schools in their jurisdiction are ineffective and mismanaged. Apparently, then, information is not reaching the board in sufficiently massive doses and with sufficiently objective verification to induce it to push the needed reforms—which inevitably would "shake up" the system a good bit. School board members, after all, tend to be victims of the system's inertia in the same way as nearly everyone else in the system. But unless board members stand the system on its head, it is hardly possible to deal with the crisis which is growing more severe in the big-city schools. A department of inspections, if it functioned effectively, conceivably might have enough impact to push board members beyond the line which separates sympathetic but cautious understanding from resolute and drastic reform.

To summarize, school districts in the big cities should establish an entirely new department responsible for identifying and correcting dysfunctions which now are tolerated in urban schools. Personnel in one of the two units in this department of inspections would operate analogously to the inspectors who perform this important function in other kinds of large-scale organizations; personnel in the second unit would function somewhat similarly to the *ombudsman*, whose job is to investigate citizen perceptions of unjust or ineffective government, but they would also process information and grievances which employees feel unable to raise through regular channels.

In establishing such units and procedures, a board of education should recognize that its decision could set in motion potentially divisive forces which might create an entirely new set of serious problems for a city's schools. Nevertheless, present organizational arrangements are proving so ineffective that perceptive and informed observers question the viability of the big city districts in their present form; these districts cannot be made to work very satisfactorily without some major changes. It is already widely recognized that big city schools must undertake thoroughgoing curriculum reform and must acquire vast new resources for housing and conducting a variety of instructional services if adequate education is to be provided for the millions of students whose future will be determined in them. In Chicago, for example, Superintendent James F. Redmond has bluntly asked the Board of Education and the public to face up to the fact that the city schools need three-quarters of a billion dollars just for buildings in the next five years.[8] It is not so widely recognized that unless equally significant innovations are made with respect to administration and organization of the big-city districts, a large proportion of these funds might as well be burned as flushed through the ineffectual system which makes the present expenditure of resources so distressingly unproductive. The establishment outside regular administrative channels of a department of inspections would constitute one such innovation.

The establishment of a department of inspections promises a number of important benefits in the social system of the big-city district. Just as the discovery by senior executives in the General Motors Corporation that it sometimes took six months to obtain suitable replies to memos led to important changes that helped make it one of the world's most successful organizations, so the dysfunctions investigated by the department of inspections would help board members and top administrators gain a fuller understanding of why the big-city schools are functioning so poorly and what it would take to improve them. Merely giving serious attention to the dysfunctions which prevent personnel at the school level from working effectively would, in itself, do much to raise morale throughout a big-city school district. A relatively independent department with direct channels to the board of education could initiate action on a number of problems which now go unsolved. At the present time, for example, new superintendents almost never try to replace department heads whose behavior and attitudes may be doing irreparable harm within the big-city districts, because to do so might cause them to lose the confidence of the entire administrative staff. Rather than waiting five or ten years for the "old palace guard" to retire or resorting to the sometimes wasteful stratagem of grafting all sorts of new positions for his own appointees on a structure handed down from a previous administration, a new superintendent might welcome arrangements which, in effect, supplied a required and independent evaluation of the adequacy of his staff. In addition, superintendents and board members served by a department of inspections could be far more effective as decision makers, for as Peter Drucker recently pointed out in the *Harvard Business Review*:

Effective decision makers . . . follow a rule which the military developed long ago. The commander who makes a decision does not depend on reports to see how it is carried out. He or one of his aides—goes and looks . . . the reason is that they learned the hard way to distrust abstract "communications."[9]

Is the structure of the educational system as now delineated in the big cities so sacrosanct as to prohibit experimentation with supplementary, semiautonomous components which might help realign and revitalize a poorly functioning bureaucracy? Educators who recognize the need for critical and continuous assessment of modern organizations in accordance with the imperatives of a rapidly changing environment will hardly think so.

Notes

1. For example, see Christopher Jencks, "Speaking Out: The Public Schools Are Failing," *The Saturday Evening Post*, April, 1966, pp. 14, 18; Martin Meyerson and Edward C. Banfield, *Boston: The Job Ahead*. Cambridge, Mass.: Harvard University Press, 1966, pp. 80–83; and Harvey Pressman, "The Failure of the Public Schools," *Urban Education*, Vol. 11, No. 2, pp. 61–81.
2. *Education U.S.A.*, January 5, 1967, p. 112.
3. William G. Scott, *The Management of Conflict*. Homewood, Ill.: The Dorsey Press, 1965, p. 124.
4. *Ibid.*, p. 28.
5. Joseph Pois, *The School Board Crisis: A Chicago Case Study*. Chicago: Aldine, 1964, pp. 88–89.
6. *Ibid.*, p. 87.
7. *Ibid.*, p. 169.
8. *The Chicago Sun-Times*, December 18, 1966, p. 1.
9. Peter F. Drucker, "The Effective Decision," *Harvard Business Review*, January-February, 1967, p. 98.

22 | The Authority Structure of the School: System of Social Exchange

James G. Anderson

Scholars in the field of educational administration have long looked upon authority as the "glue" that holds an organization together. Anderson's article considers the functioning organization as an authority structure. The question is asked: On what basis does an organization invest authority in members? how much? at what levels? Anderson concludes that relatively little authority is granted to teachers by administrators, and to pupils by teachers. This severely limits the exercise of authority by teachers and pupils in contributing to the achievement of the schools' goals.

Organizational Authority as a System of Social Exchange

Formal organizations arise in order to coordinate the efforts of individuals in the pursuit of a common goal. Such coordination implies central direction of organizational activities. Power—the ability to influence the behavior of members of the organization in accordance with the wishes of a leader or administrative staff—makes such collective effort possible.[1]

Max Weber suggests that the legitimacy of such power must be recognized by the society in which the organization functions if officials of an organization are to perform their duties.[2] According to him, such legitimation of authority may be accomplished in one of three ways. First, it may be based upon a charismatic leader with extraordinary powers.[3] A body of disciples, assigned specific duties by him carries out his directives. Second, authority may be traditional, based on a body of customs handed down from generation to generation. The leader and his staff achieve a certain status in this instance by virtue of these traditions.[4] Third, it may be based on a body of general rules that delineate and circumscribe the behavior of members of the organization. Weber terms this final form of authority "legal-rational."[5]

Chester I. Barnard defines authority within formal organizations as that character of an order which causes it to be accepted by a member of the organization as a determinant of his behavior. The two essential features are

James G. Anderson, "The Authority Structure of the School: A System of Social Exchange," *Educational Administration Quarterly* III, No. 2 (Spring, 1967), 130–148. Reprinted by permission.

249

the acceptance of the order by the subordinate and the character of the order making it acceptable to him. For Barnard, acceptance of the authority by the individual is essential and is dependent upon an exchange system. The organization offers certain inducements for an individual's contributions to the organization. It can maintain authority over members only so long as this balance is favorable for the individuals participating. Consequently, much of the administrative effort must be directed at maintaining a favorable balance of inducements for the individual so that he will accept the authority of the organization and provide the necessary contributions.

Additionally, Barnard equates the "system of communication" within the organization with the institution's "lines of authority." This system functions to provide information to positions of authority within the organization so that orders may be issued. Maintenance of an attitude conducive to acceptance of orders by subordinates requires a careful structuring of the lines of communication from higher positions to lower ones.[6]

This notion of viewing a member's participation within an organization in terms of an exchange between the individual and the organization has been further developed by James S. Coleman.[7] He suggests that, in formal organizations, role expectations and role obligations constitute an exchange system based on a deferred payment plan. The structure is built around expectations and obligations for each individual occupying a position in the organization. Although such a set exists between each pair of role partners within the organization, direct reciprocity between the two is not necessary, and payment of obligations may occur over an extended period of time. Formal organizations consist of series of these asymmetric role relationships, which are then balanced by the organization itself. The institution guarantees that the role expectations of members will be met. It supplements those intrinsic rewards received by the individual from his interpersonal relations with the organizational members with whom he has role relations and with clients that the organization serves with extrinsic institutional rewards.

An example from the schools is the role relationship between a teacher and a student. From a student's (and his parent's) standpoint, expectations include qualified instruction, citizenship training, character formation, safety while under the auspices of the school, extracurricular opportunities, educational certificates, etc. His corresponding obligations are regular attendance, proper behavior, minimal effort, etc.

The teacher expects remuneration, status, security, and administrative support, in addition to enforcement of those obligations already specified for the student. His obligations include meeting to the best of his ability those expectations held by the student and his parents in addition to other purely institutional obligations and duties, such as continued professional development, discipline and control of students, compiling records and reports, sponsoring student activities, etc.

Both the teacher and the student look to the organization to balance this exchange and to enforce obligations. The school as an institution provides the teacher with remuneration and status, ensures attendance and acceptable behavior on the part of the student, and guarantees competence on the part of the teacher and an acceptable educational program. The organization also satisfies those expectations of the student and those of the teacher which are not intrinsic to their role relationship such as social intercourse and collegiality.

Not only does an exchange relation develop between members of the organization and its clients (in the case of the school, teachers and students) but several systems of exchange also develop within the institution. At first, as Barnard has suggested, an individual member submits to the authority of the organization in exchange for the rewards that organizational membership offers. But once he is established as a member of the organization, the individual begins to submit to managerial authority because of emerging social norms that evoke social disapproval of opposition. In short, he exchanges compliance with institutional authority for the approval of his social peers, as Blau points out.[8]

Such a pattern emerges because of the distinctive feature of institutionalized authority that causes it to be enforced not only by superiors but by individual members of the organization. For, although voluntary, social constraints make compliance imperative for the individual and preclude departure from accepted norms, rules, and directives. These social constraints arise as a result of a second form of exchange: that of the group to which the individual belongs which exchanges compliance with orders for a share of the rewards that the organization offers for such compliance and for group contributions. If these rewards exceed what is considered as a "fair exchange" for the cost of compliance and contributions, the collective approval of this exercise of control over the group's actions legitimates it.[9]

Thus, the collective obligations incurred for these rewards resulting from managerial actions and group approval of the exchange of compliance and services for them, creates group pressures that enforce compliance with institutional authority. To a large extent such social sanctions obviate the necessity for organizational sanctions.[10]

Moreover, coordination of group activities often involves social credit.[11] Employees are willing to comply with administrative demands in excess of their obligations with the expectation of a reward at some later date. If the administration is effective in securing greater rewards for them that would not have been obtained otherwise, this success buttresses superior claims to greater compliance in the future. In effect, it establishes credit which can be called upon at will.

Notwithstanding the exchange processes already described, Coleman has identified a third one that takes place within organizations: that of delegation of authority. It is this model that will be dealt with at some length.

Weber in characterizing a bureaucracy describes an incumbent of a particular office as limited to a sphere of competence with clearly defined jurisdiction. This requires a detailed specification of the responsibility for accomplishing some institutional subgoal for each position within the organization. However, concomitantly the organization must provide each imcumbent with the requisite means to carry out this responsibility by providing him with the necessary authority and means of compulsion as well as with norms governing their use.

If we now look at this as an investment of authority by the organization in subordinates, we can analyze authority within an organization as investments in roles or offices as means for the accomplishment of the institutional goals. Responsibility or obligations then are the required return on the investment.[12] Since the incumbent may occupy the office for an extended period of time, a continued return on the investment is required. At the same time there is a continuing delegation or investment of authority in him.

The amount of authority invested, the expected return on the investment, and the time required for return on investment will vary within and between organizations. Consequently, it is possible to differentiate between organizations and between offices within an organization on this basis. One may ask on what basis does an organization invest authority in members at different levels of the hierarchy? Also how does it know how much authority to invest at each level? What is a sound investment? In all organizations these decisions are made and authority relations are prescribed for each office. In order to answer these questions we must focus attention on the investment decision itself.

The Investment Decision

Gain

In any organization authority may be centralized in key positions and little authority invested in subordinates at lower levels. This tendency to restrict investments appears to arise out of the organization's need to guarantee responsible action, to coordinate the performance of participants so that they will contribute to the accomplishment of the overall goals of the organization, and to utilize expert opinion in making decisions.

On the other hand, there is a countervailing tendency toward decentralization of authority and investment in subordinates. This seems to arise from the fact that much of the information relevant to decision making within the organization originates at the lower levels where the goal activities are carried on. Also, separation of decision making from these primary activities of an organization is time consuming, costly, and sometimes dysfunctional. Finally, there is an expectation of gain on the part of the administration in investing authority due to the utilization of the experience of participants, greater motivation and commitment, flexibility, and reinforcement of the organizational goals by the individuals involved.[13]

If an investment of authority is made, it may in turn be reinvested by the recipient. For example, if a broad investment of authority is made in a teacher, he can in turn invest it in his students. In this investment there is both the possibility of greater gain and of greater loss.

One of the examples that Coleman discusses is one in which the teacher reinvests authority in his students.[14] If the investment is made in such a way as to utilize the social organization of the classroom, the goals of the teacher will be reinforced and the teacher gains authority through the investment.

The same thing is true of the organization's investment of authority in the teacher. If a broad investment is made, the organization may gain from the reinforcement of the institution's goals by drawing upon the teacher's experience, knowledge, and initiative. Also the teacher may reinvest this authority in his students with the possibility of an additional gain for the school. Nevertheless, as in all investments, the possibility of loss is greater also. If the teacher is incompetent or if the students usurp the teacher's prerogatives, the school may lose through the investment.

The period of time between the investment of authority and the review of a subordinate's performance (this can be thought of as the requirement for an accounting or a return on the investment) is an indication of how much authority is invested or the level of his responsibility in the organization.[15] Lower participants are likely to have their performance evaluated quite often (a relatively short-term investment of authority) while a person occupying a more responsible position in the organizational hierarchy may only have his performance evaluated once a year (a much longer term investment).

In the schools this measure is quite valid in that new probationary teachers are subject to frequent observation and supervision by subject-matter specialists, department chairmen, and principals; but once a teacher has achieved tenure, he may be subject to supervision as little as once a year. The awarding of tenure and the autonomy accorded these teachers are indicative of a long-term investment of authority.

Furthermore, reinvestment will occur from time to time. If the expected rate of return on the investment is met over a period of time, there is the likelihood that more authority will be invested with the expectation of greater gain. Again this can be illustrated in those cases where a teacher is very successful and manages to attract the attention of his superiors. Over a period of time he may be permitted to teach brighter classes and may be given a great deal more latitude in subject-matter emphasis, text selection, and methods of instruction than the average teacher. However, those teachers who do not provide an adequate return on the investment may experience a withdrawal of authority over the same period of time as evidenced by closer supervision, a more rigid prescription of subject matter and teaching methods, etc.

In the case of the school these considerations appear to obtain. Since teaching is carried out by the lowest participants of the organization and is of an esoteric nature, a certain degree of authority must be delegated if the goals of the organization are to be met. The amount of authority delegated will depend upon expectations of gain for the organization resulting from the investment.

Let us examine the investment decision for a particular case, that of the secondary school teacher in the public schools. The administrator's decision concerning the scope of the investment in teachers is first a function of the anticipated gain from such an investment. In appraising potential gain, the first consideration is that of the competence of teachers in performing their tasks. Such an appraisal is complicated by the failure to date to devise generally acceptable measures of teaching effectiveness or to measure a particular teacher's influence on a group of students.[16] It is further compounded with vague esoteric goals such as character formation, problem solving ability, intellectual curiosity and a general lack of evaluative information concerning the efficacy of various teaching methods and curricula.

As a result, the administration limits its investment in teachers and instead relies on centralization of authority. Through rules it structures the action of teachers and relationships between them and other participants within the organization. Since the determining factor in accomplishment of the goals of the school is the contact between students and teachers in the institutional framework of the school, the main control that the organization has over the action of teachers in the accomplishment of the school's goals is the enforcement of rules concerning teacher behavior. Thus, the administrator can measure teacher compliance with these norms rather than teacher effectiveness since, unfortunately, for many administrators the two are synonymous.

In short, the decision in this case to limit the scope of the investment in teachers seems to be, to a great extent, a result of this inability to measure the gain that might be realized by making such an investment.

A second consideration in anticipating gain from an investment is an estimation of the commitment of the participants to the pursuit of the organization's goals. In this case we are dealing with the perception of motivation by the administration. This problem arises especially in large cities where teaching positions are not as desirable as in suburban areas or in private schools. Here the problem of producing some measurable change in the child's skill or knowledge, the problems of maintaining order and control, and the problem of morally accepting unaccustomed behavior of students make these positions undesirable. As a result, administrators perceive a lack of motivation on the part of teachers. This observation is reinforced by the large number of requests for transfers and the difficulty in recruiting qualified teachers to fill vacant positions.[17]

Since the administration is not assured that its interests will be preserved in delegating authority, the decision appears to be to restrict the investment in teachers. As before, authority is centralized with the development of a body of rules and procedures in order to prescribe behavior for teachers. One function of these rules is directional. They operate as guidelines for behavior so that an individual can participate as a member of the organization.[18] In order to orient the contributions of members toward the fulfillment of organizational goals, obligations are specified and authority is delineated. Rules, then, communicate the expectations of the administration to those administered.

Rules may also be used to expand or contract the authority invested in teachers through several functions that they serve within organizations. First, they can legitimate the use of punishment by warning teachers of the probable consequence of improper behavior.[19] For example, the punishment for not submitting grades and attendance records at the close of the school year may be the withholding of a teacher's pay check. Resorting to warnings of punishment to achieve proper behavior in a sense represents a withdrawal of investment in teachers. Instead the institution resorts to coercion, since one might say that no real alternative remains other than the prescribed one if punishment is to be averted.

However, an administrator may expand the investment in teachers by intentionally failing to enforce such rules prescribing punishment.[20] By refraining from exercising his legitimate power he creates an obligation on the part of the teacher, if you will, a social credit which can be called upon sometime in the future.[21] For example, a principal may choose not to enforce rules concerning signing in and out of school in return for acceptance of extracurricular assignments that require a great deal of time before and after school hours. This phenomenon may be considered as a periodic short-term investment by administrators in teachers. In this case the investment is limited and variable, the return is specific, and the period of investment is short.

Finally, in education there is one other factor that limits the realization of anticipated gain from an investment of authority in teachers, that is, the imbalance between authority and expected gain. There is usually an underinvestment of authority in the teacher at the same time that there is an overexpectation of gain. This occurs because the teacher's responsibility almost invariably exceeds his authority. Although he is responsible for demonstrating the progress of his students, he has little or no authority to control the environmental factors (social, political, and economic) that operate in and on the school and that have a decided bearing on the progress of students and affect the realization of the teacher's goals. Moreover, he has little choice of curricula or textbooks, has nothing to do with assignment to ability groups, can do little more than suggest that a child may need psychiatric counseling, and does not have the authority to curb severe behavioral problems by suspension or expulsion.

For example, a teacher assigned a basic class consisting of emotionally disturbed children, low-ability students, and discipline cases has no authority to control the innumerable variables that seriously affect the progress of these children, yet is responsible for each child's progress.

Risk

The decision concerning how much authority is to be invested also depends upon the risk involved for the institution. In evaluating risk for an investment one must assess the anticipated gain and weigh it against the possible loss. This estimation of risk then will affect the terms under which authority is invested, the amount invested, the anticipated return on the investment, and the period of investment. Homans has suggested that an individual, a group, or an organization will only act when the probability of realizing the anticipated gain from such an action exceeds that of the possible loss.[22] As a result, to a large extent, the investment decision will depend upon the range of consequences of actions taken by different members of the organization. Since actions of a particular participant in the institution may affect persons at higher and at lower levels of the hierarchy, when this range is wide, the higher levels of the organization must be assured that subordinates will behave in a manner so as to preserve their interests for the two levels. Or it may be assured by the technical competence and high commitment of those to whom authority is delegated. Nevertheless, in order to accomplish the goals of the organization, some authority must be delegated to the lower levels. If the possible loss to the organization is high, the institution may not choose to take the risk involved in a broad investment of authority in participants. In those areas where actions may have adverse affects for the institution, rules and procedural specification may be used to limit the scope of an individual's jurisdiction. If we again turn to the example of the school teachers, we may examine this factor in analyzing the investment of authority in teachers.

One of the reasons that an extensive investment of authority in teachers is considered to involve a high risk is the public belief in the critical nature of education. In our society the belief that students can be permanently influenced during the formative years of adolescence is prevalent. This is certainly evidenced by the repeated censorship of texts, criticism of social studies curricula, accusations of subversion among school teachers, etc. Due to this public concern and their idealistic expectations for the school, such as teaching citizenship, character formation, and group participation, there is the feeling among administrators that investing authority in teachers and allowing them to use their own judgment in educational matters involves a high risk, with a poor investment resulting in permanent damage to the student and in adverse criticism from society. Since students at this age are generally not considered mature enough to make individual value choices, an effort is made to insulate them from anything which is controversial or which requires an ethical choice. As a result, little authority is invested in teachers and many of their functions are specified, especially in social studies.

Moreover, the public may communicate its view of education through lay boards of education and state legislatures, thus directly affecting school program and policies. Notwithstanding these channels, parents whose child has been severely disciplined or injured or who strongly object to school policies may seek redress through the courts and may put pressure on school administrators through the newspaper, the PTA, as well as through organized interest groups.

Since the range of consequences of individual actions is great in this instance, affecting all levels of the public educational system, the necessity for restricting the authority of teachers appears evident, at least to most school administrators.

There may be another factor in the reluctance of school administrators to invest authority in teachers, due to the necessity for legitimating administrative authority. This reluctance may be motivated by the instability of the authority relationship between teachers and administrators. Instability is manifested in the functional supervision of teachers who are accountable both to subject-matter specialists and to the principal at the secondary level. Since the principal does not feel competent to judge the technical aspects of the teacher's performance, this job is relegated to specialists and curriculum coordinators.

Also, the formation of teacher organizations, such as unions, as countervailing forces to the administration and the reluctance of such organizations to admit school administrators suggests a further conflict between teachers and school administrators.[23]

Teachers identify school administrators with the bureaucratic structure of the schools, with its centralization of authority and tight prescription of behavior. Realizing their limited ability as individuals to affect changes in personnel policies, salary schedules, instructional procedures, etc., teachers are turning increasingly to group action. Through such action they attempt to modify the conditions under which they work as evidenced by the militancy of growing teacher unions.[24]

One might reasonably expect that this insecurity in the authority relationship between administrators and teachers (essentially a conflict between bureaucratic authority and professional autonomy) would result in a reluctance to invest authority in teachers.[25] Since there is some evidence that the interests of the higher levels of educational institutions are not coincident with those of teachers, especially in matters such as collective bargaining, there is a great deal of reluctance to invest authority. As a result, authority is centralized at the higher levels of the organization and teachers are viewed merely as employees of the school system, hired to carry out a prescribed job, and not as professionally responsible members of a profession.

Cosigners for the Investment

Another factor in the estimation of risk is the existence of cosigners who will offer collateral security for the investment. In the absence of permanent ties or a multiplicity of ties between the organization and the individual, collateral becomes the basis for security for investments. If we consider collateral in an intangible sense, educational institutions and professional associations through certification and licensing may be considered as cosigners for the investment of authority in an individual. When a bad investment is made, the cosigner may or may not be able to rectify the loss.

A profession traditionally renders a public service in return for which the public gives the profession a mandate to control admission and expulsion from the profession. This self-regulation presupposes that members acquire a certain expertise that can only be judged by their colleagues. It is then the profession's responsibility to prescribe and proscribe actions in accordance with a professional code of ethics. The profession rewards its members for the services they render to the public, which better enables clients to contribute to the community, which in turn awards the profession its mandate and status.[26]

To be admitted to a profession, an individual must heavily invest his resources in order to gain the necessary expertise and credentials (usually educational certificates and a professional license). Those individuals selected for admission, then, are strongly committed to the profession, in many cases irrevocably. Such a commitment impedes mobility and gives the professional association a great deal of power over its members due to their fear of sanctions or ultimate expulsion with the attendant loss of the resources that the individual has invested in gaining entry (money, time, effort, ego, etc.).[27]

Consequently, we may look at the reluctance of school systems to invest authority in teachers as a problem of professional autonomy. In general, professional autonomy pertains to a wide variety of decisions concerning conduct of members which are left to the discretion of the professional group. In delegating authority, the recipient of the authority is allowed to use his discretion since his training and experience allow him to make a more expert decision than the person delegating the authority. Therefore, professional autonomy means the latitude allowed the practitioner due to his expert skill and knowledge.

In most professions, the professional association and the educational institutions that offer the professional training act as cosigners for the investment of authority in an individual. Since they traditionally control entry into, and expulsion from, the profession, they provide some security for an investment of authority in an individual. This is due to the selective process and requirements for admission to the profession as well as the power of the association in sanctioning members who do not fulfill their obligations to a particular institution. Also, in the major professions the association controls the accreditation of schools which train practitioners for the profession. Consequently, they too provide security for an investment of authority in individuals by a particular organization.[28]

However, in education the lack of similar cosigners to provide security for investment in teachers is a decided limiting factor. Since there is widespread disagreement as to the role of the teacher, it is difficult to define what his expert professional functions comprise.

Furthermore, education, unlike other professions, generally does not control entry and expulsion through a board of practitioners of the profession. Rather state certification boards, usually state boards of education, are composed primarily of laymen in all but a few states and teachers possess a very limited representation on such boards. In this respect education even differs from other occupational groups such as barbers, beauticians, and architects where state licensing boards are composed entirely of practitioners.[29] Also unlike education, appointments to these boards are typically made by the professional association or from a list submitted by the association. This lack of professional representation on licensing boards for teachers is partially the result of laws in a number of states expressly prohibiting educators from serving on such boards.[30] Such policies have been defended repeatedly as necessary in order to preserve local control over the schools and to keep them responsive to the community.

A further limitation on the professional mandate accorded education by the public is the lay control over certification or licensing requirements, again a practice that differentiates education from the other professions. Teacher training institutions usually offer programs that satisfy minimal state certification requirements established both by the state legislature and by the state board of education. This arrangement attenuates local pressures and further weakens the professional associations' ability to guarantee expertise and competence.

After completing his study of teacher training programs in seventy-seven institutions in sixteen states, James Bryant Conant concluded that:

> The policy of certification based on the completion of state-specified course requirements is bankrupt; of this I am convinced. Unfortunately, the newer approved-program approach, which is intended to afford increased flexibility and freedom, involves the state department to such a degree that the dominant public school forces can use it to impose their own orthodoxy as easily as they used the older system. The specific course requirements and the approved-program approach as it is now developing have critical defects in common; they cannot be enforced in such a manner that the public can be assured of competent teachers, and they involve the states in acrimonious and continuous political struggles, which may not serve the public interest.[31]

Again, contrast this arrangement for licensing with that of other professions that license only after passage of a rigorous examination at the end of a lengthy formal education.[32]

Moreover, requirements for entry into the profession are appallingly low. Many states require in effect, less than a good baccalaureate program in the liberal arts (if the student majors in education at the undergraduate level) and little that the public considers as specialized professional training. To make matters worse, certification requirements are not rigidly enforced. On the pretense of filling shortages in instructional staffs, many local school districts easily circumvent state requirements by requesting "emergency" or "temporary" certificates.

Such diversity in the licensing requirements, minimal academic requirements, and the variety of certificates awarded in education drastically impede the mobility of teachers and give little assurance of the competency of teachers licensed in various states.

Finally, lack of professional control over the accreditation of professional training programs further reduces confidence in the educational profession in regards to certifying teacher competence.[33] Generally, there are three different means of accrediting professional schools: through a board of practitioners under the auspices of the professional association, through an agency created by the professional schools themselves, and through a council composed of representatives of both the association and the schools.[34] The stronger professions such as medicine, law, chemistry, and public health resort to the first means of guaranteeing quality in professional training.

Business administration, music and nursing employ the second means; while engineering, dentistry, and pharmacy utilize the third.

Along with state and regional accreditation, departments and schools of education and their programs are evaluated by a joint council known as the National Council for the Accreditation of Teacher Education (NCATE). However, the disproportionate representation on the council of members from the very institutions being accredited (appointed by the American Association of Colleges for Teacher Education) and state school officials who are responsible for the establishment and operation of teacher education programs (appointed by the Council of Chief State School Officers, the National Association of State Directors of Teacher Education and Certification, and the National Commission on Teacher Education and Professional Standards), makes the adoption of rigorous criteria for accreditation inconceivable, since to do so would prevent many states from fulfilling their insatiable demand for additional teachers.

With little direct control over certification requirements and licensing, except through the lobbying of public school organizations, and with a professional accreditation agency primarily composed of persons who are directly involved in establishing or administering teacher education programs, the teaching profession has been unable to regulate the teacher education institutions upon which it relies for the professional training of practitioners. This has resulted in the admission to the profession of teachers with questionable training and competence.[35] Since the teaching profession cannot guarantee the competence of its members, there is, in effect, no reliable cosigner to substantiate the judgment of supervisors or administrators in evaluating the capabilities of teachers and differentially investing authority in them. Consequently, authority, due to the lack of security for an investment, is parcelled out sparingly and there is no general broad investment in practitioners as there is in other callings such as medicine and law that rely heavily on professional norms to curb abuses of professional autonomy and guarantee professional responsibility as the return on the investment.

Investment and Risk in the Schools: A Summary

From the preceding discussion it would appear that Coleman's investment model for authority in organizations focuses attention on the essential factor in institutional authority relations, the investment decision. An insight into the functioning of the organization is gained by asking such questions as: On what basis does an organization invest authority in members? How much authority does it invest at each level? What does the organization consider as the criteria for a sound investment? One can then differentiate between organizations and between different levels within an organization on the basis of the terms of the authority investment, such as its magnitude, the required return, and the time allowed for the return.

In examining the role of the school teacher in relation to this model, a number of factors militating against and limiting the investment of authority were identified. Limiting the expected gain from the investment are the inability to measure performance and results, the distrust of teachers' motivation, the use of coercive measures, variability of investment, and the imbalance between authority and expected return. Contributing to the possibility of loss are the public's view of the critical nature of education, the wide range of consequences of actions of teachers, the instability of the authority relationship between teachers and administrators, the formation of informal teachers' groups as countervailing forces within the organization, and the absence of reliable cosigners (professional associations) for the investment.

The result appears to be a withdrawal of authority invested in teachers due to the perceived risk involved. Increasingly teachers are part of a bureaucratic organization in which their conduct is circumscribed by rules. The result is two conflicting sources of authority—professional and bureaucratic.[36]

The knowledge, skills, and norms acquired through extensive professional training ideally permit the vesting of authority in individual practitioners rather than in a centralized authority communicated through a hierarchical structure. Self-determination and self-responsibility are the norms, with each practitioner exercising a great deal of autonomy in the performance of his professional speciality.[37]

However, in the schools these professional expectations of teachers receive little support. State boards of education and local school boards do not look to the teacher's professional association in licensing, recruiting, and promoting teachers. The teacher is rather an employee of the board of education whose welfare depends upon conformance to the bureaucratic authority exercised by the school administrators.

The overwhelming danger is that many teachers whose professional expectations are frustrated abandon them, accepting instead a more rewarding bureaucratic orientation characterized by apathy, a rigid legalistic adherence to rules and regulations, an impersonal attitude toward students, and an "upward-looking posture" that looks to school administrators for cues before decisions are made. These unprofessional attitudes, although decried by school administrators, school boards, and the public, are unanticipated results of bureaucratically structured school systems that inadvertently foster and reward such behavior.[38]

Another indirect consequence of the limited investment of authority in teachers is the teacher's inability to reinvest the limited authority he has in the students. Since little authority is invested, students assume little responsibility for their own education outside of attendance and a certain minimal compliance with regulations concerning their behavior in school. Rather than holding students responsible for independent effort, the responsibility for somehow getting them through resides with the teachers. In many schools department chairmen or principals regularly review grades and require teachers to account for marks that, in their estimation, are too low. Additionally, automatic promotion policies provide further evidence of the limited investment of authority in teachers and students.

Again the system has unanticipated consequences—the lack of motivation of students who create their own adolescent society with norms and values in many instances directly antithetical to those of the school.[39] This failure to invest authority results in a total inability of the schools to draw upon the powerful societal structure of the student subculture in the accomplishment of educational goals. In fact, it makes it more difficult and in some cases impossible to do so.

Notes

1. Kenneth D. Benne, *A Conception of Authority* ("Contributions to Education," No. 895; New York: Teachers College, Columbia University, 1943), pp. 2, 39. Herbert Goldhammer and Edward A. Shils, "Types of Power and Status," *American Journal of Sociology*, XLV (September, 1939), 171–178.
2. For an excellent discussion of Weber's concept of institutionalized authority see the introduction to A. M. Henderson and Talcott Parsons (eds.), *Max Weber: The Theory of Social and Economic Organization* (New York: Oxford University Press, 1947), pp. 56–77.
3. *Ibid.*, pp. 358–373. Also see H. H. Gerth and C. Wright Mills (eds.), *From Max Weber: Essays in Sociology* (New York: Oxford University Press, 1958), pp. 245–252.
4. A. M. Henderson and Talcott Parsons, *op. cit.*, pp. 341–358.
5. *Ibid.*, pp. 329–341. Also H. H. Gerth and C. Wright Mills, *op. cit.*, pp. 196–244.
6. Chester I. Barnard, *The Functions of the Executive* (Cambridge, Mass.: Harvard University Press, 1954), pp. 161–184.
7. James S. Coleman, "Systems of Social Exchange" (Johns Hopkins University, Baltimore, Md., February, 1963), pp. 20–21. (Mimeographed.)
8. Peter M. Blau, *Exchange and Power in Social Life* (New York: John Wiley & Sons, Inc.), p. 200.
9. *Ibid.*, p. 207.
10. *Ibid.*, pp. 208–209.
11. *Ibid.*, p. 135; George C. Homans, *Social Behavior: Its Elementary Forms* (New York: Harcourt, Brace & World, 1961), pp. 297–299.
12. Coleman, *op. cit.*, pp. 22–23.
13. Herbert A. Simon, *Administrative Behavior* (New York: Macmillan Co., 1947), p. 157.
14. Coleman, *op. cit.*, pp. 24–26.
15. Elliott Jaques, *Measurement of Responsibility* (London: Tavistock Publications, 1956), pp. 32–42.
16. For two good summaries of attempts to measure teaching effectiveness see A. S. Barr *et al.*, *Wisconsin Studies of the Measurement and Prediction of Teacher Effectiveness* (Madison, Wis.: Dembar Publishing Co., 1961) and

Dwight E. Beecher, *The Evaluation of Teaching: Backgrounds and Concepts* (Syracuse, N.Y.: Syracuse University Press, 1949).

17. For a good discussion of the effect that these three problems have on teachers' career patterns see Howard S. Becker, "The Career of the Chicago Public School Teacher," *American Journal of Sociology*, LVII (March, 1952), 470–477.

18. For an extended discussion of the role played by rules in formal organizations see James G. Anderson, "Bureaucratic Rules: Bearers of Organizational Authority," *Educational Administration Quarterly*, II (Winter, 1966), 7–34. Also for what he calls the "explicational" function of rules see Alvin W. Gouldner, *Patterns of Industrial Bureaucracy* (New York: Free Press, 1954), pp. 162–164.

19. See Anderson, *op. cit.*, p. 22 and Gouldner, *op. cit.*, p. 170, for discussions of the "punishment legitimating" function of rules.

20. This function of rules is termed the "bargaining function" by Anderson, *op. cit.*, pp. 22–23 and the "leeway function" by Gouldner, *op. cit.*, pp. 172–174.

21. Blau, *op. cit.*, p. 206, notes that a superior may extend his control by refraining from exercising his formal power. Using this strategy, the superior exchanges some of his power for greater voluntary control over subordinates who are then obligated to him.

22. Homans, *op. cit.*

23. For a good discussion of the emergence of informal groups in organizations see Philip Selznick, "An Approach to a Theory of Bureaucracy," *American Sociological Review*, VIII (February, 1943), 47–54.

24. See Robert Dubin, "Decision Making by Management in Industrial Relations," *American Journal of Sociology*, LIV (January, 1949), 292–297.

25. For a good brief discussion of this conflict in authority see Chandler Washburne, "The Teacher in the Authority System," *Journal of Educational Sociology*, XXX (May, 1957), 390–394.

26. For this observation see Blau, *op. cit.*, pp. 262–263.

27. *Ibid.*, p. 161.

28. For an excellent discussion of the problem of professional autonomy, certification, and accreditation see Myron Lieberman, *Education as a Profession* (Englewood Cliffs, N.J.: Prentice Hall, Inc., 1956), pp. 87–184.

29. Lieberman (*Ibid.*, pp. 93–95) has reproduced several tables from *Occupational Licensing in the States* (Chicago: Council of State Governments 1952), pp. 84–87 to illustrate this point.

30. Data contained in: U.S. Office of Education, Federal Security Agency, *State Boards of Education and Chief State School Officers* (Washington, D.C.: Government Printing Office, 1951), pp. 17–18, indicate that in 1951 ten states expressly prohibited professional educators from serving on state boards of education.

31. James Bryant Conant, *The Education of American Teachers* (New York: McGraw Hill, 1964), pp. 54–55.

32. See Lieberman, *op. cit.*, pp. 124–156 for a good discussion of the results of this practice.

33. *Ibid.*, pp. 157–184.

34. T. M. Stinnett, "Accreditation and the Professionalization of Teaching," *Journal of Teacher Education*, III (March, 1952), 30–39.

35. The study entitled *Secondary School Science Characteristics and Service Loads* (Washington, D.C.: U.S. Government Printing Office, NSF 63–10, 1961) conducted by the National Association of State Directors of Teacher Education

and Certification and the American Association for the Advancement of Science for the National Science Foundation estimates that almost half of the biology classes are taught by teachers who have completed less than thirty semester hours in their field. The percentages for mathematics in grades 9–12 and mathematics, general science and physics in grades 7–8 are much lower. Here it is estimated that twenty-three percent of the physics teachers and thirty-four percent of the math teachers have completed less than nine semester hours in their fields.

36. Washburne, *op. cit.*, pp. 390–394.
37. For two good discussions of how the typical bureaucratic structure of an organization is altered when authority is decentralized and professionalization of participants is relied upon see Arthur L. Stinchcombe, "Bureaucratic and Craft Administration of Production: A Comparative Study," *Administrative Science Quarterly*, IV (September, 1959), 168–187, and Amitai Etzioni, "Authority Structure and Organizational Effectiveness," *Administrative Science Quarterly*, IV (June, 1959), 43–67.
38. See Anderson, *op. cit.*, for an exploration of the dysfunctional consequences of bureaucratically structuring educational systems. For an empirical examination of this problem see James G. Anderson, "Applicability of the Bureaucratic Model to the Organizational Structure of the School," U.S. Office of Education, Cooperative Research Project, S-043, 1964.
39. See James S. Coleman, *The Adolescent Society* (New York: The Free Press, 1961).

The Context of Organizational Behavior: A Conceptual Synthesis for the Educational Administrator

E. G. Bogue

The structure for organization is not the sole determinant of how members will behave. Bogue suggests a model of organizational behavior which is useful for the administrator in developing guidelines for his own behavior as he integrates personnel, material, and ideas into a productive unit.

Since the German sociologist Max Weber first outlined the characteristics of a bureaucracy, the literature on organizational theory has been growing with exponential rapidity. The recent books by Bass,[1] Thompson,[2] Scott,[3] and March[4] manifest the interest commanded by this relatively new field of inquiry. And the diversity of organizational inquiry is revealed by the variety of disciplines participating in both separate and interdisciplinary ventures. Economists, sociologists, psychologists, management specialists, educators, and mathematicians have initiated studies into one or more phases of organizational theory.

For the educational administrator, the array of research and reporting in organizational theory presents a dilemma not unlike that faced by the teacher confronting the literature of educational psychology. From the research and writing of the behavioral, stimulus-response, cognitive, neuro-physiological, and developmental psychologists, the teacher searches for those conceptual threads which he may weave into the fabric of his classroom teaching. Constructing a conceptual framework which can serve as a guide to more enlightened practice proves to be a formidable task.

A similar challenge faces the educational administrator as he surveys the literature of organizational theory, which is as diverse as that of educational psychology. The orchestration of personnel, material resources, and ideas which leads to the harmonious integration of man and organization is a complex task. It is natural, therefore, that the practicing administrator

E. G. Bogue, "The Context of Organizational Behavior: A Conceptual Synthesis for the Educational Administrator," *Educational Administration Quarterly*, 5 (Spring 1969), pp. 58–75. Reprinted by permission.

would also search for those concepts and principles which would assist him in developing a more commanding professional competency.

Certainly there are considerable risks in any attempt to distill the numerous points of inquiry found in organizational theory. Entire books have dealt with the topics of job satisfaction, motivation, communication, supervisory behavior, organizational conflict, and decision-making processes. A paper of this length could hardly capture the full impact of these topics. Yet our conviction is that we may profitably consider a portion of organizational inquiry of immediate utility to the practitioner—whether he be an elementary school principal, school superintendent, or university president.

Principal focus of the paper will be on the determinants of organizational behavior. We will suggest a simple model composed of four elements and then proceed to examine the relationship of each element to individual behavior. The reader will readily discern considerable interaction among the elements, but for purposes of exposition we have chosen to treat them separately. Our objective is to provide a concise conceptual framework of value to the educational administrator.

A Simplified Model of Behavior Determinants

In the literature of organizational theory, one can find research and theorizing related to a number of organizational concepts. Since this paper is an attempt to capsule some of these concepts into a more concise scheme, we present a highly simplified model involving four elements.

As Figure 1 indicates, we are suggesting that individual behavior in organizations can be viewed in terms of four perspectives: management philosophy, organizational structure, group membership, and individual personality. Each of these elements has important implications for practice as the educational administrator develops structures and relationships designed to free the creative energies of those with whom he works.

Individual Behavior Within Organizations			
Management Philosophy	Organizational Structure	Group Membership	Individual Personality

Figure 1.   Simplified Model of Behavior Determinants

The Influence of Management Philosophy

Our thesis in this discussion is that management philosophy is a keystone variable in influencing individual behavior within the organization. In treating management philosophy, we mean to consider those value dispositions and assumptions which managers hold about the nature of man and his work. We will suggest that management philosophy has changed significantly over the past half century, primarily as a result of intense research into the nature of leadership and organizations.

Three rather distinct periods of thought may be discerned in the literature of administration and management. The first of these is often called "scientific management." Scientific management was born in the late 19th century and flourished in the early 20th century, principally as a result of the research and writing of Frederick Taylor.[5] Based predominantly on the philosophy of Adam Smith, the focus of scientific management was on the economic nature of man. In essence, scientific management embraced the study of work specialization and wage analysis. Jobs were dissected in order to find the most efficient way of doing a particular task and for the purpose of setting a fair wage. Some of the assumptions about the nature of the average worker were not very noble, and the central theme was that money was the principal motivator.

Although scientific management produced a number of more effective management practices, its influence began to wane in the 1920's as industrial psychologists began to reveal that the problem of motivation-satisfaction was not as simple as the economic model assumed by scientific management. At the Western Electric Company, the now familiar Hawthorne studies by Elton Mayo and his colleagues committed mayhem on many hallowed assumptions held about the attitudes of workers toward their jobs. These and other studies also punched large holes in the concept of an organization as a blue print in action, as a series of line and staff relationships with fixed job responsibilities and closely specified interrelationships as initially proposed by Weber.

Organizations were revealed as social systems composed of both formal and informal elements, of grapevines and cliques, of overt and covert power structures, of both logical and non-logical behaviors. The economic assumption of the scientific management era was not adequate to account for the diverse need patterns uncovered, among which were the psychological needs for recognition, for security, for accomplishment, and for involvement.

Out of the research of the industrial psychologists in the 1920's and 1930's emerged the "human relations" movement. This movement stressed the notion that if managers became more sensitive to the diversity of human needs, they could deal more effectively with the problems of motivation and conflict within organizations.

A host of training and development programs for executives and supervisors were developed in human relations. Reaching its zenith in the 1950's, the movement began to lose some of its momentum, however. Human relations was the first movement to introduce in a systematic way the findings of behavioral science into management practice, and this represents no small contribution. Perhaps its demise in recent years may be attributed to lack of hard research validating the effectiveness of human relations training and the inhospitable environment to which many managers trained in human relations returned.

"Industrial humanism" is the rubric which describes the current trend in management philosophy.[6] The writing of scholars such as Chris Argyris, Douglas McGregor, and Rensis Likert provide much of the empirical and theoretical bases for this movement. Relying heavily upon the hierarchial need structure proposed by the psychologist Maslow, these theorists have suggested a number of concepts which merit serious reflection.

A brief digression to consider the motivation theory of Maslow may prove of value for our continued discussion. Maslow proposed a hierarchy of human needs beginning with the basic physiological needs and culminating in the higher social and ego needs, such as need for self-actualization.[7] The need for self-actualization can be described as a desire to feel that one's abilities are being fully utilized in some worthwhile and creative manner. We shall see in a moment how this theory makes a contribution to contemporary management philosophy.

Returning now to our discussion of industrial humanism, we should recall that one of the traditional assumptions about man and his work was that man is generally opposed to work. Notions of control and authority have therefore occupied prominent positions in traditional management philosophy. Scholars of the industrial humanist movement suggest that restrictive managerial control, coupled with inadequate opportunities for self-actualization, inhibits the development of trust among managers and between managers and employees. This paucity of trust and honesty in human relationships leads to serious dysfunctional consequences.

An experienced administrator has observed such dysfunctional consequences many times. Consider the following example of how trust and communication may be related. If there exists no feeling of trust between the administrator and the employee, then communication is filtered as information moves both up and down in the organizational hierarchy. The results are as follows. Failure to communicate downward means that employees are prevented from relating their individual and group objectives to the overall organizational objectives. Failure of employees to communicate upward prevents the administrator from obtaining accurate information about the true status of organizational operations. Eventually, of course, organizational productivity is affected.

We can begin to see how the motivation psychology of Maslow has had an impact on management philosophy, for Maslow has suggested that once the physiological needs are satisfied, the higher level needs become operative. Opportunity for self-actualization—for using his full array of talents in a creative venture—may transform work into an activity from which the individual may derive real pleasure and satisfaction.

In developing his Theory X and Theory Y notions of management in *The Human Side of Enterprise* McGregor leans heavily on Maslow's theory.[8] There are traces of the theory to be found also in Likert's *New Patterns of Management* emphasizing the participative approach to management.[9] And the influence of Maslow is to be seen in the theoretical presentation of Argyris' *Integrating the Individual and the Organization*.[10] The essential theme of these scholars is that relationships encouraging dependence, submissiveness, conformity, and imposed evaluation must give way to relationships which hold opportunity for development of trust, for independence of action, for risk taking, and for self-evaluation. The thrust of the industrial humanist movement thus encourages development of greater interpersonal competency on the part of managers. In addition, therefore, to learning more about the rational approaches to management—decision theory, operations research, simulation, etc.—managers must learn to work at the "gut level" of feelings and emotions.

As we close our discussion of management philosophy, we do not wish to leave the reader with the notion that contemporary management thought abandons the ideas of authority and control in organizational relationships. As we have pointed out in this discussion, it seems apparent that the trend in management thought is toward the development of more positive approaches to the motivation of man in organizational situations, with emphasis on trust and participation as vehicles for developing opportunity for self-actualization.

Yet the literature is equally clear on another point. It is that rigid and stereotyped notions of management styles belong, to borrow a phrase from Galbraith, in the museum of irrelevant ideas. There is no personality syndrome characteristic of all effective leaders nor a management style appropriate for all organizational situations. Flexibility is the key word. There is a time for independence and a time for control, a time for participation and a time for authority. Contrary to what some may think, flexibility in management style demands a greater competency than does a single approach. Flexibility requires the development of a broad knowledge base, the exercise of balanced judgment in matching style with situation, and careful consideration of values so that flexibility does not degenerate into opportunism.

We append a brief postscript to this discussion of motivation and management philosophy to mention another approach to the study of motivation in modern organizations, one which the reader may find particularly provocative. Whereas our analysis of the changing mood of human motivation and management philosophy has proceeded from a psychological base, in *The New Industrial State* Galbraith suggests that the motivation of men in organizations has changed; but the basis of his argument is economic rather than psychological. Briefly, he says that:

> Power in economic life has over time passed from its ancient association with land to association with capital and then on, in recent time, to the composite of knowledge and skills which comprises the technostructure. Reflecting the symmetry that so conveniently characterizes reality, there have been associated shifts in the motivations to which men respond. Compulsion has an ancient association with land. Pecuniary motivation had a similar association with capital. Identification and adaptation are associated with the technostructure.[11]

Here the word "technostructure" is a term coined by Galbraith to describe the organized intelligence found in the various groups of highly trained specialists providing the motive power in modern organizations. Though his analysis proceeds from a basis of economic change rather than from a consideration of psychological needs, the results are strikingly parallel. Compulsion is the motivation of authority. Pecuniary motivation is that of money. Identification and adaptation are the motivations associated with the merging of individual goals and aspirations with the organization's goals.

From whatever framework one may view contemporary management philosophy—whether from an economic, psychological, or sociological perspective—it is apparent that the concepts of trust, participation, and self-actualization are key elements in all frames of reference. Having thus briefly explored management philosophy as one of the determinants of individual behavior, we turn now to the second element of our simplified model, organizational structure.

The Effect of Structure

In contemporary society, a term frequently tossed about is "bureaucracy." Most often the context of its use will be an unfavorable one. Yet the various forms of bureaucracy found today are perhaps the most efficient means that man has found for accomplishing complex tasks.

Indeed, we might even observe that bureaucracy represents a kind of innovation in human relationships. It is apparent, however, that the formal and static kind of structure described by Weber has significant limitations when measured against the demands of contemporary society. In this discussion, we will mention four such limitations which illustrate how organizational structure has an impact on individual behavior.

Reduces Opportunity for Individual Psychological Success

One of the most critical indictments of contemporary organizational patterns is that they reduce the opportunity for individuals to achieve psychological success. This point of view is especially prominent in the research and writings of Chris Argyris.[12] The concept is essentially this. Modern hierarchial structures are based on the principles and philosophy of scientific management—which includes the familiar ideas of chain of command, span of control, task specialization, etc. And, as we have pointed out in the previous section, the prevalent managerial philosophy is that man is opposed to work. Thus, a combination of restrictive managerial controls and jobs fragmented by technology and specialization act to reduce opportunities for individual challenge and psychological success—especially at the lower levels in the hierarchy.

Thus, at some levels in our organizational structures we have so fragmented job responsibilities that employees are using only a narrow range of their talents. Faced with the frustration which comes from lack of challenge, employees may react in a variety of ways by expending much of their energy in non-productive activities. Expenditure of energy in these adaptive activities reduces the productive output of the organization. And the cycle is made complete, because these types of employee behaviors convince administrators that more controls are needed.

Here then is a vivid example of interaction between management philosophy and organizational structure. The results of rigid management, lack of opportunity for participation, and narrowly conceived responsibilities are becoming painfully apparent to many educational administrators today. Teachers and students are becoming more forceful in making known their objections to such approaches.

Contributes to Organizational Inertia

Another serious criticism of contemporary organizational structures is that they contribute to inertia by reducing opportunity for change. John Gardner has pointed out the need for continued "self-renewal" at both the individual and organizational level and has clearly explained that a readiness to grow and change is critical in contemporary society.[13] Yet those familiar with the workings of large organizations know that the rigidity which comes with formalization of activities is difficult to surmount. One of the mechanisms of the impedance is explained by Thompson:

> Hierarchial relations overemphasize the veto and underemphasize approval of innovation. Since there is no appeal from the superior's decision, a veto usually ends the matter. However, an approval will often have to go to the next higher level where it is again subject to veto. A hierarchial system always favors the status quo.[14]

Thus, communication is often inhibited in the hierarchial structure. Of course, there are other more complex concepts involved in this problem of resistance to change. We refer especially to the problem of individual status and role expectations associated with hierarchial structures. The basic idea is, however, that organizational inertia is encouraged by the "chain of command" concept inherent in contemporary patterns.

Inhibits Effective Decision Making

Today's society is one of specialization and increased interdependence, but we find it difficult to integrate specialists into hierarchial organizational patterns. In times gone past, the "boss" usually had come up through the ranks so that he knew every job under his supervision better than anyone working for him. This, of course, is no longer true. The diversity of organizational activities makes it impossible for one man to know it all. What school principal, school superintendent, or college president can possess an effective command of the variety of activities that take place in modern educational organizations?

Galbraith emphasizes the contribution of specialization as he points out that:

> The real accomplishment of modern science and technology consists of taking ordinary men, informing them narrowly and deeply and then through appropriate organization, arranging to have their knowledge combined with that of other specialized but equally ordinary men.[15]

He goes on to emphasize the need for coordination:

> Finally, following the need for this variety of specialized talent, is the need for its coordination. Talent must be brought to bear on the common purpose. More specifically, on large and small matters, information must be extracted from the various specialists, tested for its reliability and relevance, and made to yield a decision.[16]

The tasks of designing an "appropriate organization" and achieving "coordination" are the ones which are made more difficult by contemporary organizational patterns.

Thompson maintains that:

> Modern bureaucracy is an adaptation of older organizational forms altered to meet the need of specialization. Modern specialization is grafted into it, but old traces of the past remain. Along with technological specialization, we find survivals of Genghis Khan and the aboriginal war chiefs. We find the latest in science and technology associated with the autocratic, monistic, hierarchial organization of a simpler time.[17]

His thesis is that in modern organizations there is a growing imbalance between ability and authority—between the right to make decisions, which is authority, and the power to do so, which is specialized ability. Through the creation of staff agencies, cabinet methods of governance, and various council and committee structures some of the limitations outlined by Thompson have been overcome, but a number of problems remain unresolved.

Encourages Mechanistic View of Organization

Finally, we mention the fact that contemporary organizational patterns encourage a mechanistic view of organizational functions. With a mechanistic perspective, little relationship is discerned among the various parts of the organization. This restricted perspective has little correspondence with the reality of organizational functions, which is that the vitality of an organization depends upon the vitality of each component.

The dysfunctional consequences of an administrator's failure to take an organic view of an organization are readily apparent. For example, the school principal who evaluates his teaching faculty without regard to the capabilities of students or availability of teaching resources is taking a mechanistic view of his organization. The school superintendent who evaluates the effectiveness of his records division without any thought to the status of his computer and data processing division is taking a mechanistic view of his school system. The college president who feels that he can develop a strong department of psychology while neglecting to build strength in departments with which psychology may relate is taking a mechanistic view of the university. Indeed, any administrator who makes decisions without careful reflection of the impact throughout the organization has a bad case of "tunnel vision" with regard to the true nature of organizations today.

What implications do these concepts of structure have for the educational administrator? What points of focus and emphasis are suggested for practice? Clearly, the administrator must address himself to the challenges of (1) defining job responsibilities so that a greater array of human talents are called into play, (2) creating a sensitive balance between organizational control and independence of action so that change and innovation are facilitated rather than inhibited, (3) designing organizational relationships so that maximum contribution of specialists can be realized, and (4) developing an organic perspective of organizations so that he remains vigilant to the interdependency of organizational components.

In closing this discussion, let us admit readily that it is easier to recommend than it is to transform recommendation into action. At the same time, however, a more professional approach to administration begins with awareness. The writer shares with other practicing administrators the obligation of translating awareness into action.

The Impact of Group Membership

Occasionally administrators fall into the habit of thinking that the most important variables related to individual behavior within organizations are those associated with the vertical relationships formally expressed in line and staff charts. However, these formal relationships are only the above-surface part of the "iceberg" of organizational structure. In the words of Iannaccone:

> For centuries, some students of organization have thought that the formal organization is only what appears on the surface of organizational life and is given lip service. They have felt that beneath the formal organization, and obscured in part by it, there lies a "real" world consisting of the way things actually get done and how people truly behave in organizations.[18]

If research into organizational life has produced any finding of significance to the practicing administrator it is that peer relationships—both formal and informal—are critical variables in organizational productivity.

The study of group dynamics has produced a number of fruitful concepts concerning human behavior. It is not our purpose in this discussion to attempt a synopsis of the fields included in the study of group dynamics. To capsule areas such as the study of communication networks, leadership styles, attitude shaping, group counseling would be impossible; but perhaps with one or two examples we may illustrate the importance of group membership on individual behavior.

One of the things known from the study of group dynamics is that every individual in an organization is a member of both formal and informal groups and that these groups can have particular impact upon his attitudes and behavior. The literature abounds with laboratory and action research studies which reveal how group pressures can affect both the quality and speed with which tasks are accomplished and how groups can influence judgement. Administrators are in no way free from such influence, for research reveals that higher levels of education provide no immunity from pressures to conform. Thus, in understanding behavior within the organization, the alert administrator must remain sensitive to horizontal and diagonal relationships, the lines of which may extend outside the framework of the organization.

In the study of community and school relationships, administrators learn to define both the overt and covert power structures in the community of which the school is a part. A sensitivity to these structures is a valuable asset in a number of ways. Perhaps, an equally attentive study of both the above-surface and the "subterranean" structures within the organization may also prove fruitful.

Since our emphasis in this discussion is predominantly on the group membership effect on individual attitudes and behavior, perhaps it would be appropriate to take a short digression for the purpose of outlining an interesting motivation psychology which has emerged from the study of group behavior. We refer to the "cognitive dissonance" theory proposed by Festinger.[19] The core ideas of this theory are rather straightforward. Individuals are often confronted with conflicting notions or "cognitions" which do not fit well tgether. For example, a teacher may feel that a strike is an appropriate professional action but at the same time may feel that such action is unfair to the student. It is easy to see how different group memberships can bring pressure to bear on this point of individual conflict or dissonance.

Or consider the dissonance generated for an administrator who finds that the organizational chart dictates that he relate directly to another administrator for whom he has an intense personal dislike, a dislike derived from an extra-organizational association. According to Festinger, these conflicts or dissonances have motivation features because the dissonance will lead to behavior designed to reduce the dissonance. The teacher may decide that a temporary sacrifice of student welfare may be necessary for the long range welfare of other students, thus weighing in favor of the strike action. The administrator may decide that his personal feelings are less important than the welfare of his division, or he may find ways to circumvent the formal line of relationships. Cognitive dissonance theory has proved to be of considerable utility in predicting a wide range of behavior, and a basic familiarity with the concepts involved could prove to be of value in understanding, and predicting, behavior.

A number of other variables have been researched with regard to their effect on group performance and individual behavior. Research has included probes into (1) task variables, such as the effect of time required and task complexity; (2) structural variables, such as size of group, opportunity for interaction, and homogeneity of group talent; (3) leadership style, such as task orientation and group maintenance functions; and (4) communications, such as the study of network composition of speed of task completion and member satisfaction. This brief discussion is highly inadequate. Yet our purpose was limited. It was to stimulate the administrator to remain sensitive to the importance of both informal and formal relationships.

The Influence of Individual Personality

A careful review of the three previous sections of this paper will reveal that the determinants of individual behavior thus far considered have been external rather than internal. In effecting a more harmonious integration of individual and organization, our emphasis has been on adjusting the external factors of management philosophy, organizational structures, and group membership.

However, there is another perspective—and associated psychology—which is in contrast to three points of view previously considered. This perspective is most clearly captured in the writings of Zaleznik, who suggests that:

> The energy and vitality that make organizations move depend upon individual initiative. Leaders with brilliant ideas and the capacity to inspire thought and action in others are the main generators of energy. The effects of their personality induce a contagion to perform that is considerably stronger in directing organizations than depersonalized systems such as interlocking committee structures or participative management. The release of individual energy and the contagion to perform occur within organizational structures. But the impulse and inspiration derive from individual personality.[20]

Zaleznik goes on to analyze man-organization interaction from a framework of Freudian psychology. His theme is that many of the problems encountered in man-organization conflict may be better understood from an internal view rather than from an external one. From the standpoint of Freudian psychology, the determinants of present behavior are to be found in the past experience of the individual. Zaleznik's thesis is that much dysfunctional behavior in organizations may be explained as a failure of the individual to achieve psychological maturity.

His exposition of leadership dilemmas, subordinancy relationships, status conflicts, and other organizational problems in terms of individual personality development is conceptually rich. Perhaps we could explore one or two concepts which illustrate the importance of this idea for the educational administrator.

Let us take as our first example, the problem of communication in administrative behavior. We may recall that there has been significant emphasis given to the development of the ability to listen creatively and to empathize. Such an emphasis has a client-centered counseling orientation as proposed by Carl Rogers.[21] Certainly, the administrator will admit to frequent situations when listening is the appropriate administrative behavior. But, as Zaleznik points out, there are also situations which call for a posture more directive in character:

> It is important for both superior and subordinate to know where one stands on issues of work or personal conflict. We usually hear that it is important to listen to the other person and understand his point of view. This is good advice as far as it goes. What gets left out to the misfortune of all concerned is the fact that competent behavior depends on the ability of the individual to know where he stands and what he would like to see happen. In particular, the authority figure may find himself tyrannized by his own vacillations. If the subordinate is confused and torn by mixed feelings, it will do him little good to find his boss is equally confused. In this sense, knowing where one stands and being prepared to take a position has a salutary effect on human relationships.[22]

Our purpose here is not to emphasize one point of view at the expense of the other. It is to reinforce the idea of flexibility which earlier we proposed in our discussion of management philosophy.

Another concept of special interest to the administrator concerns the relationship of "personality orientation and executive functions." One of the really significant findings of behavioral research is that there is no personality syndrome characteristic of all effective leaders. Another way of saying this is to point out that research has suggested that effective leadership is often as much determined by situational variables as by personality variables. In his book *Management by Objectives*, Odiorne makes the point clear by analogy.[23] He suggests that effective management is similar to effective acting. The successful actor, knowledgeable of his strengths and limitations, pays attention to the selection of the play so that it will be compatible with his strengths and limitations. Likewise, the administrator should learn to assess his abilities so that he can achieve a harmonious and productive match of personality with function. Zaleznik neatly illustrates the interaction between administrator personality and administrative functions by the following diagram:

Executive Functions–Organizational Requisites

		Homeostatic	Mediative	Proactive
	Investment In			
	Persons	1	2	3
Personality Orientation	Persons & Tasks	2	1	3
	Ideas & Tasks	3	2	1

1-Major Performance
2-Secondary Performance
3-Avoided Performance

Figure 2.   The Interaction of Executive Functions and Personality Orientations.[24]

The interaction model of Figure 2 may be interpreted as follows. There are three types of organizational requisites or functions—homeostatic, mediative, and proactive. Homeostatic functions are passive in character and are associated with maintaining the internal stability of the organization. On the opposite end of the continuum are the proactive functions, which are those more active functions necessary for adapting the organization to its environment. These are change-oriented functions required for modifying organizational goals or the means by which the goals are achieved. Occupying an intermediate position on the continuum are the mediative functions.

Corresponding to these three types of organizational functions are three types of personality orientation. For example, the individual who is person-oriented will most probably give his major attention to the homeostatic organizational activities. In contrast, the idea and task oriented personality will find his major challenge and satisfaction in the proactive functions of the organization. There is a rough analogy here with some of the findings from group dynamics which suggest that two types of leaders may emerge within a group, a task oriented leader and a group maintenance leader. The task leader keeps the group focused on goals, whereas the maintenance leader insures the coherence and stability within the group.

The important implication of this model is that a match of personality with organizational function may be critical for both organizational productivity and individual personality development. Thus, a person-oriented individual thrust into an organizational position requiring a focus on tasks and goals may experience stress arising from the incompatibility of his personality and the organizational function. The same would be true of a task-oriented person finding himself in a position calling for a primary focus on interpersonal relations. These comments are not meant to suggest that individuals may be neatly and finally categorized in disregard of growth and change in personality. They do suggest, however, that it is inappropriate to ignore personality orientation in the integration of individual and organizational function.

This particular concept also relates to a suggestion which Zaleznik makes earlier in his book. It is that the administrator must develop a strong sense of identity:

The exercise of leadership requires a strong sense of identity—knowing who one is and who one is not. The myth of the value of being an "all-around guy" is damaging to the striving of an individual to locate himself from within and then to place himself in relation to others. This active location and placement of oneself prevents the individual from being defined by others in uncongenial terms. It prevents him also from being buffeted around the sea of opinion he must live within. A sense of autonomy, separateness, or identity permits a freedom of action and thinking so necessary for leadership.

Not the least significant part of achieving a sense of identity is the creative integration of one's past. There is no tailor who can convert a hayseed into a big-city boy—anymore than a dude can become a cowboy for all the hours he spends on the range. Coming to terms with being a hayseed or a dude permits the development of a unique person who goes beyond the stereotypes offered to him as models.[25]

The message is clear. Before he can hope to direct effectively the action of others, the administrator must first acquire a mastery of himself.

We have hardly circumscribed the full range of concepts which are embodied in this emphasis on individual personality. But hopefully, the illustrations presented were sufficiently pertinent to reveal the importance of individual personality in the influence of individual behavior at all levels of the organizational hierarchy.

Summary

In closing this paper it is appropriate that we ask what points of emphasis are suggested for the educational administrator aspiring to develop a more commanding professional competence. Among the many concepts which may be extracted from our discussion, we deem these to be most important.

Perhaps it is a trivial point, but it bears repeating that the causes of individual behavior in organizations are multivariate. The administrator needs to remember, therefore, that the determinants of behavior emerge from a matrix composed of management philosophy, organizational structure, group memberships, and individual personality.

As we consider the elements of this matrix, we find that contemporary research and theorizing in management philosophy indicate that the most productive relationships are those in which dependence, submissiveness, conformity, and external evaluation give way to relationships which hold opportunity for the development of trust, for independence of action, for risk taking, and for self-evaluation. The latter elements are essentials in providing organizational opportunity for the individual to achieve self-actualization.

This is not to suggest that the notions of authority and control are absent in current thought. It does mean that rigid and stereotyped ideas of administrative style must be replaced by a more flexible perspective which encourages matching style with situation. Such administrative flexibility requires the development of a strong interpersonal competency, and this competency derives from a broad knowledge base and a willingness to work at the "gut level" of feelings and emotions where there are few rational guides for action. Finally, a flexible administrative style demands also the development of a carefully considered value framework which prevents flexibility from degenerating into opportunism.

We have also seen that contemporary hierarchical organizational patterns often tend to impede (1) the achievement of individual self-actualization, (2) the occurrence of change and innovation, (3) the effective use of specialists in decision making, and (4) the development of an organic view of the organization. While it is easier to verbalize about these limitations than it is to suggest remedies, the administrator must confront the challenge of designing organizational patterns and relationships so that a greater array of human abilities are called into play, of creating a sensitive balance between control and independence so that change and innovation are facilitated, of overcoming rigid notions of relationships so that efficient use of specialists in decision making is achieved, and of developing an organic perspective of organizations so that the interdependence of organizational components is seen.

From a consideration of group membership on individual behavior, the administrator learns to acquire a sensitivity to the importance of diagonal and horizontal relationships within the organization. Individuals in the organization are members of groups, both informal and formal, whose lines of influence may extend well beyond the formal boundaries of the organization. An awareness, then, of both the overt and covert power relationships— of the above-surface and subterranean aspects of the organization—is indispensable for the administrator interested in understanding and predicting individual behavior.

Although what we have said thus far emphasizes the importance of external forces on individual behavior, a point not to be forgotten is that powerful internal forces for action are present in the personalities of individuals. The energy which moves organizations comes from individuals *acting on their environment*. It is not particularly proper, therefore, to see members of an organization simply as passive elements, moving to and fro at the whim of external forces. A harmonious integration of individual and organization is more likely to emerge when careful attention is given to the interaction between individual personal orientation and the various organizational tasks.

Notes

1. Bernard M. Bass, *Organizational Psychology* (Boston: Allyn and Bacon, 1965).
2. Victor Thompson, *Modern Organizations* (New York: Alfred Knopf, 1961).
3. William G. Scott, *Organization Theory: A Behavioral Analysis for Management* (Homewood: Richard Irwin, Inc., 1967).
4. J. G. March (ed.), *Handbook of Organizations* (Chicago: Rand McNally, 1965).
5. Frederick Winslow Taylor, *Scientific Management* (New York: Harper and Row, 1947).
6. Scott, *op. cit.*, p. 43.
7. Abraham H. Maslow, *Motivation and Personality* (New York: Harper and Brothers, 1954).
8. Douglas McGregor, *The Human Side of Enterprise* (New York: McGraw-Hill, 1960).
9. Rensis Likert, *New Patterns of Management* (New York: McGraw-Hill, 1961).
10. Chris Argyris, *Integrating the Individual and the Organization* (New York: John Wiley and Sons, 1964).
11. John Kenneth Galbraith, *The New Industrial State* (Boston: Houghton Mifflin, 1967), p. 143.

12. Argyris, *op. cit.*
13. John Gardner, *Self-Renewal* (New York: Harper and Row, 1964).
14. Thompson, *op. cit.*, p. 61.
15. Galbraith, *op. cit.*, p. 62.
16. *Ibid.*, p. 63.
17. Thompson, *op. cit.*, p. 5.
18. Laurence Iannaccone, "An Approach to the Informal Organization of the School," *Behavioral Science and Educational Administration: The Sixty-third Yearbook of the National Society for the Study of Education, Part II*, Daniel E. Griffiths, editor (Chicago: University of Chicago Press, 1964), p. 223.
19. Leon Festinger, *Theory of Cognitive Dissonance* (Evanston, Illinois: Peterson and Company, 1957).
20. Abraham Zaleznik, *Human Dilemmas of Leadership* (New York: Harper and Row, 1966), pp. 3–4.
21. Carl Rogers, *Client Centered Therapy* (New York: Houghton Mifflin, 1951).
22. Zaleznik, *op. cit.*, p. 68.
23. George S. Odiorne, *Management by Objectives* (New York: Pitman Publishing Corporation, 1965).
24. Zaleznik, *op. cit.*, p. 191.
25. *Ibid.*, pp. 41–42.

Chapter Eight

Educational Administration:
The Process

The term "process" implies the conversion of resources into a product through a continuing variety of activities. As such, a "process" involves five elements: (1) complex goal(s); (2) resources, both animate and inanimate; (3) activities and interactions within and among those resources; (4) time; and (5) product(s). Listed in this manner these elements are vague and abstract. However, the addition of an adjective, for example "educational," to the term process places boundaries around these elements. No longer is any complex goal implied, but instead an explicit goal is sought through an education program. Similarly, the range of resources and the activities and interactions involved is reduced.

The term "educational administration process" has the same five elements but again with constraints imposed by the modifiers. For example, the development of skills and the mastery of subject matter are among the goals that would be implied by the term "educational process." In contrast, the goals of the "educational administration process" would be the establishment and efficient operation of a particular type of institution.

Literature on the process of educational administration has identified numerous subprocesses, which parallel the five elements listed above. As detailed in the literature these subprocesses concentrate primarily on the activities involved and secondarily on the material items—the equipment, people, materials, etc. This concentration can be seen in the POSDCORB statement of Gulick and Urwick,[1] the DPCCR analysis of Litchfield,[2] and DPSCA as discussed by Campbell, Corbally and Ramseyer.[3]

By conceptualizing a "process" as a dynamic set of activities with associated goals and materials, theorists have created a parallelism between the

---

[1] Luther Gulick and L. Urwick, eds., *Papers on the Science of Administration* (New York, 1937).

[2] Edward H. Litchfield, "Notes on a General Theory of Administration," *Administrative Science Quarterly*, I (June, 1956), pp. 3–29.

[3] Roald F. Campbell, John E. Corbally, Jr., and John A. Ramseyer, *Introduction to Educational Administration*. Boston: Allyn and Bacon, 1966, pp. 144–151.

terms "process" and "system." Griffiths' article, "Use of Models in Research," discusses the systems construct. In it he presents a definition attributed to Floyd Allport.

> . . . any recognizably delimited aggregate of dynamic elements that are in some way interconnected and interdependent and that continue to operate together according to laws and in such a way as to produce some characteristic total effect.[4]

That that definition could apply to either "process" or "system" becomes clear as the rest of Griffiths' statement is studied.

The subprocesses which comprise educational administration according to Campbell, Corbally, and Ramseyer are: deciding, planning, stimulating, coordinating, and appraising. Further elaboration of three of these, planning, stimulating, and coordinating, is presented by content in other chapters in this book (planning in the Setting, A Philosophical Base, and Organization; stimulating and coordinating in The Man, The Job, and Organization). The other two, deciding and appraising, are examined through readings in this chapter.

Decisions are choices between alternatives. They have a prerequisite—information—a commodity obtained by the administrator through three activities: (1) insightful analyses of prior experiences; (2) research; and (3) evaluation. Little is written about the first of these. That does not, however, discount its importance. The latter two activities have been examined over a lenghy period of time and are currently taking on new dimensions as shown in the articles presented in this chapter by Guba, Stufflebeam, and Worthen.

Insights from professional experience, research, and evaluation are all prone to bias. Seldom is it possible for an individual to be completely objective in analysis of his experiences. Research activities are structured to overcome subjectivity. In doing so, however, other biasing factors and additional problems are encountered. The information generated in an evaluation is situation-bound. Like research, it attempts to control subjectivity, but there are inherent problems of generalizability. Together these three activities provide a check and balance system in the provision of information, a system analogous to the check and balance written into our Constitution in the form of the Legislative-Executive-Judicial division of power. The administrator should recognize that, as in government, reliance on one source of information for decision-making is likely to contribute to bias in the appraising subprocess.

[4] Floyd H. Allport, *Theories of Perception and the Concept of Structure* (New York: John Wiley and Sons, Inc., 1955), p. 469.

24 | Use of Models in Research

Daniel E. Griffiths

In exploring the idea that administrative decisions are derived from the total organization and its environment, the concept of systems theory presents perhaps the most cogent positive statement. Systems theory constitutes one aspect of this paper, "Use of Models in Research," by Daniel E. Griffiths. Points concerning the qualities of input-output, open systems, and feedback all have implications for the school administrator as he is concerned with the decision-making process.

System-Theory

What is called "system-theory" is an outgrowth of relatively new organismic conceptions as reflected in the work of von Bertalanffy and Goldstein and in certain aspects of Gestalt psychology. It opposes simple reaction theories, where a virtual automaton is seen to respond discretely to stimuli.

A "system" is simply defined *as a complex of elements in mutual interaction.* System is a construct which has been used in almost every area of science for a long period of time. Floyd Allport offers a more comprehensive definition of system indicating it to be:[1]

> . . . any recognizably delimited aggregate of dynamic elements that are in some way interconnected and interdependent and that continue to operate together according to certain laws and in such a way as to produce some characteristic total effect. A system, in other words, is something that is concerned with some kind of activity and preserves a kind of integration and unity; and a particular system can be recognized as distinct from other systems to which, however, it may be dynamically related. Systems may be complex; they may be made up of interdependent sub-systems, each of which, though less autonomous than the entire aggregate, is nevertheless fairly distinguishable in operation.

A more succinct definition is that of Hall and Fagen: "A system is a set of objects together with relationships between the objects and between their

Daniel E. Griffiths, "Use of Models in Research," *Educational Research: New Perspectives,* Jack A. Culbertson and Stephen P. Hencley, eds. (Danville, Illinois: The Interstate Printers and Publishers, Inc., 1963), pp. 129–40. Reprinted by permission.

attributes."[2] This means that a system is composed of *objects* which are the parts of the system and that there are relationships among the objects and their attributes which tie the system together. Systems may be *open* or *closed*. An open system is related to and exchanges matter with its environment, while a closed system is not and does not. Further, a closed system is characterized by entropy or a state of equilibrium, while open systems may tend toward the steady state. All systems except the smallest have sub-systems and all but the largest have supra-systems which are their environments.

Properties of organismic, open systems. Open systems, of course, have the properties of systems in general, but open systems have certain characteristics which distinguish them from closed systems.[3]

1. Open systems exchange energy and information with their environments; that is, they have *inputs* and *outputs*.

2. Open systems tend to maintain themselves in *steady states*. A steady state is characterized by a constant ratio being maintained among the components of the system. A burning candle is often used to illustrate one aspect of a steady state. Upon being lighted the flame is small, but grows rapidly to its normal size. It maintains this size as long as the candle and its environment exist.

3. Open systems are *self-regulating*. In the preceding illustration, a sudden draft will cause the flame to flicker, but with the cessation of the draft the flame regains its normal characteristics.

4. Open systems display *equifinality*; that is, identical results can be obtained from different initial conditions.

5. Open systems maintain their steady states, in part, through the *dynamic interplay of sub-systems operating as functional processes*. This means that the various parts of an open system function without persistent conflicts which can neither be resolved nor regulated.

6. Open systems can maintain their steady states through *feedback* processes.

7. Open systems display *progressive segregation*.[4] This process occurs when an open system divides into a hierarchical order of subordinate systems which gain a certain independence of each other.

Hearn summarizes the properties of open, organismic systems in this manner:[5]

There is a dynamic interplay among the essential functional sub-processes or sub-systems in the organismic system which enables it to maintain itself in a homeostasis steady state. Assuming a sufficient input of material from its environment, the organism develops toward a characteristic state despite initial conditions (equifinality). All of this is accomplished through an automatic self-regulatory process.

Statement of assumptions. Two very general assumptions are made concerning administrative performance:[6]

1. *Administrative performance is a generalized type of behavior to be found in all human organizations.* "Administration" is a term used to describe an aspect of behavior in a social organization. Since there are few aspects of behavior unrelated to some social organization, administrative performance is a vital and pervasive aspect of all human behavior. An extension of this point-of-view is that the adjectival varieties of administrative performance are alike rather than different. Administrative performance in a business enterprise, a hospital, a military unit, an industrial plant, or a school has some apparent unique variance, but the common variance of the performance among different settings is a valid area for theoretical focus. Further, administrative performance is not to be thought of in terms of the behavior of a single person: "the administrator." Administrative performance is, rather, an abstraction of behavior present in organizations even though there is no one formally designated as an administrator.

2. *Administrative performance involves the directing and controlling of behavior in a social enterprise.* Administrative performance has as its purpose the implementation of the goals for which an organization is designed. The implementation is effected through (a) establishing criteria for the performance of individuals as they interact in the organization, and (b) establishing controls to make certain that performance agrees with plans. Administrative performance is not an artificial function superimposed on the normal activities of human beings; it rather involves the process (cycle of events) engaged in by the members of a social organization in order to control and direct the activities of the members within the organization. It can be said that administration is not the production of the organization. Barnard stated this quite clearly when he said, "Executive work is not that *of* the organization, but the specialized work of *maintaining* the organization in operation."[7]

A theory of administrative performance. It is proposed that system-theory serve as a model for a theory of administrative performance. As was just indicated, any system exists with sub-systems and with supra-systems;

all this means is that there are related systems of different sizes. A school district is a system comprised of human interactions which maintains a definite boundary. The school district exists in a larger system of human interactions called the school community. Existing within the school district is the system of human interactions occurring at the school building level. Thinking only of the system at the building level, attention is to be focused upon the administrative performance system. It is located at the point of tangency of the boundaries of the school building system, the school district system, and the school community system.

An individual, of course, may be considered to be a system—an open, organismic system.[8] But the principal as a person system is not the focus of attention here. Rather the focus is upon the administrative performance system which at many points, but not all, may coincide with a system of a specific person. In most instances, the administrative performance system is comprised of many people; however, this discussion deals with research based on an instance in which there is but one administrator, making it the simplest form of an administrative performance system.[9]

Relation of model. The first question to be raised is, "Is the administrative performance of school principals isomorphic to system-theory?" In other words, can administrative performance be conceptualized as a system? The test to be applied is to raise the question, "Is it possible to state certain propositions derived from system-theory which may be demonstrated to apply to a school principal?"

Performance as a system. In order for *performance* to be considered as a system, it must exhibit the properties of a system. The description of administrative performance has been the major concern of the afore-mentioned research study. The findings of the study are summarized in a general way by the eight primary factors and the two second-order factors found in the analysis of the in-basket work of the principals. Seven properties of open, organismic systems were noted. It is of interest to compare the findings of the study with the formal properties of an open system.

1. Input-Output.

Administrative performance is conceptualized as a system existing at the point of tangency of several systems, including the school community, the school district, and the school building unit. All open, organismic systems exhibit an input-output function. Evidence of input-output are certainly clear in the administrative performance system. Factor A, Exchanging Information, is clearly an input-output factor. The performance system exchanges information with the school unit system, the school district, and the community. Factor G, Responding to Outsiders, indicates not only exchanging information with the community system, but also responsiveness to the demands of that system. Output dimensions are noted in Factor H, Directing Others, and Factor C, Complying with Suggestions. There is abundant evidence that the administrative performance system does exchange energy and information with its environment. It has an input and an output.

2. Steady States.

A steady state is evidenced by a constant ratio being maintained among the components of the system. Many of the findings of the study can be understood as expressions of a system maintaining itself in a steady state. The school principals who were studied displayed a singular lack of concern with organizational changes or the initiation of new procedures. It may be that it is necessary to consider leadership and administration as separate and distinct. One way to understand such a dichotomy is in terms of the maintenance of a steady state within a performance system. While a steady state was observed, it must be noted that this was not a constant state. There was *some* change, generally as a result of stimuli from the environment.

Since the study was essentially cross-sectional in nature and no feedback was introduced, little can be said about the steady state. A study employing simulation, but longitudinal in nature, should be undertaken. It would then be possible to study the characteristics of this steady state over a period of time.

3. Self-Regulation.

When a system is disturbed, but re-establishes itself, selfregulation is apparent. There is little evidence from the study which can be brought to bear on this property. The same comments are appropriate here as are made under number 2.

4. Equifinality.

This property refers to the observed fact that identical results can be obtained from different initial conditions. We note the position of the performance system as being tangential to the other three systems. The function of the performance system is to handle information and energy from all sources and to make decisions on what are perceived as problems. Factor X is noted to be a decision factor (see Table 1). This factor was found to involve all of the primary factors, except Factor E, Maintaining Relationships. The important point to note is that the average performance of administrators can be plotted on the continuum from "Preparing to Decide" through to "Taking Terminal Action." Taking terminal action on a problem may be viewed as the final step of the process described as administrative performance. There is no indication that all principals go through all the stages of decision-making, but that once a problem is perceived, the terminal decision appears to be the end to be reached by entry at any place in the stages of decision-making. This is not to say, however, that the same final decision could be expected by entering the decision continuum at different places.

5. Sub-systems.

The sub-systems of the administrative performance system were not directly identified by the study. There are some leads, however. The factors can be considered as suggesting sub-systems; thus, there might be a communications system, a leadership system, and a group maintenance system. Sub-systems might be construed in more traditional terms as the functions of an organization, and so there might be a supervision system, a planning system, and the like. While it seems clear that there are sub-systems, just what they are is not clear.

6. Feedback.

Factor A, Exchanging Information, Factor C, Complying with Suggestions, Factor E, Maintaining Relationships, and Factor G, Responding to Outsiders, all reflect the presence of feedback activities, that is, responses to disturbance in the steady state. This study has little evidence to bear on feedback as a dynamic aspect of the administrative performance system, since the subjects received no feedback from their own work. Another study is needed to provide evidence of this nature.

7. Progressive segregation.

Little information has been gained concerning the structuring of the sub-systems of the administrative performance system. Evidence on this property of open systems will have to wait on later reserach. Once sub-systems are identified, it is predicted that they will tend to fall into a hierarchial order.

Propositions. As Meadows has pointed out:[10]

The scientist wishes to predict, and the model becomes thus a device by which assumptions are transformed into postulates. Models, then, are techniques of inference-making.

TABLE 1* Stages in Decision-Making with Appropriate In-Basket Scores and Their Loadings on Factor X

Stages in Decision-Making	In-Basket Scoring Categories	Loadings on Factor X
1. Recognizes a problem		
2. Prepares to clarify the problem	Arrives at a procedure for deciding	.69
	Requires further information for deciding	.63
3. Initiates work on the problem	Work scheduled for same or next day	.61
	Discusses with subordinates	.60
	Asks subordinates for information	.56
	Takes leading action	.41
4. Organizes and judges facts and opinions	Conceptual analysis	.24
	Tentative or definite plans only	.16
	Delays, postpones	.15
5. Selects alternative solutions	Follows lead by superiors	.09
	Follows lead by subordinates	—.10
6. Decides and acts	Concluding decisions	—.51
	Terminal action	—.62

* Taken from John Hemphill, Daniel Griffiths, *et al.*, *Dimensions of Administrative Performance*, Contract No. 214 (6905) Cooperative Research Branch, U.S. Office of Education, Department of Health, Education, and Welfare, May, 1961, p. F. 10.

The system model presented here could lead to a number of propositions, all of which would need more research. Two propositions will be discussed simply as illustrations.

A question of major importance is, "By what means is the steady state of the administrative performance system maintained?" The structure of the system and its tangential location to other systems cause it to avoid extreme positions and to prefer a relatively even keel. This leads to proposition 1.

Proposition 1. The steady state of the administrative performance system is maintained by a decision process in which satisfactory alternatives are selected rather than optimal alternatives.

Discussion. Simon has suggested that administrative man satisfices rather than maximizes. As he has said,[11]

1. While economic man maximizes—selects the best alternatives from among all those available to him; his cousin, whom we shall call administrative man, satisfices—looks for a course of action that is satisfactory or "good enough." Examples of satisficing criteria that are familiar enough to businessman, if unfamiliar to most economists, are "share of the market," "adequate profit," "fair price."

2. Economic man deals with the "real world" in all its complexity. Administrative man recognizes that the world he perceives is a drastically simplified model of the buzzing, blooming confusion that constitutes the real world. He is content with this gross simplification because he believes that the real world is mostly empty—that most of the facts of the real world have no great relevance to any particular situation he is facing, and that most significant chains of causes and consequences are short and simple. Hence, he is content to leave out of account those aspects of reality—and that means most aspects—that are substantially irrelevant at a given time. He makes his choices using a simple picture of the situation that takes into account just a few of the factors that he regards as most relevant and crucial.

   What is the significance of these two characteristics of administrative man? First, because he satisfices, rather than maximizes, administrative man can make his choices without first examining all possible behavior alternatives and without ascertaining that these *are* in fact all the alternatives. Second, because he treats the world as rather "empty" and ignores the interrelatedness of all things (so stupefying to thought and action), administrative man is able to make his decisions with relatively simple rules of thumb that do not make impossible demands upon his capacity for thought.

Simon regards this explanation of administrative decision-making as verified both by common sense reasoning and through work with machine simulated thought processes.[12]

Several of the scoring categories are related to the choice of alternatives. Such categories as Following Leads by Superiors and Subordinates, Making Concluding Decisions, and Taking Terminal Action could be considered as indicating that the principals restricted their world to their immediate associates and made decisions in terms of what they learned from them. Such categories as Conceptual Analysis and Uses Program Values could be considered as indicating that the principals attempted to analyze the item, to see its broad implications, and to relate the item to background information or to other items. The former was much more prevalent than the latter.

It would appear that the steady state of the administrative performance system is one in which there is more satisficing than maximizing.

Proposition 2. Administrative systems respond to continuously increasing stress first by a lag in response, then by an over-compensating response, and finally by a catastrophic collapse of the system.[13]

Discussion. There is some evidence which indicates that moderate stress lifts performance above ordinary levels, but that extreme stress may cause performance to deteriorate. In the study the subjects indicated that, during the test week, they were under more stress than usual, but that they produced more than normally. The intriguing question is, "How much stress can the administrative performance system take before it collapses?" Another way of putting the question is, "What is the optimum stress which should be placed on a system so as to produce optimum performance?" There is no definitive evidence on this at present, but a rigorous testing of this proposition would provide extremely important information.

Assumptions Underlying the Use of System-Theory

What assumptions underlie the use of open, organismic system as a model for the study of administration? Meadows presents one assumption which is back of the use of system as a model for research in general.[14]

1. The first assumption is rarely stated by those who employ the system as a model, namely that "reality exists in systems."[15] The argument establishing system as the way in which reality exists was summarized by the biologist Henderson. "It is in systems that all forms of activity manifest themselves. Therefore, any form of activity may be produced by a suitable system."[16]
2. It has frequently been noted that several sciences have "discovered" independently the same phenomenon or principle. This leads one to assume that a theory developed in one field might be useful in several. The assumption is, then, that the various physical and non-physical scientific disciplines constitute an interdependent whole and as such contribute to one another's knowledge.[17]
3. The assumption as regards the nature of the universe is that it is continually expanding and that it is an open system.
4. It is assumed that while man may be referred to as a species, he exists in great variety. Kluckhohn and Murray have said that "every man is in certain aspects (a) like all other men, (b) like some other men, and (c) like no other man."[18]
5. If man has a nature, it is to create a more perfect relationship between himself and his environment. He is not content merely to adjust. Man is able to acquire and transmit knowledge and to gain increasing control over his environment.
6. It is assumed that human behavior is always the result of interaction between the biological organism and its environment. All individuals are participants in a number of interlocking networks of interaction, and the organizational behavior of an individual can be understood only by reference to these networks.

The adoption of the open, organismic system as a model for the study of administration might have as wide an influence as the earlier adoption of the machine by Strayer, Cubberley, and Spaulding. If this is so, then we might well be on the threshold of a new organizational structure for public education.

Notes

1. Floyd H. Allport, *Theories of Perception and the Concept of Structure* (New York: John Wiley & Sons, Inc., 1955), p. 469.
2. A. D. Hall and R. E. Fagen in *General Systems—Yearbook of the Society for the Advancement of General Systems Theory*, Ludwig van Bertalanffy and Anatol Rapoport (eds.) (Ann Arbor: Braun-Brumfield, 1956), p. 18.
3. Adapted from Gordon Hearn, *Theory Building in Social Work* (Toronto: University of Toronto Press, 1958), pp. 44–50.
4. Ludwig von Bertalanffy, "An Outline of General Systems Theory," *British Journal for the Philosophy of Science*, Vol. I, 1950, p. 148.
5. Hearn, *op. cit.*, pp. 48, 49.
6. For an elaboration of these assumptions in a different framework, see Daniel E. Griffiths, *Administrative Theory* (New York: Appleton-Century-Crofts, Inc., 1959).
7. Chester I. Bernard, *The Function of the Executive* (Cambridge: Harvard University Press, 1938), p. 215.
8. James G. Miller, "Towards a General Theory for the Behavioral Sciences," *The American Psychologist*, Vol. X, 1955, p. 521.
9. John Hemphill, Daniel Griffiths, Norman Frederiksen, *Administrative Performance and Personality* (New York: Teachers College Bureau of Publications, 1962).
10. Meadows, *op. cit.*, p. 8.
11. Herbert Simon, *Administrative Behavior* (New York: the Macmillan Co., 1957), pp. xxv–xxvi.
12. *Ibid.*, pp. xxvi–xxviii.
13. Miller, *op. cit.*, p. 525.
14. Meadows, *op. cit.*, pp. 3–4.
15. *Ibid.*, p. 3.
16. L. J. Henderson, *The Order of Nature* (Cambridge: Harvard University Press, 1917), p. 172.
17. Assumptions 2, 3, 4, and 5 are discussed in greater detail in Hearn, *op. cit.*
18. Clyde Kluckhohn and Henry A. Murray, *Personality in Nature, Society and Culture* (2nd ed.) (New York: Alfred A. Knopf, Inc., 1953), p. 53.

25 | The Expanding Concept of Research

Egon G. Guba

Some see research only as experimentation. It is more than that. It is the systematic investigation engaged in by individuals who wish to enhance the general understanding of specific phenomena. It encompasses a range of methodologies from histories, descriptive surveys, and case studies, through unobtrusive quasi-experiments, to true experiments. Guba discusses this methodological expansion along with the development of new research-related specialties.

Educational research is expanding in many ways. Enormous increases in research and development funds and a comparable expansion in the number and kinds of agencies engaged in educational research and development are familiar indicators of this burgeoning. A further measure is the projection of needed educational research and development manpower recently furnished by Clark and Hopkins under an Office of Education grant.[1] Their conservative estimates indicate that by 1972, more than 40,000 full-time equivalent personnel will be needed to man only those programs of research and development funded by the Federal Government or by foundations.[2] No provision is made in these statistics for the expansion at the state and local level in education or for the vast industrial investments in this area.

Educational research has not remained unaffected by these sudden changes. With these new demands and challenges, educational researchers have become increasingly introspective about what they are doing and why. They have become increasingly concerned because education has not been as affected by research as one might expect. More than thirty years ago, Paul Mort called attention to the fifty-year lag between school practice and the best available knowledge. Educational researchers wonder why such a lag exists and what to do about it. Thus, as the research *enterprise* has increased in size and complexity, the *concept* of what research is and how it may be utilized to affect educational practice is under considerable scrutiny. This self-evaluation by researchers may, in the long run, result in more sig-

Egon G. Guba, "The Expanding Concept of Research," *Theory Into Practice* VI (April, 1967), 57–65. Reprinted by permission.

nificant changes in educational research than could be accounted for simply by increased size.

Three areas of concern are emerging. First, it is clear that the traditional techniques of research are not adequate to handle the many questions that can or should be asked about education. Classic models of experimentation, although extremely useful, cannot handle the full range of inquiry. Second, there is a developing interest in establishing better linkages between research and practice. Models of such linkage systems are being proposed and used. They are also forming the basis for projections about the kinds of middle-men roles likely to emerge and the kinds of training experiences necessary to prepare the potential incumbents of those roles. Finally, there is a shift away from questions of mere technique and methodology in research to those concerning the nature of problems, the place of theory, and other aspects of the research activity. These latter activities, which were viewed as the "softer" or "more arty" aspects of research, are emerging as substantial issues which can be attacked in the same rigorous and systematic ways as issues of methodology. Another way to characterize this latter movement is to label it as a shift from more methodologically based thinking to more substantively based thinking about research.

New Methodologies

Research has often been equated with a particular form of inquiry known as "experimentation." Experimentalism has characterized the physical sciences, with unparalleled success. It is accepted as *the* mode of inquiry in most scientific areas, including the behavioral sciences. What are the characteristics of this approach?

Consider an example. Galileo, contrary to others of his day, believed that all objects, regardless of weight, would fall through an equal distance in equal time. He reached this conclusion by theorizing about the constancy of gravitational pull (although he did not use that particular concept explicitly). To "prove" his assertion he is reputed to have dropped two objects from the Tower of Pisa, and they reached earth at the same time.

From this short example, the following crucial characteristics of an experiment can be identified:

1. Experiments involve variables (i.e., characteristics that may vary from subject to subject) identified *a priori*, e.g., weight, time, and distance.

2. Experiments are intended to test assertions, usually called hypotheses, about certain relationships that are said to exist among the variables (e.g., all objects fall equal distances in equal times regardless of their weights).

3. Experiments give the investigator control over both the variables of interest (in this case, weight, distance, and time), as well as over other variables that might be suggested as accounting for the observed phenomenon (so-called confounding variables). Thus, if anyone had suggested that it was really the *shape* of the object that determined its speed of fall, Galileo could have used objects of different shapes to refute the contention.

4. Experiments involve *interventions* on the part of the investigator. The phenomena he studies do not typically occur by themselves but are arranged for. Thus, Galileo arranged to drop the objects, released them simultaneously, and timed their fall independently. He determined which variables were included and which were excluded, and what the conditions of the test would be.

5. Experiments are public, empirical, and replicable. Any investigator of equal competence must be able to produce the same data in a replication of the experiment.

This experimental model has general validity for many situations. But is experimentation useful in every kind of inquiry situation that might come up in educational research, and when it is used, does the intervention of the investigator in fact predetermine the findings to some extent, especially with human subjects? These questions relate to the first four of the characteristics outlined above. Thus, can experimentation be used in situations in which the relevant variables cannot be defined *a priori*, when hypotheses cannot be formulated, or when the institution of controls may be impossible or undesirable for some reason? Does the intervention of the experimentor produce data with a laboratory bias? Typically, no objection is raised with regard to the fifth characteristic, replicability.

What are some situations in which these questions might be raised? Suppose we are interested in the teacher-student interaction in the classroom. Many variables must be considered to account for observed interactions, including teacher and pupil personalities, motivational factors, situational factors, task factors, and others, so it would be difficult to formulate powerful hypotheses or to identify the crucial variables in advance. While no one would argue that it might be impossible to manage these matters *eventually*, serious doubts may be raised about the utility of an experimental approach early in the game.

Or, what if it were proposed to introduce a variety of new materials into a school to find what uses the children might make of them? An experimentalist would be prone to contrive a number of different uses which children *might* make of the materials and, then, instruct certain groups to use each alternative. Thus, each alternative could be studied and the particular educational outcomes of each determined. Obviously, we would never discover by this approach what the children *themselves* would do if left to their own devices. It is possible they might evolve entirely different alternatives than the experimentor. If our interest were in the latter alternatives, the imposition of the experimental design would obviously be undesirable.

Or, consider that a new method of teaching language to culturally disadvantaged children is to be studied in a school. The experimentor would be prone to select certain *experimental* schools (i.e., schools in which the new method would be used) and certain *control* schools (i.e., other schools in which the new method would not be used but in which comparative data would be collected). The experimentor would have to insist that (1) the method tested must be used consistently throughout the experimental period, and (2) no other deviations from "normal" practice be permitted during that period lest the effects of the new method be influenced by the other new elements. These conditions place severe restrictions on the educator as he operates in the school. First, the educator wants to feel free to make continuous improvement in the new method as he gains insights into how it works. Second, he wants to feel free to do what he can to help alleviate the situation of the culturally disadvantaged child. Thus, he may find the experimentor's imposition of controls intolerable; he may even insist that he cannot ethically agree to them because they will not permit him to do his best for each child.

The experimentor answers these objections by saying that the imposition of such conditions and controls is simply the price society must be willing to pay for new knowledge. After all, half of the children in the Salk vaccine test did not get protective vaccine, but distilled water. They were as prone to polio as ever, but it was their susceptibility that proved how good the vaccine was. Some children were allowed to contract polio so others might be saved. The fact that this ethical problem is encountered does not in the final analysis warrant giving up experimental inquiry altogether.

One additional objection may be raised that is more difficult to cope with, viz., that the very act of intervention by the experimentor so changes the data, that they have a "laboratory bias" and no longer represent what "normally" happens in the "real world." This argument has been presented by Barker,[3] and has been further explicated in relation to research by my own studies of educational change.[4]

To illustrate the problems of bias that arise in social inquiry when the experimental method is used, Barker cites the following example, which makes the point quite well (the italics are mine):

> Some years when I was a student of Kurt Lewin, he and Tamara Dembo and I carried out some experiments upon frustration. The findings of these experiments have been verified by others and they have become a part of the literature of scientific psychology. The experiments provided basic information about

the consequences for children of frustration, as defined in the experiments, and about the processes that produce these consequences. Time passed. In due course *I* had a student, and he undertook to study frustration. So far, so good. All in the grand tradition! My student, Clifford L. Fawl, did not replicate the earlier study; he did not contrive frustration for his subjects; he pioneered, and extended the investigation from children *in vitro*, so to speak, to children *in situ*. He searched our specimen records of children's everyday behavior for instances of this allegedly important phenomenon without psychologists as operators. Here are the words of his report . . . "The results . . . were surprising in two respects. First, even, with a libeal interpretation of frustration fewer incidents were detected than we expected. . . . Second . . . meaningful relationships could not be found between frustration . . . and consequent behavior such as . . . regression . . . and other theoretically meaningful behavioral manifestations. . . ." In other words, frustration was rare in the children's days, and when it did occur it did not have the behavioral consequences observed in the laboratory. It appears that the earlier experiments simulated frustration very well as we defined it and prescribed it for our subjects (in accordance with our theories); but the experiments did not simulate frustration as life prescribes it for our children.[5]

It appears that the data resulting from an investigation depend heavily upon the mode of inquiry used by the investigator. Experimental inquiry seemingly produces information about the range of possible relationships between several variables *defined a priori in accordance with some theory* or, that is, about the *possible relationships* that might exist in a laboratory setting. There is a second kind of inquiry, however, exemplified by the conduct of Barker's student, Clifford Fawl, in which the investigator does not intervene at all but simply keeps a close record of what occurs. This second mode—which Barker called "Type T" inquiry and which I call "aexperimental" inquiry—delivers a real-life correspondence not available in the laboratory. On the other hand, the laboratory offers a degree of precision and control that can never be approximated in a field study.

If a naive view with respect to this example of Barker's were to be taken, this question could be posed: "Which are the 'real' data concerning children's reaction to frustration—Barker's experimental data or Fawl's aexperimental data?" Such a question is fruitless. Both forms of inquiry provide valuable information. The experimental approach yields information about a toal range of relationships, focuses attention on a highly restricted number of variables as indicated by theory, maintains careful controls, and is highly generalizable because it is, by design, quite context free. The aexperimental approach yields information about relationships as they actually occur in nature, focuses attention on many variables at once, provides a certain flexibility for adjusting to situations that the rigid controls of experimentalism make impossible, and yields a rich and detailed supply of information about a particular happening in a particular context. The laboratory tells what happens in the best of all possible worlds, while the aexperiment tells what happens in the worst.

Thus, experimentalism and aexperimentalism are complementary—representing two sides of the same coin. There are times when each is appropriate, depending upon the investigator's intent, the degree of pre-existing knowledge about the phenomenon being studied, and the relative degree of control or flexibility that may be desirable.

It appears there are two problems with the experimental approach: (1) it is not always possible or desirable to maintain the degree of control required by the laboratory-oriented experimental approach in a real-life setting, such as that represented by the school, and (2) data from experiments do not answer all questions that might be asked. As this is understood, the educational research community is reaching out to devise new methods and approaches appropriate when experimentalism may not be.

Regarding the first problem, lack of control, considerable headway has already been made in the so-called quasi-experimental designs proposed by Campbell and Stanley.[6] They are intended for situations in which the assumptions underlying the classic research designs cannot be met, as is often true in education. The second problem is somewhat more difficult. About all that can be said is that the educational researcher is becoming aware of the necessity for aexperimental research, but aexperimental designs analogous to experimental designs have not yet been developed.

Perhaps the most promising tool available to those conducting an inquiry in the aexperimental mode is the computer, which monitors many variables at once. If one can collect information on a large scale and have it instantaneously available for recall and comparison with new data, it is possible to detect the effects of any change at once by noting in what particulars the data about the monitored variables have altered. It is as though a physician could have available instantaneously a wide variety of data about a patient; then, when given a drug, the physician could know at once its effects on the patient by noting changes in temperature, blood sugar count, level of adrenalin, etc. Similarly, if a new method of teaching were introduced into a classroom, it would be possible to tell almost at once (and continously) the effects of the new method by noting changes in such monitored variables as children's motivation, achievement, relationships with the teacher, etc.

No doubt these computer applications are in the future. But whether or not these particular techniques ever receive widespread use, it is clear that experimentalism is no longer sufficient to deal with all the questions the educational researcher must ask. At the methodological level at least, the concept of what educational research is continues expanding considerably to admit new techniques and to search assiduously for additional novel methods.

Linkages Between Research and Practice

A second concern for the educational research community is the massive lag between research and practice. In our struggle to upgrade education in the post-Sputnik era, it is clear that the schools have not taken full advantage of the knowledge produced by educational research.

Why? For more than a decade, it was fashionable for the researcher and the practitioner to blame each other. Practitioners accused researchers of residing in ivy towers, studying problems of no practical significance. Simultaneously, researchers insisted that the development of applications from research was the practitioner's responsibility. The orderly transition of knowledge from a theoretical into a practical state has suffered.

The real problem was that the educational community had never made provisions for development. It would never occur to the Bell Telephone Company, for example, that the basic research being conducted in its laboratories would find its way into improved switchboards or better handsets unless someone bore the specific responsibility for seeing that this happened. In education, however, the assumption was blithely made that educational research, once published, would by some mysterious process be turned into a practical teaching method or new curriculum.

A whole series of functions intervene between research and practice, and these are only now being identified. An example of one taxonomy of such intermediate functions is shown in Table 1.[7] Each function has its own particular purpose and will probably require a specially trained person to carry it out.

The general activity labeled "development" is concerned with identifying problems, inventing solutions to those problems, engineering the proposed solutions into practical form, and field testing these packages. Those carrying out these functions may be thought of as educational engineers in a very literal sense. Like the engineers of the hard sciences, they are concerned with utilizing the knowledge produced by the researchers in order to develop practical answers to operating problems. Special training, skills, techniques, and resources are obviously required.

These developmental engineers are concerned with four activities:

1. *Gathering operational and planning data.* This activity has often been called institutional research. Its main purpose is to describe and analyze what is going on so that breakdowns can be quickly detected and diagnosed. This activity also provides a general baseline of data which can be used effectively in the evaluation of any proposed innovation (new solution to a problem).

2. *Inventing solutions to operating problems.* If the first step described is working as it should, operating problems will be quickly detected. Once

TABLE 1   *Schema of Functions Necessary to a Program of Planned Improvement in an Institution or Social Process Field*

Activity	Function	Purpose
D E V E L O P M E N T	1. *Gathering* Operational and Planning *Data*	1. To identify operational problems
	2. *Inventing Solutions* to Operating Problems	2. To solve operational problems
	3. *Engineering* Packages and *Programs* for Operational Use	3. To operationalize solutions
	4. *Testing* and Evaluating Packages and *Programs*	4. To assess the effectiveness and efficiency of the packages and programs
D I F F U S I O N	5. *Informing* Target Systems About Packages and Programs	5. To make potential adopters aware of the existence of packages and programs
	6. *Demonstrating* the Effectiveness of the Packages and Programs	6. To convince the adopter of the efficiency of the packages or programs
	7. *Training* Target Systems in the Use of the Packages and Programs	7. To develop a level of user competence with the packages or programs
	8. Servicing and *Nurturing* Installed Innovations	8. To complete the institutionalization of the invention

identified, the problem must be solved through the intervention of an inventor or a team of inventors and such a team will depend on research data to suggest possible solutions. This activity implies an intimate knowledge of research and the ability to translate it into applied form.

3. *Engineering packages and programs for operational use.* Basic research findings and inventions share a common characteristic—for the most part, they are unusable by the practitioner. The proposed solution must be

turned into some convenient package which can be applied by him. Knowing something about the mechanics of vacuums, or, that the principle of the vacuum can be used to pick up objects does not really help the housewife clean her rug—she needs a preengineered vacuum cleaner to get the job done. This engineering or pre-packaging does not imply a large, inflexible, all-or-none program; packages may be designed creatively with a substantial degree of built-in adaptability. Regardless of the flexibility of the package, ideas have to be engineered before they are usable in the practical situation.

4. *Testing and evaluating packages and programs.* This refers to the specific task of testing the effectiveness and efficiency of a particular package or program. Testing and evaluation will take place continually regarding each of the functions of Table 1 (e.g., one may well evaluate the process of gathering operational and planning data), but a formal field test is logically called for at this stage. Packages designed for widespread applicability in a number of school settings require elaborate evaluations to assure that they are valid and warrantable. Without the hard evidence of a rigorous evaluation, one cannot be sure an innovation will perform as specified, and the innovator cannot in good conscience offer it as a viable professional alternative.

Diffusion informs about packages and programs and demonstrates them, offering training in their use and assisting in their installation. Again, a variety of new educational middlemen is required. These diffusion engineers are also concerned with four activities:

1. *Informing target systems about packages and programs.* The process of diffusion cannot occur unless target systems (i.e., potential users) are aware of an innovation. Until recently, educational innovations occurred so rarely there was little need for such an informing function. But with new developments available on an increasingly larger scale, the function of informing is becoming important even to very sophisticated school systems. Suddenly faced with a variety of alternatives, practitioners are now clamoring for more information about them. This information must be made available in ways to help the practitioner make a sensible professional judgment. The innovations must not be given the "hard sell" but must be presented simply, as one additional way in which some objective can be reached. The approach must be less huckstering and more "consumer report."

2. *Demonstrating the effectiveness of packages and programs.* Demonstration, like informing, can easily be turned into evangelism. In the past the typical demonstration was set up to convince the practitioner of something by showing him it was feasible. But these traditional demonstrations often failed; first, because they tended to be set up in situations lacking credibility from the practitioner's viewpoint (e.g., university laboratory schools), and second, because they did not provide the opportunity for evi-

dential assessment of the innovation by the practitioner. The function of the demonstrator is to create credible situations in which the practitioner can gather information about the operation and the consequences of the innovation. Conviction that the innovation will perform as specified does not, of course, lead to automatic adoption, but rather to its consideration as an alternative among all other innovations or existing practices which are also warrantable.

3. *Training target systems in the use of the packages and programs.* The training of potential adopters makes sense because the innovation will undoubtedly require new skills and knowledge to make it work effectively. On psychological grounds, few persons are so secure that they will risk their reputations by trying an innovation in whose performance they are not expert. It seems likely that the availability of such in-service training accounts in great measure for the success of such recent innovations as the curricular materials in mathematics and science.

4. *Servicing and nurturing installed innovations.* At some point, an innovation must be converted by the target system into a non-invention, into a regular part of the ongoing operation. This is usually easier said than done, since many inventions require something of the institution in the form of physical or personnel resources which were not required by earlier practice. In addition, the initial flash of enthusiasm for the innovation usually wanes, and the deficit created by lowered efficiency must be compensated for by further resources and support. If an innovation is to achieve continuity, become accepted and valued, and thoroughly integrated into normal routines, means must be devised to achieve local servicing and nurturing. Unless such resources are to be made available on a regular basis, there is little point in adopting the innovation in the first place.

If this depiction of emergent functions is at all valid, it is clear that a variety of new roles and techniques will soon emerge (and are in fact emerging now) to which the research community must relate. If research is to successfully undergird these other activities, new linkages must be forged. Without research, new solutions to operating problems can be based solely upon judgment, opinion, and experience; and while these are valuable guides they cannot replace the hard facts and knowledge provided by good research. As it struggles to achieve this new relationship the research community is confronted with a series of difficult questions. Among the more important are:

1. How can research provide what is needed to carry out the intermediate function described in Table 1 (or similar functions)? If research is to be the fountainhead from which new solutions to operating problems are drawn, engineered, and disseminated, how can we be sure that research exists which is relevant to the urgent problems of the school? It is said that educational research is irrelevant to practical problems; that available research on any

topic is conflicting or unavailable; that there is no real feedback mechanism to the researcher to let him know what the important problems are (or if there is such feedback, that the researcher is not responsive to it). To whatever extent these allegations are true, some changes or improvements must be made.

2. How can research continue to be creative and inventive if it exhibits great concern for practical problems? The genius of research in all fields has been that the researcher can go wherever his inquiry leads him, pursuing an idea to its logical conclusion. If the research community takes seriously the mandate expressed in Question 1 is it not possible that research will degenerate into a mere problem-solving activity? Will we not, as Cronbach has suggested,[8] witness the action of a kind of perverse Gresham's Law in which the bad questions drive out the good?

3. Can research be protected against subversion by the dissemination activity which has, as Cronbach has again pointed out,[9] an element of built-in hucksterism? If the researcher allows himself to become too intimate with these emergent functions he may well find himself being used by unscrupulous disseminators who see their function as selling, not inquiring into value, validity, or utility. What can the researcher do to force dissemination into a professional posture? Can dissemination take the form of opening viable professional alternatives rather than pushing a particular one? Can the research community help to develop criteria and methods of applying them that will permit a more sensible decision to be made by the consumer?

4. Can and should the educational research community become involved with the training of the large numbers required to fill these emergent research-related roles? As noted earlier, over 40,000 full-time equivalent personnel will be needed by 1972 to man federal and foundation-supported programs of educational research and development. Some 86 per cent of these persons will fill the new linking roles. The models for training the traditional researcher seem to provide only a scant base on which to project the training programs of developers of diffusors. Instructional materials are nonexistent. What can be done?

Educational researchers, while not pretending to have any clear answers to these questions, are approaching them with intelligence and responsibility. And, as the questions are answered, the concept of what research is will again be enlarged.

The Scientific Development of the Process

A third concern manifesting itself in the research community is the rigorous development in the research process of what might be called non-methodological or, at least, non-procedural aspects.

If he is asked to judge the value of a piece of research, the typical educational researcher will probably apply methodological criteria in arriving at his judgment. He will raise questions concerning how the variables were operationalized (how they were measured), the representativeness of the sample, the adequacy of the statistical design, the rigor of field controls and the like. He is very *unlikely* to raise questions concerning the nature of the problem investigated, the significance of that problem, the nature of the particular objectives of the research, or the nature of the theoretical framework within which the research was carried on. These are typically regarded as "soft" questions, depending a great deal upon the "art" which the researcher brings to his inquiry. Even the research critic who seeks to ask such questions is not likely to be able to respond with very good judgments because criteria are lacking and standards are undefined.

Any prudent reader of research proposals knows that the majority of professional researchers have no clear concept of the nature of a researchable problem. Problems often are mistaken for statements of condition, e.g., that there are a very large number of disadvantaged youth who are unable to profit from the normal experiences provided by the schools. This is certainly so, but no fact is by itself a problem. It becomes a problem only as it is a barrier or hindrance to some desirable goal. Thus, if we didn't care what happened to the disadvantaged youth, or if their inability to profit from school experience did not have some disastrous consequences for society, the fact that there were many of them would be of no concern.

Problems are also often confused with objectives. The researcher may be able to state with reasonable clarity what he wants to do, but not why. A common phenomenon found in research proposals is what I have come to call the "great proposal shift." Many funding agencies require a proposal to follow a particular format—begin with a problem, follow with a statement of objectives, and follow that by a statement of hypotheses or questions. If the researcher confuses the problem with the objectives, his problem statement usually turns out to be a series of objectives (the purpose of this research is to . . .) which, of course, immediately produces an awkwardness with regard to the required following statement of objectives. The researcher usually resolves this problem by stating his questions or hypotheses instead.

When he reaches the section on questions or hypotheses, he is usually in deep trouble, a problem which he typically resolves by restating or paraphrasing either the original objectives or the earlier statement on hypotheses. Objectives are thus shifted to the problem section, and hypotheses to the objectives section; the large vacuum left in the hypotheses section is filled (badly) by a restatement of earlier material.

Problems are also likely to be confused with statements of significance or justifications for the research proposed. As a result, a researcher calls for research in relation to cases of reading disability because that deficiency is so dysfunctional for other schoolwork, because poor readers may develop a negative self-image, or because the lack of ability to read deprives the subject from many enjoyable reading experiences. While all of these reasons may be valid they hardly define a problem.

As researchers have become aware of these deficiencies, they have begun to ask whether it is not possible to develop better operational definitions of what a problem is and better criteria or standards for determining whether a problem has in fact been enunciated. Clark, Guba, and Smith, for example, have suggested that a problem arises out of an anomaly, a series of contradictory "facts," unverified findings, or an uncharted area.[10] Gephart suggests that problems arise from the adaptation of a means to an end, the lack of understanding of the character of an object or event, or the existence of an unexpected event.[11] Other and more systematic definitions will undoubtedly arise as work advances in this area.

In addition to this problem with problems, researchers also have notorious difficulty in setting out objectives (ends or goals) of the research activity which they propose to undertake. Sometimes the objectives are simply pulled out of the air with no evident relationship to a problem. At other times, they bear no evident relationship to the procedures, for the procedures proposed could not possibly result in data that have a bearing on the announced objectives. But even when these deficiencies do not occur, a more fundamental problem does arise, i.e., the objectives are not derived systematically with regard to the problem so that all objectives can be examined and certain particular ones chosen on the basis of some sensible criteria.

A great many things can obviously be done in relation to any problem. Suppose the problem of concern arises out of an anomaly—a palm tree growing at the Arctic Circle, to take an absurd example. Palm trees do not usually grow in such a locale—how can we account for this? A meteorological study might be conducted—perhaps there are perverse warm winds. Or, this tree could be a sport of some kind, and this would call for a genetic investigation. Is there some peculiar soil condition?

If it were possible to detail all of the possible objectives in relationship to the problem, it might then be possible to select from among them in some systematic way, e.g., selecting the most heuristic, the most socially significant, the sensible next step in a programmatic development, the most interesting to the particular researcher, etc.

Such a detailing could clearly only be done within the framework afforded by some explicit theory; otherwise, the number of objectives might easily be infinite. This leads directly to a third major problem confronting researchers: how to select a theory that has promise of being "powerful" in relation to the problem under investigation. Most educational researches have been conducted in the absence of an explicit theory; however, it is clear that some theoretical formulations must guide (even if only "hunches"), since not all phenomena may be observed at once nor may all data be collected at once. Thus, some principles of selectivity may always be identified, even if only implicitly. If there must be some guiding theory, why not make it explicit so that its assumptions are known and can be taken into account?

How are explicit theories selected? Given a problem, how can one tell whether a given theory has utility for studying it? Or, suppose no theory can quickly be identified; how can a theory be developed for the purpose? These are nagging questions indeed, and little progress has been made in relationship to them. The work of the Maccias indicates that educational theories can be developed by analogy to powerful theories from other fields, and they have been able to develop some specific theories of unusual promise.[12]

The questions raised here concerning the problem, the objectives, and the theoretical framework illustrate another dimension along which the concept of educational research is rapidly expanding. Once the educational researcher was likely to be a person well trained in statistics and methodology whose major concern was the rigorous collection and analysis of data. Now his interests are being broadened to consider other parts of the research process as amenable to equally rigorous analysis. Apparently, more systematic procedures can be devised and appropriate criteria developed. It seems safe to assume that over the next decade there will be a substantial development along this dimension and a consequent enlargement of the research concept.

Summary

Educational research is expanding in many ways—it is now standing on the brink of what will undoubtedly be its most important decade in history.

Mere size and vast resources are not the only indicators of the marked change in educational research. The very *concept itself* has undergone significant alterations. First, traditional methods, while not inappropriate, are now seen as insufficient for dealing with the broad range of questions and conditions that must be confronted in education. New approaches are being developed. Second, a whole new series of roles is being defined which will link research much more solidly to educational practice than it has ever been. Third, the total process of research is being subjected to the same rigorous analysis and definition that only the methodological aspects before received.

These alterations and accommodations are not without cost, of course. Healthy argumentation is going on. Questions are being asked. Solutions are being tested. Time and resources are being committed. And, it seems likely that the research community will be as inventive meeting these new challenges as it has been in pursuing problems of other sorts—this decade's most speculative stock will probably turn out to be the next decade's blue chip investment.

Notes

1. Clark, David L., and Hopkins, John. "Roles for Research, Development, and Diffusion Personnel in Education," Cooperative Research Project No. X-022, Indiana University, 1966.
2. Compare this figure with the approximately 4,000 names currently listed in the the *National Register of Educational Researchers.*
3. Barker, Roger G. "Explorations in Ecological Psychology," *American Psychologist*, 1965, 20, 1–14.
4. Guba, Egon G. "Methodological Strategies for Educational Change," a paper presented to the Conference on Strategies for Educational Change, sponsored by the Ohio State University and the U.S. Office of Education, Washington, D.C., 1965.
5. Barker, *op. cit.*, p. 5.
6. Campbell, Donald T. and Stanley, Julian C. "Experimental and Quasi-Experimental Designs for Research on Teaching," in *Handbook of Research on Teaching*, N. L. Gage, editor. Chicago: Rand, McNally and Co., 1963.
7. This table and much of the related discussion are drawn from Egon G. Guba and David L. Clark, "Effecting Change in Institutions of Higher Education," presented to the UCEA International Inter-Visitation Program, Ann Arbor, Michigan, October 1966.
8. Cronbach, Lee J. "The Role of the University in Improving Education," *Phi Delta Kappan*, June 1966, 47, 539–45.
9. *Ibid.*
10. Clark, David L.; Guba, Egon G.; and Smith, Gerald R. "Functions and Definitions of Functions of a Research Proposal or Research Report," Columbus, Ohio: The Ohio State University, 1962. Mimeographed.
11. Gephart, William J. "Criteria for Methodological Adequacy in Educational Innovation Diffusion Research," a paper presented to the Conference on Strategies for Educational Change, sponsored by The Ohio State University and the U.S. Office of Education, Washington, D.C., 1965.
12. See E. S. Maccia, G. S. Maccia, and R. E. Jewett, *Construction of Educational Theory Model* (C.R.P. No. 1623). Washington, D.C.: Office of Education, 1963; and E. S. Maccia and G. S. Maccia, *Development of Educational Theory Derived From Three Educational Theory Models* (C.R.P. No. 5–0638). Washington, D.C., Office of Education, 1966.

26 | Toward a Science of Educational Evaluation

Daniel L. Stufflebeam

Evaluation and research have long been equated. Careful examination of the purposes served by each of them has contributed to a differentiation. Research activities contribute knowledge that is generalizable across situations and time, while evaluations contribute knowledge applicable to a specific situation and decision. With this differentiation has come awareness of weaknesses and voids in our understanding of the concept "evaluation" and in methodology. Stufflebeam's article attempts to explicate evaluation as it is today.

A Rationale

If decision-makers are to make maximum, legitimate use of their opportunities, they must make sound decisions regarding the alternatives available to them. To do this, they must know what alternatives are available and be capable of making sound judgments about the relative merits of the alternatives. This requires relevant information. Decision-makers should, therefore, maintain access to effective means for providing this evaluative information. Otherwise, their decisions are likely to be functions of many undesirable elements. Under the best of circumstances, judgmental processes are subject to human bias, prejudice and vested interests. Also, there is frequently a tendency to over-depend upon personal experiences, hearsay evidence, and authoritative opinion; and, surely, all too many decisions are due to ignorance that there is a need for a decision or that viable alternatives exist. To summarize this chain of reasoning:

(1) the quality of programs depends upon the quality of decisions in and about the programs;

(2) the quality of decisions depends upon decision makers' abilities to identify the alternatives which comprise decision situations and to make sound judgments of these alternatives;

(3) making sound judgments requires timely access to valid and reliable information pertaining to the alternatives

Daniel L. Stufflebeam, "Toward a Science of Educational Evaluation," *Educational Technology* (July 30, 1968), 6–12. Reprinted by permission.

(4) the availability of such information requires systematic means to provide it; and

(5) the processes necessary for providing this information for decision-making collectively comprise the concept of evaluation. Given this rationale, a definition of evaluation will now be presented.

Evaluation Defined

Generally, evaluation means the provision of information through formal means, such as criteria, measurement, and statistics, to serve as rational bases for making judgments in decision situations. To clarify this definition, it will be useful to define several key terms. A decision is a choice among alternatives. A decision situation is a set of alternatives. Judgment is the assignment of values to alternatives. A criterion is a rule by which values are assigned to alternatives, and optimally such a rule includes the specification of variables for measurement and standards for use in judging that which is measured. Statistics is the science of analyzing and interpreting sets of measurements. And, measurement is the assignment of numerals to entities according to rules, and such rules usually include the specification of sample elements, measuring devices and conditions for administering and scoring the measuring devices. Stated simply, evaluation is the science of providing information for decision-making.

The methodology of evaluation includes four functions: *collection, organization, analysis,* and *reporting of information.* Criteria for assessing the adequacy of evaluations include *validity* (is the information what the decision-maker needs?), *reliability* (is the information reproducible?), *timeliness* (is the information available when the decision-maker needs it?), *pervasiveness* (does the information reach all decision-makers who need it?), and *credibility* (is the information trusted by the decision-maker and those he must serve?).

Since the purpose of evaluation is to provide information for decision-making, one must have some knowledge of the decision situation to be served. To assist in developing a parsimonious classification system for educational decision situations in programs such as Title I and Title III, it is useful initially to focus exclusively on the functions of decisions.[1] The functions of decision situations in education may be classified as *planning, programming, implementing* and *recycling. Planning* decisions are those which focus needed improvements by specifying the domain, major goals, and specific objectives to be served. *Programming* decisions specify procedure, personnel, facilities, budget, and time requirements for implementing planned activities. *Implementing* decisions are those in directing programmed activities. And, *recycling* decisions include *terminating, continuing, evolving,* or *drastically modifying activities.*

Four Strategies for Evaluating Educational Programs

Given these four kinds of educational decisions to be served, there are also four kinds of evaluation. These are portrayed in Figure 1 as Context, Input, Process, and Product Evaluation (CIPP). Since these evaluation strategies have been detailed elsewhere,[2] we will only summarize them here. We will focus exclusively on the objectives of each of the four kinds of evaluation. The method of each kind of evaluation and its relation to decision-making in the change process is summarized in Figure 1, but, in the interest of brevity, will not be discussed in this paper.

Context Evaluation

Context evaluation would be used when a project is first being planned. The major objective of context evaluation is to define the environment where change is to occur, the environment's unmet needs, problems underlying those needs, and opportunities for change.

For example, the environment may be defined as the inner-city elementary schools of a large metropolitan area. Study of such a setting might reveal that the actual reading achievement levels of children in this area are far below what the school system expects for them. This would be the identification of a need, i.e., the context evaluation would have revealed that the children's reading achievement levels need to be raised. As a next step in the context evaluation, the school would attempt to identify the reasons for such a need. Are the students receiving adequate instruction? Are the instructional materials appropriate for them? Is there a major language barrier? Is there a high incidence of absenteeism? Is the school's expectation for these students reasonable? These are what is meant by problems. They are potential dilemmas which prevent the achievement of desired goals and thereby result in the existence of needs.

Information from context evaluation leads ultimately to the establishment of program goals and objectives.

Input Evaluation

To determine how to utilize resources to meet the program goals and objectives it is necessary to do an input evaluation. The objective of input evaluation is to identify and assess relevant capabilities of the proposing agency, strategies which may be appropriate for meeting program goals and designs which may be appropriate for achieving objectives associated with each program goal. The end product of input evaluation is an analysis of alternative procedural designs in terms of potential costs and benefits.

Specifically, alternative designs are assessed in terms of their resource, time and budget requirements; their potential procedural barriers; the con-

FIG. 1 The CIPP Evaluation Model (A Classification Scheme of Strategies for Evaluating Educational Change)

Strategies:	Context Evaluation	Input Evaluation	Process Evaluation	Product Evaluation
Objective	To define the operation context, to identify and assess needs in the context, and to identify and delineate problems underlying the needs.	To identify and assess system capabilities, available input strategies, and designs for implementing the strategies.	To identify or predict, in process, defects in the procedural design or its implementation, and to maintain a record of procedural events and activities.	To relate outcome information to objectives and to context, input, and process information.
Method	By describing individually and in relevant perspectives the major subsystems of the context; by comparing actual and intended inputs and outputs of the subsystems; and by analyzing possible causes of discrepancies between actualities and intentions.	By describing and analyzing available human and material resources, solution strategies, and procedural designs for relevance, feasibility and economy in the course of action to be taken.	By monitoring the activity's potential procedural barriers and remaining alert to unanticipated ones.	By defining operationally and measuring criteria associated with the objectives, by comparing these measurements with predetermined standards or comparative bases, and by interpreting the outcome in terms of recorded input and process information.
Relation to Decision-Making in the Change Process	For deciding upon the setting to be served, the goals associated with meeting needs and the objectives associated with solving problems, i.e., for planning needed changes.	For selecting sources of support, solution strategies, and procedural designs, i.e., for programming change activities.	For implementing and refining the program design and procedure, i.e., for effecting process control.	For deciding to continue, terminate, modify or refocus a change activity; for linking the activity to other major phases of the change process, i.e., evolving change activities.

sequences of not overcoming these barriers; the possibilities and costs of overcoming them; relevance of the designs to program objectives; and overall potential of the design to meet program goals. Essentially, input evaluation provides information for deciding whether outside assistance should be sought for meeting goals and objectives, what strategy should be employed, e.g., the adoption of available solutions or the development of new ones, and what design or procedural plan should be employed for implementing the selected strategy.

Process Evaluation

Once a designed course of action has been approved and implementation of the design has begun, process evaluation is needed to provide periodic feedback to project managers and others responsible for continuous control and refinement of plans and procedures. The objective of process evaluation is to detect or predict, during the implementation stages, defects in the procedural design or its implementation. The overall strategy is to identify and monitor, on a continuous basis, the potential sources of failure in a project. These include interpersonal relationships among staff and students; communication channels; logistics; understandings of and agreement with the intent of the program by persons involved in and affected by it; adequacy of the resources, physical facilities, staff, and time schedule; etc.

Product Evaluation

Product evaluation is used to determine the effectiveness of the project after it has run full cycle. Its objective is to relate outcomes to objectives and to context, input, and process, i.e., to measure and interpret outcomes.

The Structure of Evaluation Design

Once an evaluator has selected an evaluation strategy, e.g., context, input, process, or product, he must next select or develop a design to implement his evaluation. This is a difficult task since few generalized evaluation designs exist which are adequate to meet emergent needs for evaluation. Thus, educators must typically develop evaluation designs de novo. What follows is an attempt to provide a general guide for developing evaluation designs. Specifically, an attempt will be made to define in general terms and to explicate the general structure of designs for educational evaluation.

Design Defined

In general, design is the preparation of a set of decision situations for implementation toward the achievement of specified objectives. This definition says three things. First, one must identify the objectives to be achieved through implementation of the design. In a product evaluation, for example, such an objective might be to make a determination of whether all students in a remedial reading program attained specified levels of specific reading skills. Second, this definition says that one should identify and define the decision situations in the procedure for achieving the evaluation objective. For example, in the remedial reading case cited above, one would want to identify the available measuring devices which might be appropriate for assessing the specified reading skills. Third, for each identified decision situation the evaluator needs to make a choice among the available alternatives. Thus, the completed evaluation design would contain a set of decisions as to how the evaluation is to be conducted and what instruments will be used.

It should be useful to evaluators to have available a list of the decision situations which are common to many evaluation designs. This would enable them to approach problems of evaluation design in a systematic manner. Further, such a list could serve as an outline for the content of evaluation sections in research and development proposals. Funding agencies should also find such a list useful in structuring their general guidelines for evaluations which they provide to potential proposal writers. Also, such a list should be useful to training agencies for defining the role of the evaluation specialist.

Figure 2 is an attempt to provide such a general list of decision situations for evaluation designs. By presenting this general list, it is asserted that the structure of evaluation design is the same for context, input, process, or product evaluation. This structure includes six major parts. There are (1) focusing the evaluation, (2) information collection, (3) information organization, (4) information analysis, (5) information reporting, and (6) the administration of evaluation. Each of these parts will be considered separately.

Focusing the Evaluation

The first part of the structure of evaluation design is that of focusing the evaluation. The purpose of this part is to spell out the ends for the evaluation and to define policies within which the evaluation must be conducted. Specifically, this part of evaluation design includes four steps.

The first step is to identify the major levels of decision-making for which evaluation information must be provided. For example, in the Title III program of the Elementary and Secondary Education Act evaluative information from local schools is needed at local, state and national levels. It is important to take all relevant levels into account in the design of evaluations since different levels may have different information require-

FIGURE 2   Developing Evaluation Designs

The logical structure of evaluation design is the same for all types of evaluation, whether context, input, process or product evaluation. The parts, briefly, are as follows:

A. *Focusing the Evaluation*

1. Identify the major level(s) of decision-making to be served, e.g., local, state, or national.
2. For each level of decision-making, project the decision situations to be served and describe each one in terms of its locus, focus, timing, and composition of alternatives.
3. Define criteria for each decision situation by specifying variables for measurement and standards for use in the judgment of alternatives.
4. Define policies within which the evaluation must operate.

B. *Collection of Information*

1. Specify the source of the information to be collected.
2. Specify the instruments and methods for collecting the needed information.
3. Specify the sampling procedure to be employed.
4. Specify the conditions and schedule for information collection.

C. *Organization of Information*

1. Specify a format for the information to be collected.
2. Specify a means for coding, organizing, storing, and retrieving information.

D. *Analysis of Information*

1. Specify the analytical procedures to be employed.
2. Specify a means for performing the analysis.

E. *Reporting of Information*

1. Define the audiences for the evaluation reports.
2. Specify means for providing information to the audiences.
3. Specify the format for evaluation reports and/or reporting sessions.
4. Schedule the reporting of information.

F. *Administration of the evaluation*

1. Summarize the evaluation schedule.
2. Define staff and resource requirements and plans for meeting these requirements.
3. Specify means for meeting policy requirements for conduct of the evaluation.
4. Evaluate the potential of the evaluation design for providing information which is valid, reliable, credible, timely, and pervasive.
5. Specify and schedule means for periodic updating of the evaluation design.
6. Provide a budget for the total evaluation program.

ments and since the different agencies may need information at different times.

Having identified the major levels of decision-making to be served by evaluation, the next step is to identify and define the decision situations to be served at each level. Given our present low state of knowledge about decision-making in education, this is a very difficult task. However, it is also a very important one and should be done as well as is practicable. First, decision situations should be identified in terms of those responsible for making the decisions, e.g., teacher, principals, the board of education members, state legislators, etc. Next, major types of decision situations should be identified, e.g., appropriational, allocational, approval, or continuation. Then, these types of decision situations should be classified by focus, e.g., research, development, diffusion or adoption. (This step is especially helpful toward identifying relevant evaluative criteria.) Next, the timing of the decision situation to be served should be estimated so that the evaluation can be geared to provide relevant data prior to the time when decisions must be made. And, finally, an attempt should be made to explicate each important decision situation in terms of the alternatives which may reasonably be considered in reaching the decision.

Once the decision situations to be served have been explicated, the next step is to define relevant information requirements. Specifically, one should define criteria for each decision situation by specifying variables for measurement and standards for use in the judgment of alternatives.

The final step in focusing the evaluation is to define policies within which the evaluation must operate. For example, one should determine whether a "self evaluation" or "outside evaluation" is needed. Also, it is necessary to determine who will receive evaluation reports and who will have access to them. Finally, it is necessary to define the limits of access to data for the evaluation team.

Collection of Information

The second major part of the structure of evaluation design is that of planning the collection of information. This section must obviously be keyed very closely to the criteria which were identified in the evaluation focus part of the design.

Using those criteria one should first identify the sources of the information to be collected. These information sources should be defined in two respects: first, the origins for the information, e.g., students, teachers, principals or parents; and second, the present state of the information, i.e., in recorded or non-recorded form.

Next, one should specify instruments and methods for collecting the needed information. Examples include achievement tests, interview schedules and searches through the professional literature. Michael and Metfessel[3] have recently provided a comprehensive list of instruments with potential relevance for data collection in evaluations.

For each instrument that is to be administered, one should next specify the sampling procedure to be employed. Where possible, one should avoid administering too many instruments to the same person. Thus, sampling without replacement across instruments can be a useful technique. Also, where total test scores are not needed for each student, one might profitably use multiple matrix sampling where no student attempts more than a sample of the items in a test.

Finally, one should develop a master schedule for the collection of information. This schedule should detail the interrelations between samples, instruments, and dates for the collection of information.

Organization of Information

A frequent disclaimer in evaluation reports is that resources were inadequate to allow for processing all of the pertinent data. If this problem is not to arise, one should make definite plans regarding the third part of evaluation design: organization of information. Organizing the information that is to be collected includes providing a format for classifying information and designating means for coding, organizing, storing, and retrieving the information.

Analysis of Information

The fourth major part of evaluation design is analysis of information. The purpose of this part is to provide for the descriptive or statistical analyses of the information which is to be reported to decision-makers. This part also includes interpretations and recommendations. As with the organization of information, it is important that the evaluation design specify means for performing the analyses. The role should be assigned specifically to a qualified member of the evaluation team or to an agency which specializes in doing data analyses. Also, it is important that those who will be responsible for the analysis of information participate in designing the analysis procedures.

Reporting of Information

The fifth part of evaluation design is the reporting of information. The purpose of this part of a design is to insure that decision-makers will have timely access to the information they need and that they will receive it in a manner and form which facilitates their use of the information. In accordance with the policy for the evaluation, audiences for evaluation reports should be identified and defined. Then means should be defined for providing information to each audience. Subsequently, the format for evaluation reports and reporting sessions should be specified. And, finally, a master schedule of evaluation reporting should be provided. This schedule should define the interrelations between audiences, reports, and dates for reporting information.

Administration of Evaluation

The last part of evaluation design is that of administration of the evaluation. The purpose of this part is to provide an overall plan for executing the evaluation design. The first step is to define the overall evaluation schedule. For this purpose it often would be useful to employ a scheduling technique such as Program Evaluation and Review Technique. The second step is to define staff requirements and plans for meeting these requirements. The third step is to specify means for meeting policy requirements for conduct of the evaluation. The fourth step is to evaluate the potential of the evaluation design for providing information which is valid, reliable, credible, timely, and pervasive. The fifth step is to specify and schedule means for periodic updating of the evaluation design. And, the sixth and final step is to provide a budget for the evaluation.

While each point in the structure for developing evaluation designs could doubtlessly be explicated in greater detail, the above should suffice to indicate clearly that the design and analysis of educational evaluation is a most complex and difficult undertaking.

Notes

1. Daniel L. Stufflebeam, "Evaluation as Enlightenment for Decision-Making," an address delivered at the Working Conference on Assessment Theory sponsored by The Commission on Assessment of Educational Outcomes, The Association for Supervision and Curriculum Development, Sarasota, Florida, January 19, 1968.
2. Ibid.
3. Newton S. Metfessel and William B. Michael, "A Paradigm Involving Multiple Criterion Measures for the Evaluation of the Effectiveness of School Programs," Educational and Psychological Measurement, 1967, 27, 931–936.

27 | Toward a Taxonomy of Evaluation Designs

Blaine R. Worthen

As the differentiation between research and evaluation is made, individuals become aware that long-standing research designs cannot always be employed in evaluations. Worthen builds on Stufflebeam's conceptualization of evaluation by describing classes of evaluation designs.

In a recent article, Stufflebeam proposed a structure which might be used to generate evaluation designs.[1] That structure is reproduced herein as Figure 1.

Deceptively simple when viewed in outline form, the structure consists of a list of no less than twenty-two decision situations which are common to most evaluation designs. Upon even cursory inspection, however, it is apparent that the structure implies much more than a simple list of twenty-two items which evaluators must keep in mind, for at each of the decision points identified in the structure, the evaluator needs to make a choice among the available alternatives. At each point, he must select the most appropriate alternative in order to generate a total set of decisions which, if followed faithfully, will yield information that will meet specified evaluative criteria of validity, reliability, pervasiveness, timeliness, and credibility.[2]

While manageable in theory, such an approach presents the evaluator with a task which is extremely difficult in practice. It requires that the selection of alternatives effects a balance between selection of the most appropriate alternative for each decision situation and the selection of a set of alternatives which can be integrated into the best over-all design. In addition, use of the structure assumes that the evaluator can either identify or generate alternatives that are relevant to each of the twenty-two decision situations—no small assumption. In short, while the proposed structure provides a general guide for developing evaluation designs, educators must still engage heavily in the laborious, painstaking process of developing each design de novo.

In such a context, it is completely understandable that one of the topics evaluators most frequently discuss is the need for some type of listing,

Blaine R. Worthen, "Toward A Taxonomy of Evaluation Designs," *Educational Technology* (August 15, 1968), 3–9. Reprinted by permission.

FIGURE 1   *Developing Evaluation Designs*

The logical structure of evaluation design is the same for all types of evaluation, whether context, input, process or product evaluation. The parts, briefly, are as follows:

A. *Focusing the Evaluation*

1. Identify the major level(s) of decision-making to be served, e.g., local, state, or national.
2. For each level of decision-making, project the decision situations to be served and describe each one in terms of its locus, focus, timing, and composition of alternatives.
3. Define criteria for each decision situation by specifying variables for measurement and standards for use in the judgment of alternatives.
4. Define policies within which the evaluation must operate.

B. *Collection of Information*

1. Specify the source of the information to be collected.
2. Specify the instruments and methods for collecting the needed information.
3. Specify the sampling procedure to be employed.
4. Specify the conditions and schedule for information collection.

C. *Organization of Information*
   Specify a format for the information to be collected.

2. Specify a means for coding, organizing, storing, and retrieving information.

D. *Analysis of Information*

1. Specify the analytical procedures to be employed.
2. Specify a means for performing the analysis.

E. *Reporting of Information*

1. Define the audiences for the evaluation reports.
2. Specify means for providing information to the audiences.
3. Specify the format for evaluation reports and/or reporting sessions.
4. Schedule the reporting of information.

F. *Administration of the evaluation*

1. Summarize the evaluation schedule.
2. Define staff and resource requirements and plans for meeting these requirements.
3. Specify means for meeting policy requirements for conduct of the evaluation.
4. Evaluate the potential of the evaluation design for providing information which is valid, reliable, credible, timely, and pervasive.
5. Specify and schedule means for periodic updating of the evaluation design.
6. Provide a budget for the total evaluation program.

classification scheme, or taxonomy of evaluation designs.[3] "Can't evaluators provide a better method than that of generating each design from scratch?" "Why not construct a comprehensive taxonomy of alternative evaluation designs—a library from which educators might select the design most appropriate for their situation?" These are simply variant forms of the same recurring question. In response, it can be said that a classification scheme of generalizable evaluation designs would certainly seem to be desirable, and very few evaluators would gainsay the tremendous utility such a device might have. But, little progress has been made toward its development.

Many evaluators have pointed to the Campbell-Stanley chapter on experimental design in Gage's *Handbook of Research on Teaching*[4] as a model which evaluation designers might follow as they attempt to devise generalizable evaluation designs. Evaluators have noted, with envy, the tremendous help this chapter provides for the researcher who is in need of an experimental design. The chapter contains a series of alternative designs relevant to experimental or quasi-experimental research. The authors have listed eight factors which jeopardize internal validity and four which jeopardize external validity. Each alternative design is discussed in relationship to the degree of control it exerts on the twelve sources of invalidity. It is a relatively simple matter to turn to the Campbell-Stanley chapter to select a design for almost any legitimate research problem for which an experimental design is required.

Of course, evaluators as a group are erudite enough to realize that experimental design per se is generally inapplicable in attempts to solve evaluation problems, but the intrinsic appeal of rigor and parsimony inherent in experimental design still seems to influence evaluators' efforts to come to grips with their own design problems. The earlier question reappears in a more specific form. "Can we devise a taxonomy of evaluation designs analogous to the Campbell-Stanley chapter?" Given such a taxonomy, the argument goes, one might simply study the extent to which alternative evaluation designs meet specified evaluative criteria and overcome the relevant procedural barriers, and then select the design which is appropriate for the specific evaluation problem under consideration.

The argument is compelling—its logic strikes a responsive chord in many evaluators. But one might legitimately ask if, given the present "state of the art" constraints, the notion of constructing a taxonomy of evaluation designs is really feasible. Should we opt for such a taxonomy at present? Is it reasonable to expect that a classification scheme of generalizable evaluation designs might be developed in the near future? In short, is it appropriate at this juncture to ask questions about a taxonomy of evaluation designs, or are such questions likely to cause evaluators to expend considerable time and energy pursuing what may well be a will-of-the-wisp?

In order to answer such a question, let us refer back to the structure for generating evaluation designs. As implied earlier, the process of designing evaluations is much more complex than it appears to be on the surface. It may be useful at this point to examine these complexities in greater detail.

Figure 1 drew attention to the fact that the logical structure of evaluation design is the same for all types of evaluation, whether context, input, process, or product. While this assertion is true in general, it is not necessarily true with regard to particulars. Each element in the structure can vary in its application to the four kinds of evaluation. One way to illustrate this would be to juxtapose the structure of evaluation designs against the four kinds of evaluation identified earlier. This would be a minimal first step in any attempt to develop a taxonomy of evaluation designs. Figure 2 shows a portion of the matrix which would result from such juxtaposition. In order to illustrate the complexity of the problem, let us focus on one row of the matrix, A3, in which criteria are defined.

One note of clarification should be inserted at the outset. There are five criteria (validity, reliability, pervasiveness, timeliness, and credibility), each of which is applicable to all four kinds of evaluation. These are criteria which are used to evaluate the evaluation, however, and are not the criteria which must be used at step A3 to select from among the proposed alternatives. Criteria at A3 are those which are generated in relation to each decision situation which is under consideration. In cell w of Figure 2, for example, the majority of decisions which can be forecast are likely to be planning decisions—decisions for which context evaluation is most appropriate. In cell x, the decisions are generally programming decisions. In cell y and z, respectively, they are primarily implementing and recycling decisions.[5] It is likely that criteria for assessing alternatives in reaching a decision will vary from one type of decision to another and, consequently, from one type of evaluation to another. In short, it is probable that criteria which are specifically relevant to a certain type of evaluation might be identified. If so, the number of emergent criteria proliferate rapidly.

For example, with reference to cell x, Caldwell[6] has listed two additional general criteria (feasibility and desirability) which are relevant to input evaluation, and has further reduced these to eight specific criteria (relevance, legality, congruence, legitimacy, compatibility, balance, practicability, and cost/effectiveness). In essence, we could divide cell x into smaller matrices reflecting the above criteria, but even then we would be guilty of oversimplification. For example, still other input criteria must be applied within this cell of the matrix when the focus of the decision situation is considered. Making no attempt to be exhaustive, it could be noted, for example, that development activities would involve additional criteria such as tractability, viability, and efficiency. Diffusion activities would be evaluated on the basis of criteria such as intelligibility, fidelity, impact, and convenience. Research and adoption would necessitate still other criteria.[7]

FIGURE 2   *A Partial Classification Scheme of Evaluation Designs*

Structure for Developing Evaluation Design	Type of Evaluation			
	Context Evaluation	Input Evaluation	Process Evaluation	Product Evaluation
A. Focusing the Evaluation				
1. Identify level(s) of decision-making				
2. Project and describe the decision situations				
3. Define criteria for each decision situation	w	x	y	z
4. Define policies				
B. Collection of Information				
1. Specify the source				
2. Specify the instruments and methods				
etc.				

The foregoing discussion relates to only one cell in a matrix comprised of eighty-eight cells. Considering that every point in the structure of evaluation designs is a variable not only across the four kinds of evaluation but also within each kind, one can begin to appreciate just how complex a taxonomy of evaluation designs would be. The number of specific designs which would be included in any attempt to develop such a taxonomy would be enormous—an almost infinite number.

What was implied earlier should perhaps be stated baldly here. Given the staggering complexity of evaluation design processes, when viewed in their entirety, it would seem that attempting to create a taxonomy of evaluation designs would be both naive and inappropriate at this point. Until much more is known about specific roles which evaluation plays in providing needed information to support decision-making at different levels of varying situations, such classification schemes would likely oversimplify the problem.

As a more rational, interim approach, immediate attempts should be made to expand the structure for developing evaluation designs (Figure 1) into a tool with maximum operational utility. This could be done readily if we could identify lists—taxonomies, if you would—of alternatives for each decision situation identified in the structure. Stated differently, the alternatives which comprise each variable need to be identified and defined.

Although taxonomies of alternatives are lacking for many of the elements in the structure, there are a number of extant classification schema which are relevant to the development of specific taxonomies of alternatives.

Figure 3 shows a few examples of extant "taxonomies" of alternatives inserted at appropriate points into the structure. No attempt has been made to be exhaustive in the choice of examples, nor have they been chosen on qualitative grounds—they are illustrative only.

In reference to point A3 of Figure 1, for example, several extant classification schemes provide relevant alternatives. The two handbooks of educational objectives compiled by groups headed by Bloom[8] and Krathwohl,[9] and Woodruff's "Task Analysis of the Seven Major Component Tasks in Teaching"[10] are useful in identifying consequential objectives and associated consequential criteria.[11] Guba and Clark[12] have developed a taxonomy of instrumental objectives and associated criteria which are related to a variety of decision situations.

At point B2 of the structure, Metfessel and Michael's[13] recent listing of multiple criterion measures for evaluation of school programs is obviously relevant, as is also Buros' catalog of standardized tests.[14]

At point C1, the Iowa Data Bank System, the Project Talent Data Bank, and the National Assessment system provide alternative formats for information organization.

At point D1 of the structure, the chapter by Tatsuoka and Tiedeman[15] represents an attempt to generate a classification system of analytic modes.

FIGURE 3	Examples of Classification Schemes of Alternatives for Several Elements in a Structure for Developing Evaluation Designs

Element	*Example of Relevant Classification Scheme*
A. Focusing the Evaluation 3. Define criteria for each decision situation by specifying variables for measurement and standards for use in the judgment of alternatives.	Bloom, B. S., et al. *A Taxonomy of Educational Objectives: Handbook I, The Cognitive Domain.* 1956. Krathwohl, D. R., et al. *Taxonomy of Educational Objectives. Handbook II: Affective Domain.* 1964. Clark, David L. & Guba, Egon G. "An Examination of Potential Change Roles in Education." 1965. Woodruff, A. D. "Task Analysis of the Seven Major Component Tasks in Teaching." 1967.
B. Collection of Information 2. Specify the instruments and methods for collecting the needed information.	Metfessel, N. S. and Michael, W. B. "A Paradigm Involving Multiple Criterion Measures for the Evaluation of the Effectiveness of School Programs," *Educ. and Psych. Measurement,* Part 2. Winter, 1967. Buros, O. K. *The Buros Mental Measurement Yearbooks,* 1949.
C. Organization of Information 1. Provide a format for the information which is to be collected.	Iowa Data Bank System; National Assessment System; Project Talent Data Bank.

D. Analysis of Information
    1. Select the analytical procedures to be employed.
    2. Designate a means for performing the analysis.
	Tatsuoka, M. M. and Tiedeman, David V. "Statistics as an Aspect of Scientific Method in Research on Teaching," in Gage, N. L. (ed.) *Handbook of Research on Teaching,* 1964.
	SHARE Library System; Biomedical Computer Programs.

At D2, one could point to the SHARE Library System or the catalog of Biomedical Computer Programs as possible examples.

These are only a few examples of existing classification schemes. If taxonomies of alternatives could be developed for each element of the structure of evaluation designs, the result would be tremendously useful to both practicing evaluation specialists and design consultants. Perhaps a compendium could be compiled, containing classification schema for each element of the structure of designs and, if possible, for each of the four kinds of evaluation as well.

Such a tool, in the hands of a skillful person, could go far toward introducing a greater measure of science into the formulation of evaluation designs. Evaluators could systematically develop designs tailored to their needs, selecting the alternatives that best fit the criteria, assumptions, etc., relating to each point in the structure of designs. The resultant designs would "fit"—there would be no risk of inappropriate selection or application of a design to a problem for which it was not suited. There would be no danger, for example, of misapplications analogous to the wide misapplication of experimental designs in innumerable situations in which their inappropriateness is patently clear. This advantage of a compendium of alternatives can hardly be stressed too much, for even if attempts to generate a taxonomy of evaluation designs resulted in a limited "set" of generalizable designs, people would still be tempted to overgeneralize their favorite designs to inappropriate settings—to engage in the fallacy Kaplan eloquently decries as "the law of the instrument."[16] While not a panacea, the use of a compendium of alternatives in building specific designs would seem vastly preferable to indiscriminate overgeneralization of "packaged" designs.

On the Other Hand

Earlier in this paper, I stated that it is naive and inappropriate at the present time to be seriously engaged in attempts to develop a taxonomy of evaluation designs per se. Then I engaged in a rather circuitous argument which led to the conclusion that a better first step is to construct a series of taxonomies of alternatives relating to each element in the broad structure of design shown in Figure 1. I argued strongly that the development of such taxonomies of alternatives is a necessary interim step—one on which the educational community may well have to depend for the next several years. However, I would submit that it is not the final answer. In fact, in one sense, this line of argument really circumvents the original question, "Should we have a taxonomy of evaluation designs" (and skirts an awesome methodological abyss in the process).

Reversing my field, then, I would take the position that in the long haul, it is not unreasonable to hope for a taxonomy of evaluation designs—

indeed, it seems most reasonable to move toward such an eventual classification scheme. It is the tremendous complexity of the undertaking which makes it prohibitive at present, and it is likely to remain a prohibitive task until we have extended our insights into the nature of decision situations and information needs for which evaluations are required.

As a result of repeated efforts to think about problems relating to the development of a taxonomy of evaluation designs, one conclusion seems particularly critical to me at this juncture. If we are ever to progress toward such a taxonomy, what we really need as a stepping stone is a taxonomy of information needs associated with differing roles which evaluation might play. Given such a taxonomy, it would be possible to focus on a particular information need and identify and develop a range of possible evaluation designs relevant to that information need. These designs could in turn be checked for relevance to other specific information needs within the same class in the "information needs taxonomy." Such testing and subsequent modification should generate a series of alternative designs which are generally relevant to any information need in that particular class. Similarly, sets of designs applicable to other classes of information needs could be generated.

If a taxonomy of information needs were to be developed, we would not necessarily have to begin to generate alternative evaluation designs de novo for each class. Some alternative designs already exist.

An excellent example of extant designs relevant to a particular class of information needs is contained in the Campbell-Stanley chapter mentioned earlier.

Experimental design was initially utilized primarily to meet the need for comparative information in the agricultural and biological sciences. Agronomists were continually asked by farmers for information about ways to increase the productivity of field crops. In order to provide the information, the researchers in agronomy conducted numerous experiments testing differences among yields of various crops, results of different methods of cultivation, and effects of various fertilizers. In short, an information need existed, and a set of designs which fit the assumptions inherent in the situation was employed.

Other classes of information requirements associated with different evaluation roles can be at least grossly identified in extant programs. For example, as Stufflebeam has noted:

> Historical review of the more highly developed forms of evaluation . . . reveals that each has developed for relatively specific applications. Program Evaluation and Review Technique was developed to aid the military in making decisions in the development of complex weapon systems. Systems analysis was developed to aid the military in making decisions in the development and implementation of military operations . . . And, initially, objective testing was utilized largely

as an aid to the military in selecting men for military service. Clearly, the development of each of these forms of evaluation was precipitated by critical decision-making needs . . .[17]

Although Stufflebeam's statement emphasizes decision-making needs, his analysis is equally applicable to the specific types of information needs which were implicit in each decision situation mentioned. While these forms of evaluation do not provide taxonomies of alternatives evaluation designs per se, it is likely that careful analysis of the information needs underlying each form could eventually lead to such alternative designs in the manner described earlier.

If a taxonomy of information needs could be established and taxonomies of evaluation designs generated successfully for each resultant class of information needs, the result would be a useful, but largely unwieldly device, little more efficient than the compendium described earlier.

A necessary next step would be to find some way to analyze similarities and differences across classes of information needs—perhaps by use of analysis using logic similar to that used in factor analysis or canonical correlations.

In short, when we get to the point of having multiple taxonomies of evaluation designs (each relating to a class of information needs), we may begin to see generalized designs emerge that are applicable across classes of information needs. As such designs are identified, instrument development becomes less problematic, since there would be infinitely fewer instruments to construct. If evaluators could learn to resist the "law of the instrument" in utilizing such a set of generalized evaluation designs, the approach outlined here may yet lead us closer to the parsimony we seem to crave.

Notes

1. Stufflebeam, D. L. "Toward A Science of Educational Evaluation," *Educational Technology*, July 30, 1968.
2. *Ibid*.
3. "Taxonomy," as used in this article, refers to any systematic attempt at classifying phenomena into categories, either in correspondence to real ordering or to arbitrary ordering among the phenomena.
4. Campbell, D. T. and Stanley, J. C. "Experimental and Quasi-experimental Design for Research on Teaching," in Gage, N. L. (ed.) *Handbook of Research on Teaching*. Chicago: Rand McNally, 1963.
5. Stufflebeam discussed these four types of decisions in the July 30 issue.
6. Caldwell, M. S. "Input Evaluation and Educational Planning." The Ohio State University Evaluation Center, 1968 (mimeo).
7. For a more comprehensive treatment of the criteria related to change processes, see the following work by Clark and Guba, who originally identified several of the criteria above: Clark, D. L. and Guba, E. G. "An Examination of Potential

Change Roles in Education." Paper presented to the NEA-CSI Seminar on Innovation in Planning School Curricula, Aerlie House, Virginia, 1965 (mimeo).

8. Bloom, B. S., *et al.*, A *Taxonomy of Educational Objectives: Handbook I, The Cognitive Domain*. New York: David McKay Co., Inc. 1956.

9. Krathwohl, D. R., et al. *Taxonomy of Educational Objectives. Handbook II: Affective Domain*. New York: David McKay Co., Inc., 1964.

10. Woodruff, A. D. "Task Analysis of the Seven Major Component Tasks in Teaching." University of Utah Bureau of Educational Research, 1967 (mimeo).

11. For differentiation between consequential and instrumental objectives, see Scriven, M. "The Methodology of Evaluation," in Tyler, et al. (ed) *Perspectives of Curriculum Evaluation*. Chicago: Rand McNally & Co., 1967.

12. Clark, D. L. and Guba, E. G., op. cit.

13. Metfessel, N. S. and Michael, W. B. "A Paradigm Involving Multiple Criterion Measures for the Evaluation of the Effectiveness of School Programs," *Educ. and Psych. Measurement*, Part 2, Winter, 1967.

14. Buros, O. K. *The Buros Mental Measurement Yearbooks*, Highland Park, New Jersey: Gryphon Press, 1949.

15. Tatsuoka, M. M. and Tiedeman, David V. "Statistics as an Aspect of Scientific Method in Research on Teaching," in Gage, N. L. (ed) *Handbook of Research on Teaching*, Chicago: Rand McNally, 1964.

16. Kaplan, A. *The Conduct of Inquiry*, San Francisco, Chandler Publishing Co., 1964, p. 28.

17. Stufflebeam, D. L. "Evaluation as Enlightenment for Decision-making." The Ohio State University Evaluation Center, 1968 (mimeo) p. 21.

Chapter Nine

Integrating a Concept of Educational Administration

The prismatic construct as it has been developed in the introductory chapter and the seven "substance" chapters of the book provides not only an analytical tool but also a vehicle useful in developing a concept of educational administration. The seven chapters fit together and are highly interdependent. As a consequence, the independent analysis of each aspect in the previous chapters is done only at the risk of losing sight of the whole concept. Thus, there may be a resultant distortion of each individual dimension. In order to reestablish the true interacting character of a given aspect, it seems necessary now to pull them back into the original highly interrelated state.

The Philosophical Base

The philosophical base for any social enterprise is predicated on the values held by those involved in the activity. Purposes, in turn, emerge from the values and thus these become the genesis of administration; school administration is dedicated to reaching the objectives or purposes of the educational institution.

In order to establish in his own mind the character of the organization he chooses to administer, the school executive must know the nature of values in the culture and the character of values in the immediate locus of his concern—the given education system. Further, he must appreciate the dynamic quality of values. In order to fully comprehend this particular dimension, the administrator must be knowledgeable as to where changes, or factors that affect change, come from, and how values change. In so doing, he can assess the values and purposes in a given setting and make predictions as to ways in which these may be changed or are likely to change.

The Administrative Theory

When values are carefully examined to ascertain purposes it is necessary to determine a direction and a way to move in order to accomplish them.

331

Administrative theory in its predictive function is a vehicle used to determine initial direction and methodology. After data have been gathered, hypotheses may be formulated and tested. On the basis of findings so derived, along with previously ascertained principles, theory may be used to determine appropriate direction.

Administrative theory is also employed by the school administrator to explain phenomena. By the application of theory, the many and seemingly unrelated elements in a specific situation are given an order and relationship. This in turn aids the administrator in "filling in" the unknowns or gaps in his understanding of the phenomenon.

The assessment or appraisal function utilizes administrative theory also. The administrator examines his actions in regard to (1) theoretical consistency and (2) workability. In the former the administrator is concerned with whether the action was consistent with other values, principles, and objectives in his total behavior. In the latter he is concerned with whether the objective was reached. After the given organizational decisions have been precipitated and the administrative process carried out, the administrator asks: Did this action enable us to meet our objectives? Did it work as we had predicted? Did it work as it did for the reasons we thought it would? Does the method used violate any of our principles in this or any other phase of operation? As he asks these questions, the school administrator is testing his theory of administration. He is determining whether or not the principles utilized in making a prediction have sufficient power to bring about the anticipated results.

As the two major assessments are made, certain negative findings may emerge. Perhaps, for example, the desired results of a given bit of administrative behavior were not forthcoming. Reasons are then determined to explain why this was so. In like manner, reasons for the successful meeting of objectives are ascertained as well: Were we successful because of the selected decision and administrative behavior or because of some factor that was unknown, unanticipated, or previously considered extraneous? Perhaps the action worked, but only partially. If so, where was it weak and why? Perhaps the desired results were reached but the methodology jeopardized administrative integrity in some other area. On the basis of these tests, the theory of administration is verified, modified, rejected, and/or extended almost constantly.

In all probability the several theories in educational administration utilized by the practitioner or the researcher are seldom verified or rejected *in toto*. Since there is no generally accepted total or comprehensive theory of educational administration, and because usually some segment of the eclectic theory employed in most practice is valid, certain portions are retained and others rejected. Thus it is important to determine where theory has fallen short. Having once ascertained this, the search for an adequate predictor in this specific area begins. The answer might come to the investigator in a "flash of insight." It might come from a theory developed in another discipline or another area. Or it might come as the investigator picks up cues from others confronted with something of the same problem.

Thus the "compleat" administrator, according to the views of the editors, is that person who employs the constant testing of propositions to determine for himself: (1) the values which give order to the environment, (2) an administrative theory to provide guidelines for administrative action, (3) the expectations and demands of the setting, (4) his own values and perceptions, skills and abilities, (5) the scope of his own authority and responsibility in the job of administration, (6) a concept of organizational structure which relates institutional expectations to needs-satisfactions of the individual, and (7) the administrative process by which the organization is facilitated in making decisions.

The theory of administration then provides an order or a structure for the several facets of educational administration. The order, however, by its very nature is dynamic and eclectic.

The Setting

Basic values are demonstrated and become manifest in a setting. In the larger society, the nature of education and the subsequent value of it is determined in the free marketplace where it competes with other forms of social action and institutions for its share of man's concern, energy, and resources. Thus the inherent values of an institution are derived from the total society. The institution has a relative (though constantly changing) significance assigned to it. In a given setting at a given time education might be assigned only the responsibility of passing on the cultural heritage, whereas in another era it might be given the monumental task of creating a new social order. The status of education is dynamic as it interacts with all other social elements.

The phenomenon of value demonstration also occurs within the confines of the local community with its own unique physical characteristics. Similar values are demonstrated in various ways due to differing physical characteristics. Thus, the importance of vocational preparation is exhibited in vocational agriculture in a rural area, whereas it takes the form of a college preparatory program in a professionally oriented community of high socioeconomic level.

The school administrator must assess the setting with its unique value and social structure for several purposes. He should ascertain whether or not he can enter into a satisfying relationship in this community having a given pattern of needs and expectations. If so, he must carefully assess, and constantly reassess, the setting in order to determine on what he must predicate propositions he would test in order to move education forward.

The Man

The administrator as a man occupies a central position. He is at that point where the antecedent factors (philosophical base, theory, and setting) meet, and where the several discernible manifestations associated with educational administration are demonstrated. Thus, the unique characteristics of man are related to his actions and those factors which determine his actions.

The educational administrator, because of his own unique makeup of values, perceptions, skills, and abilities, interacts with the larger social system. His pattern of behavior is a dynamic one since both he and expectations for him are in a constant state of change.

The unique qualities of the man are most discernible in the way in which he meets the perceived expectations. He might play the role as the director—an expert who sets goals and directs subordinates in their several responsibilities that contribute to reaching predetermined goals. Or, he might act as a group coordinator and implementor. In this role he would coordinate the work of the staff, facilitating the work of the composite parts so each can best operate to reach the organization's goals agreed upon by the group. A third pattern of administrative behavior might be that of the group-oriented leader. This administrator confronts the staff with propositions regarding both method and direction to be tested by the group. Through this process he enables them to test their thinking and to develop their own bases for action.

Assuming that the educational administrator has some professional decisions to make, it becomes important to learn how these are made. These decisions have significance as they in turn become discernible aspects of administrative behavior. A primary factor to be considered is that the administrator as a man must make these decisions. As he acts, the phenomenon of administration is demonstrated. However, a secondary consideration is important as well. That is, the phenomenon has its genesis in the antecedent factors (philosophical base, theory, and setting). The administrator as a man sifts these through his own screen of values, perceptions, skills, and abilities and thus demonstrates administrative behavior in dimensions of job, organization, and process.

On the operational level it is apparent that not only does the job make the man, but also the man makes the job. The above analysis has been dedicated largely to the second part of the proposition, i.e., that the administrator has a significant role in determining the character of his job. However it seems that a more pressing question is that relating to whether the man has the freedom to determine his own administrative behavior (and on what base this determination is made).

In the practice of school administration, the practitioner must resolve the question (and the implicit subquestion): Can I be true to my own values, and in believing that the schools belong to the people, administer them according to the people's wishes? The administrator as a man is thus in the crucial position of answering this question before he can adopt a relevant pattern of administrative behavior.

The administrator must, in the broader sense, determine how he is governed, yet he is free to determine his own course of action. He must ascertain not only what freedoms are appropriate but also the degrees within which he may operate.

The Job

As a conceptualization, the job of the educational administrator is related to the antecedent factor, the social setting. The environment and values of the setting produce needs which are expressed as expectations or demands. These in turn form the framework for the conceptualization of the job as they are perceived and valued by the administrator.

These expecations are fulfilled and made applicable by relating them to and incorporating them in an institution. They are spelled out in terms of responsibilities and authority and so became limits on action.

In recent years social scientists have verified the thesis that there is considerable variation in the nature of expectations held for the school as an institution and consequently for those who administer it. The expectations may be ambivalent in terms of (1) institutional purpose, (2) tasks to be performed, (3) appropriate processes, and (4) leader behavior. Expectations in these areas vary significantly among teachers, board members, and laymen.

Individuals and groups with their own unique perceptions develop expectations on any one or a combination of these bases. However, these expectations held by the many publics are very difficult to interpret because the publics in the social setting are dynamic. Each of these social elements is subject to change within itself as well as to change in relation to others of the social system. Consequently the perceptions or expectations held are changing both in the ways expectations are viewed, and in what is expected.

Another level of variability of job expectation is encountered when one considers that the administrator must visualize his own job through his own eyes. In other words he must ask himself, "What is my perception of the several publics' perceptions of my job?" It follows then that the administrator living in the social system, being subject to the shifts and changes of society will experience change in his own image of the publics' expectations also.

The development of a concept of his job is imperative to the school administrator for several reasons. First, a well-defined job perception is necessary because it serves as a general criterion for job selection. One can ask himself, "Is this the kind of position in which I will feel productive and not be forced to subvert some of my principles and convictions?"

It is necessary for one to develop a reasonably accurate concept of the job in order to get and keep such a position. No community will retain the services of a school administrator who does not meet at least some of their expectations.

As the administrator is concerned with improvement of educational opportunity, he needs a reference point, e.g., "What do people in the community perceive good education to be?" Such a determination provides a point of departure. He can then decide which are the strategic areas (in light of this as well as other assessments) in which he can move the program forward.

Lastly, personal satisfactions in a large part are derived from the degree of acceptance one receives. Acceptance might be equated to the degree that one, through his job perception, meets expectations. The expectations may include those of the community, the board of education, the staff, the students, the profession, and the administrator himself.

The Organization

The educational administrator as a man and as a professional has responsibility in initiating the structure of the educational organization; that is, establishing and maintaining the pattern of human relationships among those persons involved in the educational enterprise. It is granted that many other forces and factors are operative in organization development as well. This responsibility must be executed within the broad structure of law provided by the state and policy provided by the local board of education. The character of this organization is dependent upon the values, perceptions, and skills of the man himself and how he perceives the community needs and demands in terms of his job as the educational administrator.

One of the primary reasons that education requires administrators rather than managers is that much organizational responsibility is not prescribed by law and policy. Thus, although a K-6-3-3 pattern of vertical organization exists and job descriptions have been meticulously worked out for all personnel depicted on a line and staff chart, the planning neither forces nor assures a given organization. Different administrators working within these same limitations might develop vastly different organizations in terms of the nature of relationships among the staff. This then suggests the behavioral rather than the structural emphasis as being of prime importance to the administrator. Since administrators are primarily concerned with people, the focus on the interrelationships of members of a group in action to achieve institutional goals seems appropriate.

The real challenge for administrators is in these crucial though nebulous dimensions of organization development. These relationships are vital but elusive. Although they bear mightily on morale, identification, and productivity of staff, the teachers and others on whom the ultimate success of the school rests can seldom identify them.

Fundamental to establishing and maintaining these relationships is the administrator's role in relating the institutional expectations to the needs-satisfactions of the individual. Naturally every time an individual becomes associated with an organization such a relationship is set up. The administrator, however, can often play a vital role in establishing the optimum relationship. Through interpretation, explanation, and clarification, he can aid the individual in more accurately assessing the institution and its expectations. He also can take overt action and specify such expectations in job descriptions and the like.

The preceding implies that people within the organization do much to determine the character of it. The administrator, although an important influencer of organization through relating institutional expectations to the needs-satisfactions of the individual staff member, cannot delude himself to think he alone creates organizational relationships. The administrator's position is one related to a transactional or mediating variable concept. He is faced with the responsibility of creating optimum organizational relationships and thus cannot be completely responsible for the nature of the ingredients which go to make up this cake. Instead he must give major concern to how he can bring the predetermined ingredients together to produce the most uniform, balanced product that is possible.

The Process

When the administrator as a man projects himself into a school organization and starts functioning to meets its objectives, the administrative process becomes manifest. However, as stated earlier, the process might be traced back to that point when the administrator influences the creation or modification of the organization by relating institutional expectations to the needs-satisfactions of the staff members.

At this juncture one might ask, "Does the organization determine administrative process or does the administrative process determine the organization?" The point of view expressed in the chapter on the administrative process suggested that process is organizational and decisional in nature. That is, the impact of administration is made through the organization; the administrative process may be viewed as the way an organization makes decisions to take action to meet its goals.

However, it is recognized that when the administrator acts, an administrative process occurs. Thus, as the administrator perceives (1) the values and objectives of education in his community, (2) a theory of administering an educational program, and (3) the expectations of and demands on the school, the administrative process has already begun. The antecedents to organizational decisions are already present and are operative. Thus the organization determines process and process likewise influences organization. The two dimensions are inextricably interwoven into the single fabric of the same larger phenomenon. The school administrator's process of long-term planning might incorporate involvement of staff as an integral part of it. As a result of this the organizational relationships are such that the staff can utilize this involvement to bring into relative congruence the institutional expectations and their own needs-satisfactions. This results in improving organizational relationships. Conversely, the staff relations might be such that to achieve the organization's objectives, a "firm hand" with much centrally imposed direction is required. Thus, the administrative process involving planning might well be dictated by the organization.

The interrelationships between administrative process and organization can be demonstrated in many other examples. All point out the vital influence that organization has on process. The school administrator cannot assume that he alone determines process. If he sees this as a unilateral decision made without considering the array of forces and factors determining the decision, the action suggested by or initiated from the decision might very well be inappropriate or inoperable. This situation could be illustrated by extending the previous example. If the school administrator in that situation were to decide, because of his own values and convictions, that he must be "democratic" and involve staff in planning (when the organizational relationships dictated the "firm hand"), the action he would be likely to initiate might well be inappropriate.

From the perspective of viewing educational administration as a process, it appears that the administrator can profitably use the concept of proposing and testing propositions in order to determine the means by which the organization moves. In this instance he determines the way he acts (administrative process) by throwing out propositions to the larger organization and having them tested, and thus he effectuates organizational decision-making and ultimate movement.

Again we might use the previous example. In the case of the group having a pattern of staff relations that seems to dictate a "firm hand" regarding long-term planning, the administrator might have the group respond to one or more of the following propositions:

1. It is vital that members of the instructional staff participate in all aspects of long-range planning.
2. There are certain key decisions regarding long-range planning that must be made by the instructional staff.

3. Certain kinds of decisions pertaining to long-range planning are better made by members of the instructional staff than by any other person or group.

A Summary and Invitation

In final summary, one can readily appreciate that a study of educational administration incorporates many complex concepts. The complexity is augmented by the fact that forces shaping educational administration are dynamic and interacting. Since it influences and is influenced by a complex society, it must be viewed from several different stances.

In the brief time since the emergence of educational administration, no easy way has been found to cope with the many problems of this inherent complexity. We have found no simple way to meet the varied and often contradictory needs, demands, and expectations of this area of endeavor. In the thinking of the editors, the most promising approach to these challenges is that of the development of a man's concept of educational administration which incorporates constant examination of facts and beliefs, developing and testing of propositions, and evaluation of goals and results.

As stated in the introductory chapter, the purpose of this book is to provide a vehicle for the formulation and testing of propositions crucial to educational administration. The book will have served its purpose if it raises questions which help a man to see himself and his goal, if it provides a means for the man to intelligently make his own decisions and thus enables him to achieve that goal as an educational administrator.

Hopefully, the study of these readings will also stimulate continuous testing of the concepts with subsequent reordering, refining, and modification of the propositions suggested by the authors and editors. In this way the practitioner may join hands with the professor in extending the art and science of educational administration.

Index

Administration: behavior, 3; defined, 5; as goal setting, 229; as instruction, 230; as management, 227; prismatic construct of, 6

Administrative: action, manifestations of, 7; decision, 12; functions, 226; performance, 287; process, 5; relationships, 6; roles, 4; tasks, 6; theory, 331

Administrator behavior, 4

Aexperimentalism, 299

Allport, Floyd H., 284, 285

Allport, Gordon W., 179

"Ambivalents" in organizations, 102

American Association of Colleges for Teacher Education, 201

American Association of School Administrators, 104

"American Way," the, 13

Anderson, Barry D., 193

Anderson, Gladys L., 179

Anderson, James G., 249

Andrews, John H.M., 198

Antecedent forces, 8

Arensberg, Conrad M., 164

Argyris, Chris, 159, 269, 270

Ait, 43

Ashby, Sir Eric, 230

Assumptions, 88

Authority, 249

Bailey, S.K., 217

Balliet, Thomas H., 205

Baltzell, Digby, 68

Barber, Bernard, 83

Barnard, Chester I., 67, 80, 84, 249

Bass, Bernard, 266

Bates, Frederick L., 84

Beck, Samuel J., 178

Blau, Peter M., 25

Blauch, Lloyd E., 84

Bloom, B.S., 325

Bobbitt, Franklin, 207

Bogue, E.G., 266

Bone, H.A., 214

Brayfield, Arthur H., 142

Brennan, Mal, 172

Briner, Conrad, 144

Brodbeck, May, 104

Bronfenbrenner, Urie, 160

Broudy, Harry S., 25, 36

Brown, Alan F., 193

Bureaucracy, 100, 146, 271

Buros, O.K., 325

Butler, Donald, 104

Button, H. Warren, 204, 207

Caldwell, M.S., 323

Callahan, Raymond E., 207

Campbell, Donald T., 300, 322

Campbell, Roald F., 67, 129, 283

Carlson, Richard, 95

Centralization, in state education, 116

Chain of command, 19, 145, 167, 273

Change, 9

Charters, W.W., Jr., 95, 149

Cheever, John, 67

Child benefit principle, 133

Church-state relations, 133

Ciardi, John, 67

Clark, David T., 295, 307, 325

Cognitive dissonance, 276

Cohen, Morris R., 53

Coladarci, Arthur P., 49

Coleman, James S., 250, 251

Committee for the Advancement of School Administration, 233

Conant, James B., 57, 260

Concept: building, 5; building, utility of, 2; definition of, 93; development, 93; of educational administration, 1; nature of a, 2

Concepts: integrating, 95; a process for developing, 3; sensitizing, 94

"Configurational thinking," 94

Cooperative Project in Educational Administration, 55, 233

Corbally, John E., Jr., 283

Corey, Stephen M., 54

Council of Chief State School Officers, 261

Crockett, Walter H., 142

Croft, Don B., 137

Cronbach, Lee J., 305

Cubberley, Ellwood, 207

Cultural relativism, 27

Cummings, L.L., 184

Cunningham, Luvern, 218

341

Dahl, R.H., 224
Decision: administrative, 11; maker, 11; making, inhibition of, 273
Decisional method of studying power, 219
Decisions: classes of, 236; responsibility for, 12; sources of approval for, 13
"Derivational thinking," 15
Development, 301
Dewey, John, 21, 51, 54
Diffusion, 303, 323
Drucker, Peter F., 68, 247
Dye, Thomas R., 109

Easton, David, 110
Economic: inputs, 114; variables, effect of, 125
Educational: administration, 5; outputs, 114
Ehrlich, Howard J., 179
Eliot, Thomas H., 110, 212
Erikson, Erik H., 67, 160
Etzioni, Amitai, 138
Evaluation: context, 312; definition of, 311; input, 312; of a model, 124; process, 314; product, 314; strategies of, 312; structure, 314
Expectations, 6
Experimentalism, 296

Fagan, R.E., 285
Fawl, Clifford, 299
Federal: aid, categorical or general, 131; programs, administration of, 131; role in education, 117; state relations, 129
Feldvebel, Alexander M., 137
Festinger, Leon, 276
Fiegl, Herbert, 87
Funk, B. Gordon, 154

Galbraith, John Kenneth, 271, 273
Game theory, 72
Gardner, John, 272
Gephart, William J., 307
Getzels, Jacob W., 49, 67, 104
Gillespie, James T., 166
Goal: achievement, 6; determination, 6; "thinking", 15
Gouldner, Alvin, 83, 95
Gregg, Russell T., 67, 212
Griffiths, Daniel E., 85, 105, 209, 284, 285
Group dynamics, 275
Guba, Egon G., 67, 295, 307, 329
Guetzkow, Harold, 83
Gulick, Luther, 283

Guthrie, Edwin R., 52

Hall, A.D., 285
Hall, Edward I., 67
Halpin, Andrew W., 55, 67, 104, 137, 143
Harlow, James G., 17
Harris, W.T., 206
Hawthorne studies, 268
Healey, James H., 170
Hearn, Gordon, 105, 286
Heller, Frank, 68
Hemphill, 99
Heroism, 42
Hopkins, John, 295
Homans, George C., 67, 251, 256
Humanities, 22
Human relations movement, 268
Hunter, Floyd, 218

Iannaccone, Lawrence, 144, 275
Indifferents in organizations, 101
Industrial humanism movement, 269
Influence and policy, 217
Inner direction, 11
Inputs, 8

James, H. Thomas, 127
Janet, Pierre, 67
Jaques, Elliot, 146
Jennings, M.K., 220
Job: 335; definition, 233-34; in educational administration, 7

Kaplan, A., 327
Kefauver, Graysen, N., 209
Kemp, C. Gratton, 178
Knezevich, Stephen J., 2
Koehler, Kathleen, 164
Krathwohl, D.R., 325
Krutch, Joseph Wood, 66

Labor: division of, 148-150; duplication of, 148-150
Larrabee, Harold W., 53
Lasswell, H.D., 214
Laws, 88
Lazarsfeld, Paul, 95, 105
Leader behavior, circular model, 195
Leadership: 12, 184; Behavior Description Questionnaire, 194; idiographic, nomothetic, and transactional, 196; Opinion Questionnaire, 190; patterns of, 219; style, 186, 189; "thinking," 15
Lebeaux, Charles N., 166
Lenzen, U.F., 53

Levine, David U., 241
Likert, Reusis, 269
Lindbloom, Charles E., 230
Line and staff, 145, 153
Lipham, James M., 152
Litchfield, Edward H., 76, 283

Man: 334; in educational administration, 7
Management: definition of, 185; philosophy, 268
March, James G., 99, 105, 266
Marx, Melvin H., 53
Maslow, A.H., 179, 269
Masters, Nicholas, 110
May, Rollo, 169
Mayo, Elton, 268
McEwen, William J., 84
McGregor, Douglas, 164, 269
Mediating variables, 8
Metfessel, Newton, 318, 325
Method, 6
Michael, William B., 318, 325
Miller, J.G., 105
Miller, Neal E., 53
Miller, Van, 11, 233
Minar, David, 216, 225
Monypenny, P., 213
Mort, Paul, 295
Moser, R.F., 196
Mumford, Lewis, 66

National Association of State Directors of Teacher Education and Certification, 261
National Commission on Teacher Education and Professional Standards, 261
National Conference of Professors of Educational Administration, 56
National Council for the Accreditation of Teacher Education, 261
National Institutes of Health, 130
National Science Foundation, 130
Newlon, Jesse H., 208
Nihilism, 37

Odiorne, George S., 278
Ombudsman, 244
Organization: 336; in educational administration, 8; formal, 144, 159; formal, basic properties of, 162
Organizational: behavior, determinants of, 267; climate, 137; inertia, 272; purpose, 19; society, 99
Organizations, rational, 163

Output, educational, 137
Outputs, 8

Paradigm, 92
Parker, Francis W., 205
Parsons, Talcott, 21, 84, 140
Patriotism, 42
Payne, W.H., 206
Perceptions, 157
Personality: 276; adjustment, 181; conflict, 91; properties of, 160
Philosophical base, 9, 331
Plato, 34, 35
Pois, Joseph, 245
Policy, 11, 12
Political: influence, 109; variables, 119, 125
Politics: definition of, 214; in education, 224
Positional method of studying power, 218
Power and decision-making, 218
Presthus, Robert, 99-100, 105
Procedural interposition, 33
Process: 337; in educational administration, 7
"Projective thinking", 15
Project on Staff Utilization, 233
Purpose: defining, 17; in education, 18

Ramseyer, John A., 283
Redmond, James F., 247
Reichenback, Hans, 51
Relativism, 31
Renshaw, Edward F., 109
Reputational method in study of power, 218
Research, new methodologies of, 296
Rogers, Carl R., 161, 277
Rokeach, Nulton, 179-81
Role: conflict, 91; of the administrator, 4, 8, 24; personality conflicts, 91

Salisbury, Robert H., 110
Schmidt, Warren, 188
School-community relations, 275
Scientific management, 268
"Scientific thinking," 15
Scott, William G., 242, 266
Selznick, Philip, 83
Setting: 333; for educational administration, 107; of educational administration, 7
Sexual behavior, 41
Shapiro, Sherman, 109
Shartle, Carroll L., 146

Siu, R.G.H., 68
Simon, Herbert A., 84, 93, 99, 163, 170, 228, 292
Situational factors, 194
Skills and abilities, 157
Smith, Gerald R., 307
Social: class, 137; forces, 8; interaction, 17; organization, 144; roles, 17; system, 135
Societal needs, 9
Sociological change, 3
Span of control, 19, 170
Specialization: 150; task, 166
Spaulding, Frank, 207
Stanley, J.C., 329
Stevenson, Charles, 27
Stogdill, Ralph M., 146, 164
Stone, Raymond G., 53
Structure in organizations, 271
Stufflebeam, Daniel L., 310, 320, 328
Sullivan, Harry Stack, 99
Sumner, Charles E., Jr., 84
Suojanen, W.W., 170
Supervisory Behavior Description, 190
System Theory, 102, 285
Systems: model, 110; open organismic, 286

Tannenbaum, Robert, 188
Tasks, 6
Tatsuoka, M.M., 325
Taylor, Frederick W., 268
Tead, Ordway, 21
Technological change, 3
Telos, 26
Theories of administration, 99

Theory: 47-48, 69; criteria for, 76; deductive approaches to, 80; defined, 85, 87; educational administration, 7; illustration of, 89; nature and meaning of, 85; practice relationship, 49; sources of, 72; terminology of, 89; test of, 89
Thomas, Lawrence G., 53
Thompson, James D., 69, 84
Thompson, Victor, 266, 272
Tiedeman, David V., 325
"Trend thinking," 15

United States Office of Education, 130
Unity of direction, 169
University Council for Educational Administration, 56, 233
"Upward-mobiles" in organizations, 101
Urwick, L., 163, 170, 283

Value judgments, 21, 27
Values: 9-10, 157; central core of, 11, 15; conflicts in, 26
Viteles, Morris J., 68

Walton, John, 226
Weber, Max, 100, 146, 249, 252, 266
White, E.E., 205
Whyte, William, 170
Wilensky, Harold L., 166
Williams, D.C.S., 169
Woodruff, A.D., 325
Worthen, Blaine R., 320
Worthy, James C., 170

Yoder, Dale, 184

Zaleznik, Abraham, 277-79